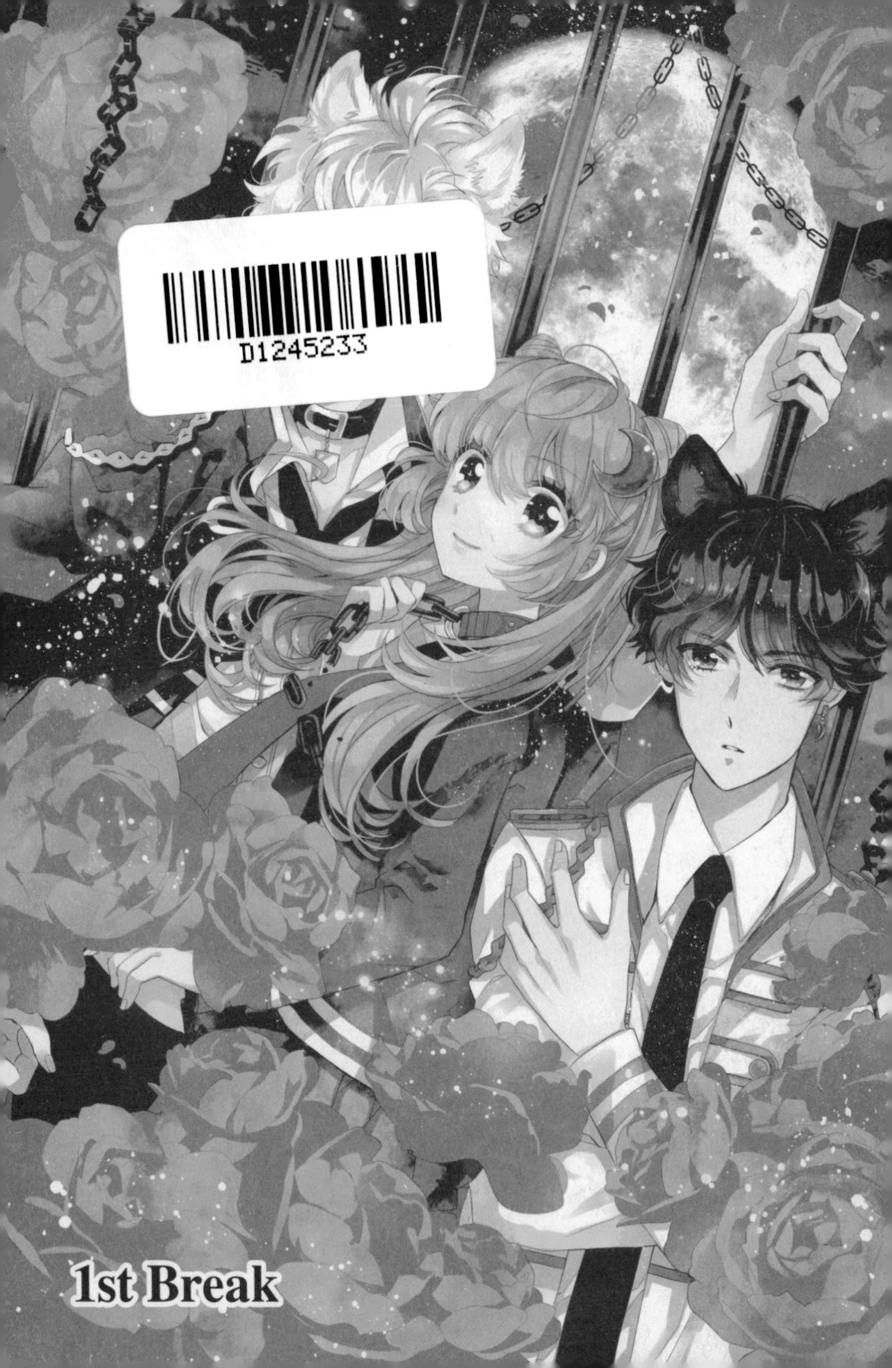
1st Break

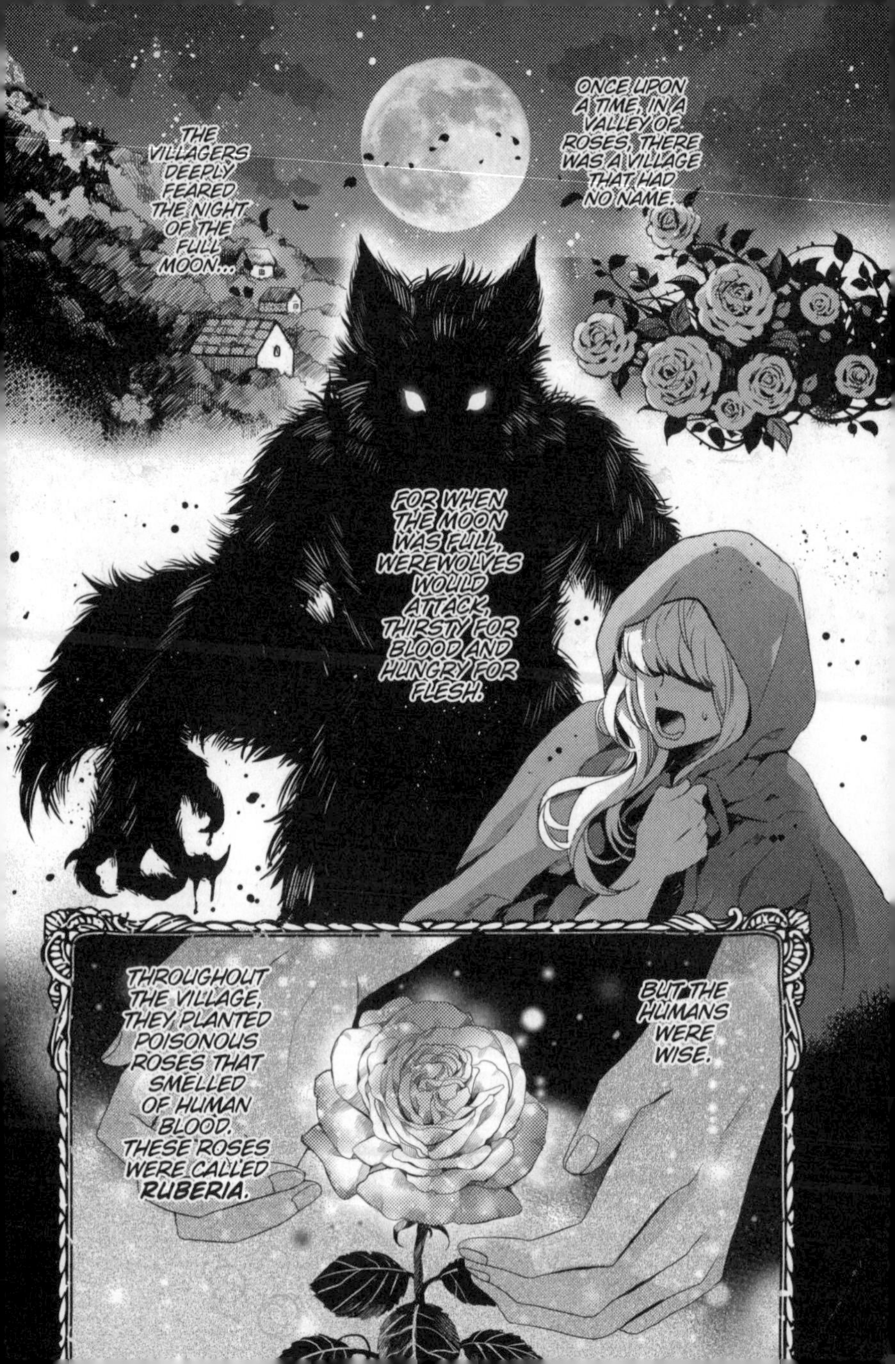
ONCE UPON A TIME, IN A VALLEY OF ROSES, THERE WAS A VILLAGE THAT HAD NO NAME.
THE VILLAGERS DEEPLY FEARED THE NIGHT OF THE FULL MOON...
FOR WHEN THE MOON WAS FULL, WEREWOLVES WOULD ATTACK, THIRSTY FOR BLOOD AND HUNGRY FOR FLESH.
BUT THE HUMANS WERE WISE.
THROUGHOUT THE VILLAGE, THEY PLANTED POISONOUS ROSES THAT SMELLED OF HUMAN BLOOD. THESE ROSES WERE CALLED RUBERIA.

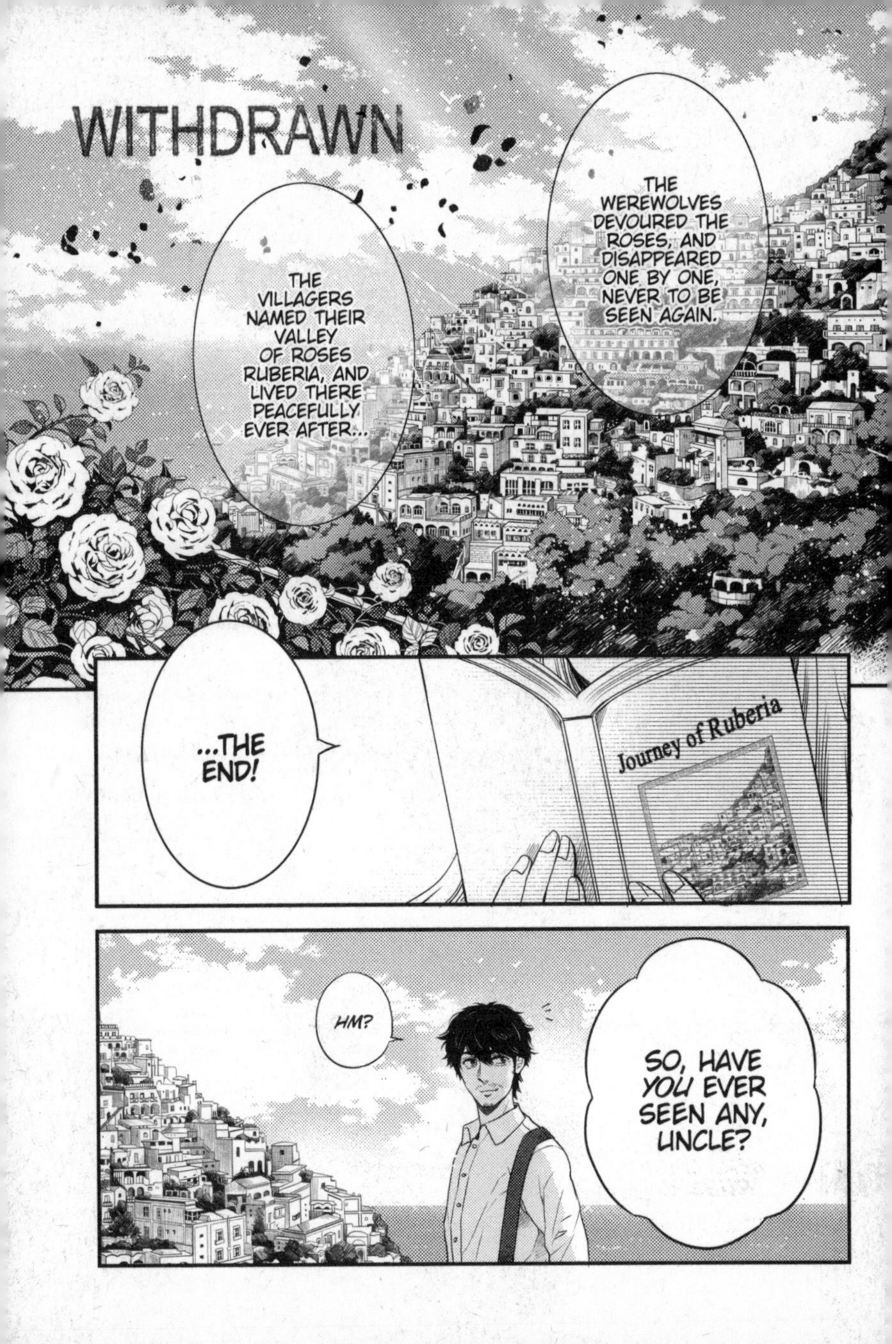
THE WEREWOLVES DEVOURED THE ROSES, AND DISAPPEARED ONE BY ONE, NEVER TO BE SEEN AGAIN.
THE VILLAGERS NAMED THEIR VALLEY OF ROSES RUBERIA, AND LIVED THERE PEACEFULLY EVER AFTER...
Journey of Ruberia
...THE END!
SO, HAVE *YOU* EVER SEEN ANY, UNCLE?
HM?

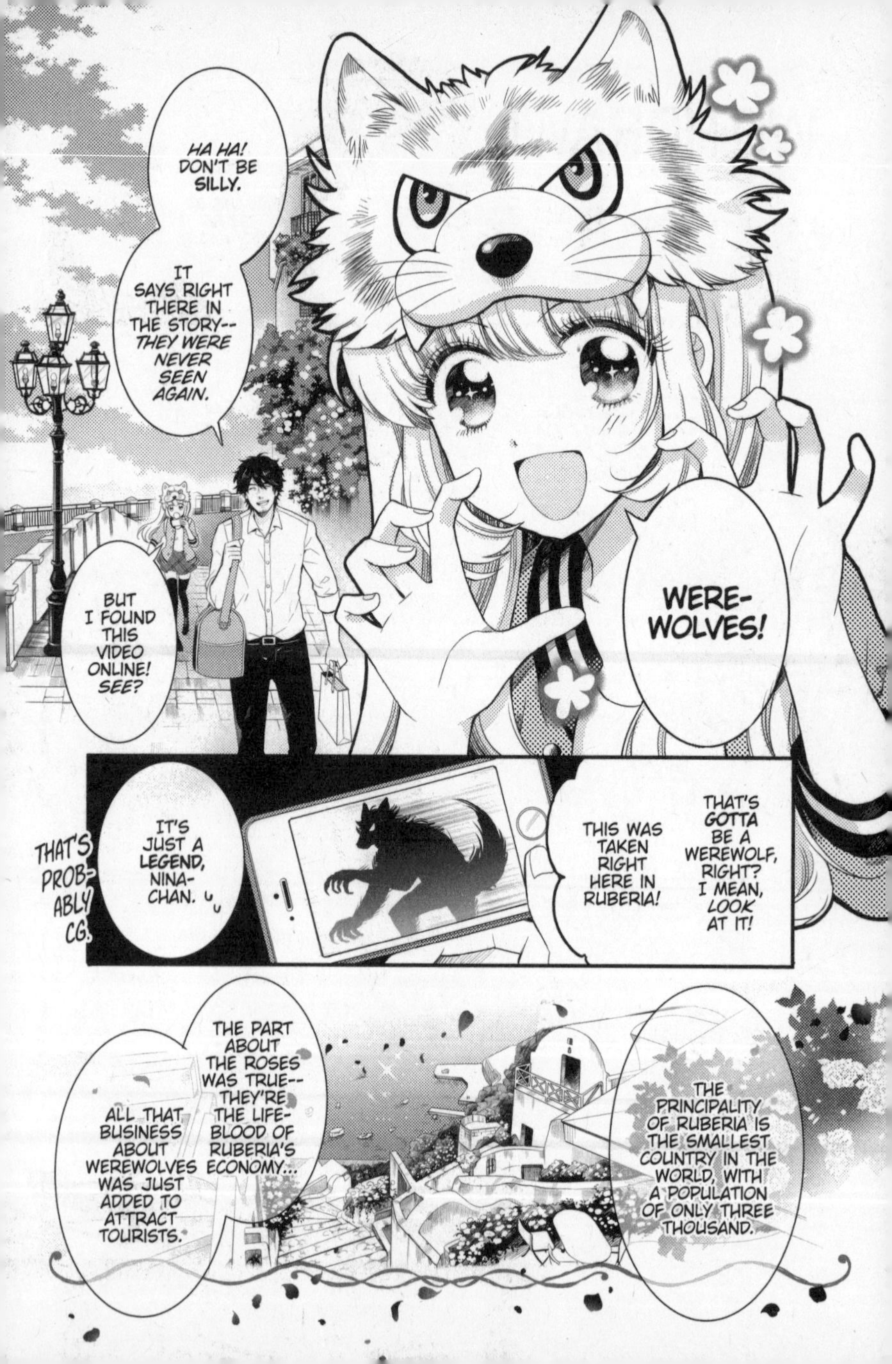
WERE-WOLVES!
HA HA! DON'T BE SILLY.
IT SAYS RIGHT THERE IN THE STORY--THEY WERE NEVER SEEN AGAIN.
BUT I FOUND THIS VIDEO ONLINE! SEE?
THAT'S GOTTA BE A WEREWOLF, RIGHT? I MEAN, LOOK AT IT!
THIS WAS TAKEN RIGHT HERE IN RUBERIA!
IT'S JUST A LEGEND, NINA-CHAN.
THAT'S PROBABLY CG.
THE PRINCIPALITY OF RUBERIA IS THE SMALLEST COUNTRY IN THE WORLD, WITH A POPULATION OF ONLY THREE THOUSAND.
THE PART ABOUT THE ROSES WAS TRUE--THEY'RE THE LIFE-BLOOD OF RUBERIA'S ECONOMY...
ALL THAT BUSINESS ABOUT WEREWOLVES WAS JUST ADDED TO ATTRACT TOURISTS.

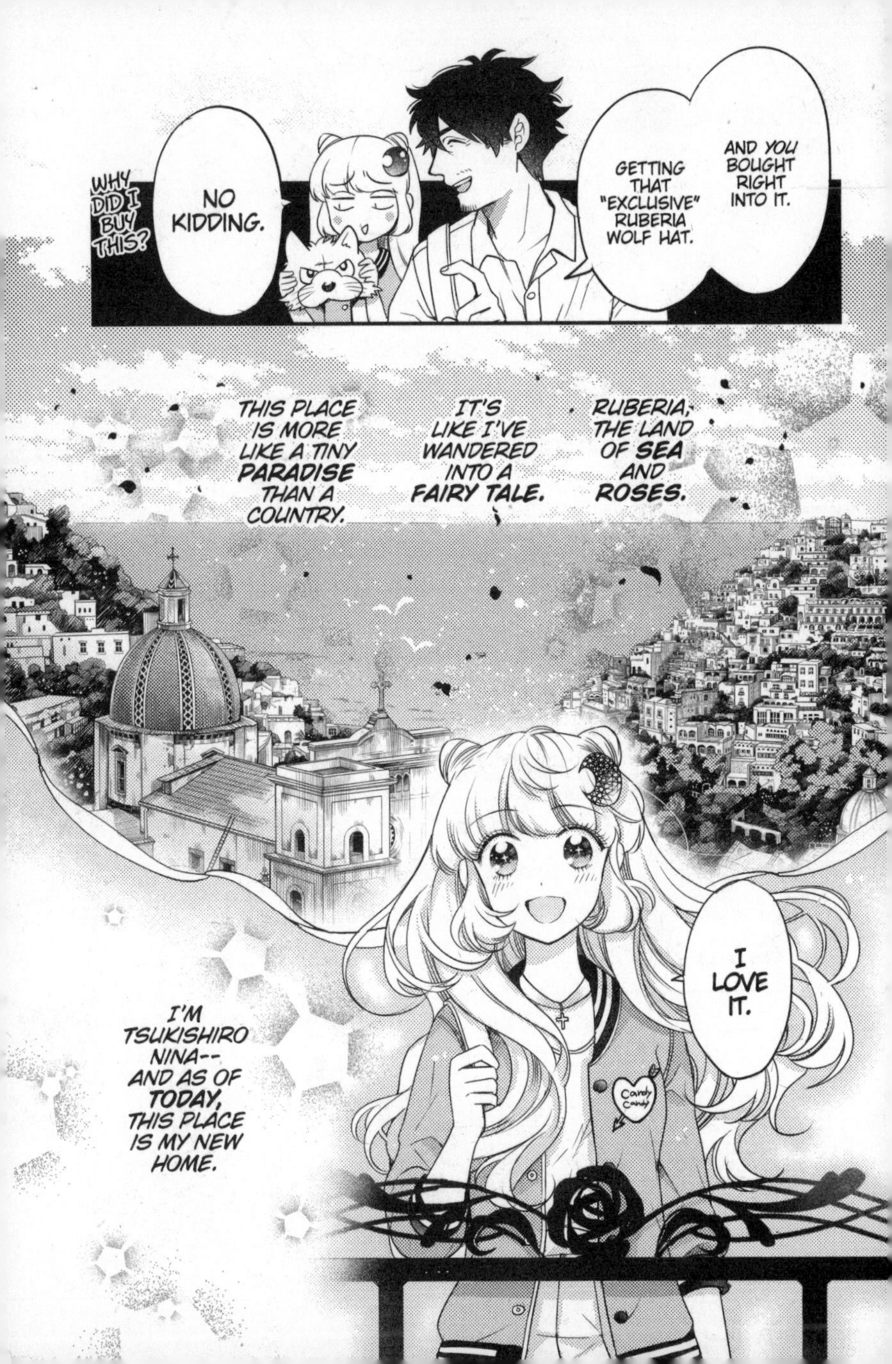
GETTING THAT "EXCLUSIVE" RUBERIA WOLF HAT.
AND YOU BOUGHT RIGHT INTO IT.
NO KIDDING.
WHY DID I BUY THIS?
RUBERIA, THE LAND OF SEA AND ROSES.
IT'S LIKE I'VE WANDERED INTO A FAIRY TALE.
THIS PLACE IS MORE LIKE A TINY PARADISE THAN A COUNTRY.
I LOVE IT.
I'M TSUKISHIRO NINA-- AND AS OF TODAY, THIS PLACE IS MY NEW HOME.

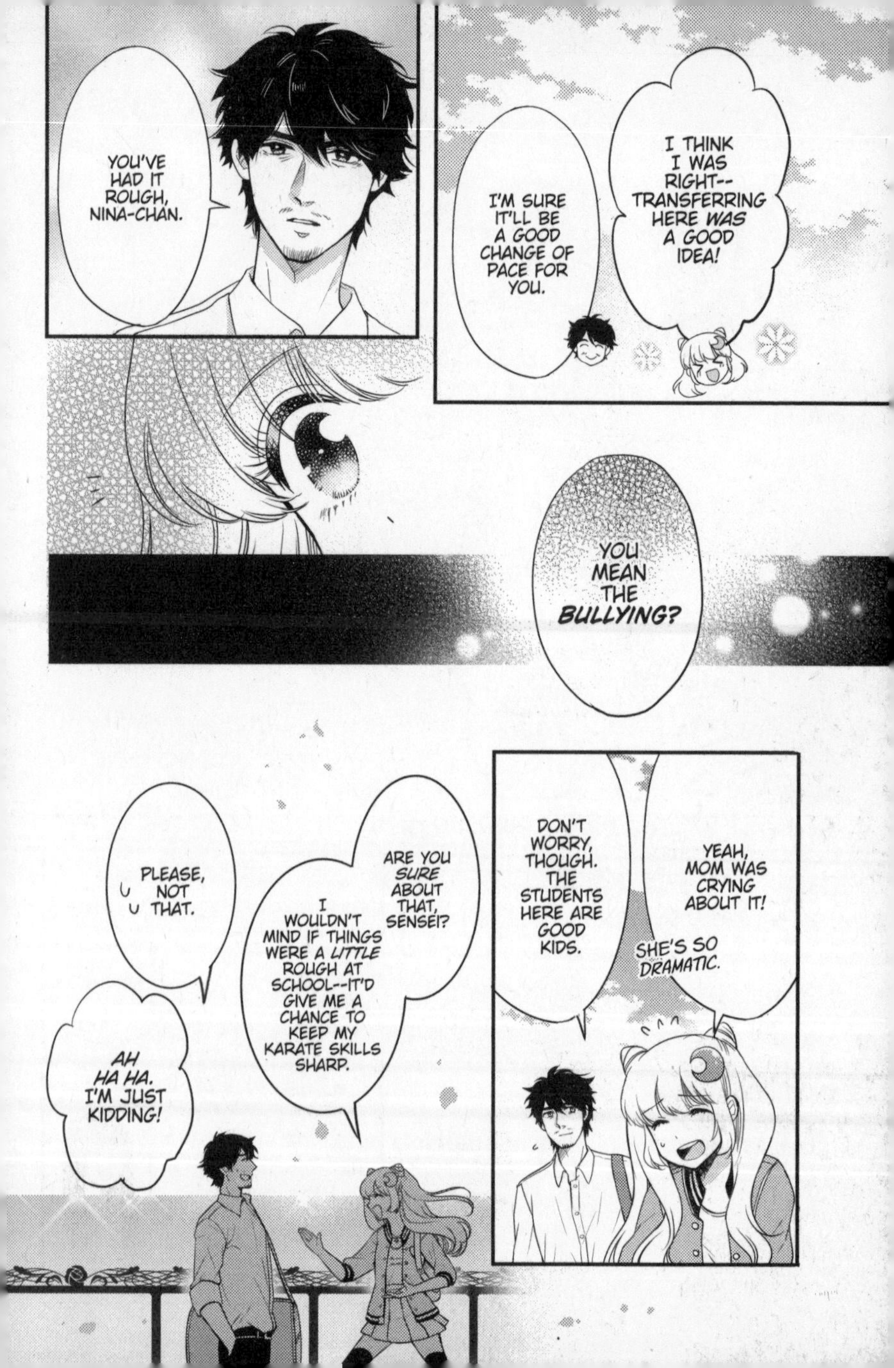
I THINK I WAS RIGHT--TRANSFERRING HERE WAS A GOOD IDEA!
I'M SURE IT'LL BE A GOOD CHANGE OF PACE FOR YOU.
YOU'VE HAD IT ROUGH, NINA-CHAN.
YOU MEAN THE BULLYING?
YEAH, MOM WAS CRYING ABOUT IT!
SHE'S SO DRAMATIC.
DON'T WORRY, THOUGH. THE STUDENTS HERE ARE GOOD KIDS.
ARE YOU SURE ABOUT THAT, SENSEI?
I WOULDN'T MIND IF THINGS WERE A LITTLE ROUGH AT SCHOOL--IT'D GIVE ME A CHANCE TO KEEP MY KARATE SKILLS SHARP.
PLEASE, NOT THAT.
AH HA HA. I'M JUST KIDDING!

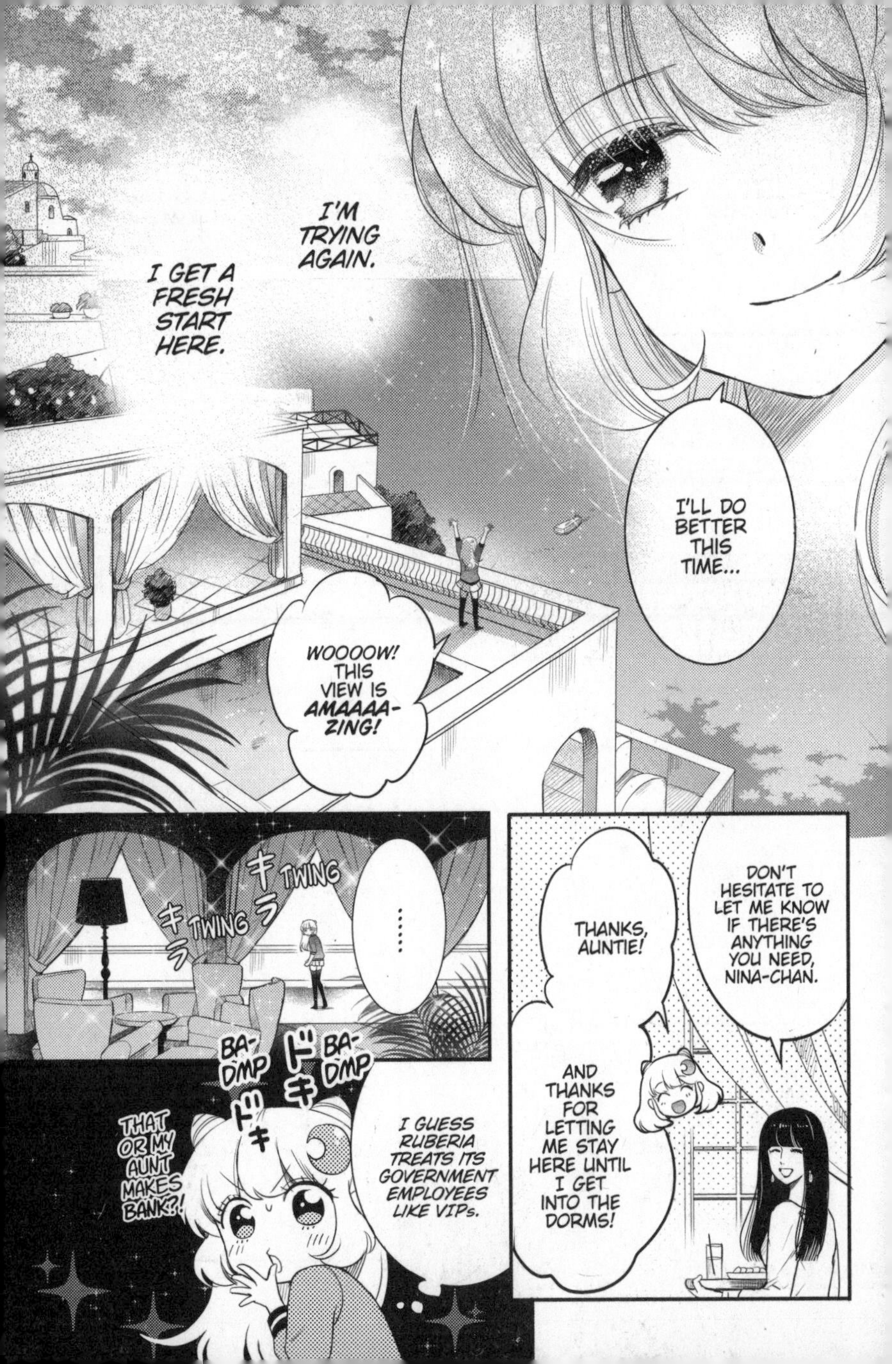
I'LL DO BETTER THIS TIME...
I'M TRYING AGAIN.
I GET A FRESH START HERE.
WOOOOW! THIS VIEW IS AMAAAA-ZING!
DON'T HESITATE TO LET ME KNOW IF THERE'S ANYTHING YOU NEED, NINA-CHAN.
THANKS, AUNTIE!
AND THANKS FOR LETTING ME STAY HERE UNTIL I GET INTO THE DORMS!
キラ TWING
キラ TWING
......
ドキ BA-DMP
ドキ BA-DMP
I GUESS RUBERIA TREATS ITS GOVERNMENT EMPLOYEES LIKE VIPs.
THAT OR MY AUNT MAKES BANK?!

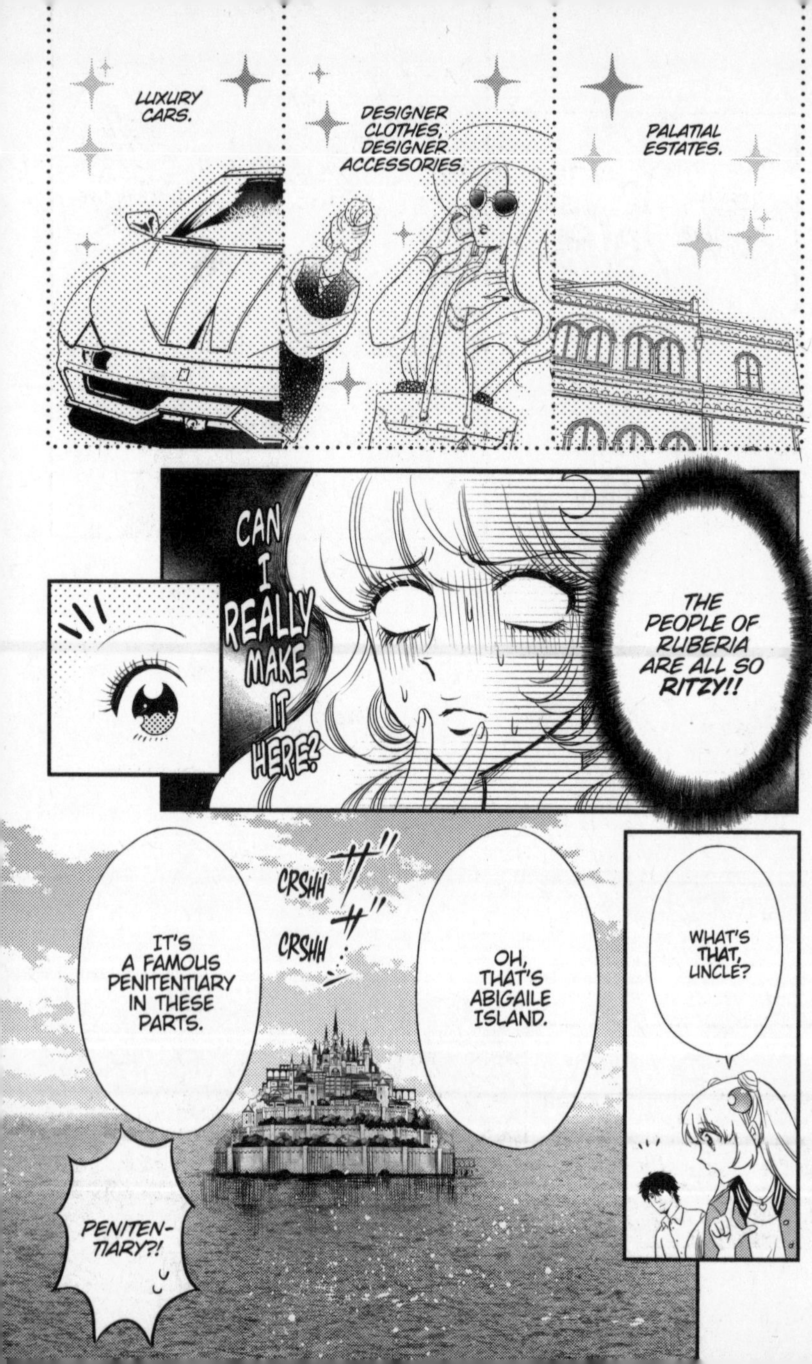
PALATIAL ESTATES.
DESIGNER CLOTHES, DESIGNER ACCESSORIES.
LUXURY CARS.
THE PEOPLE OF RUBERIA ARE ALL SO RITZY!!
CAN I REALLY MAKE IT HERE?
WHAT'S THAT, UNCLE?
OH, THAT'S ABIGAILE ISLAND.
CRSHH
CRSHH
IT'S A FAMOUS PENITENTIARY IN THESE PARTS.
PENITEN-TIARY?!

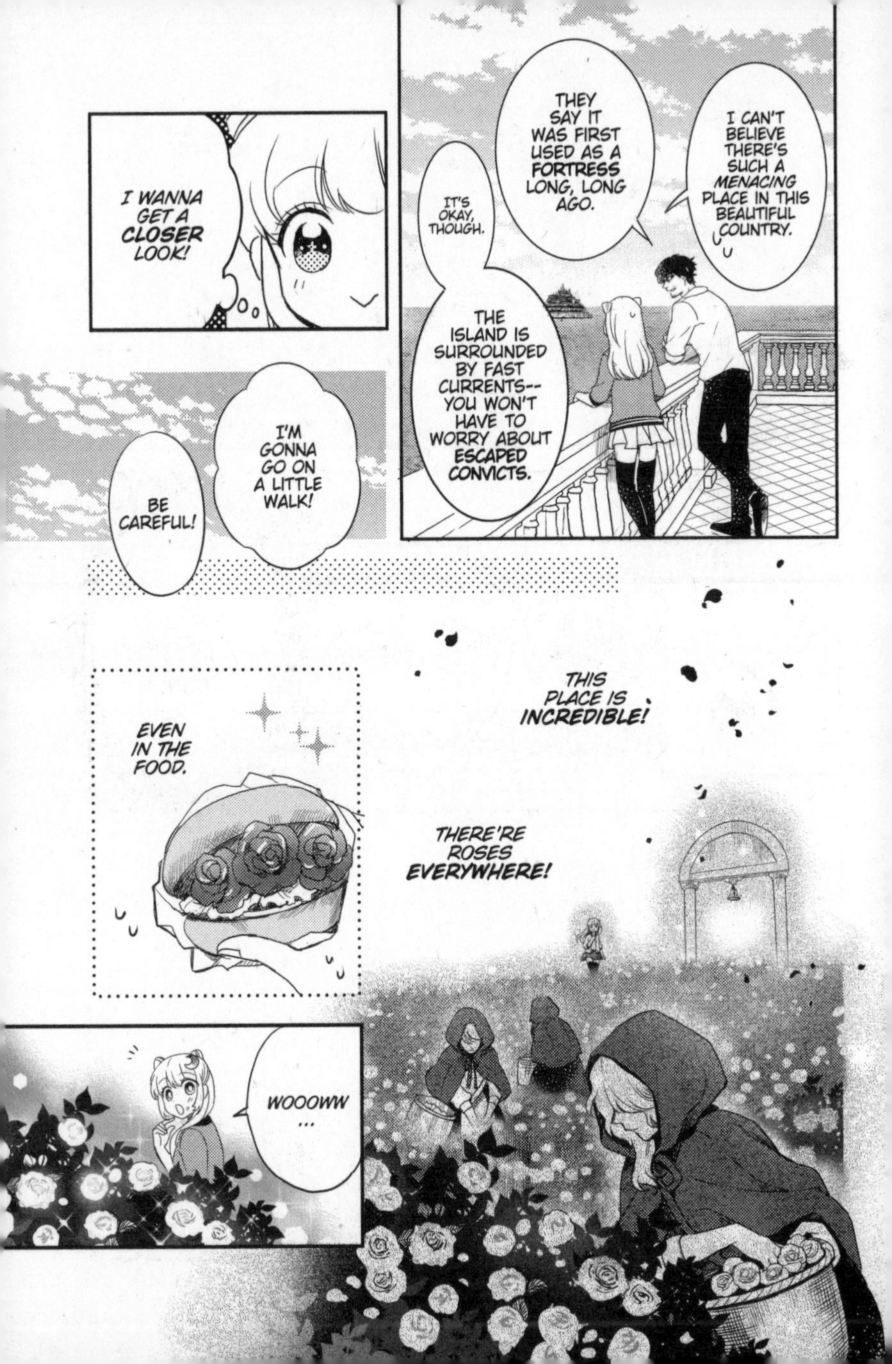
I CAN'T BELIEVE THERE'S SUCH A MENACING PLACE IN THIS BEAUTIFUL COUNTRY.
THEY SAY IT WAS FIRST USED AS A FORTRESS LONG, LONG AGO.
IT'S OKAY, THOUGH.
THE ISLAND IS SURROUNDED BY FAST CURRENTS--YOU WON'T HAVE TO WORRY ABOUT ESCAPED CONVICTS.
I WANNA GET A CLOSER LOOK!
I'M GONNA GO ON A LITTLE WALK!
BE CAREFUL!
THIS PLACE IS INCREDIBLE!
THERE'RE ROSES EVERYWHERE!
EVEN IN THE FOOD.
WOOOWW ...

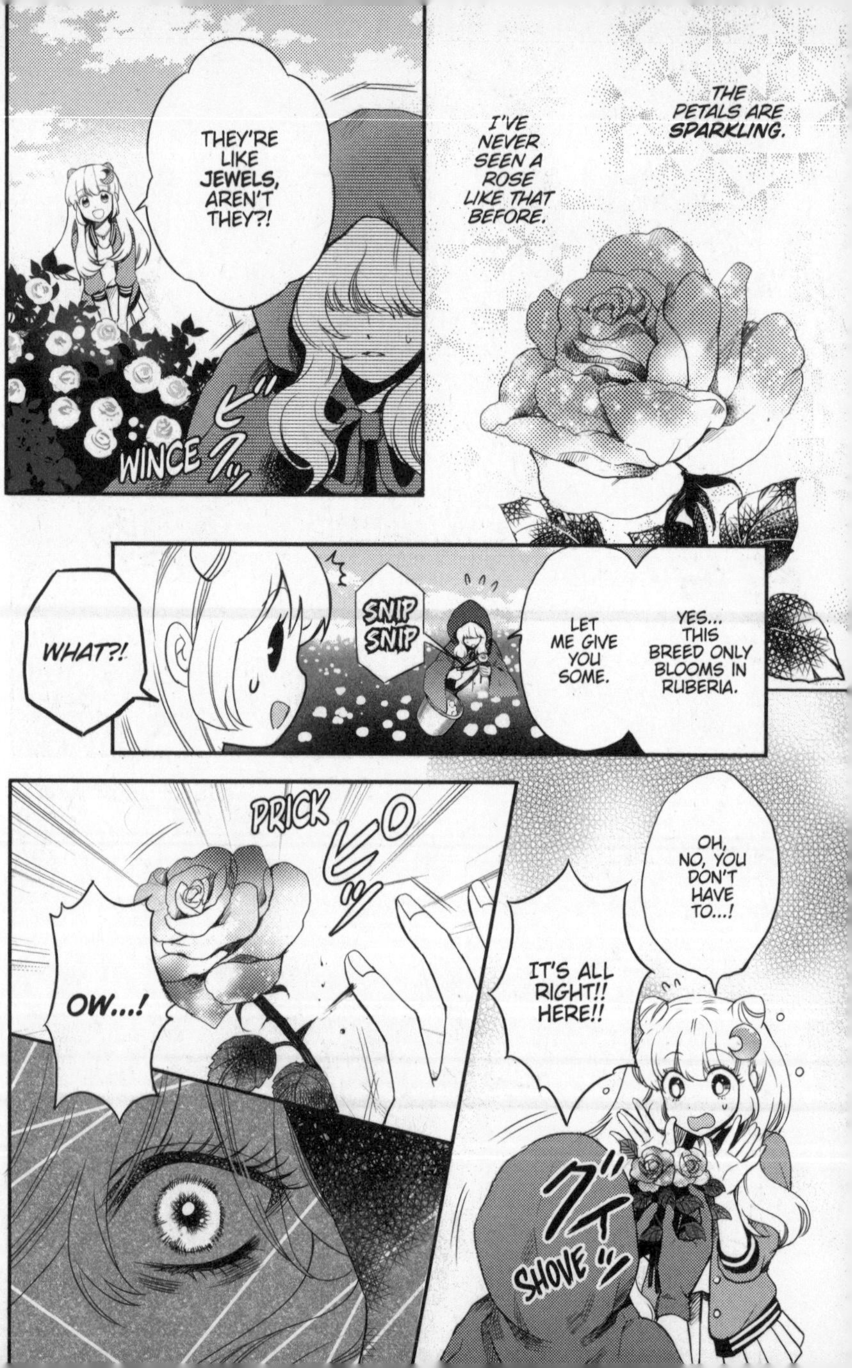
THE PETALS ARE SPARKLING.
I'VE NEVER SEEN A ROSE LIKE THAT BEFORE.
THEY'RE LIKE JEWELS, AREN'T THEY?!
WINCE
YES... THIS BREED ONLY BLOOMS IN RUBERIA.
LET ME GIVE YOU SOME.
SNIP SNIP
WHAT?!
OH, NO, YOU DON'T HAVE TO...!
IT'S ALL RIGHT!! HERE!!
SHOVE
PRICK
OW...!

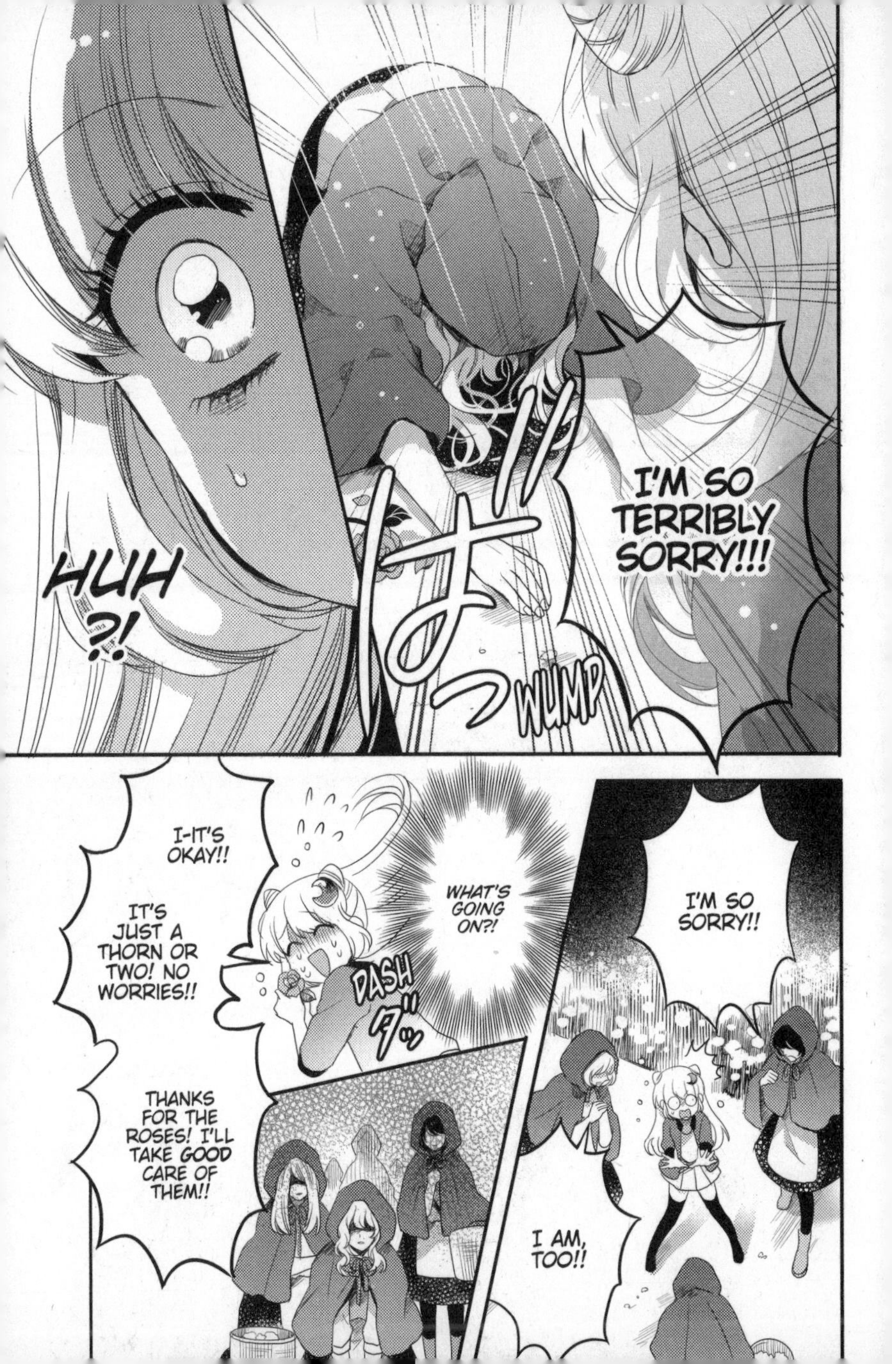
I'M SO TERRIBLY SORRY!!!
はっ
WUMP
HUH ?!
I'M SO SORRY!!
I AM, TOO!!
WHAT'S GOING ON?!
I-IT'S OKAY!!
IT'S JUST A THORN OR TWO! NO WORRIES!!
DASH
ダッ
THANKS FOR THE ROSES! I'LL TAKE GOOD CARE OF THEM!!

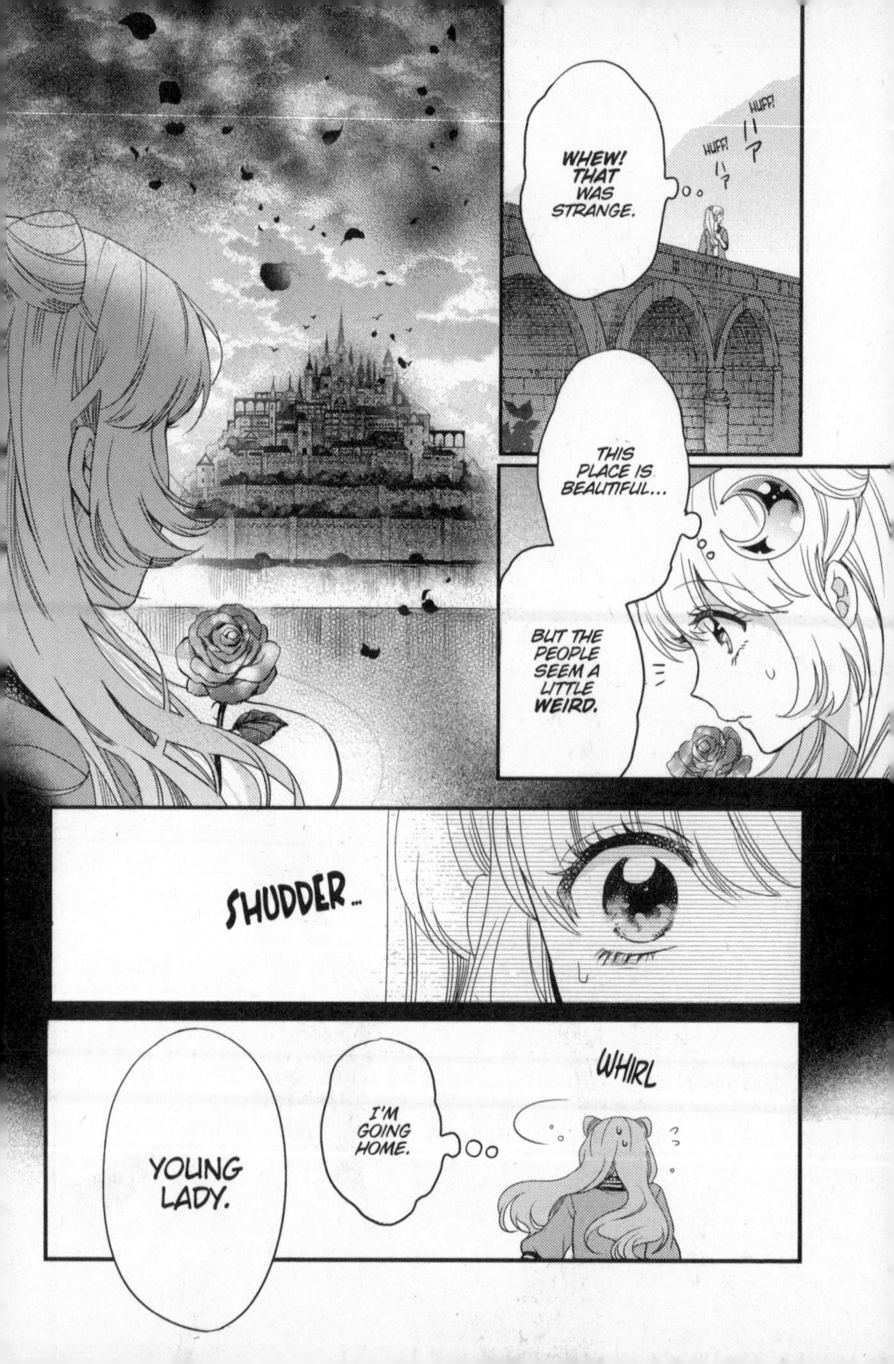
HUFF!
ハア
HUFF!
ハア
WHEW! THAT WAS STRANGE.
THIS PLACE IS BEAUTIFUL...
BUT THE PEOPLE SEEM A LITTLE WEIRD.
SHUDDER...
WHIRL
I'M GOING HOME.
YOUNG LADY.

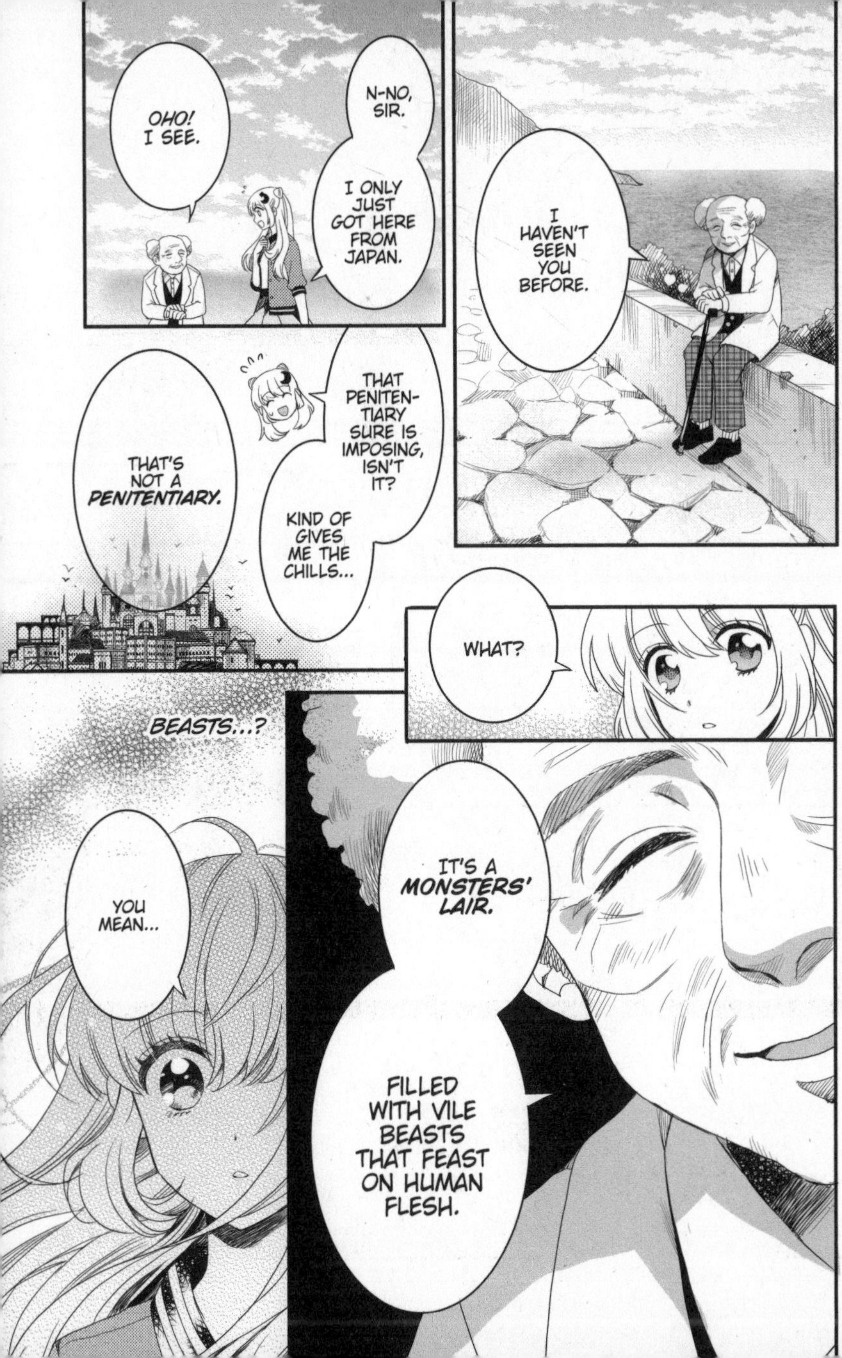
I HAVEN'T SEEN YOU BEFORE.
N-NO, SIR.
I ONLY JUST GOT HERE FROM JAPAN.
OHO! I SEE.
THAT PENITENTIARY SURE IS IMPOSING, ISN'T IT?
KIND OF GIVES ME THE CHILLS...
THAT'S NOT A PENITENTIARY.
WHAT?
IT'S A MONSTERS' LAIR.
FILLED WITH VILE BEASTS THAT FEAST ON HUMAN FLESH.
BEASTS...?
YOU MEAN...

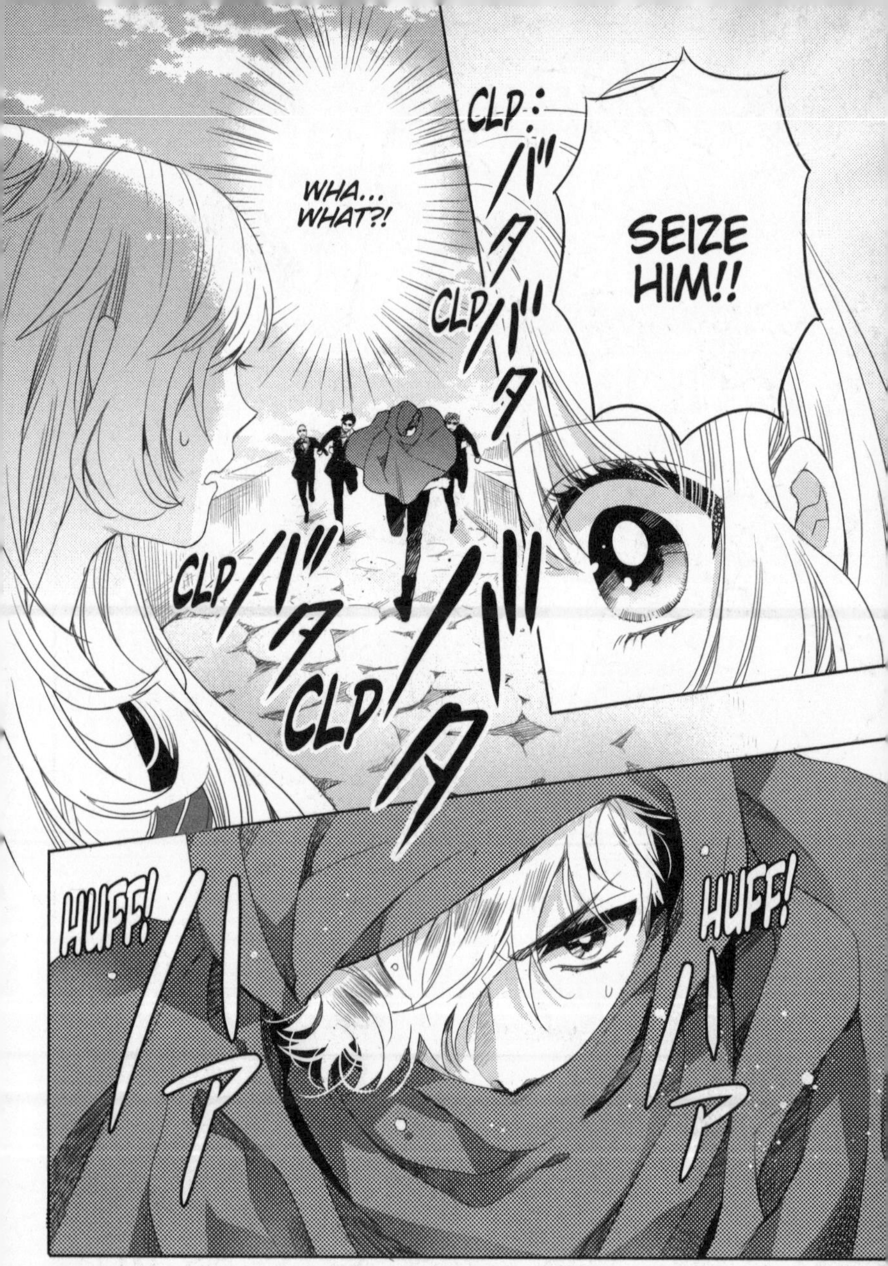
SEIZE HIM!!
CLP
バタ
CLP
バタ
WHA... WHAT?!
CLP
バタ
CLP
バタ
HUFF!
ハァ
HUFF!
ハァ

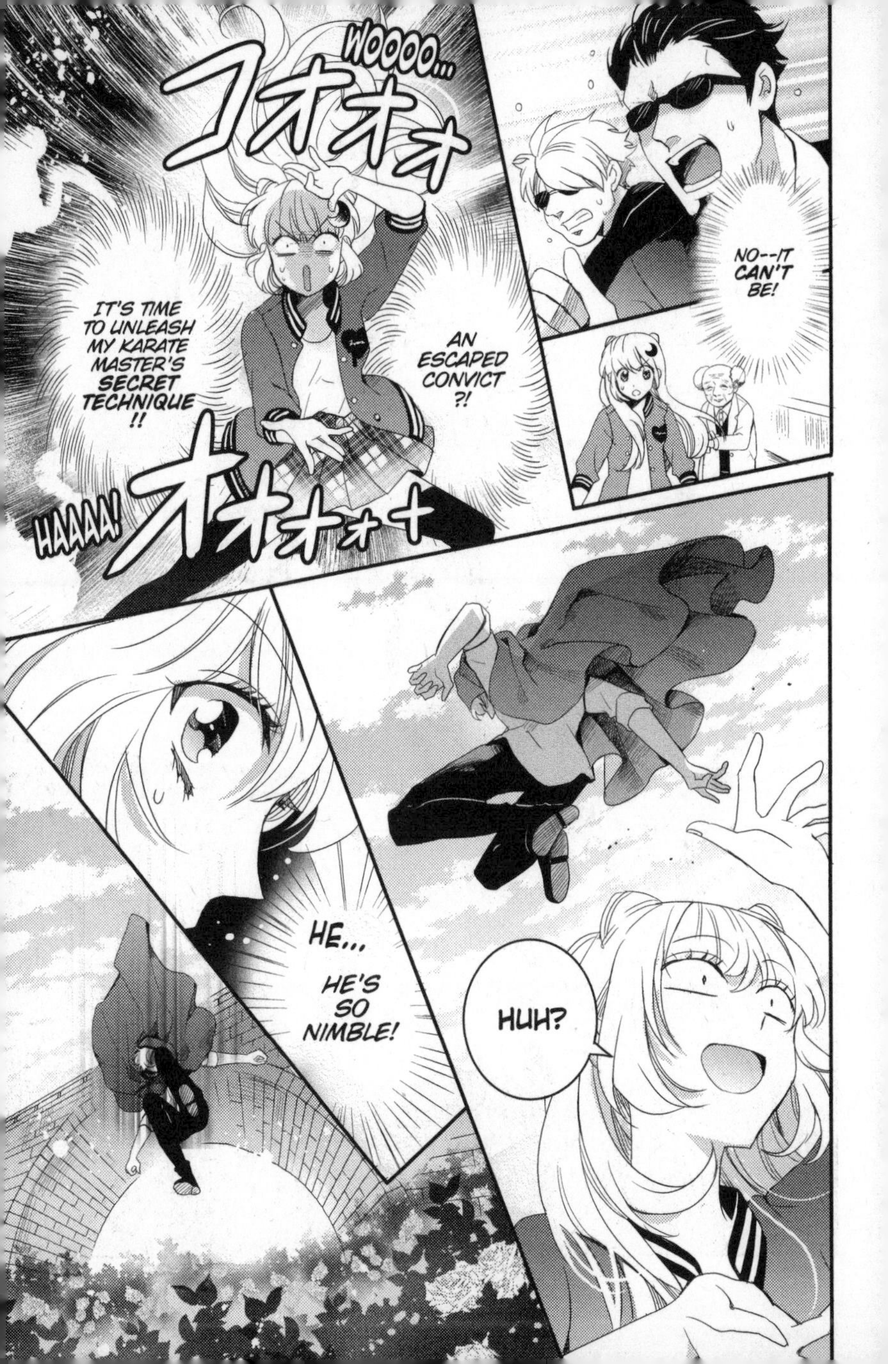
NO--IT CAN'T BE!
WOOOO...
コオオォ
AN ESCAPED CONVICT?!
IT'S TIME TO UNLEASH MY KARATE MASTER'S SECRET TECHNIQUE!!
HAAAA!
オオォォォ
HUH?
HE...
HE'S SO NIMBLE!

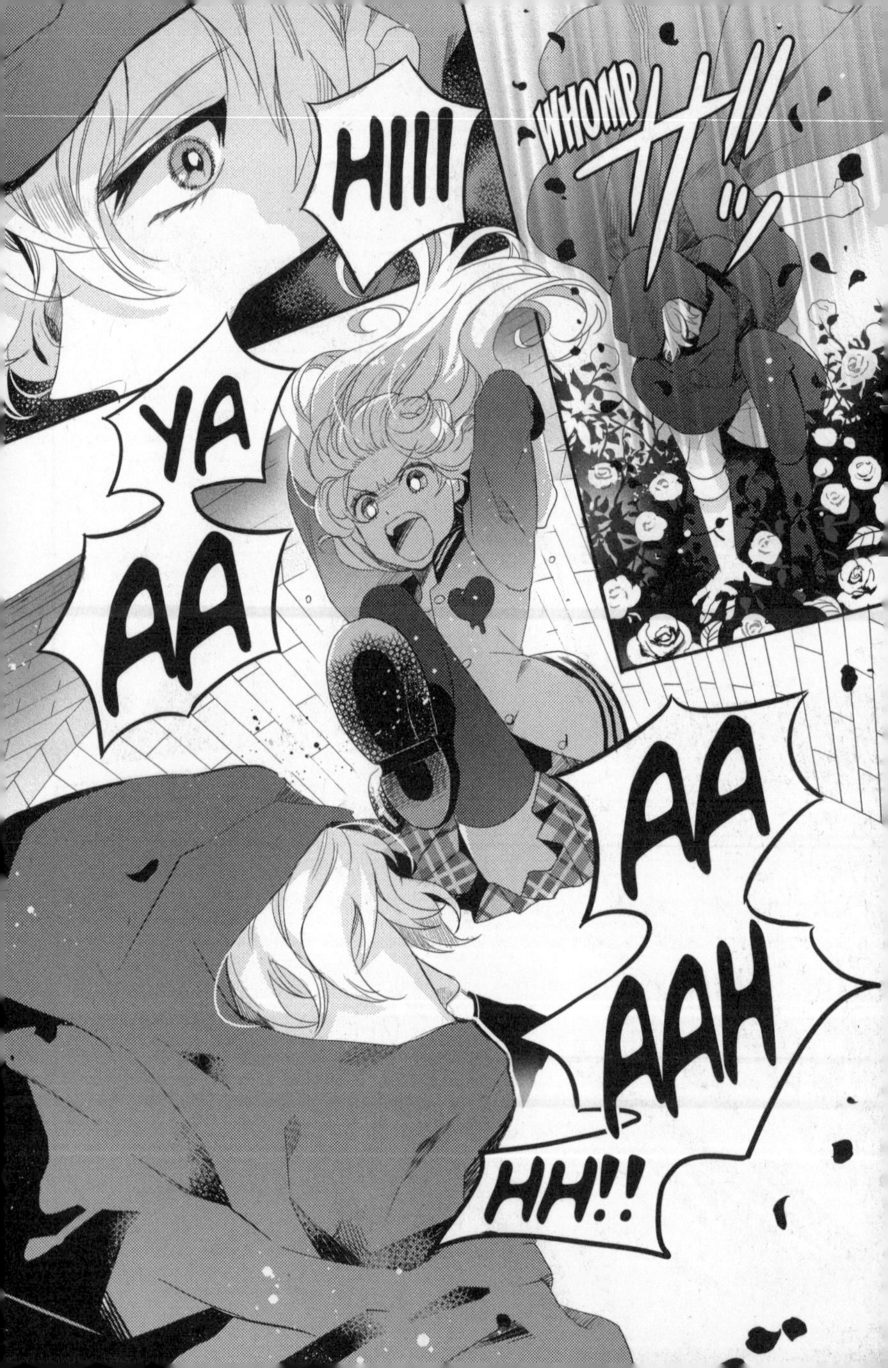
WHOMP
HIII
YA
AA
AA
AAH
HH!!

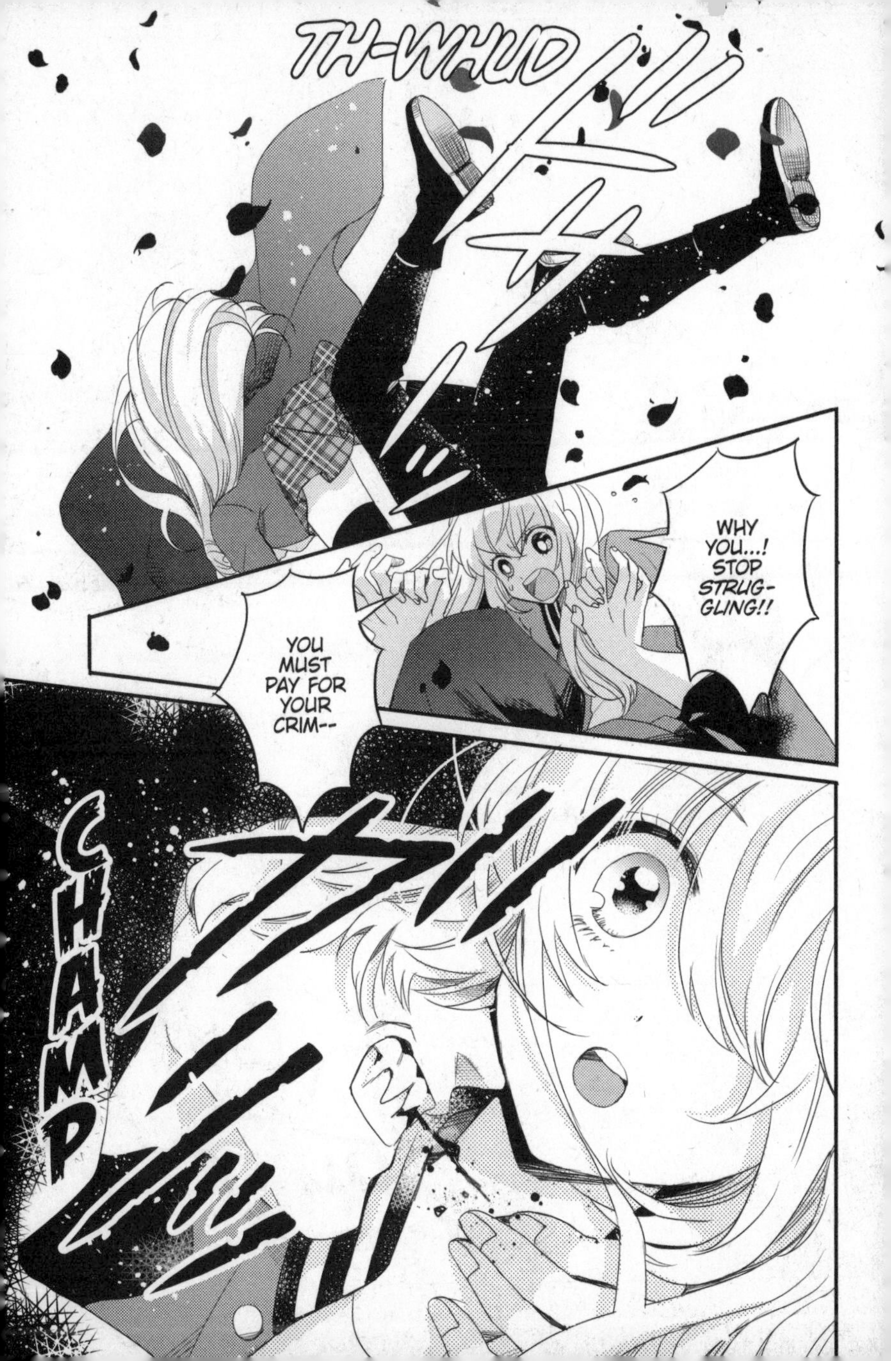
TH-WHUD
WHY YOU...! STOP STRUG-GLING!!
YOU MUST PAY FOR YOUR CRIM--
CHAMP

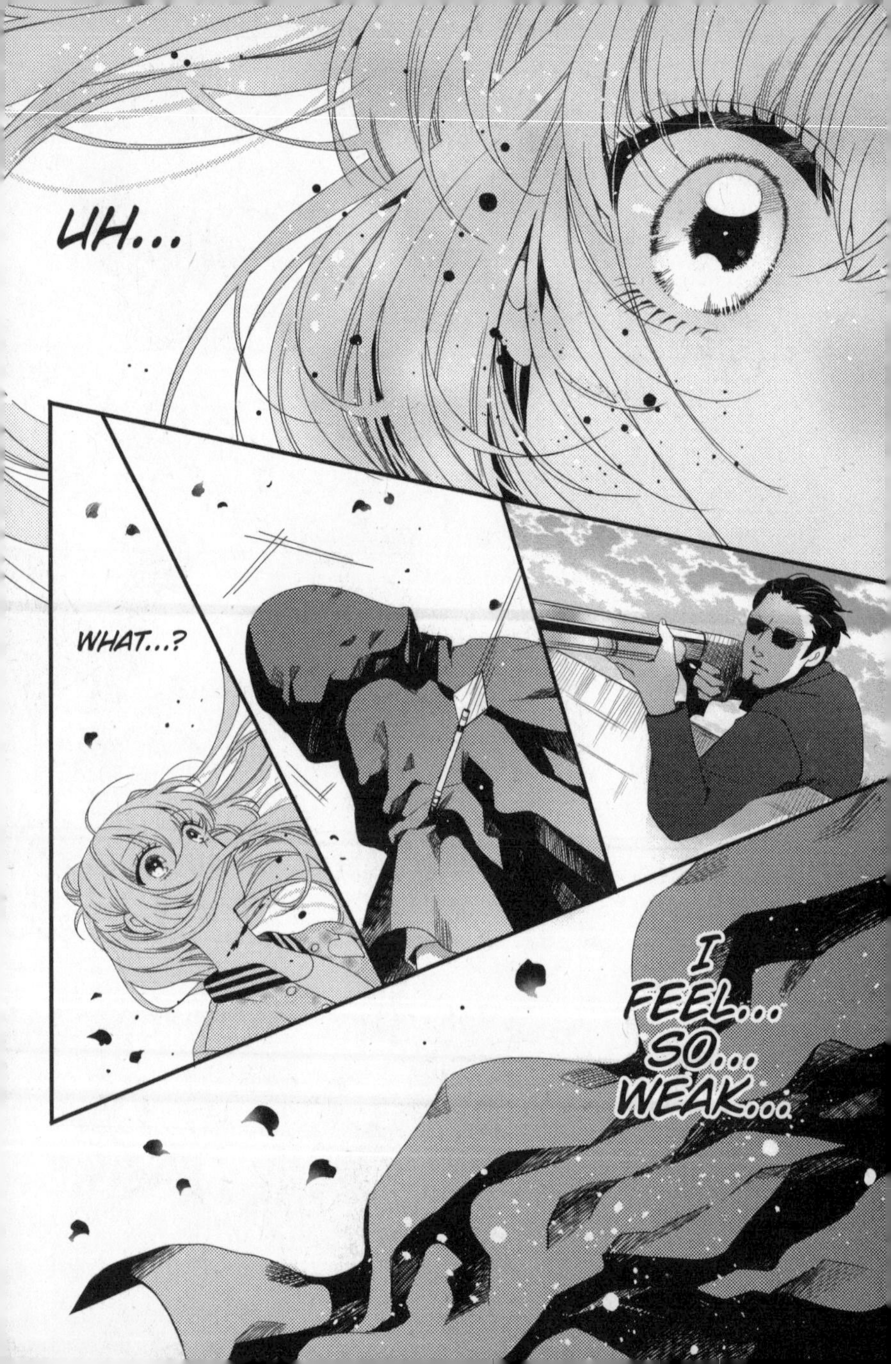
UH...
WHAT...?
I FEEL... SO... WEAK...

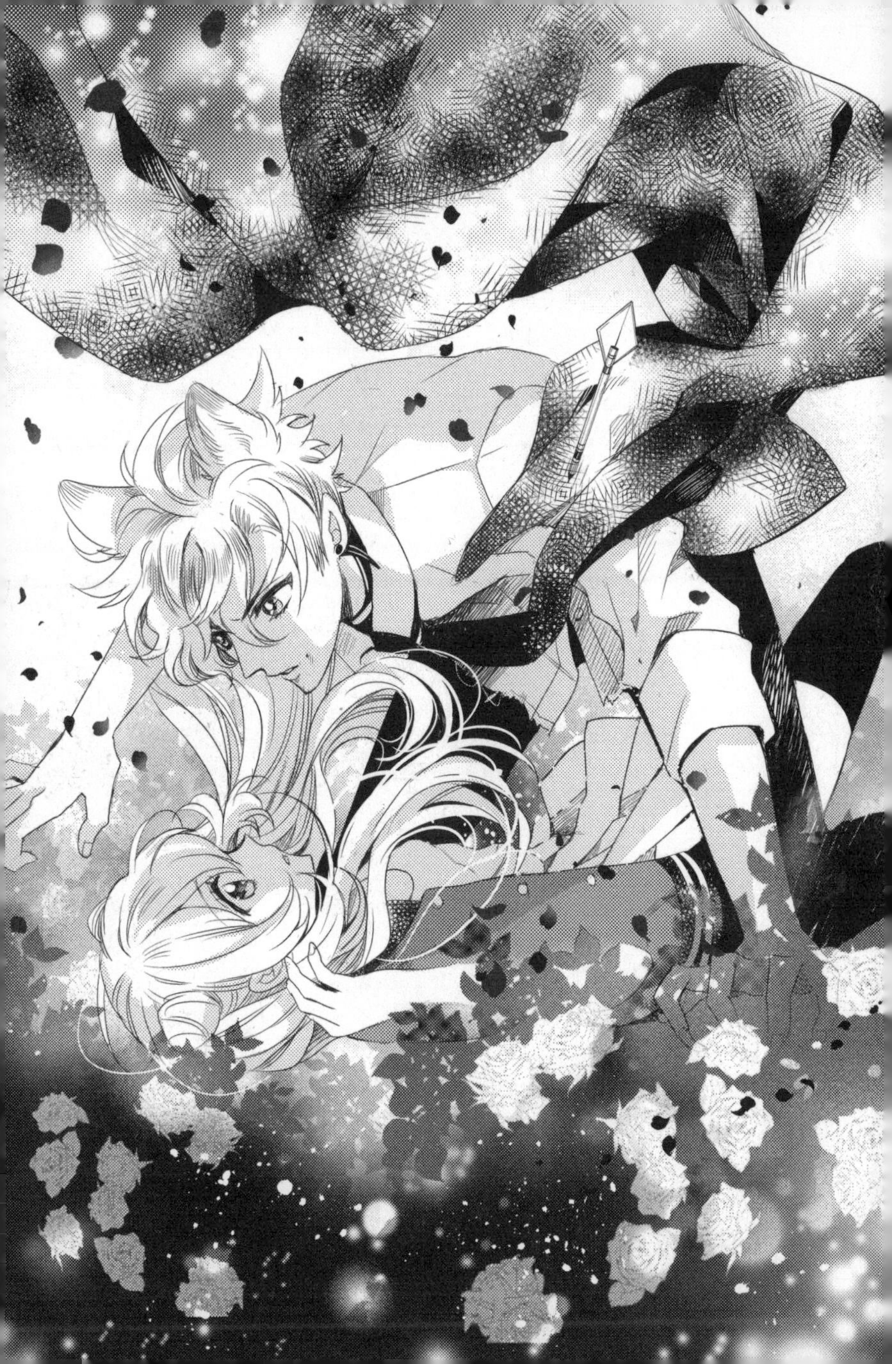

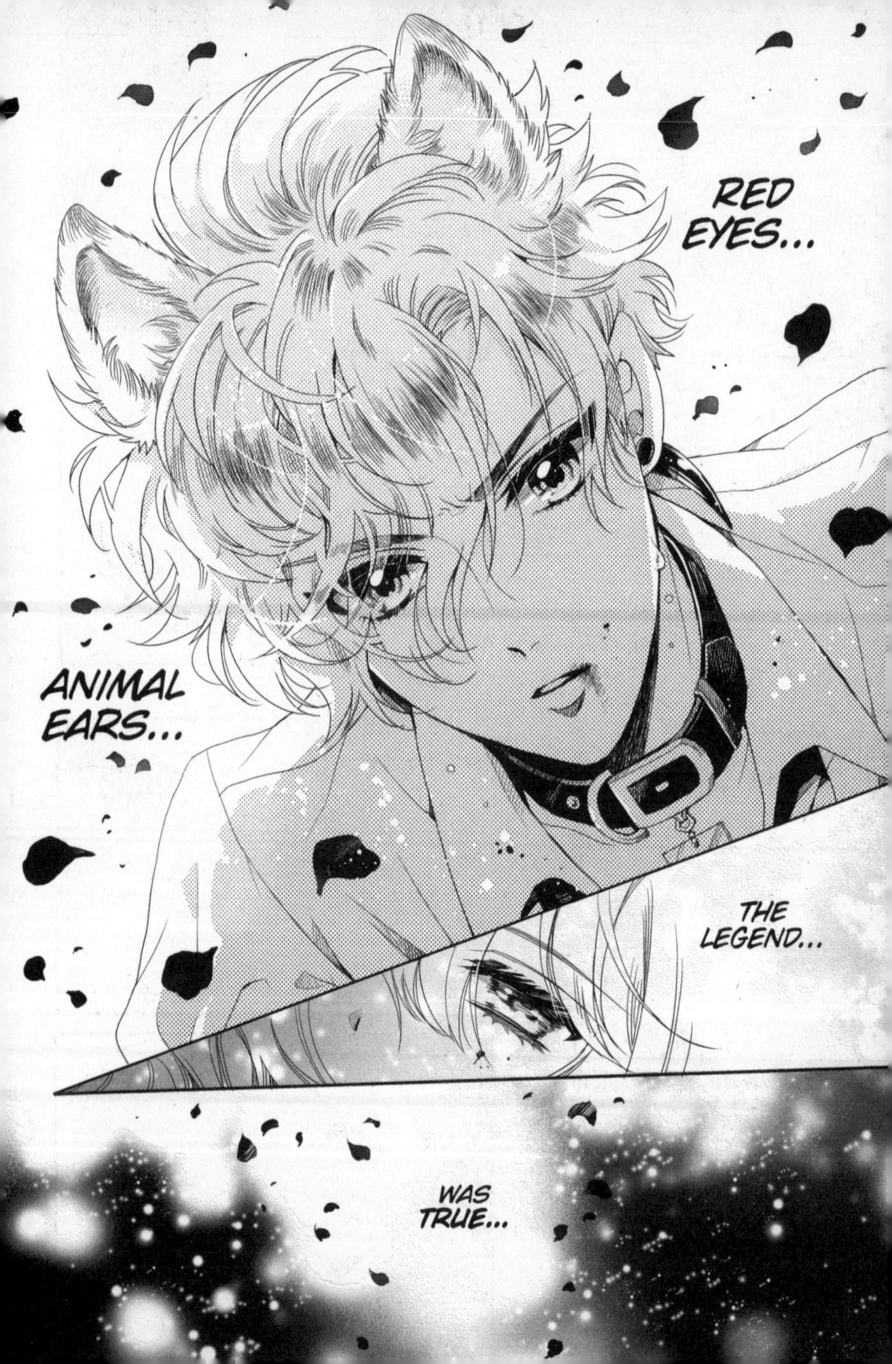
RED EYES...
ANIMAL EARS...
THE LEGEND...
WAS TRUE...

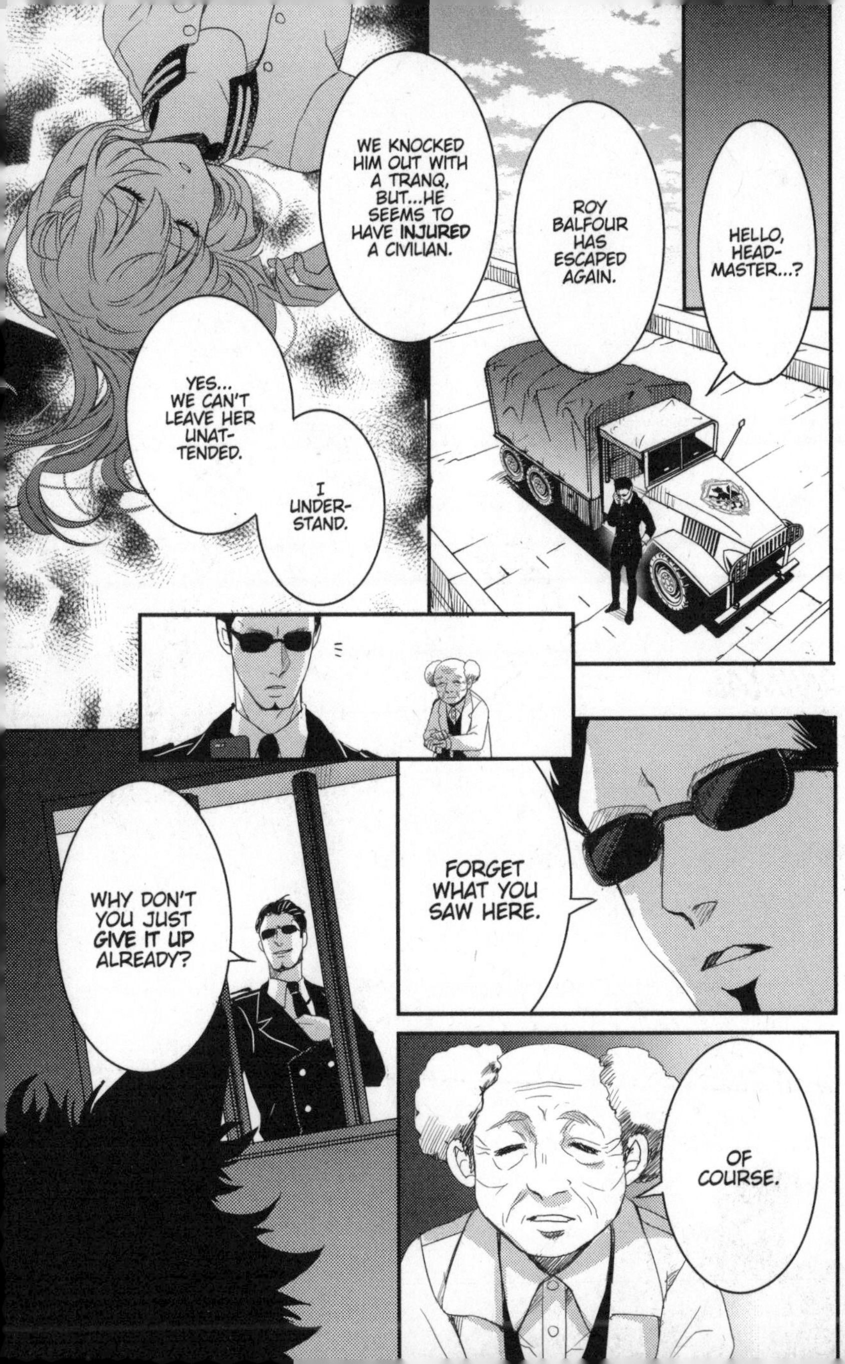
HELLO, HEAD-MASTER...?
ROY BALFOUR HAS ESCAPED AGAIN.
WE KNOCKED HIM OUT WITH A TRANQ, BUT...HE SEEMS TO HAVE INJURED A CIVILIAN.
YES... WE CAN'T LEAVE HER UNAT-TENDED.
I UNDER-STAND.
FORGET WHAT YOU SAW HERE.
WHY DON'T YOU JUST GIVE IT UP ALREADY?
OF COURSE.

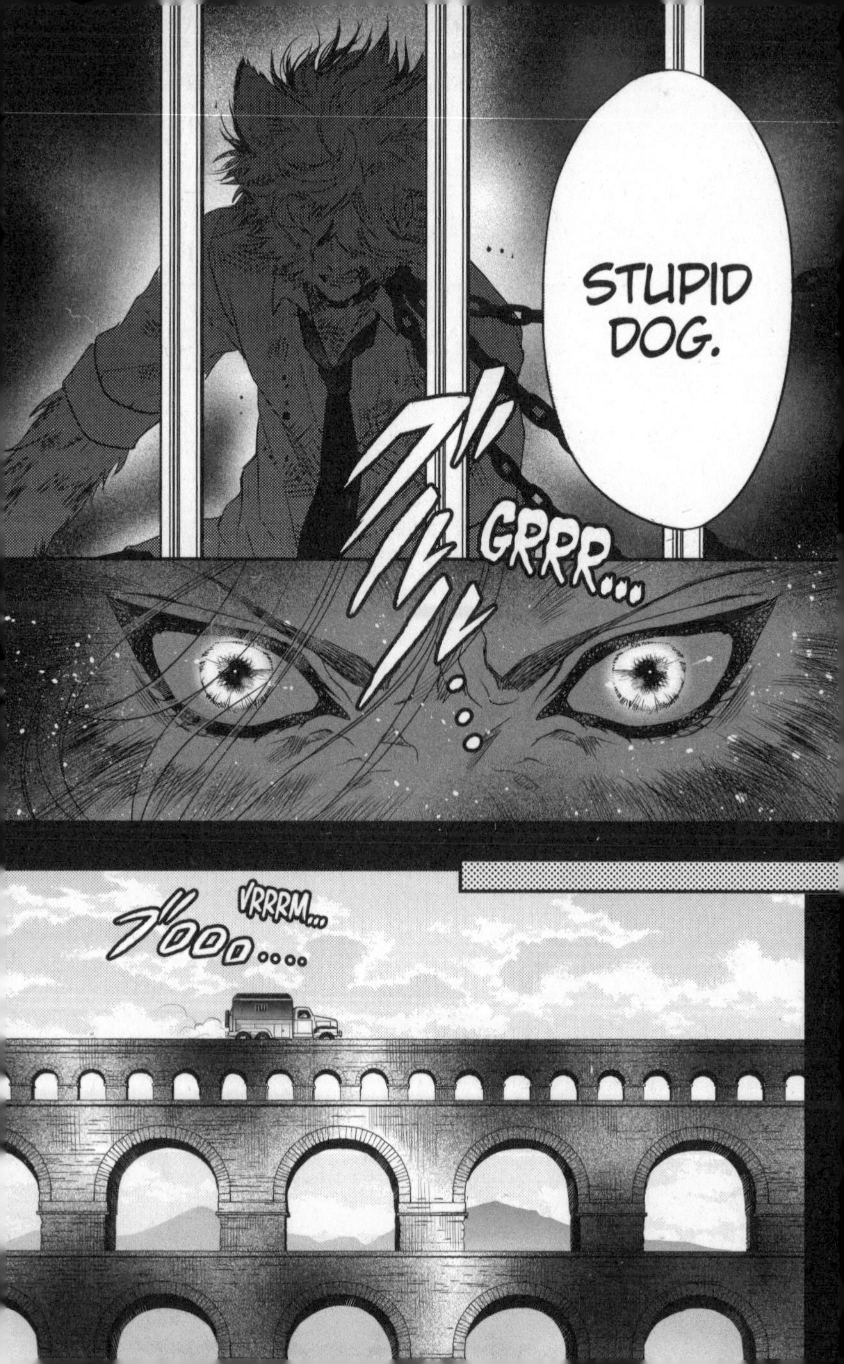
STUPID DOG.
GRRR...
VRRRM...
ブロロロ....

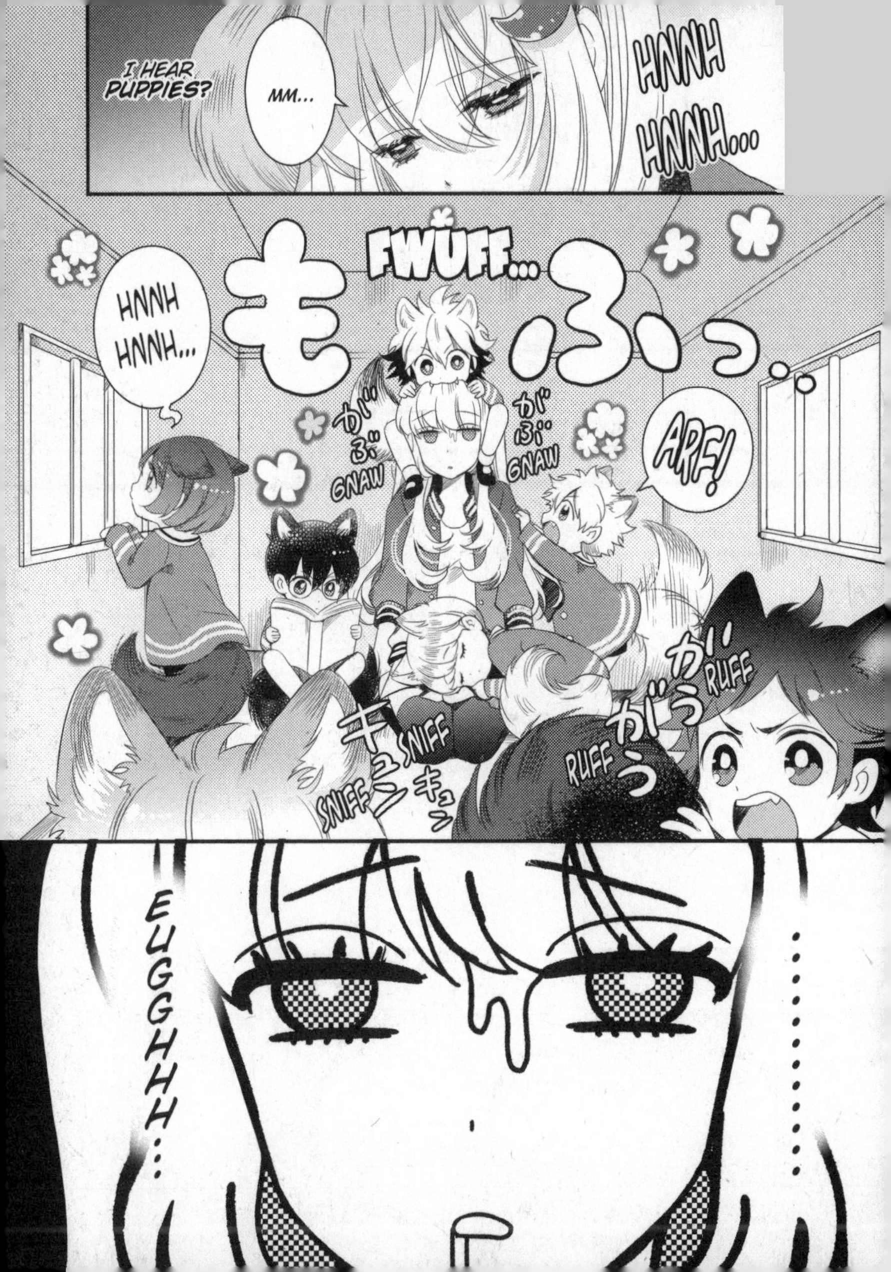
HNNH HNNH...
MM...
I HEAR PUPPIES?
もふっ..
FWUFF...
ARF!
がぶ GNAW
がぶ GNAW
HNNH HNNH...
がうがう RUFF RUFF
キュンキュン SNIFF SNIFF
......
EUGGHHH...

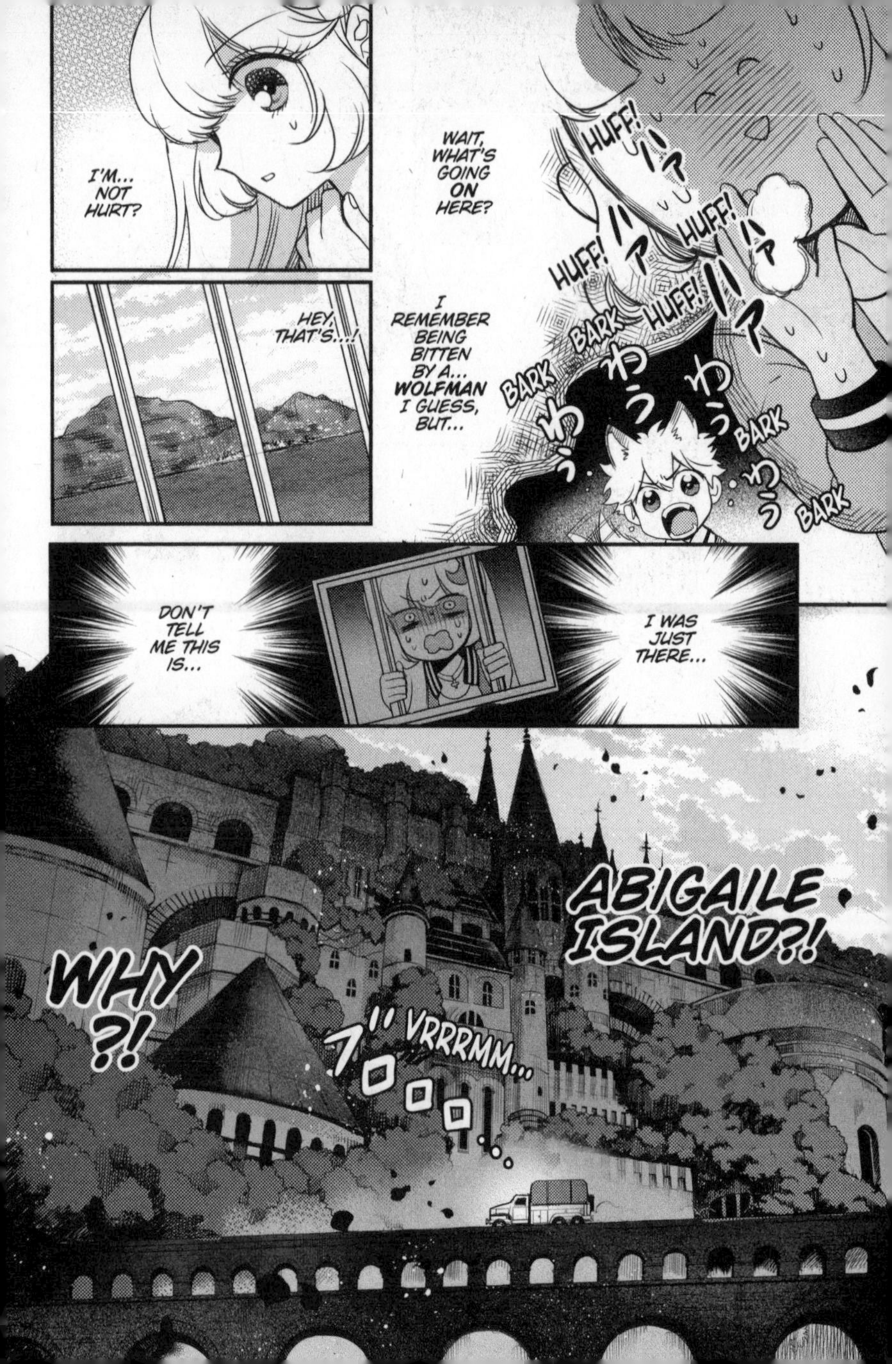
HUFF! ハァ
HUFF! ハァ
HUFF! ハァ
HUFF! ハァ
BARK わぅ
BARK わぅ
BARK わぅ
BARK わぅ
WAIT, WHAT'S GOING ON HERE?
I REMEMBER BEING BITTEN BY A... WOLFMAN I GUESS, BUT...
I'M... NOT HURT?
HEY, THAT'S...!
I WAS JUST THERE...
DON'T TELL ME THIS IS...
ABIGAILE ISLAND?!
WHY ?!
ブロロロ... VRRRMM...

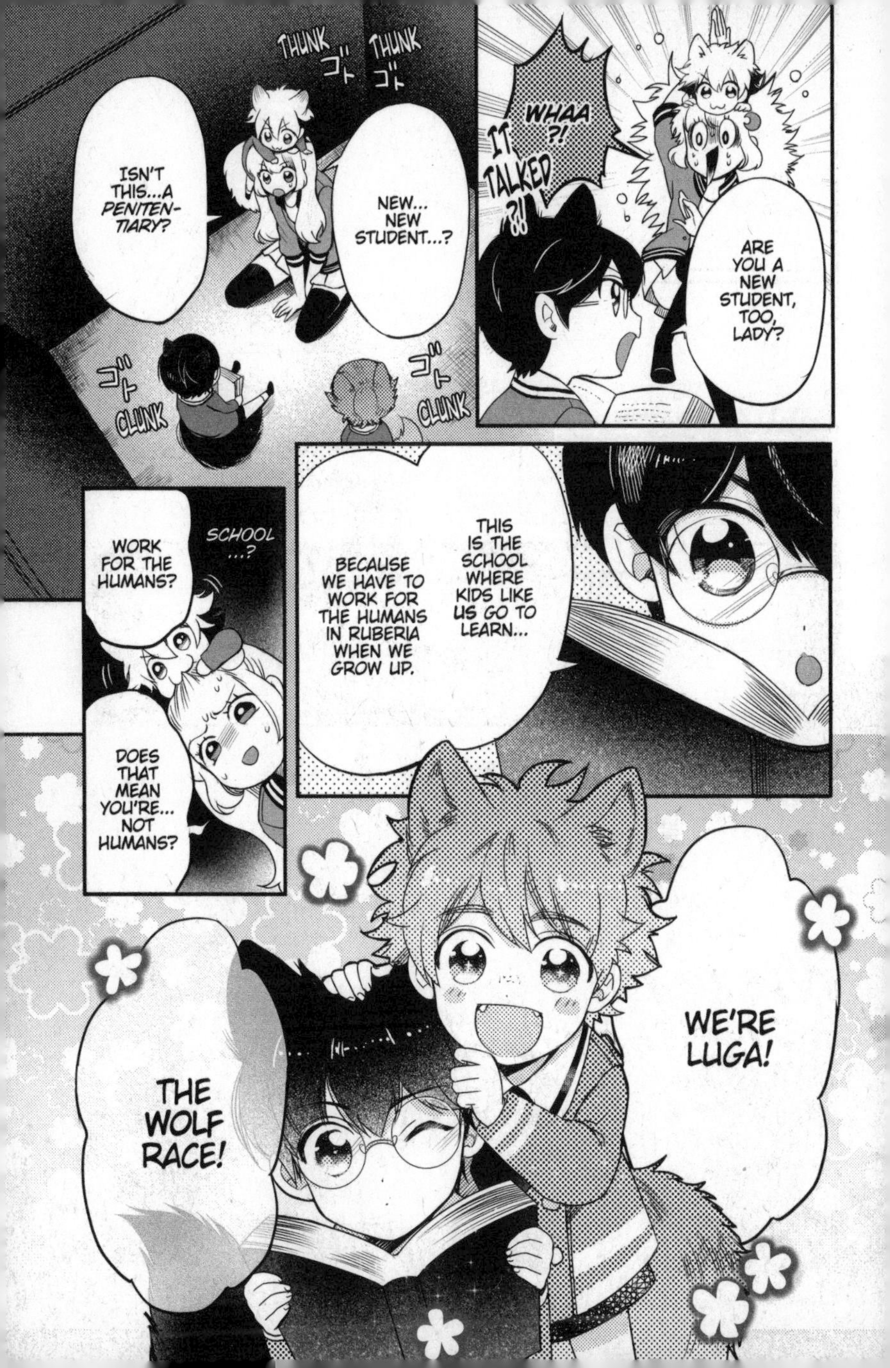
WHAA ?!
IT TALKED ?!!
ARE YOU A NEW STUDENT, TOO, LADY?
THUNK ゴト
THUNK ゴト
NEW... NEW STUDENT...?
ISN'T THIS...A PENITENTIARY?
ゴト CLUNK
ゴト CLUNK
THIS IS THE SCHOOL WHERE KIDS LIKE US GO TO LEARN...
BECAUSE WE HAVE TO WORK FOR THE HUMANS IN RUBERIA WHEN WE GROW UP.
SCHOOL ...?
WORK FOR THE HUMANS?
DOES THAT MEAN YOU'RE... NOT HUMANS?
WE'RE LUGA!
THE WOLF RACE!

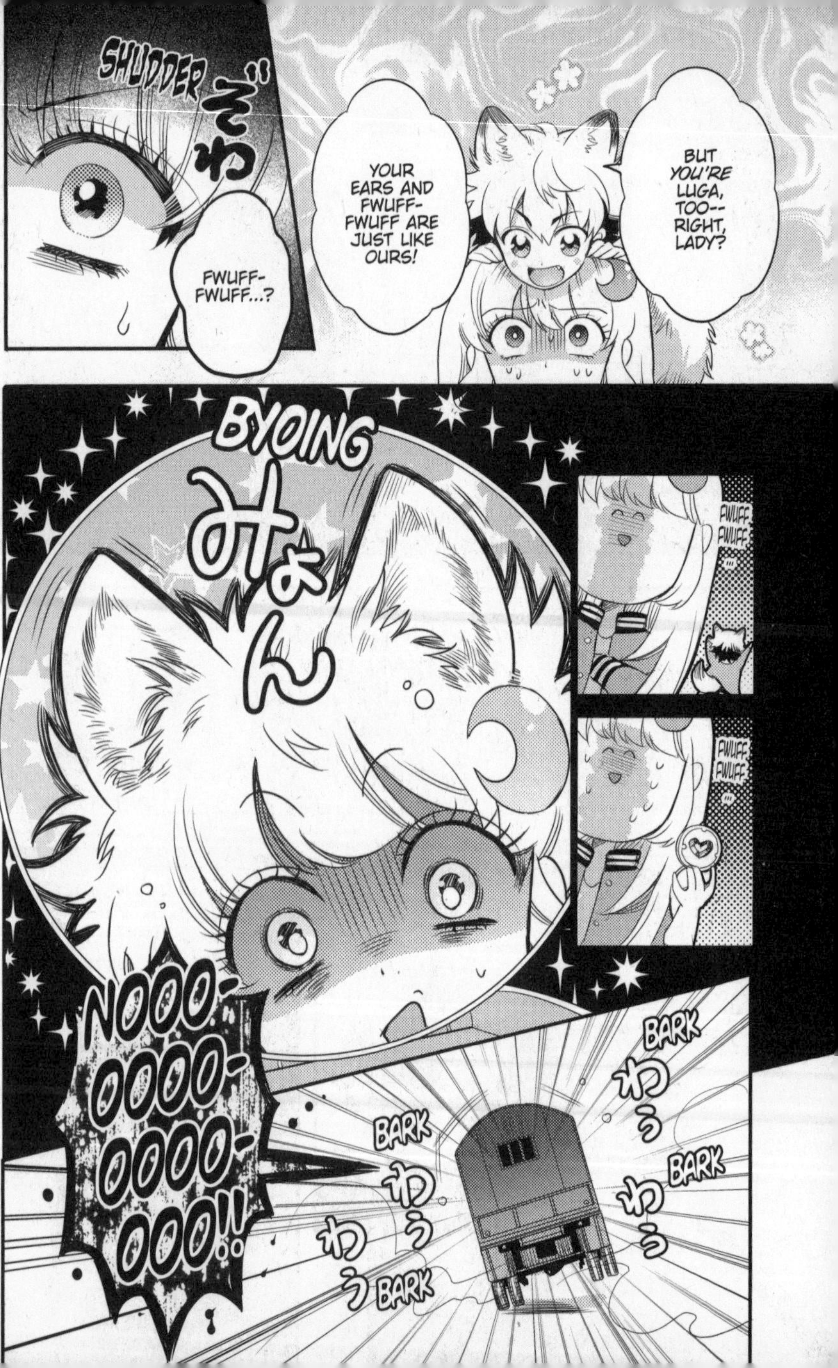
BUT YOU'RE LUGA, TOO--RIGHT, LADY?
YOUR EARS AND FWUFF-FWUFF ARE JUST LIKE OURS!
SHUDDER
ぞわ
FWUFF-FWUFF...?
FWUFF FWUFF ...
FWUFF FWUFF ...
BYOING
みょん
BARK
わう
BARK
わう
BARK
わう
BARK
わう
NOOOO-OOOOO-OOOOO-OOO!!

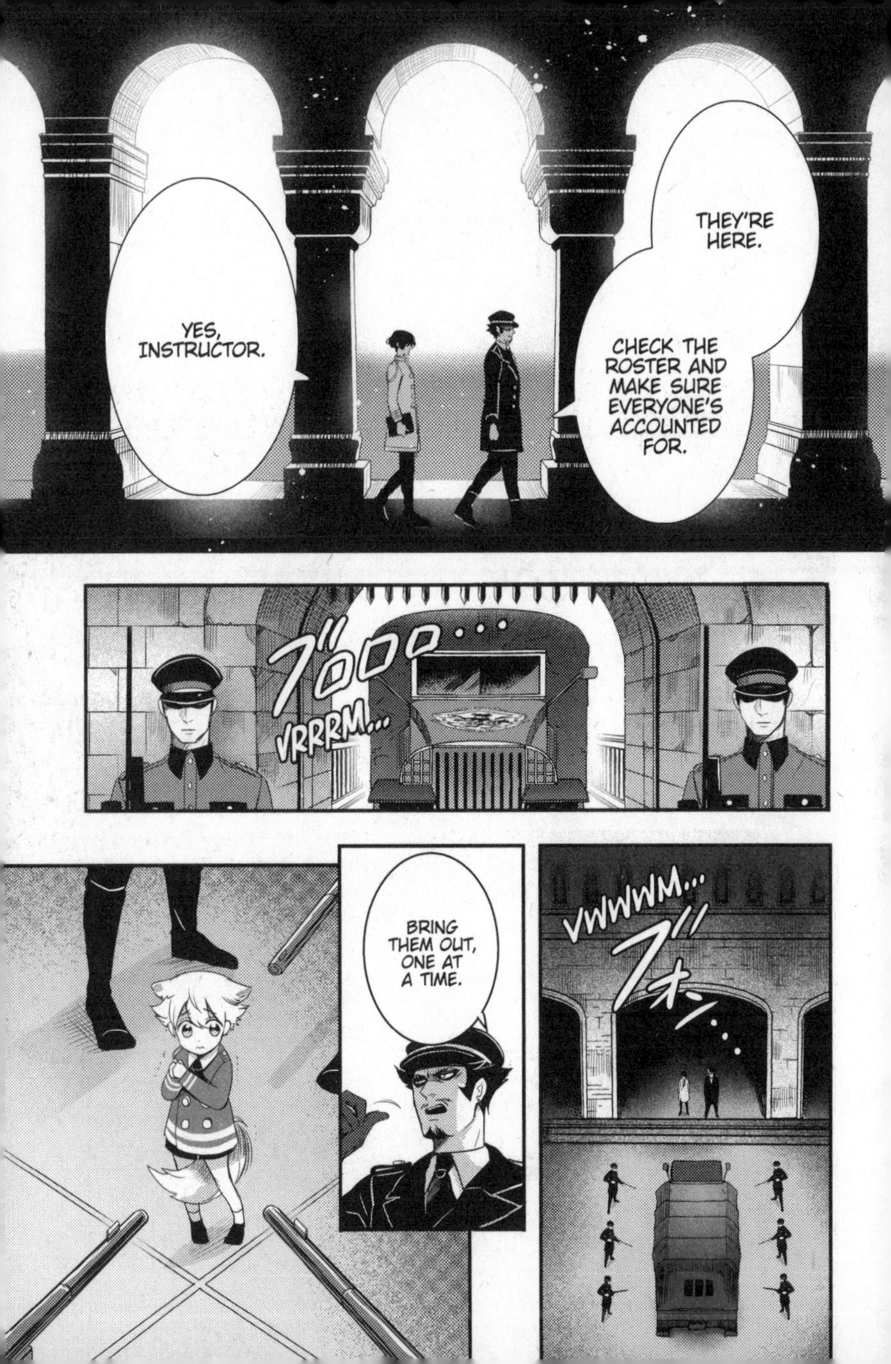
THEY'RE HERE.
CHECK THE ROSTER AND MAKE SURE EVERYONE'S ACCOUNTED FOR.
YES, INSTRUCTOR.
ブロロロ…
VRRRM...
VWWWM...
ブォン…
BRING THEM OUT, ONE AT A TIME.

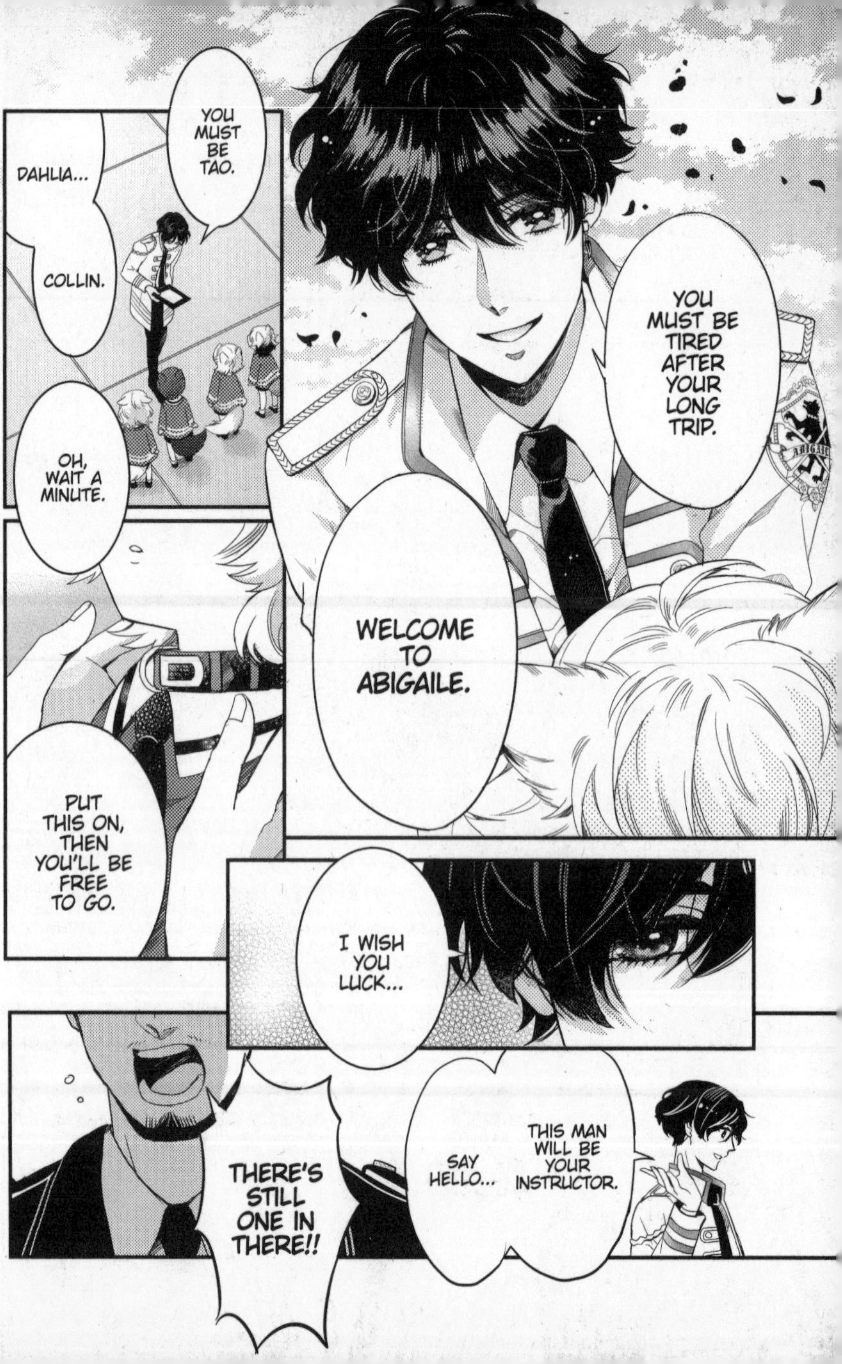
YOU MUST BE TIRED AFTER YOUR LONG TRIP.
WELCOME TO ABIGAILE.
YOU MUST BE TAO.
DAHLIA...
COLLIN.
OH, WAIT A MINUTE.
PUT THIS ON, THEN YOU'LL BE FREE TO GO.
I WISH YOU LUCK...
THIS MAN WILL BE YOUR INSTRUCTOR.
SAY HELLO...
THERE'S STILL ONE IN THERE!!

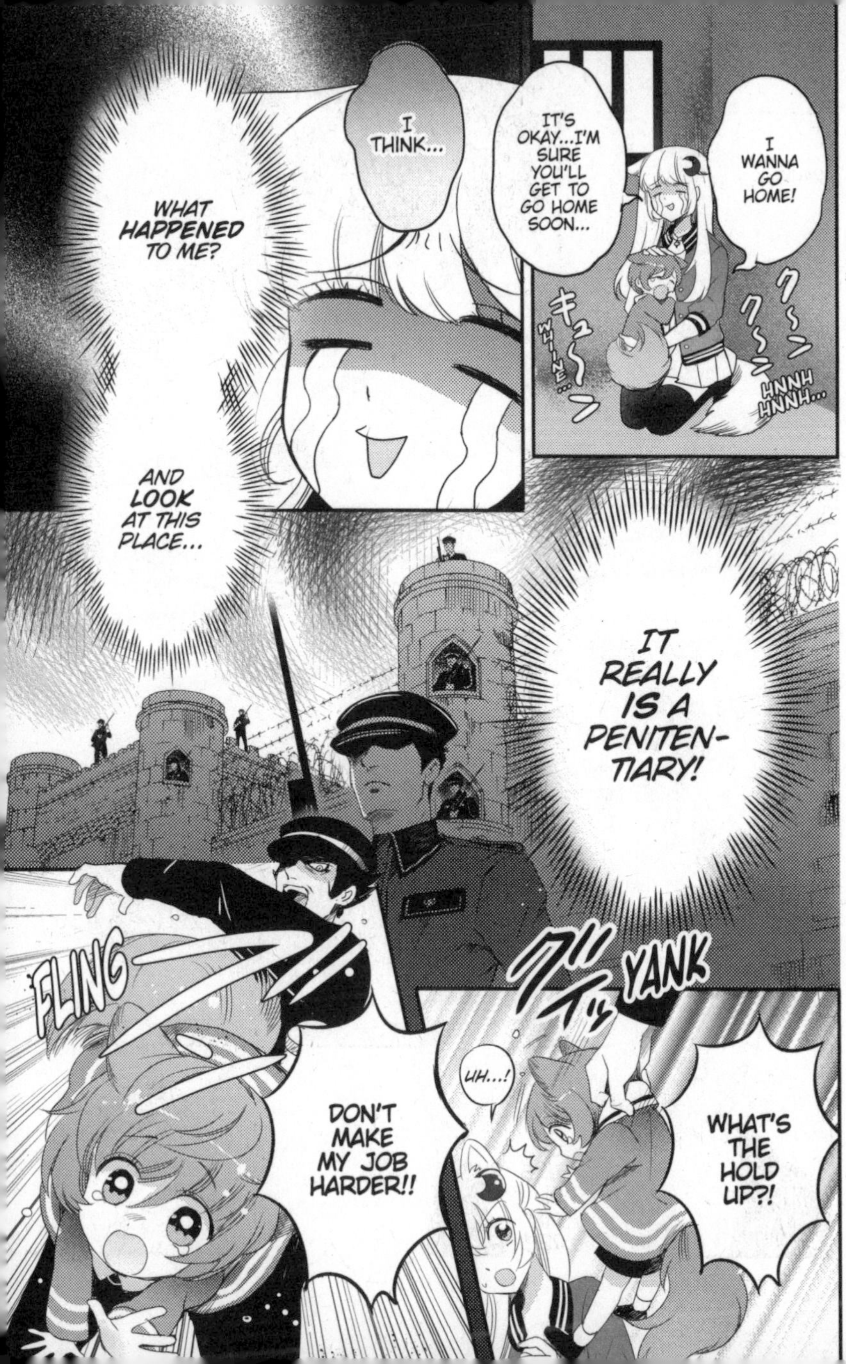
I WANNA GO HOME!
IT'S OKAY...I'M SURE YOU'LL GET TO GO HOME SOON...
HNNH HNNH...
WHINE...
I THINK...
WHAT HAPPENED TO ME?
AND LOOK AT THIS PLACE...
IT REALLY IS A PENITENTIARY!
YANK
WHAT'S THE HOLD UP?!
UH...!
DON'T MAKE MY JOB HARDER!!
FLING

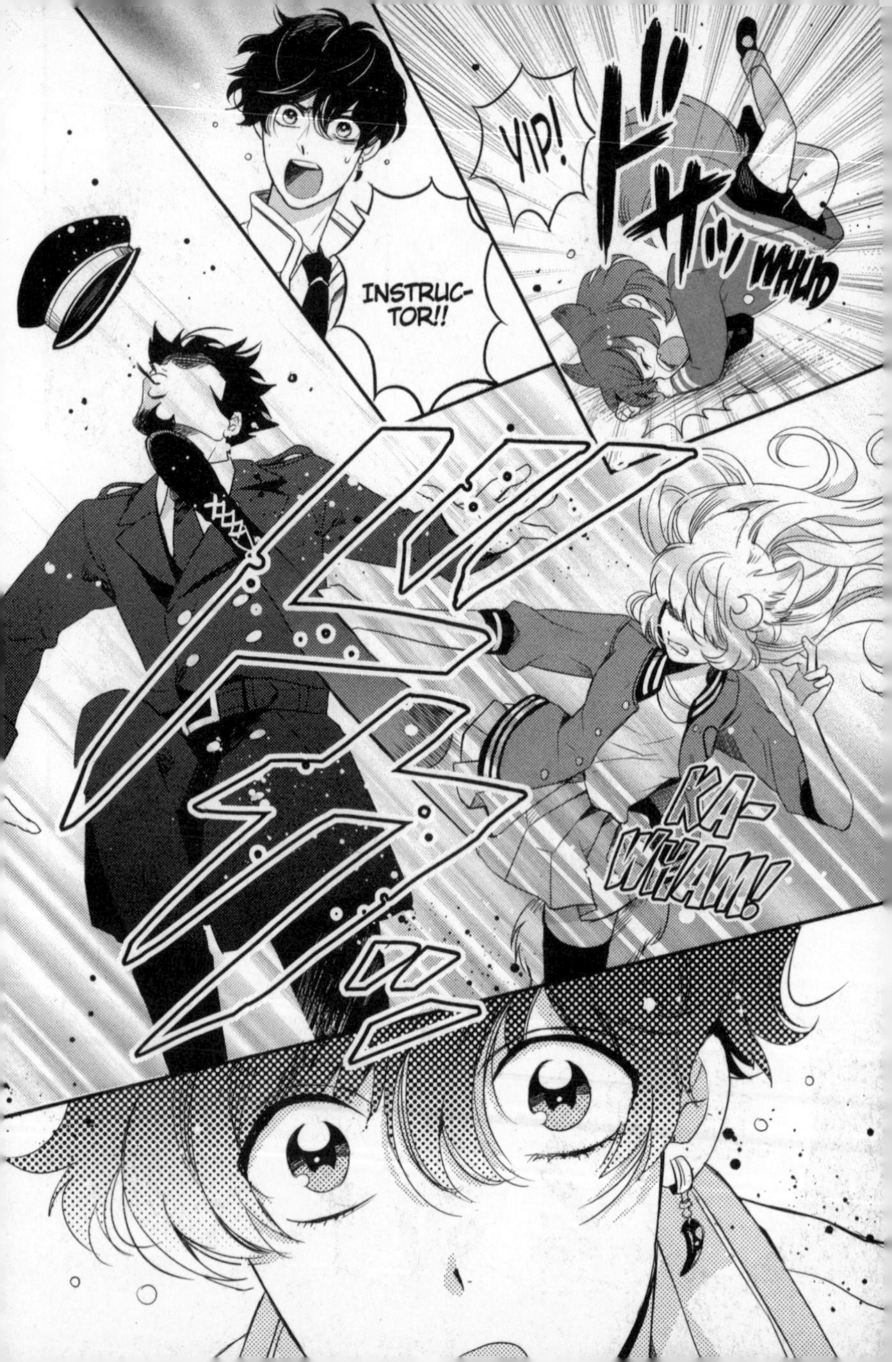
YIP!
WHUD
INSTRUC-
TOR!!
KA-
WHAM!

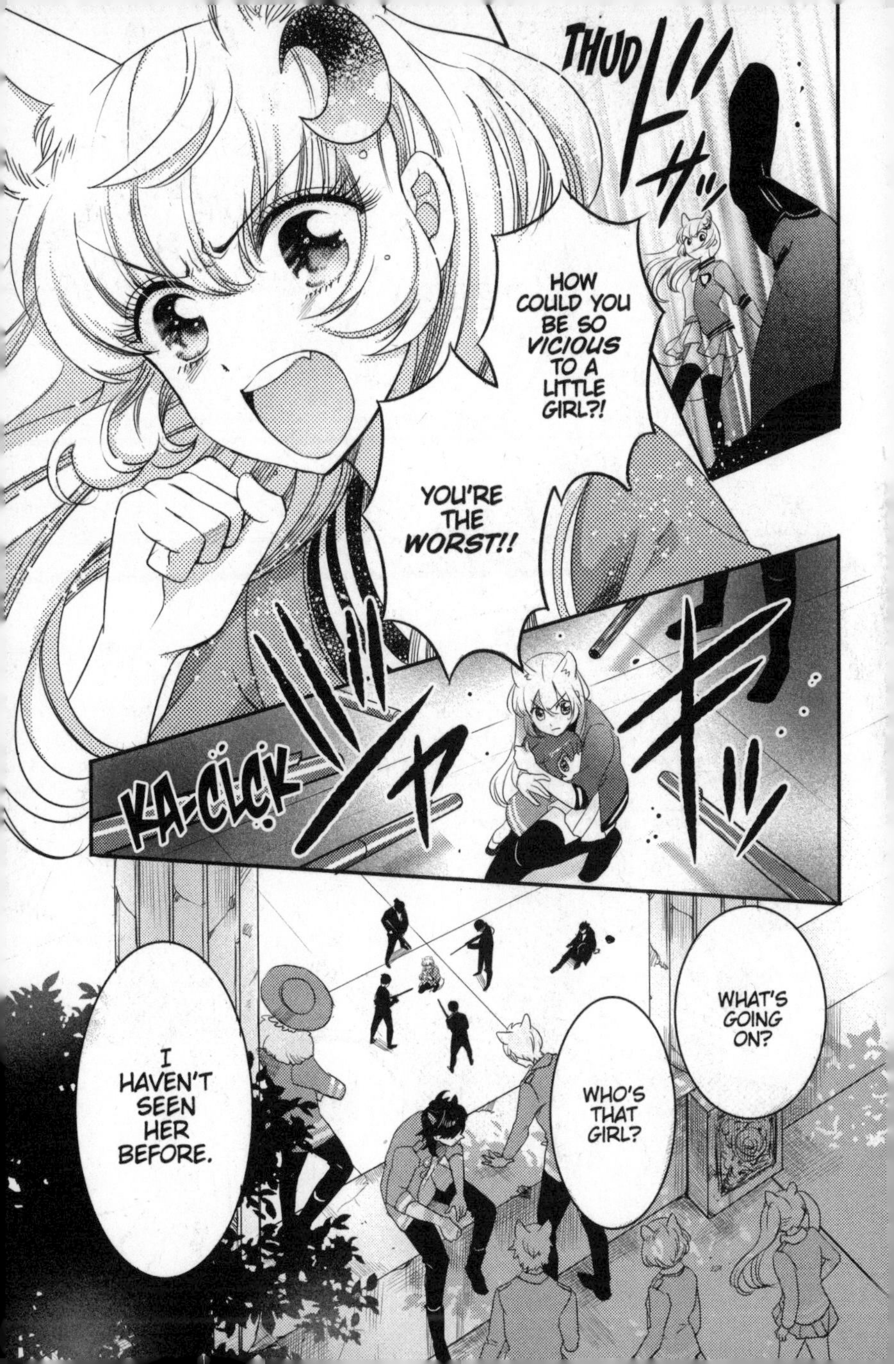
THUD
HOW COULD YOU BE SO VICIOUS TO A LITTLE GIRL?!
YOU'RE THE WORST!!
KA-CLICK
WHAT'S GOING ON?
WHO'S THAT GIRL?
I HAVEN'T SEEN HER BEFORE.

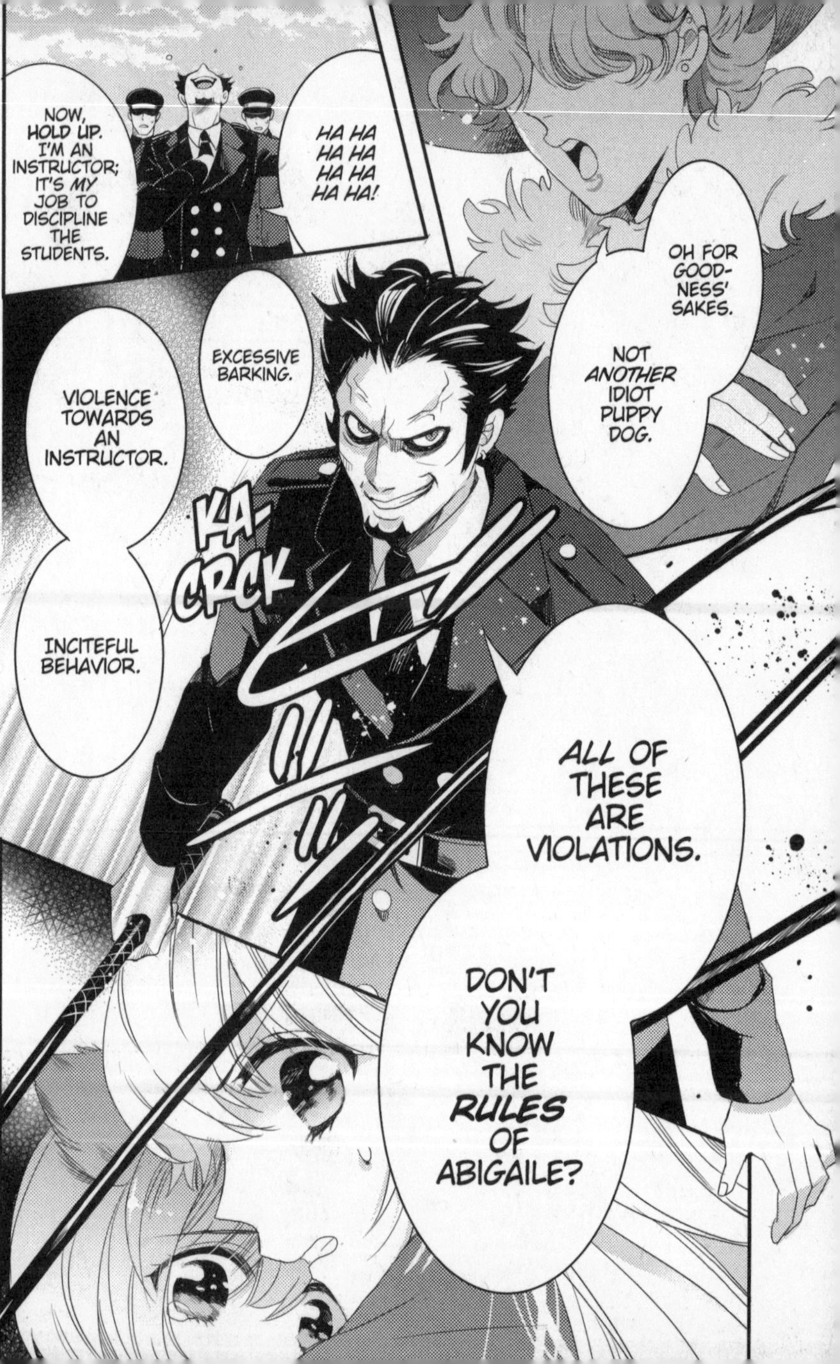
OH FOR GOODNESS' SAKES.
NOT *ANOTHER* IDIOT PUPPY DOG.
HA HA HA HA HA HA HA HA!
NOW, HOLD UP. I'M AN INSTRUCTOR; IT'S MY JOB TO DISCIPLINE THE STUDENTS.
EXCESSIVE BARKING.
VIOLENCE TOWARDS AN INSTRUCTOR.
INCITEFUL BEHAVIOR.
KA-CRCK
ALL OF THESE ARE VIOLATIONS.
DON'T YOU KNOW THE *RULES* OF ABIGAILE?

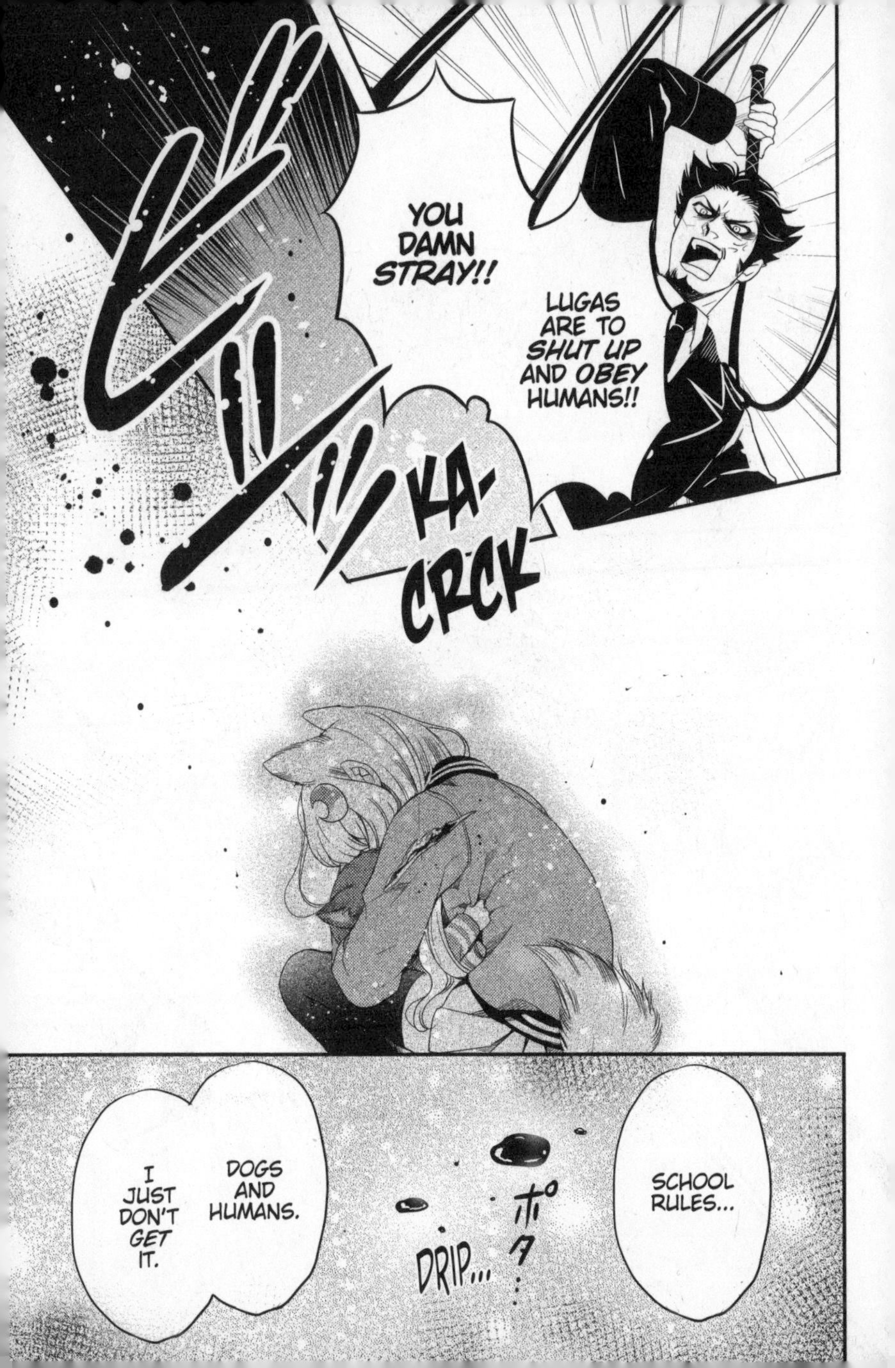
YOU DAMN STRAY!!
LUGAS ARE TO SHUT UP AND OBEY HUMANS!!
KA-CRCK
SCHOOL RULES...
DRIP...
ポタ
DOGS AND HUMANS.
I JUST DON'T GET IT.

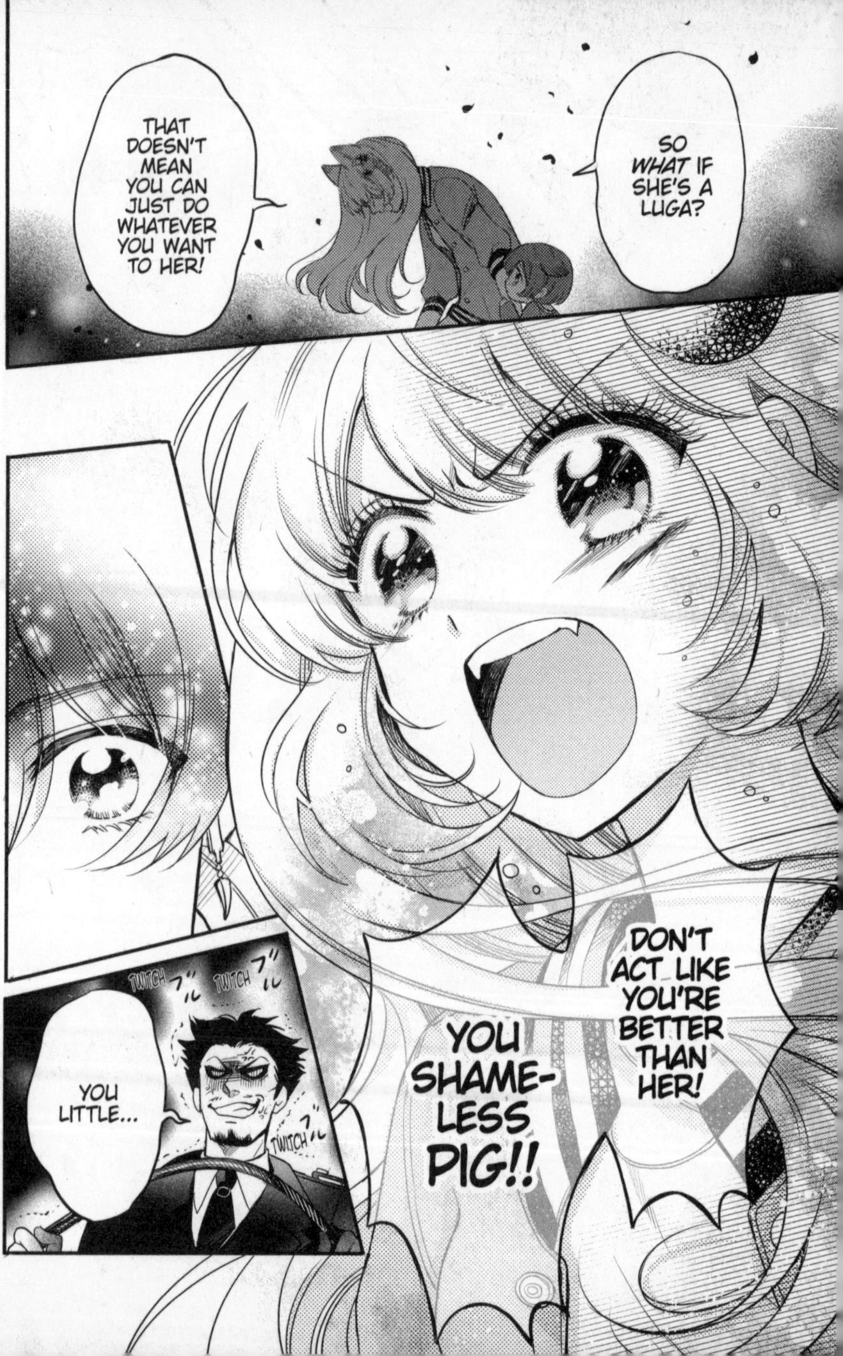
SO *WHAT* IF SHE'S A LUGA?
THAT DOESN'T MEAN YOU CAN JUST DO WHATEVER YOU WANT TO HER!
DON'T ACT LIKE YOU'RE BETTER THAN HER!
YOU SHAMELESS PIG!!
TWITCH
TWITCH
YOU LITTLE...
TWITCH

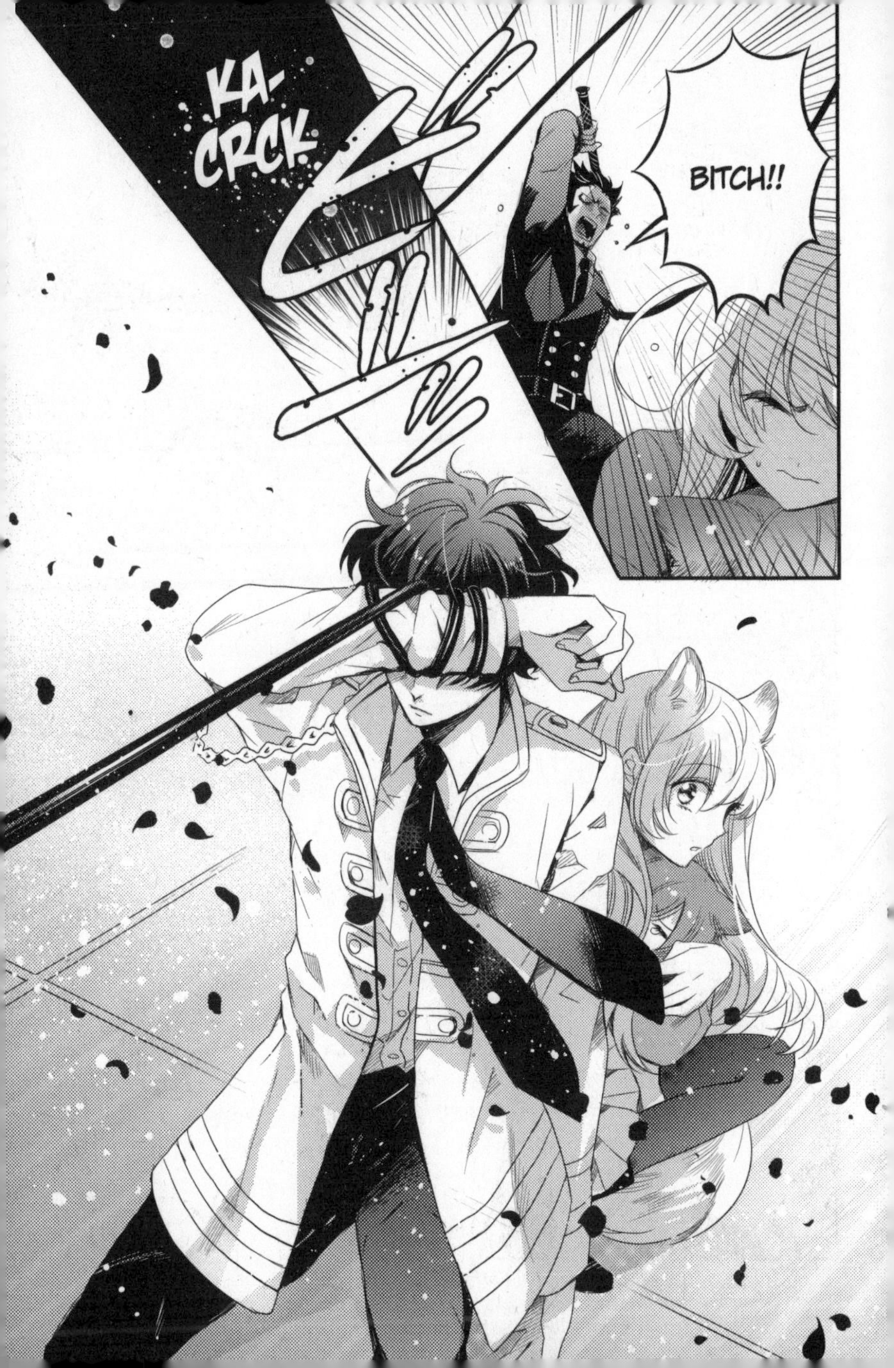
BITCH!!
KA-CRCK

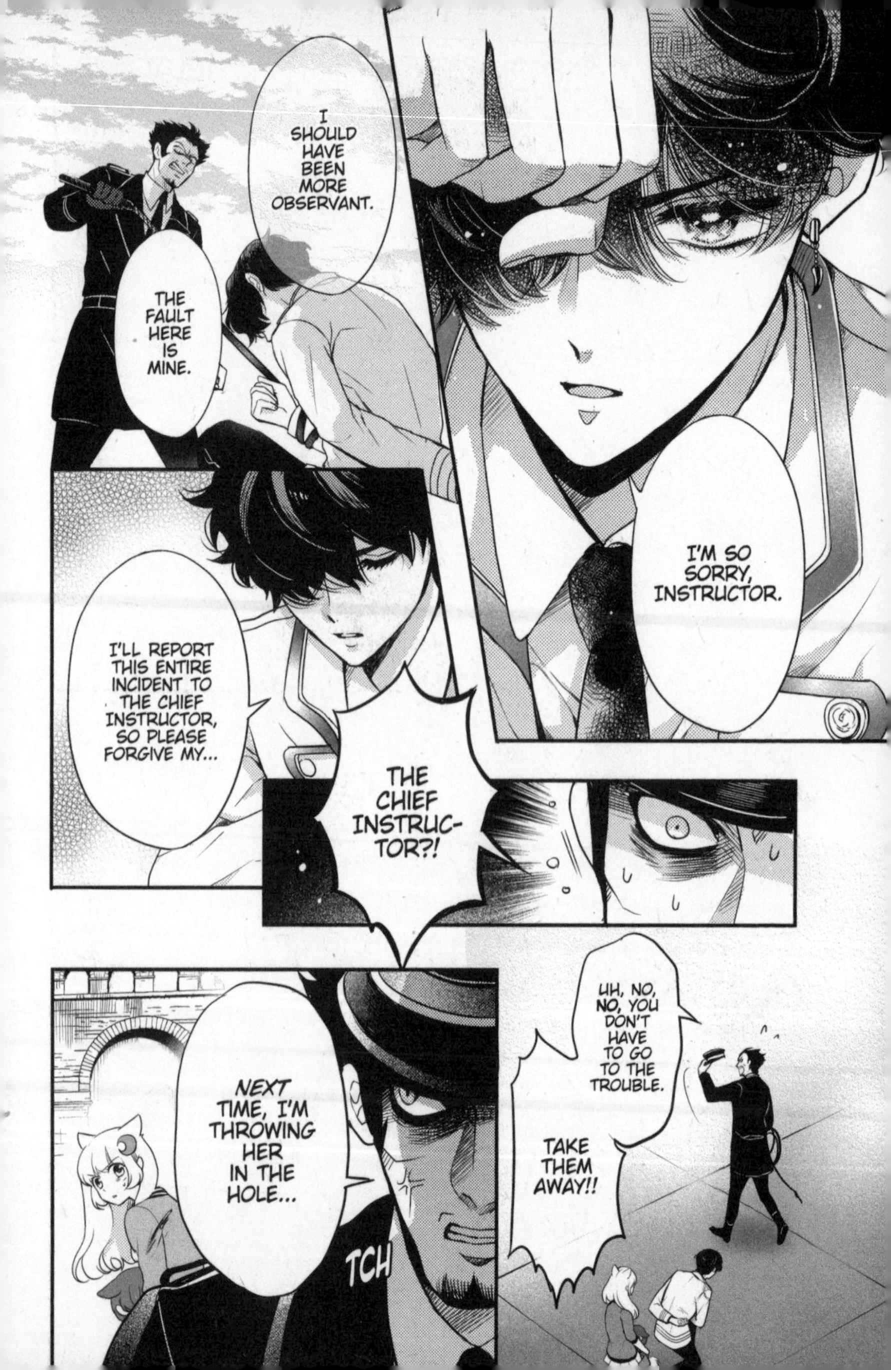
I'M SO SORRY, INSTRUCTOR.
I SHOULD HAVE BEEN MORE OBSERVANT.
THE FAULT HERE IS MINE.
I'LL REPORT THIS ENTIRE INCIDENT TO THE CHIEF INSTRUCTOR, SO PLEASE FORGIVE MY...
THE CHIEF INSTRUCTOR?!
UH, NO, NO, YOU DON'T HAVE TO GO TO THE TROUBLE.
TAKE THEM AWAY!!
NEXT TIME, I'M THROWING HER IN THE HOLE...
TCH

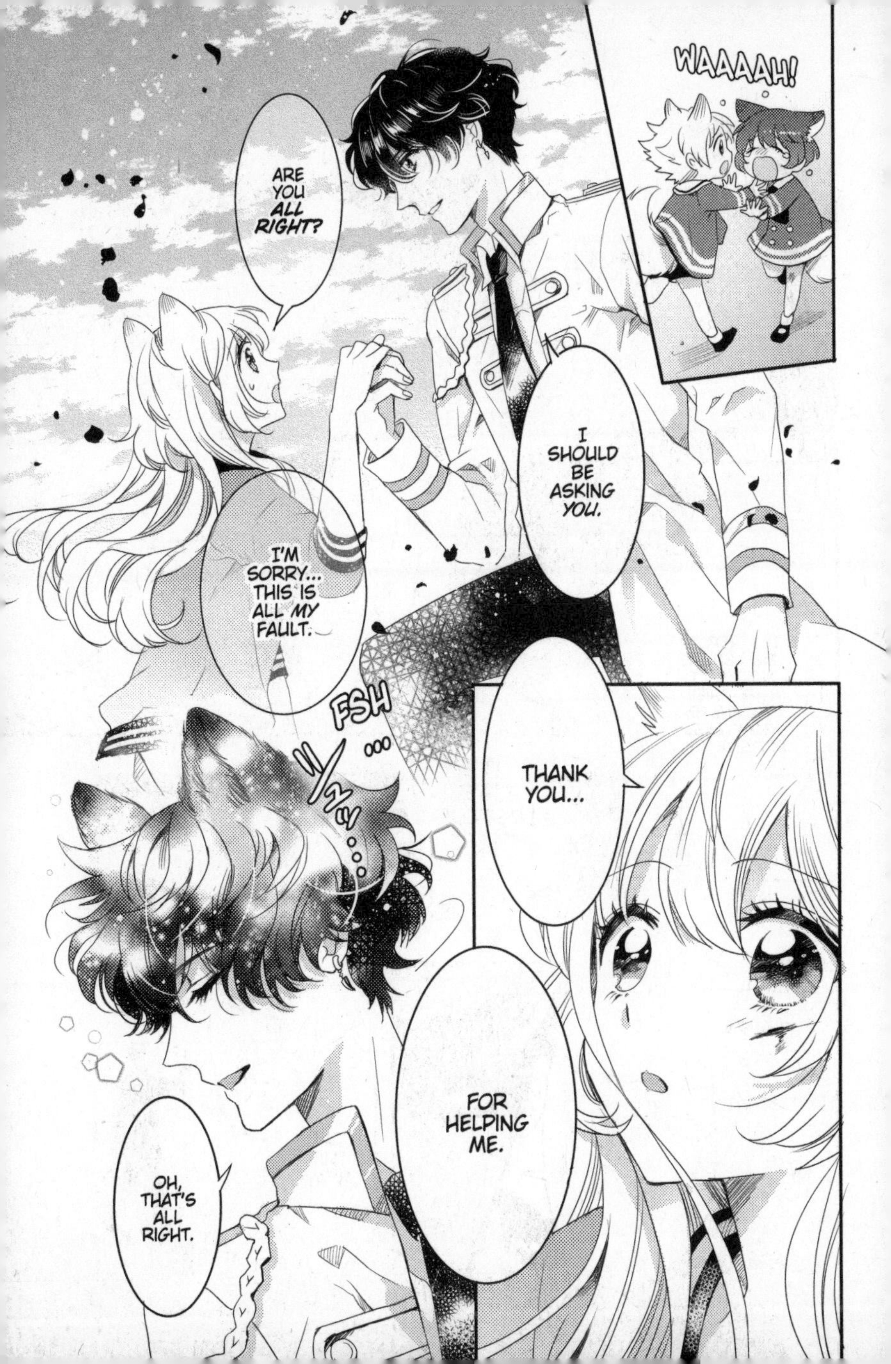
WAAAAH!
ARE YOU ALL RIGHT?
I SHOULD BE ASKING YOU.
I'M SORRY... THIS IS ALL MY FAULT.
THANK YOU...
FOR HELPING ME.
FSH
OH, THAT'S ALL RIGHT.

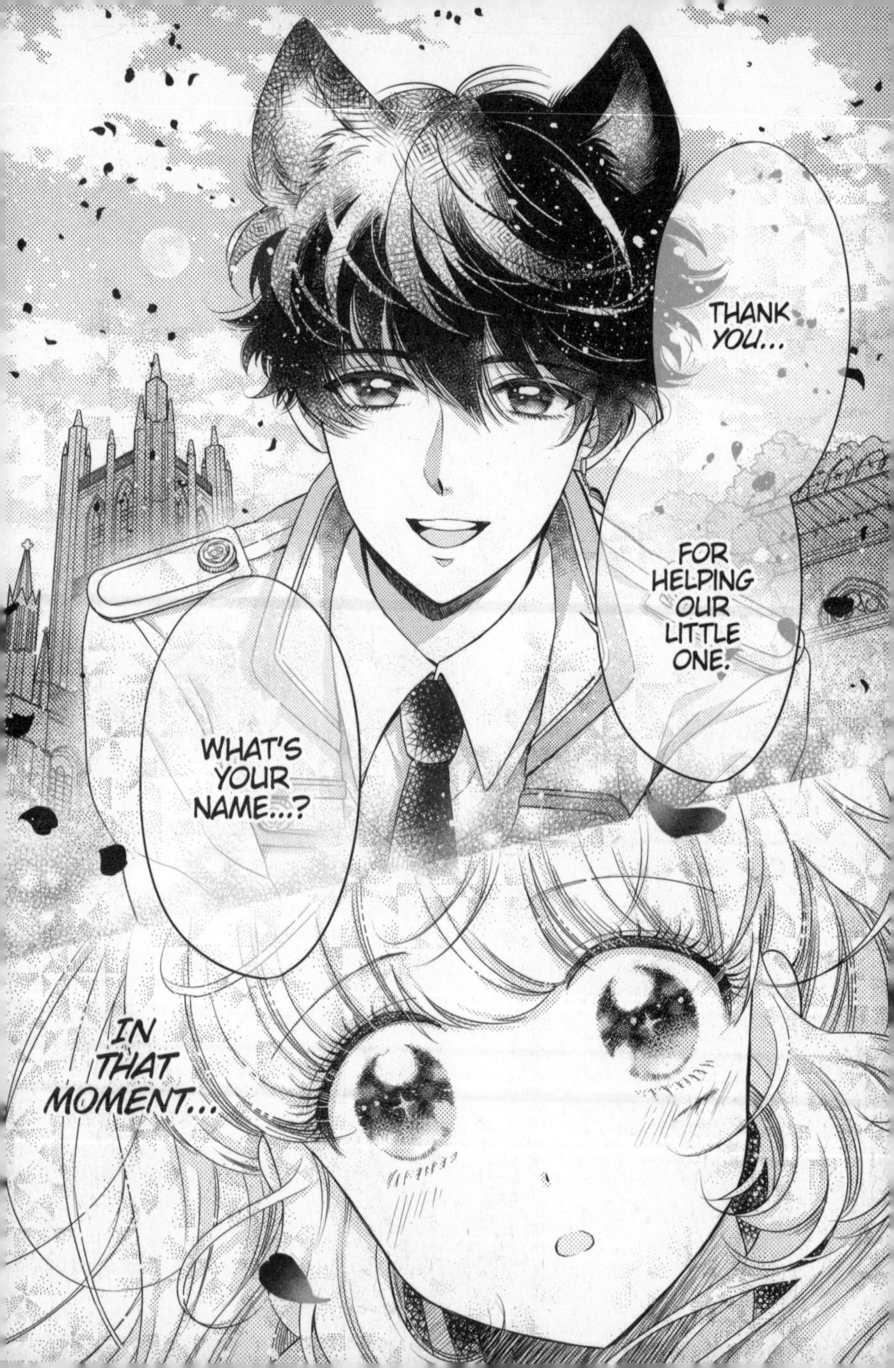
THANK YOU...
FOR HELPING OUR LITTLE ONE.
WHAT'S YOUR NAME...?
IN THAT MOMENT...

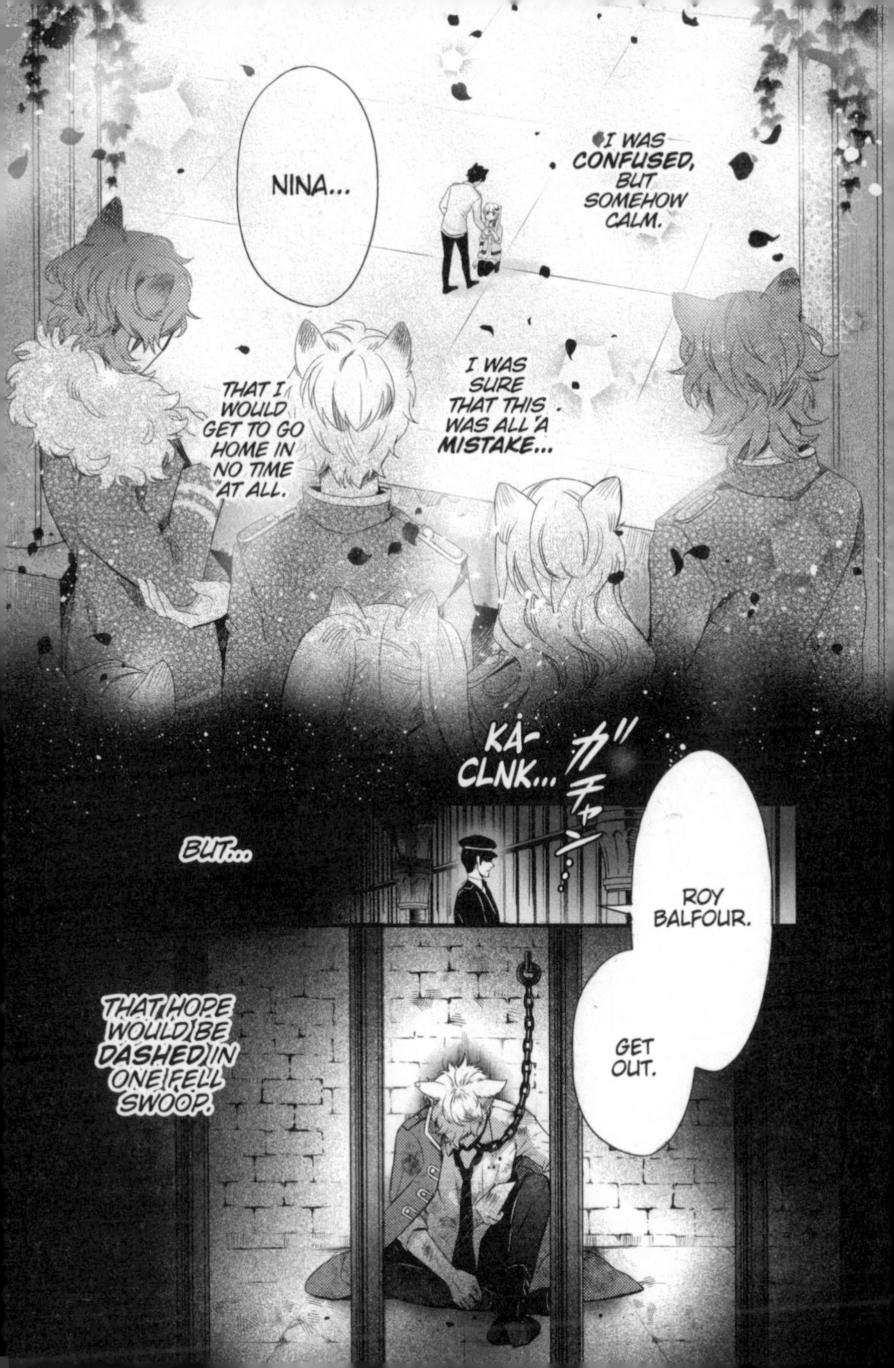
I WAS CONFUSED, BUT SOMEHOW CALM.
NINA...
I WAS SURE THAT THIS WAS ALL A MISTAKE...
THAT I WOULD GET TO GO HOME IN NO TIME AT ALL.
KA-CLNK...
ガチャン
ROY BALFOUR.
GET OUT.
BUT...
THAT HOPE WOULD BE DASHED IN ONE FELL SWOOP.

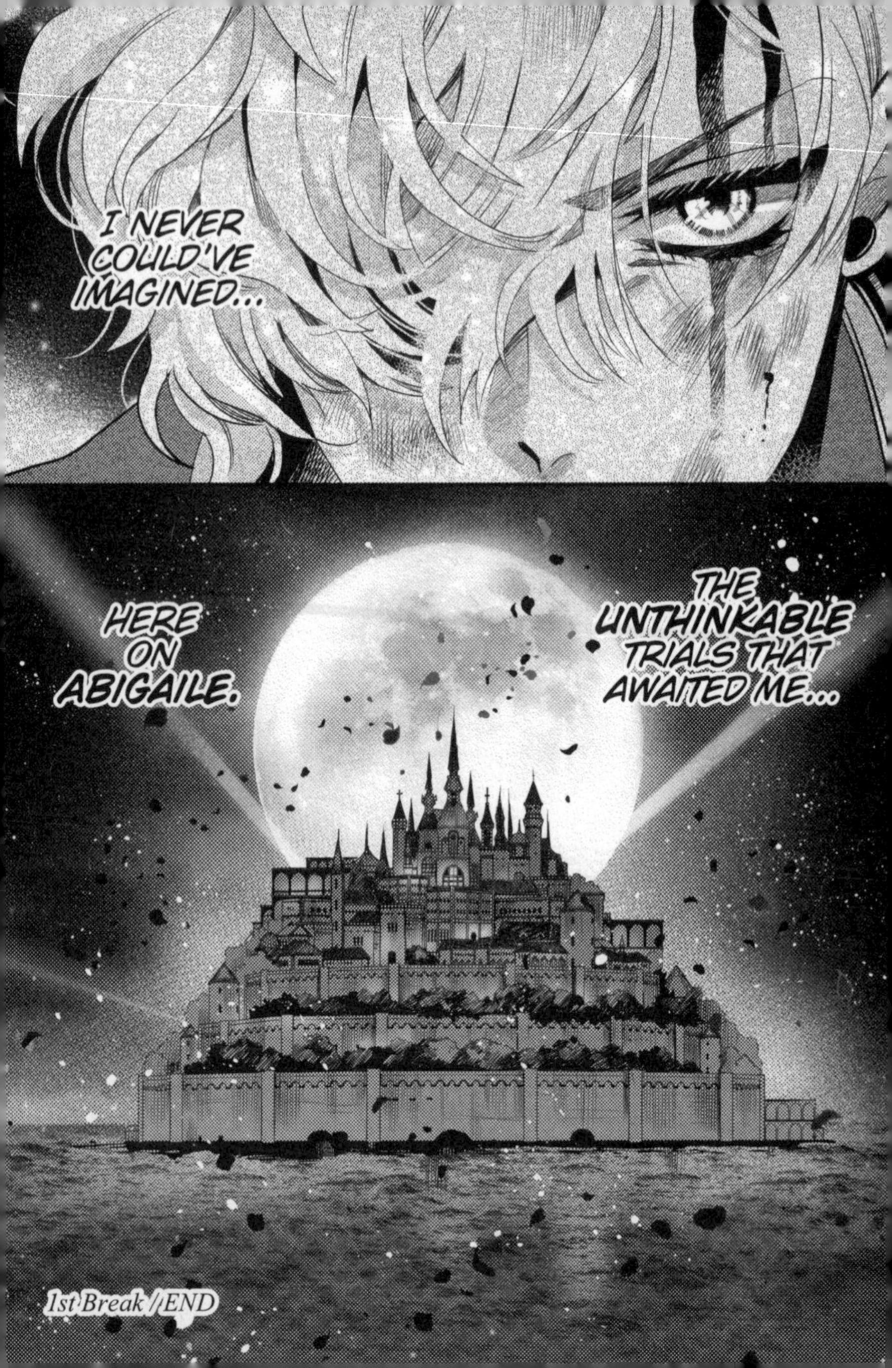
I NEVER COULD'VE IMAGINED...
THE UNTHINKABLE TRIALS THAT AWAITED ME...
HERE ON ABIGAILE.
1st Break / END

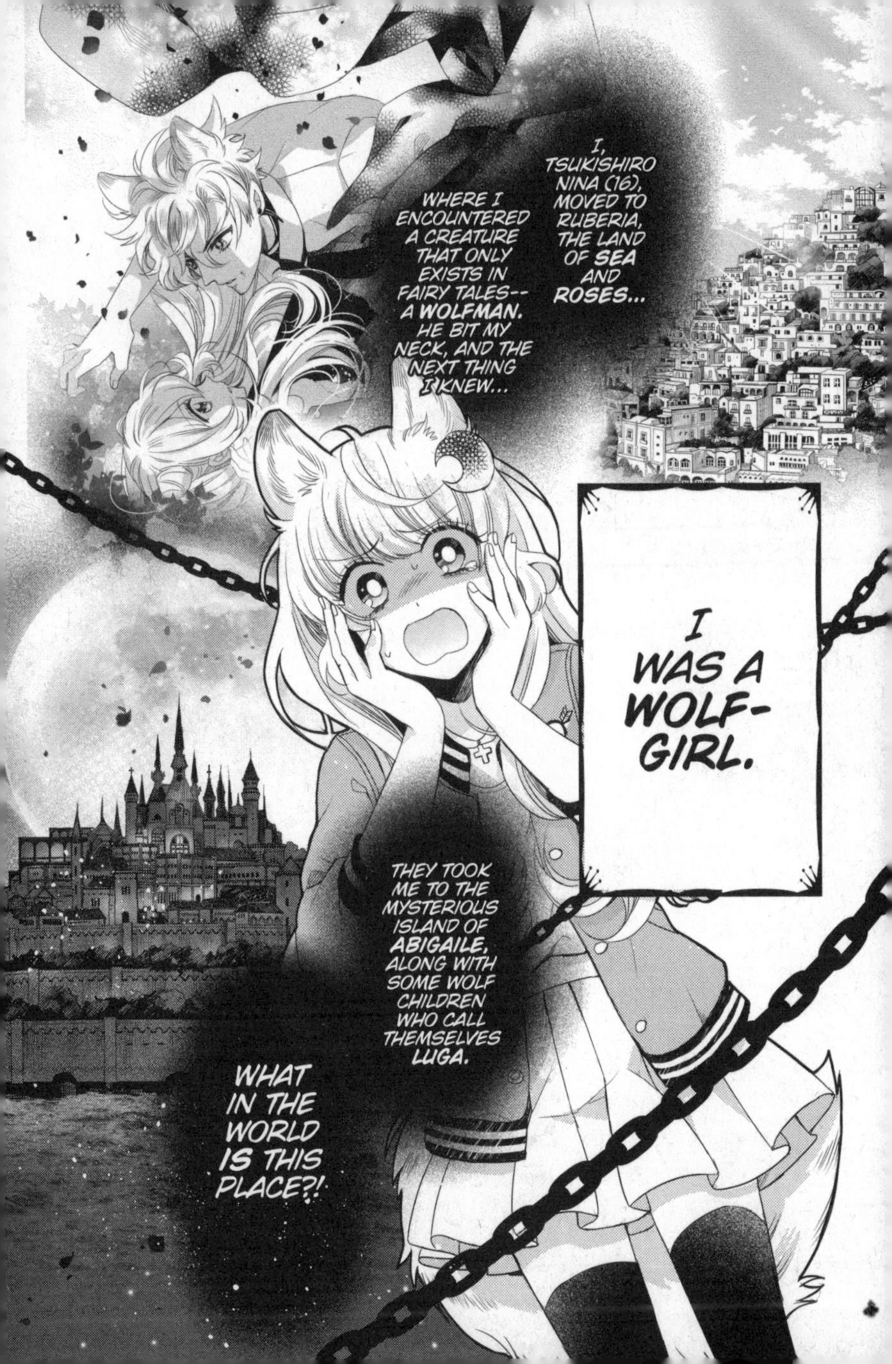
I, TSUKISHIRO NINA (16), MOVED TO RUBERIA, THE LAND OF SEA AND ROSES...
WHERE I ENCOUNTERED A CREATURE THAT ONLY EXISTS IN FAIRY TALES-- A WOLFMAN. HE BIT MY NECK, AND THE NEXT THING I KNEW...
I WAS A WOLF-GIRL.
THEY TOOK ME TO THE MYSTERIOUS ISLAND OF ABIGAILE, ALONG WITH SOME WOLF CHILDREN WHO CALL THEMSELVES LUGA.
WHAT IN THE WORLD IS THIS PLACE?!

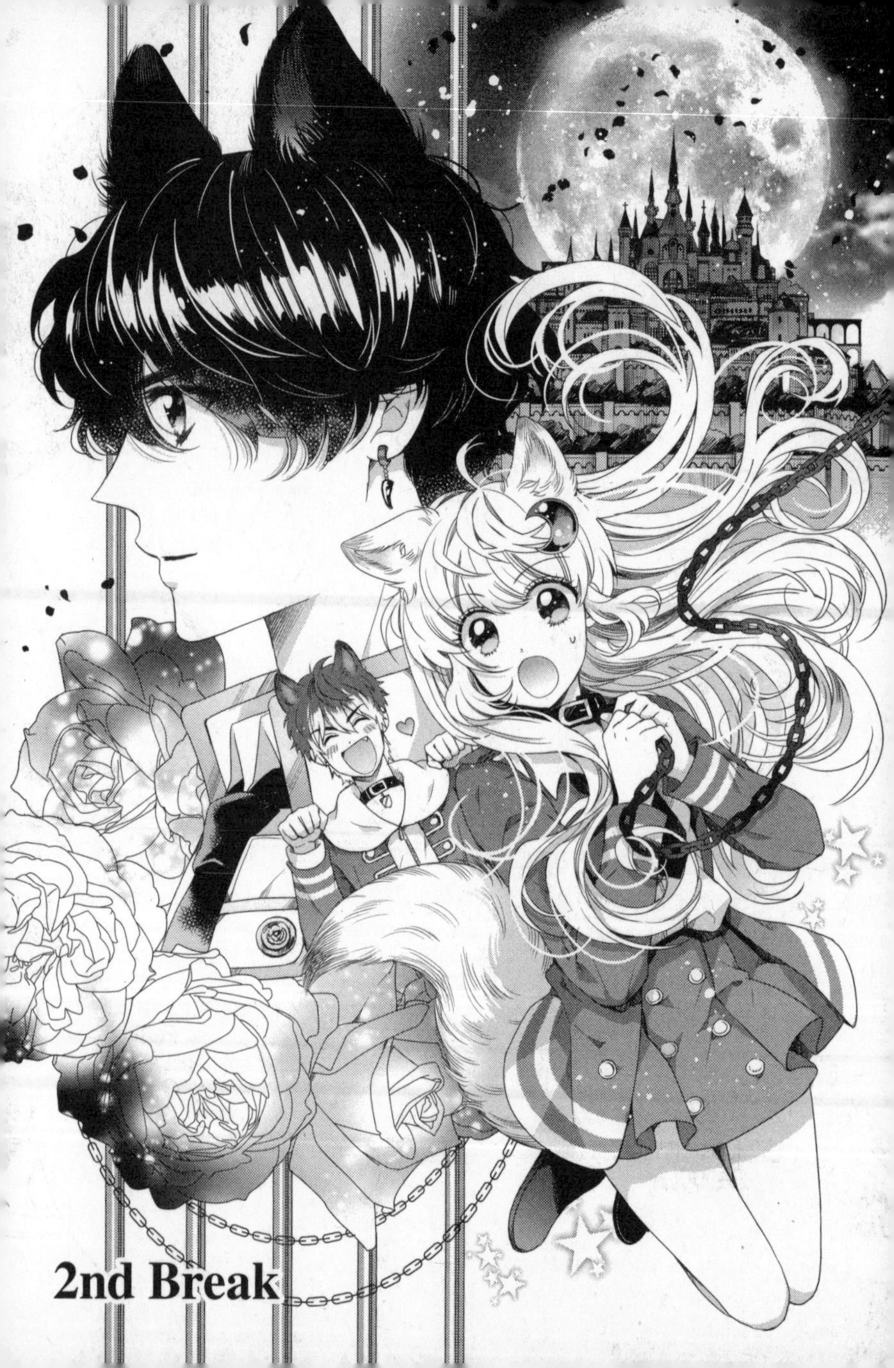

2nd Break

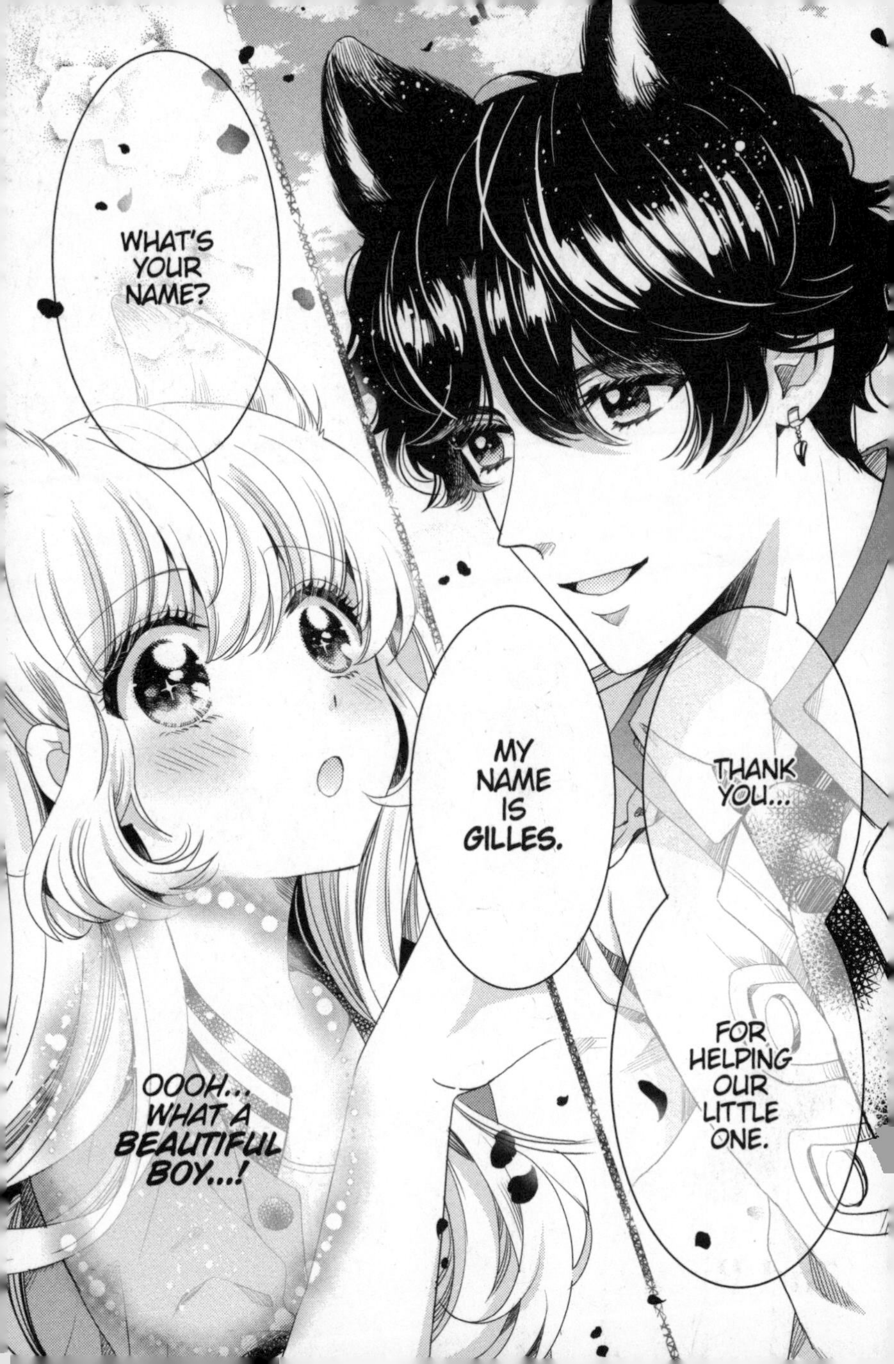
WHAT'S YOUR NAME?
MY NAME IS GILLES.
THANK YOU...
FOR HELPING OUR LITTLE ONE.
OOOH... WHAT A BEAUTIFUL BOY...!

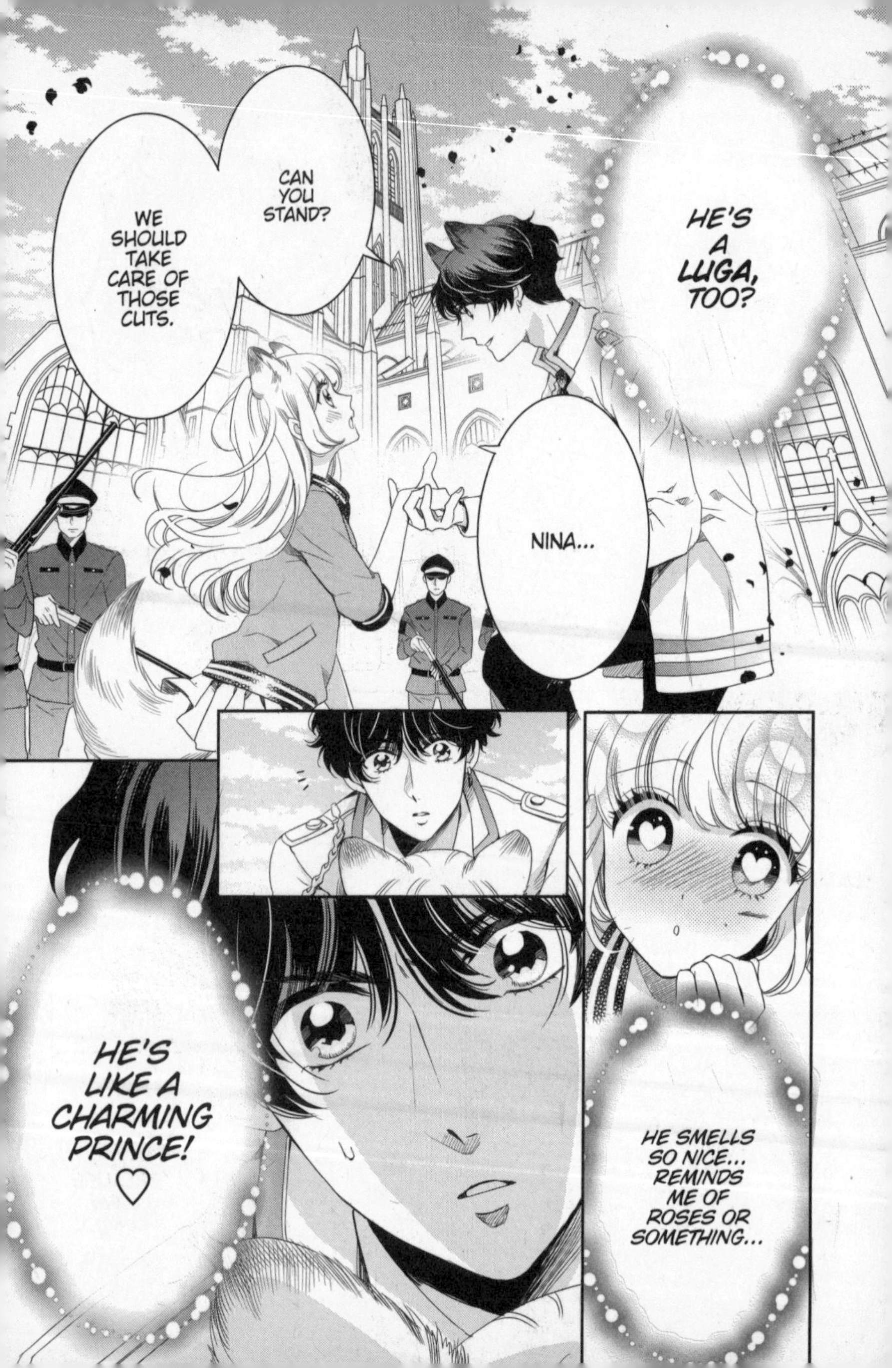
HE'S A LUGA, TOO?
CAN YOU STAND?
WE SHOULD TAKE CARE OF THOSE CUTS.
NINA...
HE SMELLS SO NICE... REMINDS ME OF ROSES OR SOMETHING...
HE'S LIKE A CHARMING PRINCE! ♡

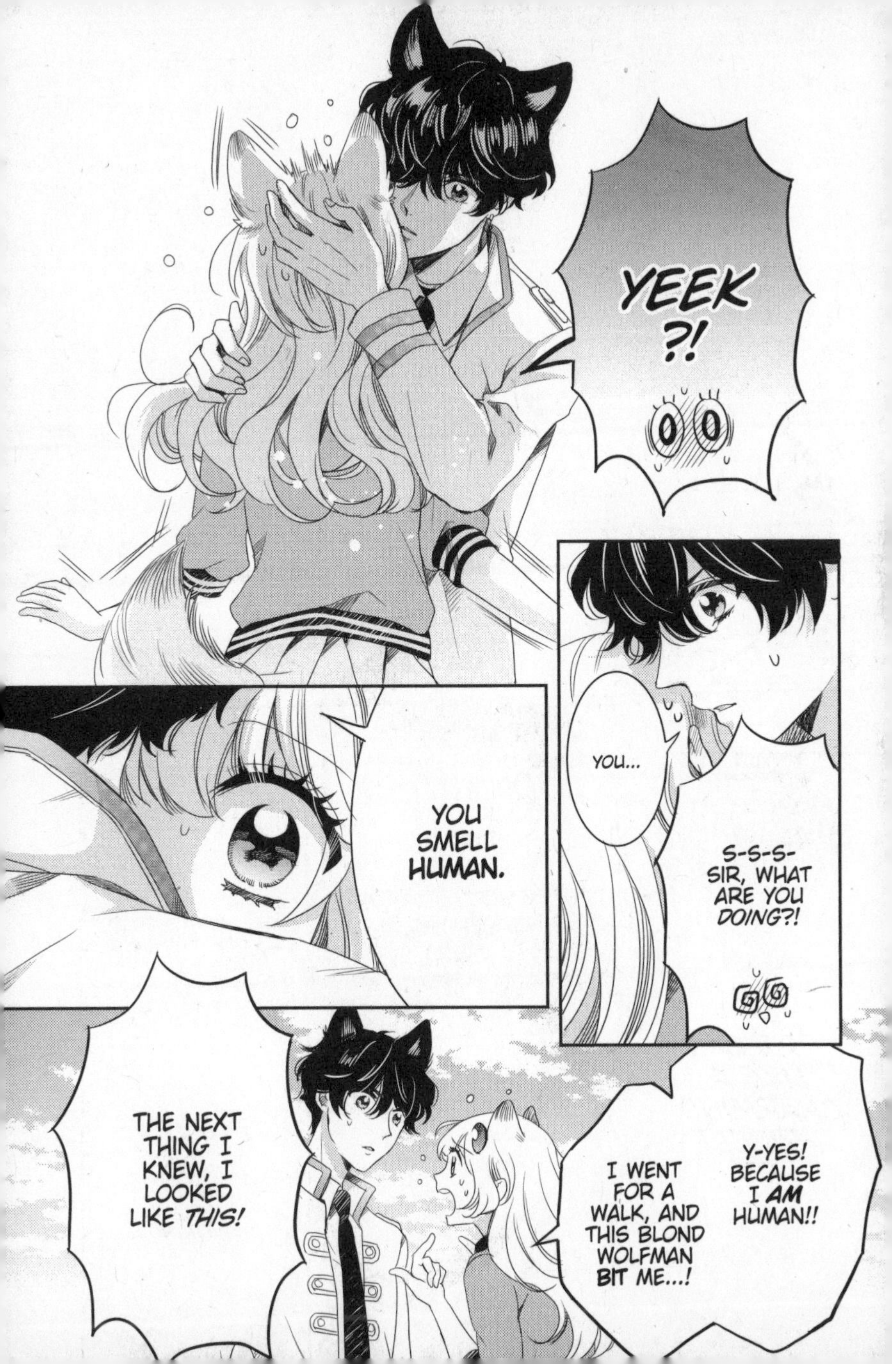
YEEK ?!
YOU...
S-S-S-SIR, WHAT ARE YOU *DOING*?!
YOU SMELL HUMAN.
Y-YES! BECAUSE I *AM* HUMAN!!
I WENT FOR A WALK, AND THIS BLOND WOLFMAN BIT ME...!
THE NEXT THING I KNEW, I LOOKED LIKE *THIS*!

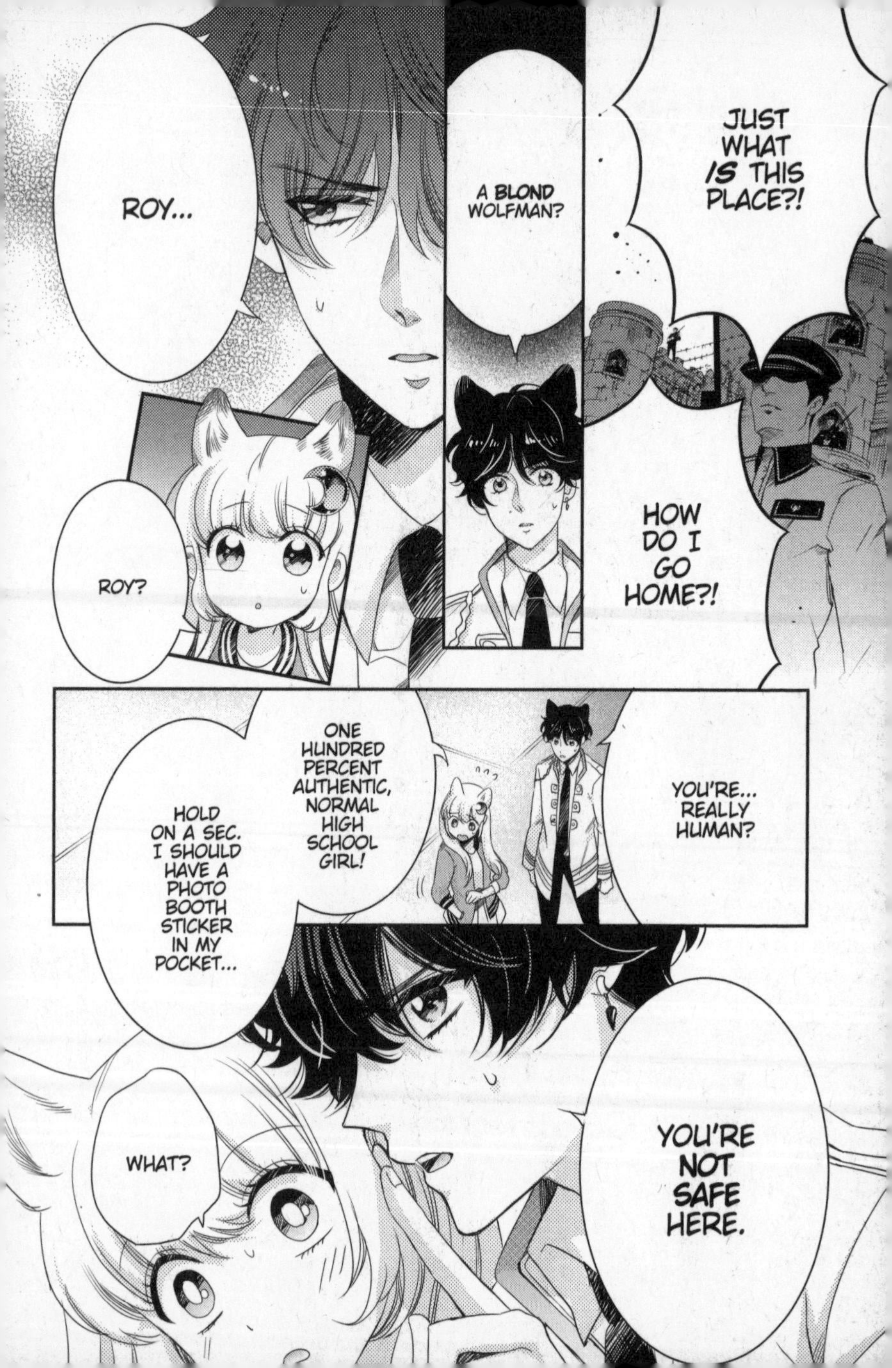
JUST WHAT *IS* THIS PLACE?!
HOW DO I GO HOME?!
A BLOND WOLFMAN?
ROY...
ROY?
YOU'RE... REALLY HUMAN?
ONE HUNDRED PERCENT AUTHENTIC, NORMAL HIGH SCHOOL GIRL!
HOLD ON A SEC. I SHOULD HAVE A PHOTO BOOTH STICKER IN MY POCKET...
YOU'RE NOT SAFE HERE.
WHAT?

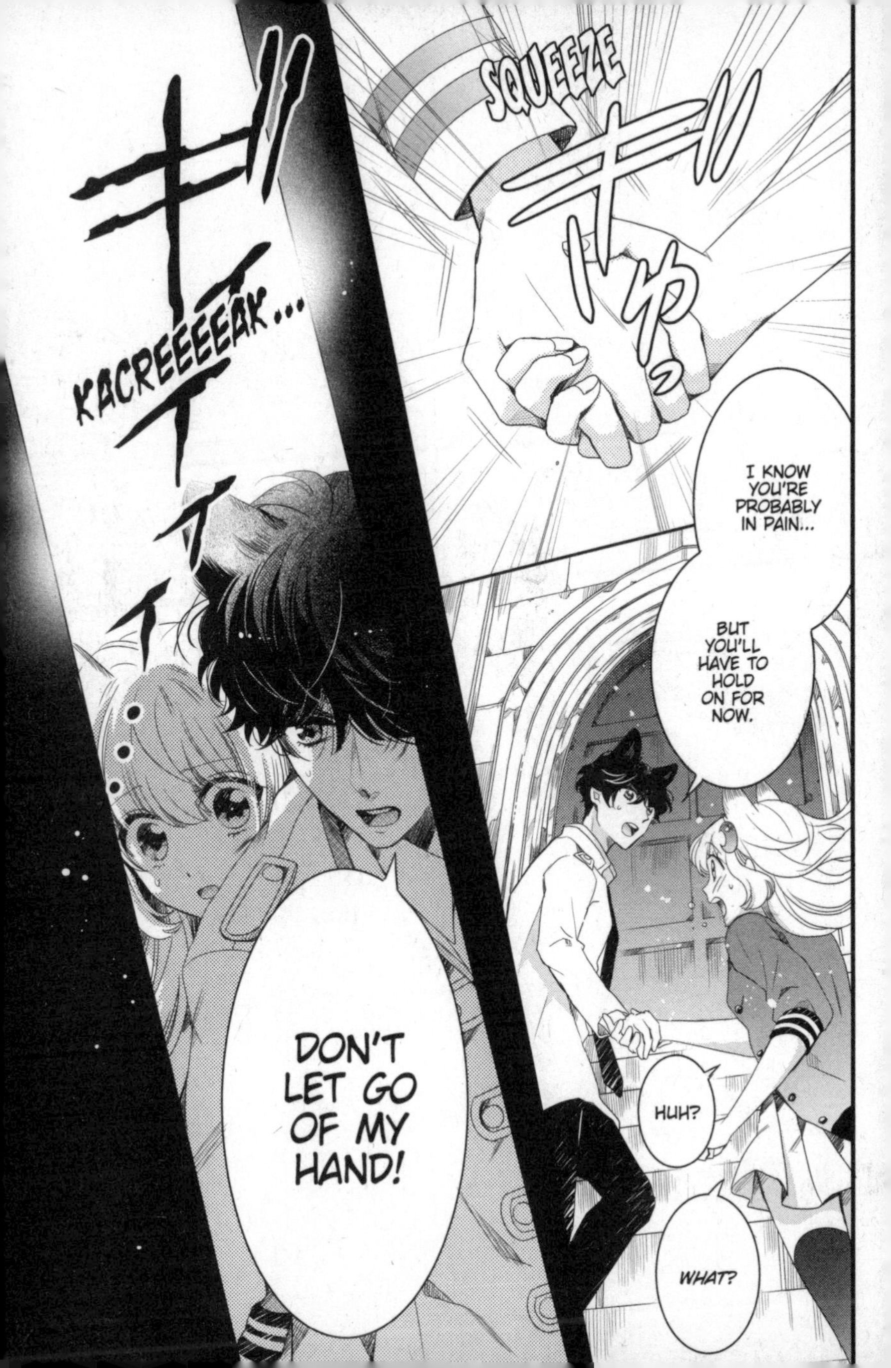
SQUEEZE
I KNOW YOU'RE PROBABLY IN PAIN...
BUT YOU'LL HAVE TO HOLD ON FOR NOW.
HUH?
WHAT?
KACREEEEEAK...
DON'T LET GO OF MY HAND!

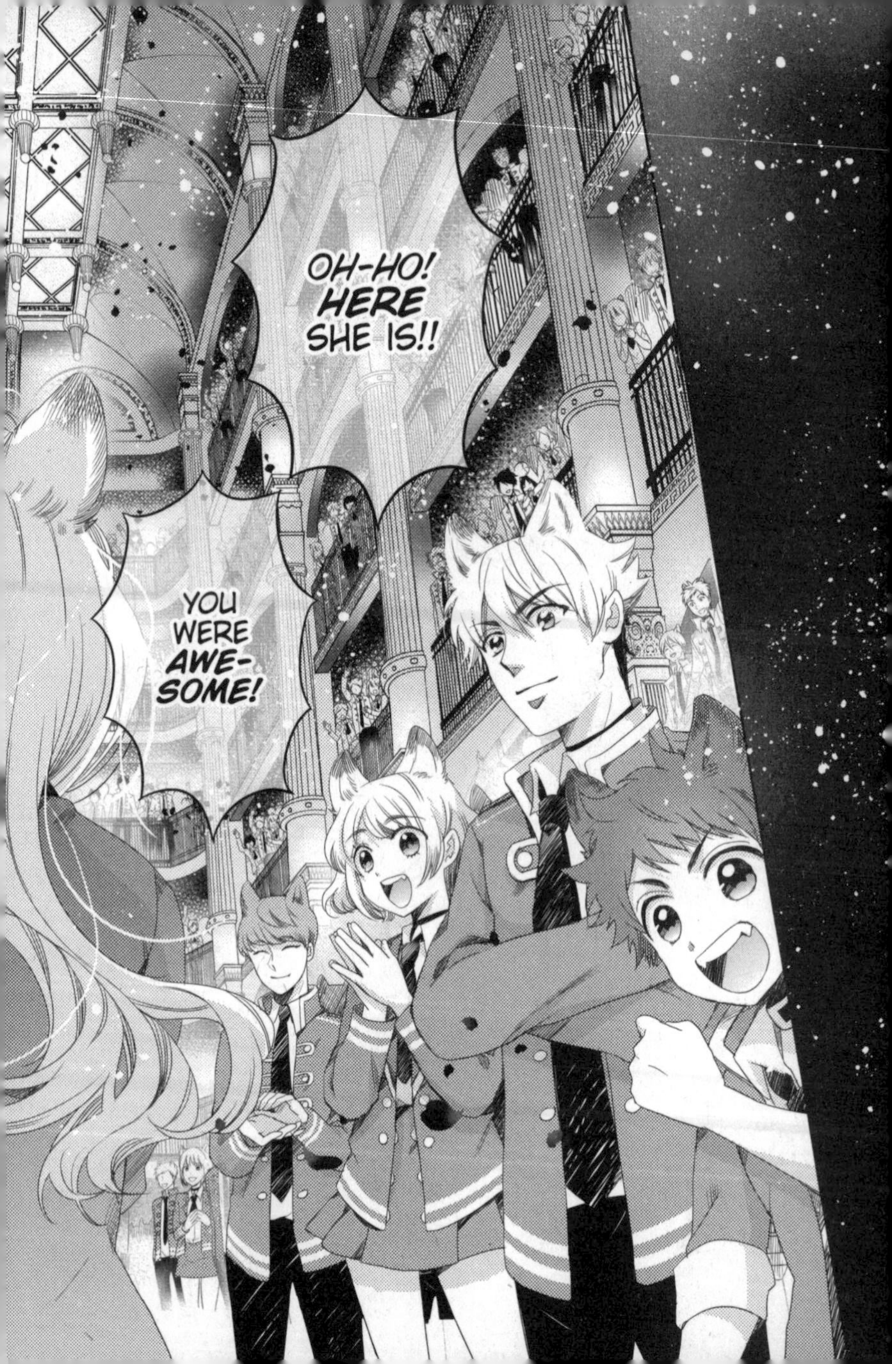
OH-HO! HERE SHE IS!!
YOU WERE AWESOME!

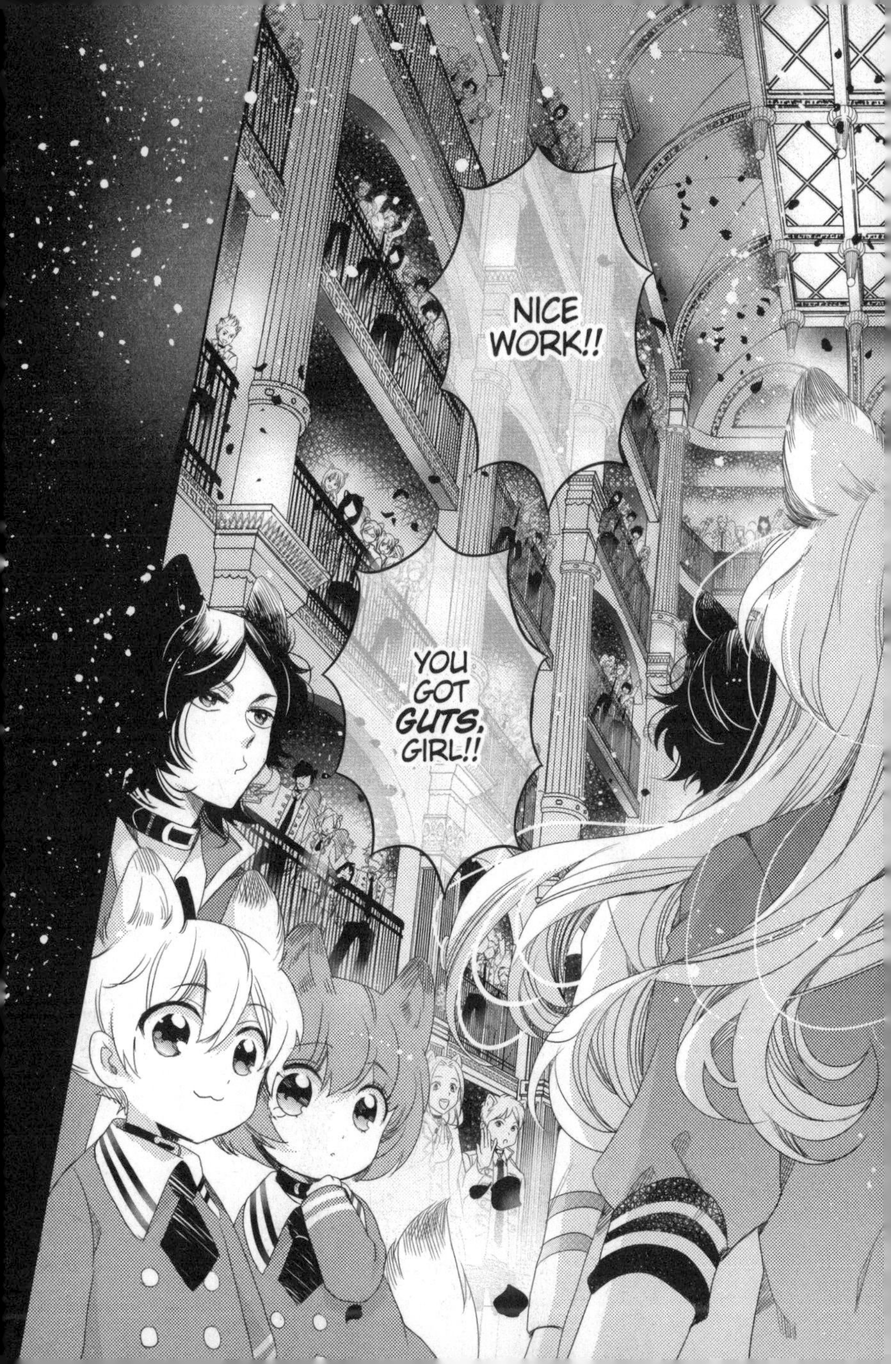
NICE WORK!!
YOU GOT GUTS, GIRL!!

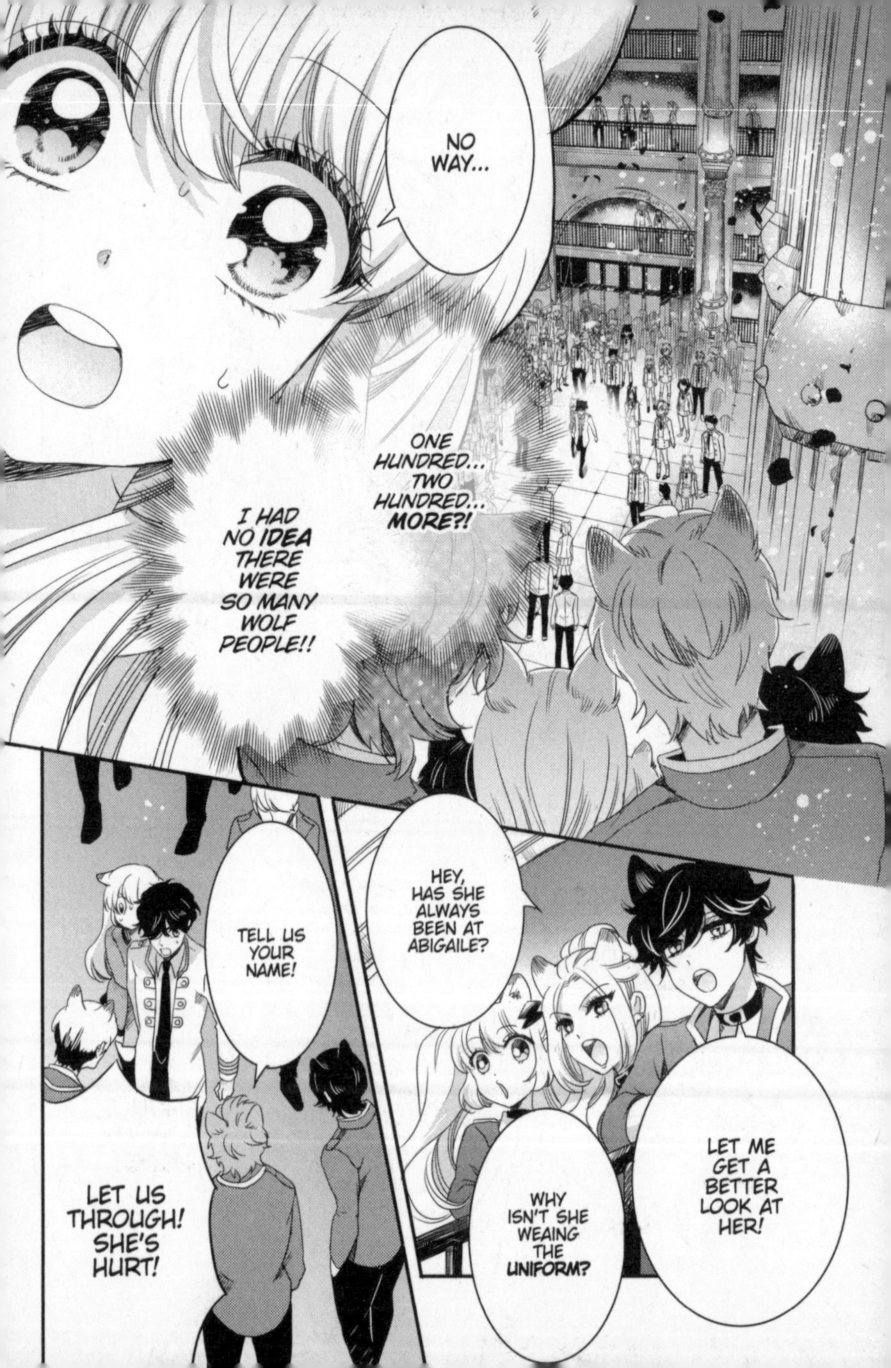
NO WAY...
ONE HUNDRED... TWO HUNDRED... MORE?!
I HAD NO IDEA THERE WERE SO MANY WOLF PEOPLE!!
HEY, HAS SHE ALWAYS BEEN AT ABIGAILE?
LET ME GET A BETTER LOOK AT HER!
WHY ISN'T SHE WEAING THE UNIFORM?
TELL US YOUR NAME!
LET US THROUGH! SHE'S HURT!

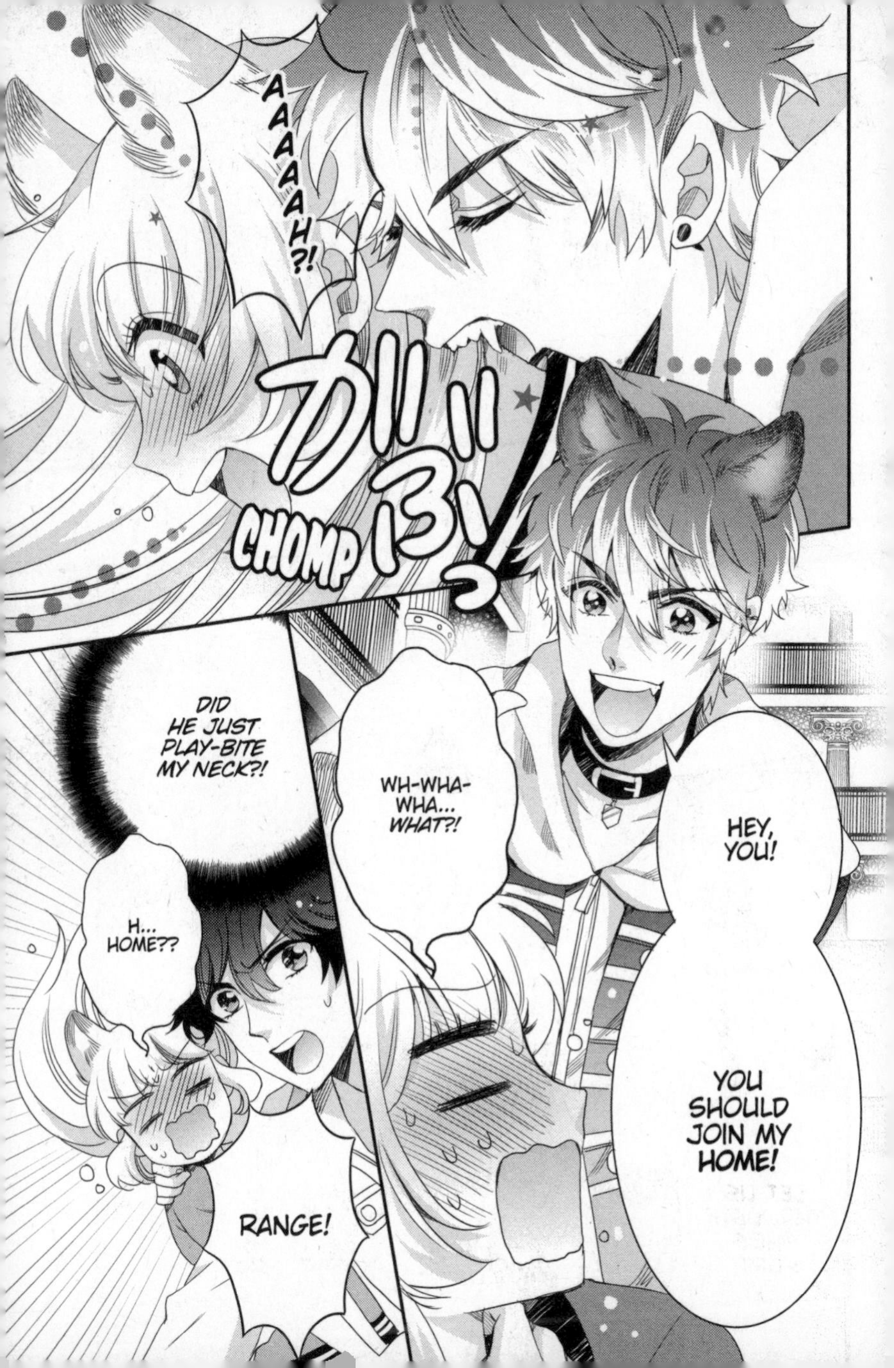

AAAAAAH?!
かぶっ
CHOMP
HEY, YOU!
YOU SHOULD JOIN MY HOME!
WH-WHA-WHA... WHAT?!
DID HE JUST PLAY-BITE MY NECK?!
H... HOME??
RANGE!

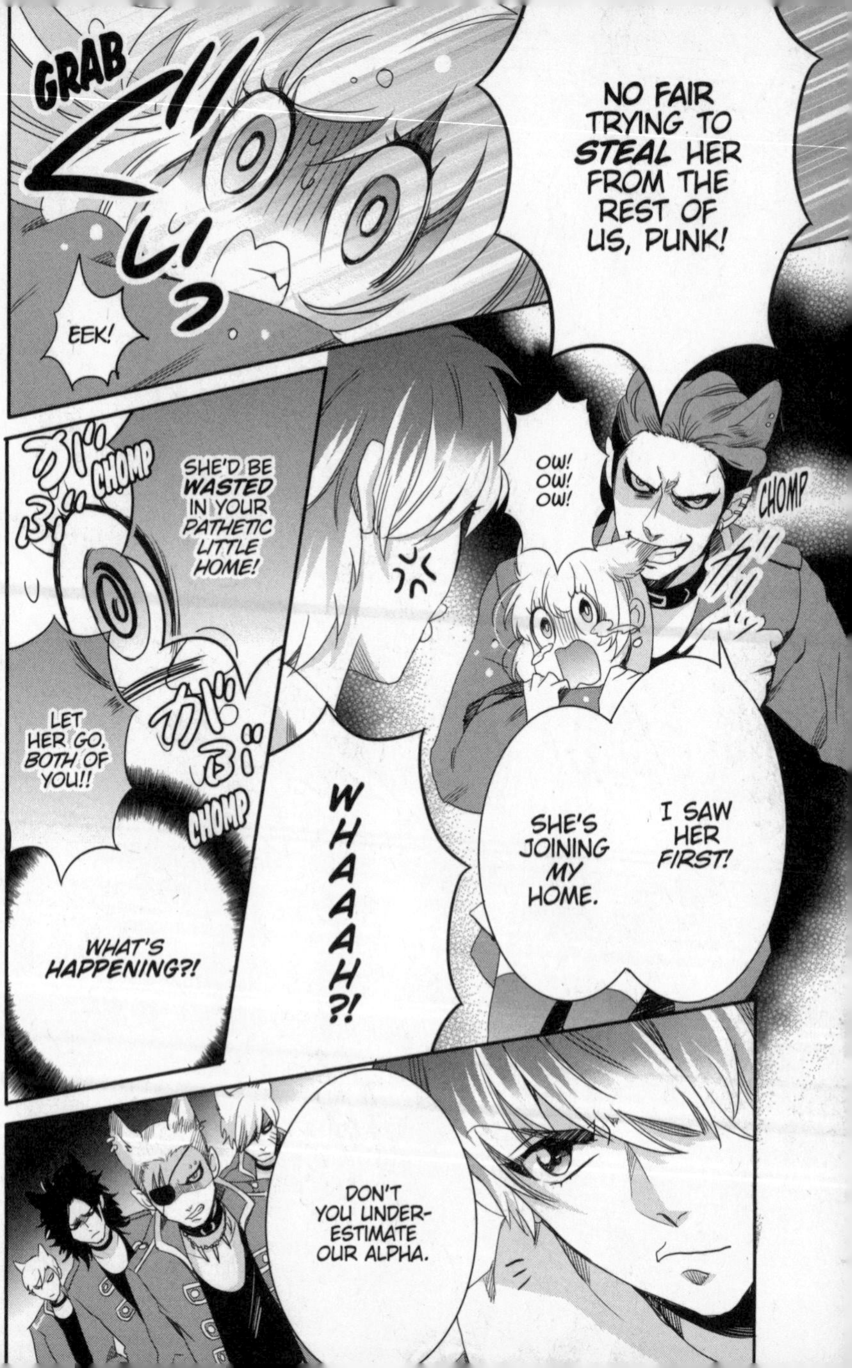
NO FAIR TRYING TO STEAL HER FROM THE REST OF US, PUNK!
GRAB
EEK!
CHOMP
OW! OW! OW!
I SAW HER FIRST!
SHE'S JOINING MY HOME.
WHAAAAH?!
SHE'D BE WASTED IN YOUR PATHETIC LITTLE HOME!
CHOMP
LET HER GO, BOTH OF YOU!!
CHOMP
WHAT'S HAPPENING?!
DON'T YOU UNDER-ESTIMATE OUR ALPHA.

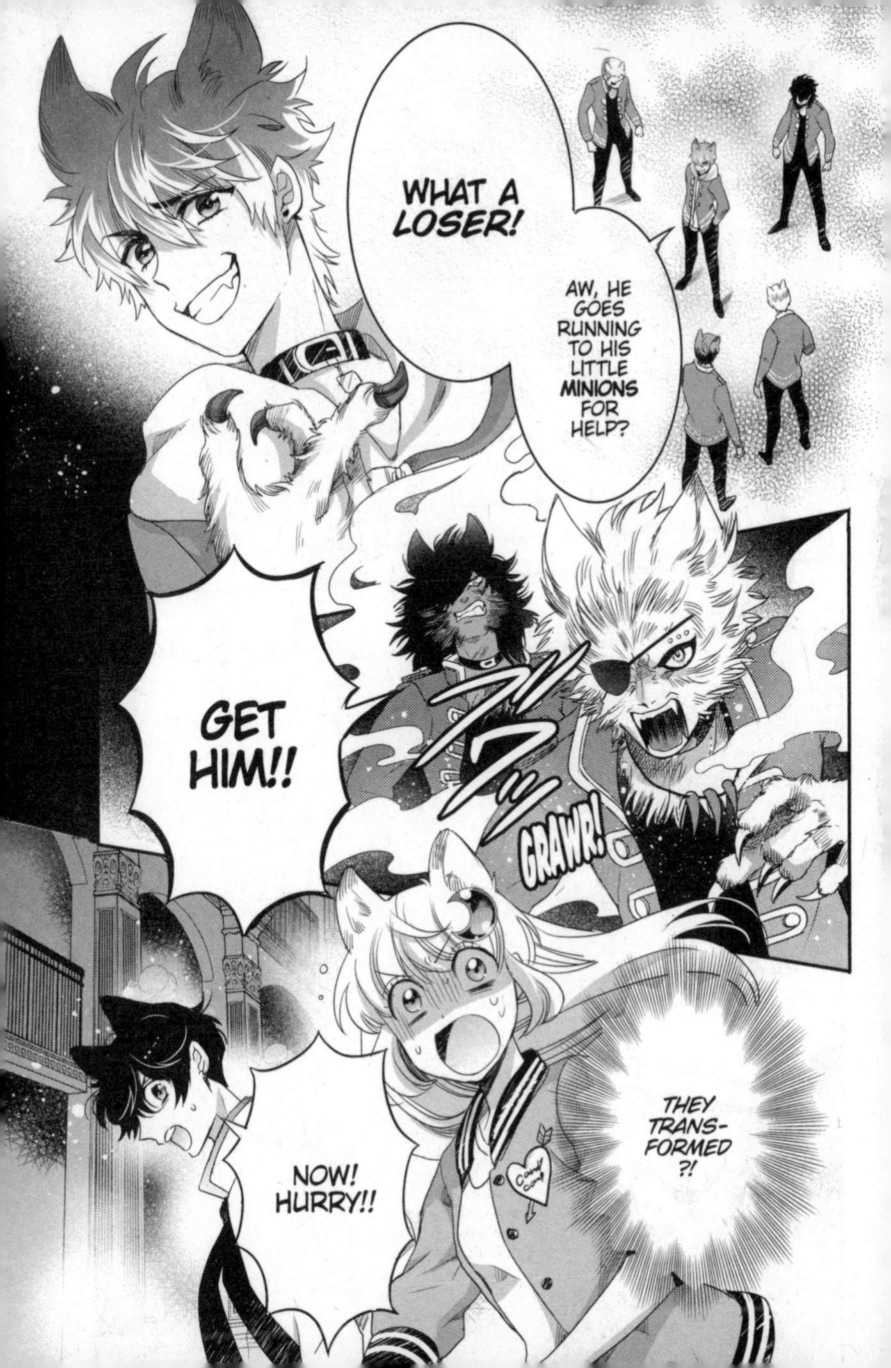
AW, HE GOES RUNNING TO HIS LITTLE MINIONS FOR HELP?
WHAT A LOSER!
GET HIM!!
GRAWR!
THEY TRANSFORMED?!
NOW! HURRY!!

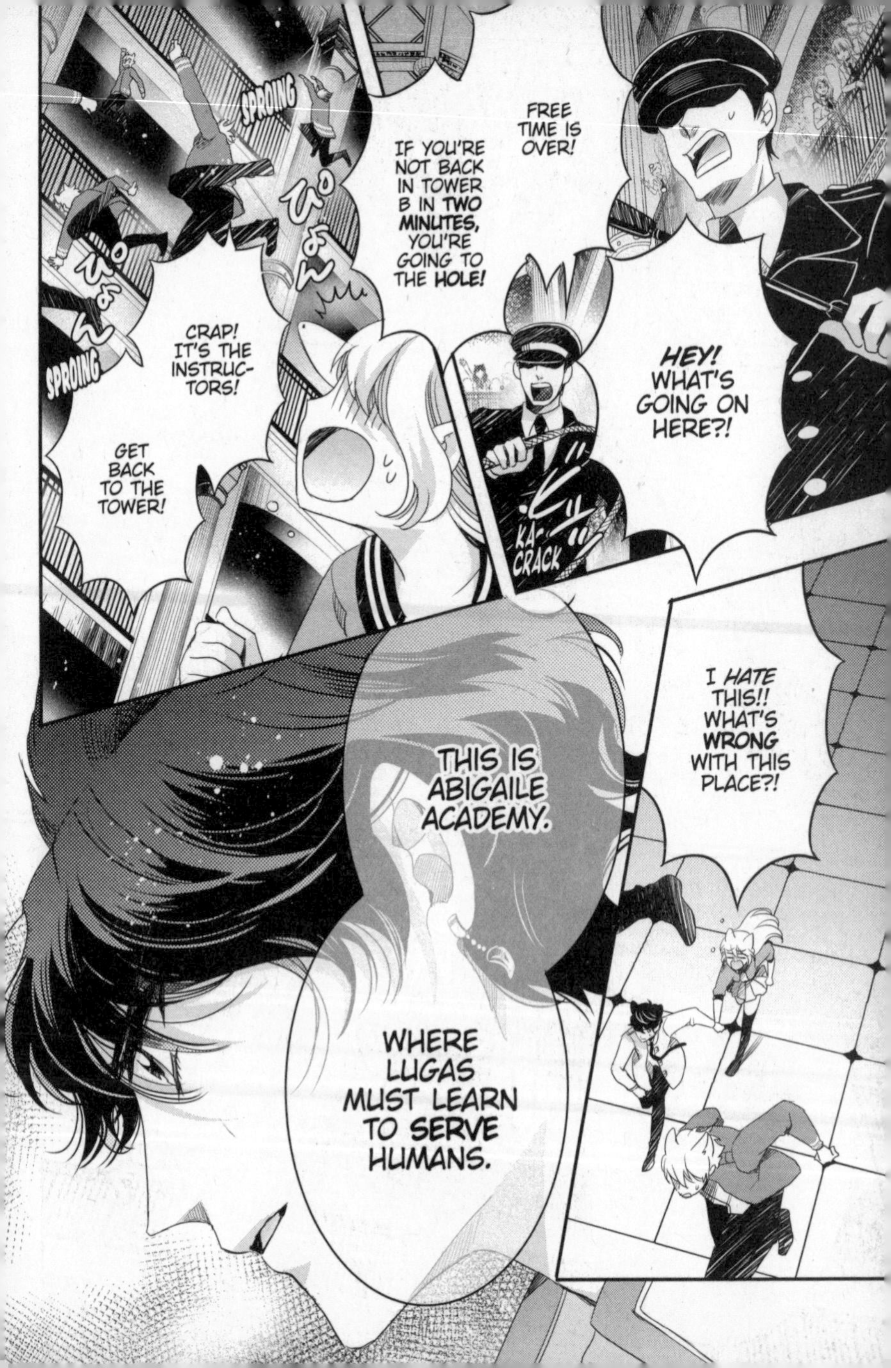
HEY! WHAT'S GOING ON HERE?!
FREE TIME IS OVER!
IF YOU'RE NOT BACK IN TOWER B IN TWO MINUTES, YOU'RE GOING TO THE HOLE!
KA-CRACK
SPROING
ぴょん
ぴょん
SPROING
CRAP! IT'S THE INSTRUC-TORS!
GET BACK TO THE TOWER!
I HATE THIS!! WHAT'S WRONG WITH THIS PLACE?!
THIS IS ABIGAILE ACADEMY.
WHERE LUGAS MUST LEARN TO SERVE HUMANS.

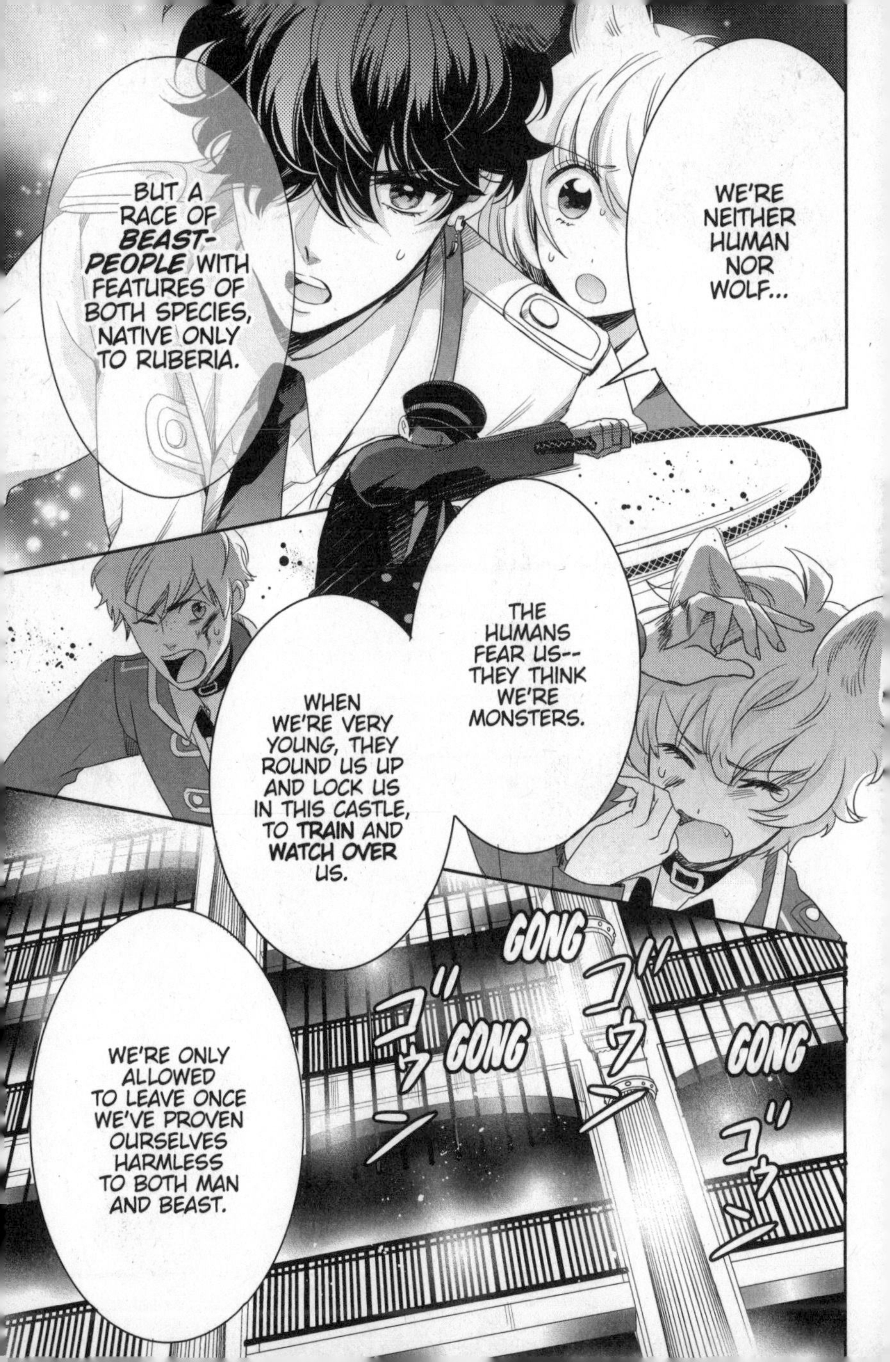
WE'RE NEITHER HUMAN NOR WOLF...
BUT A RACE OF BEAST-PEOPLE WITH FEATURES OF BOTH SPECIES, NATIVE ONLY TO RUBERIA.
THE HUMANS FEAR US-- THEY THINK WE'RE MONSTERS.
WHEN WE'RE VERY YOUNG, THEY ROUND US UP AND LOCK US IN THIS CASTLE, TO TRAIN AND WATCH OVER US.
GONG
GONG
GONG
WE'RE ONLY ALLOWED TO LEAVE ONCE WE'VE PROVEN OURSELVES HARMLESS TO BOTH MAN AND BEAST.

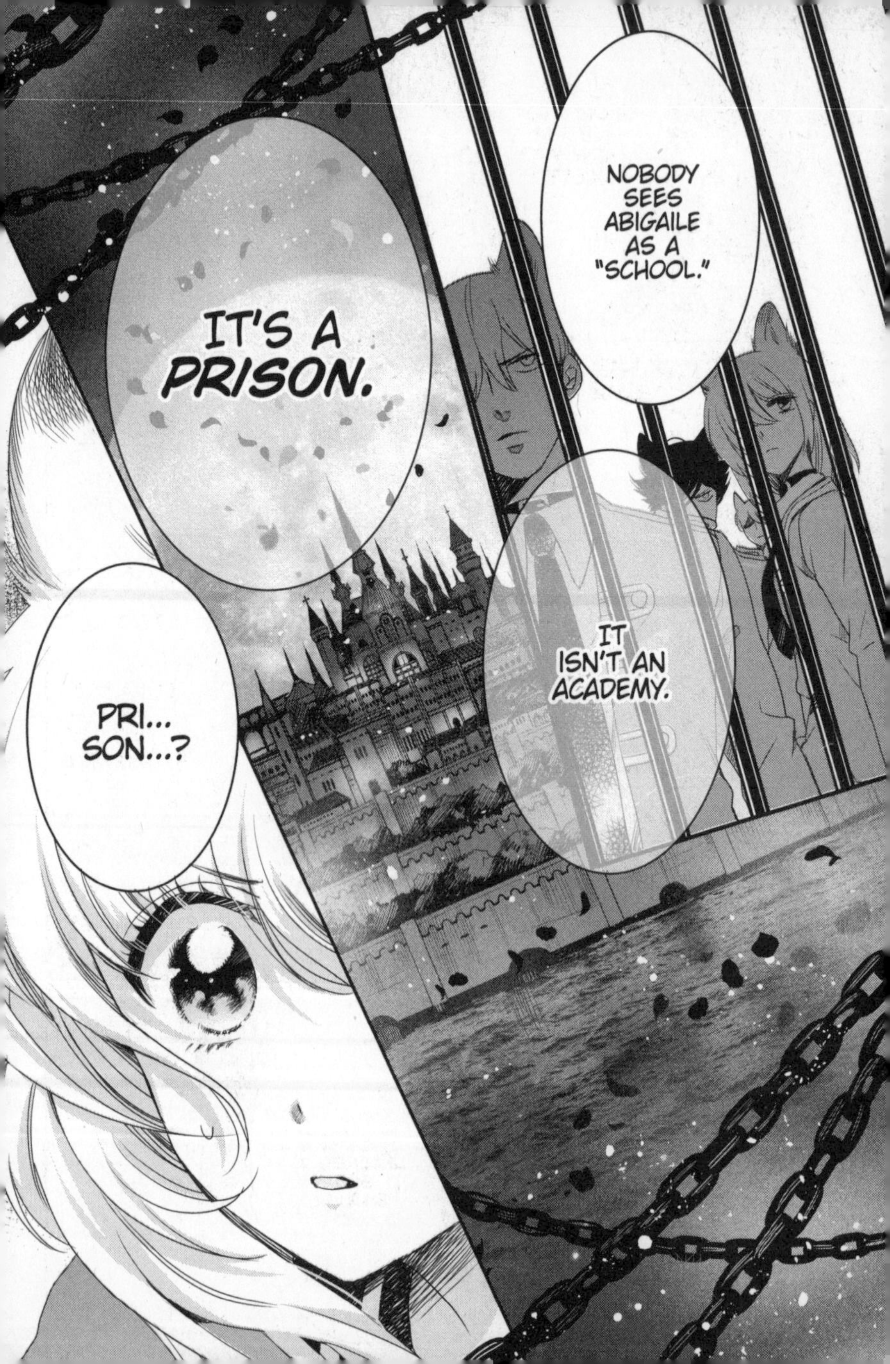
NOBODY SEES ABIGAILE AS A "SCHOOL."
IT ISN'T AN ACADEMY.
IT'S A PRISON.
PRI... SON...?

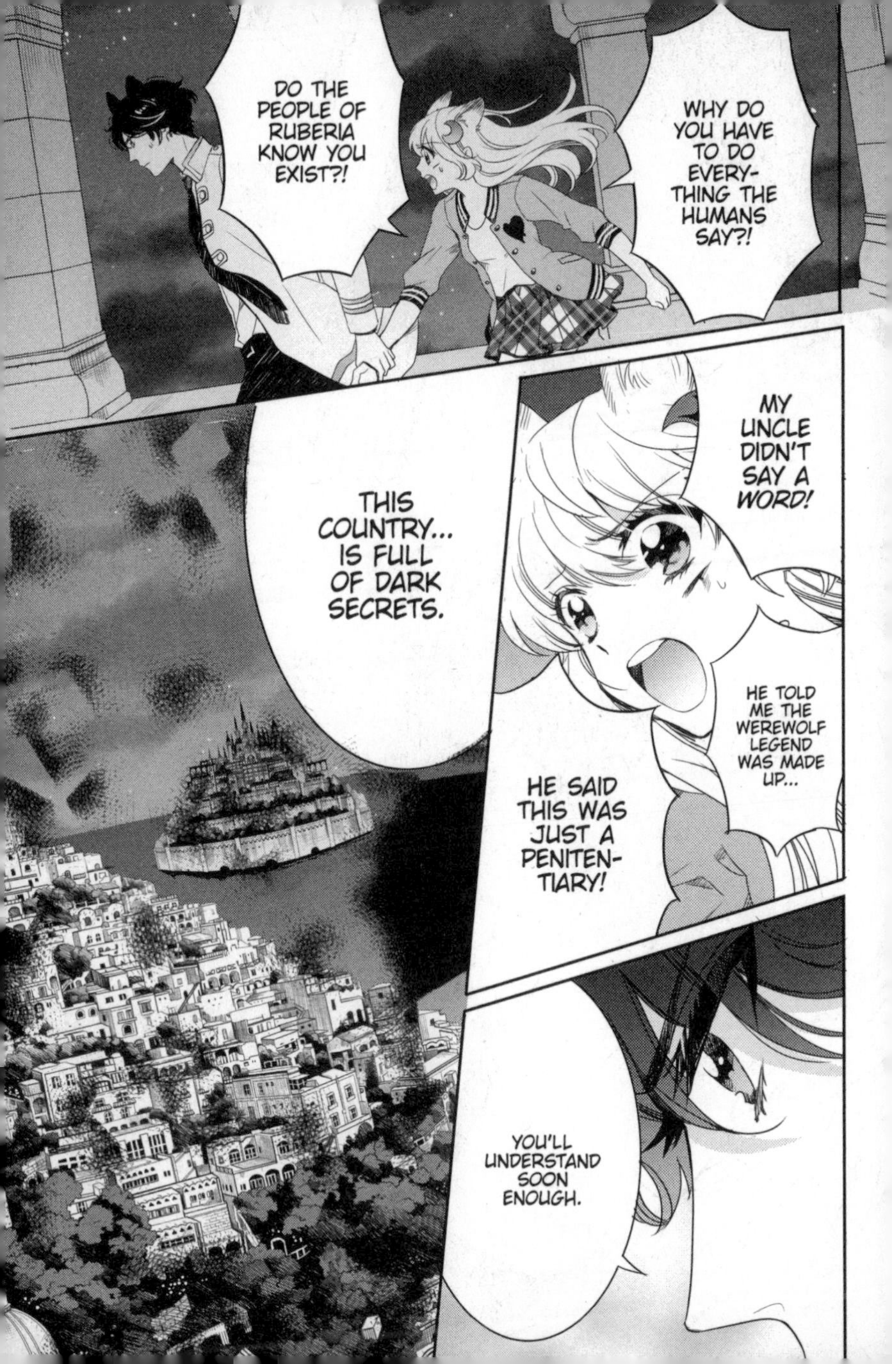
WHY DO YOU HAVE TO DO EVERY-THING THE HUMANS SAY?!
DO THE PEOPLE OF RUBERIA KNOW YOU EXIST?!
MY UNCLE DIDN'T SAY A WORD!
HE TOLD ME THE WEREWOLF LEGEND WAS MADE UP...
HE SAID THIS WAS JUST A PENITEN-TIARY!
YOU'LL UNDERSTAND SOON ENOUGH.
THIS COUNTRY... IS FULL OF DARK SECRETS.

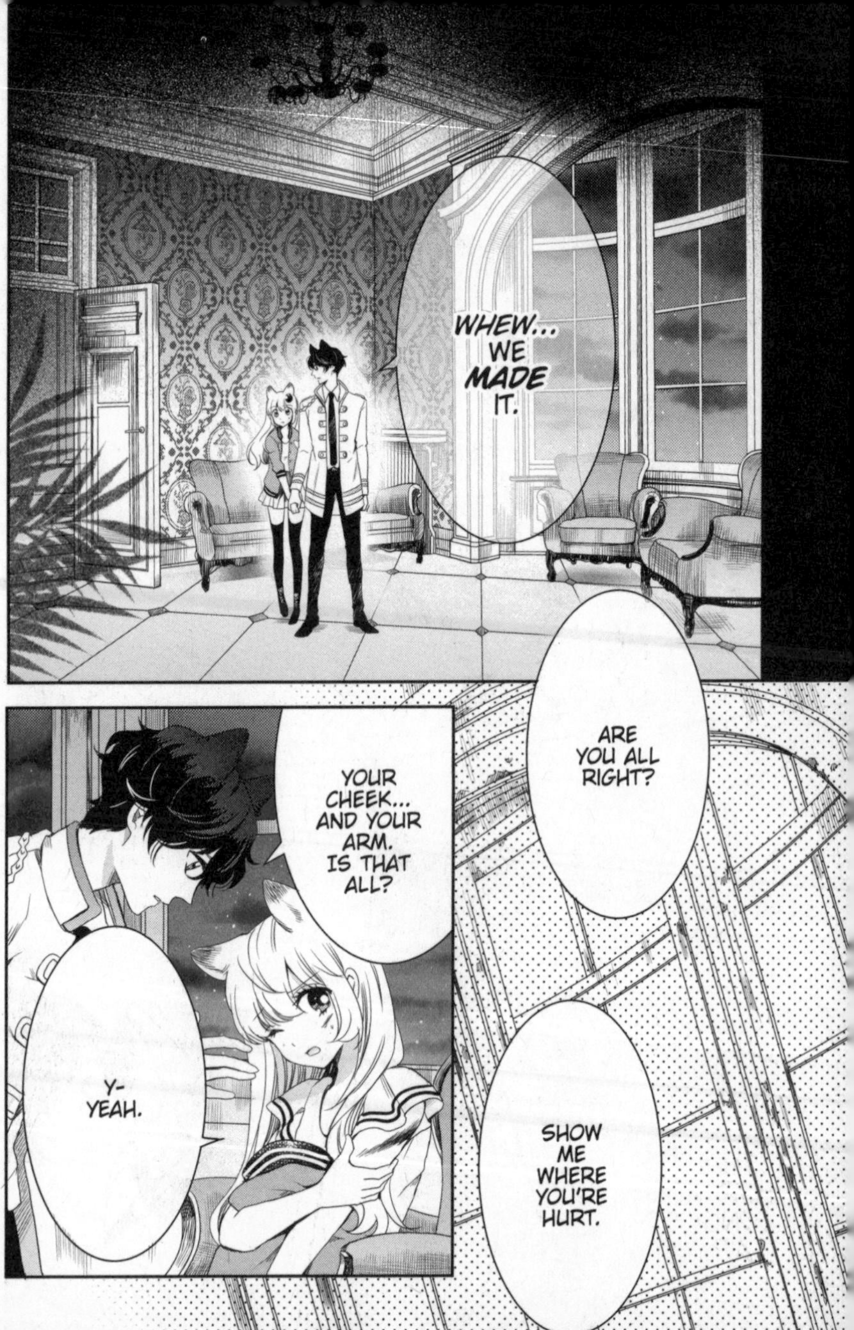
WHEW... WE MADE IT.
ARE YOU ALL RIGHT?
SHOW ME WHERE YOU'RE HURT.
YOUR CHEEK... AND YOUR ARM. IS THAT ALL?
Y- YEAH.

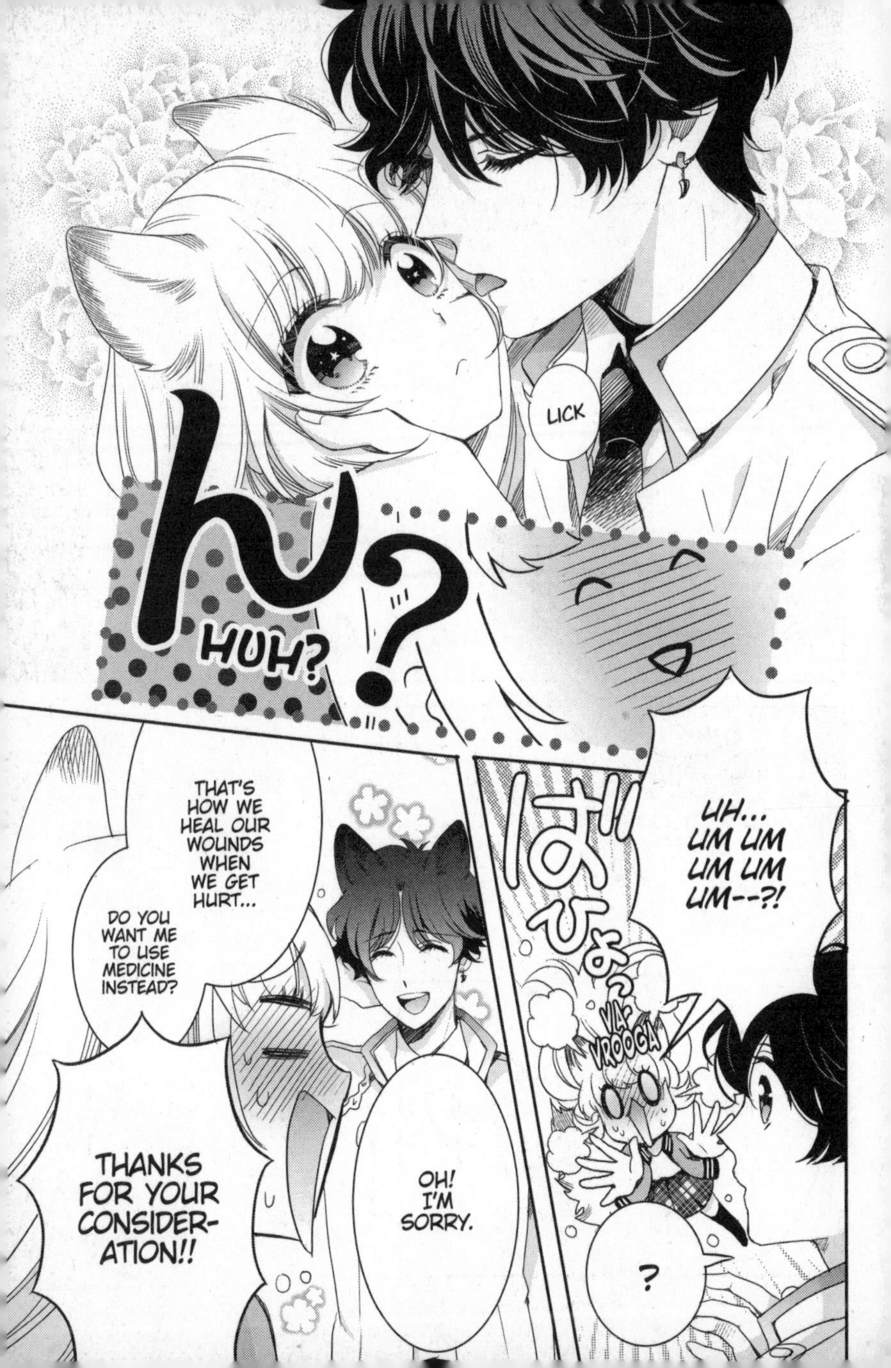
LICK
ん?
HUH?
UH... UM UM UM UM UM--?!
ばひょっ
VLA-VROOGA
?
THAT'S HOW WE HEAL OUR WOUNDS WHEN WE GET HURT...
DO YOU WANT ME TO USE MEDICINE INSTEAD?
OH! I'M SORRY.
THANKS FOR YOUR CONSIDER-ATION!!

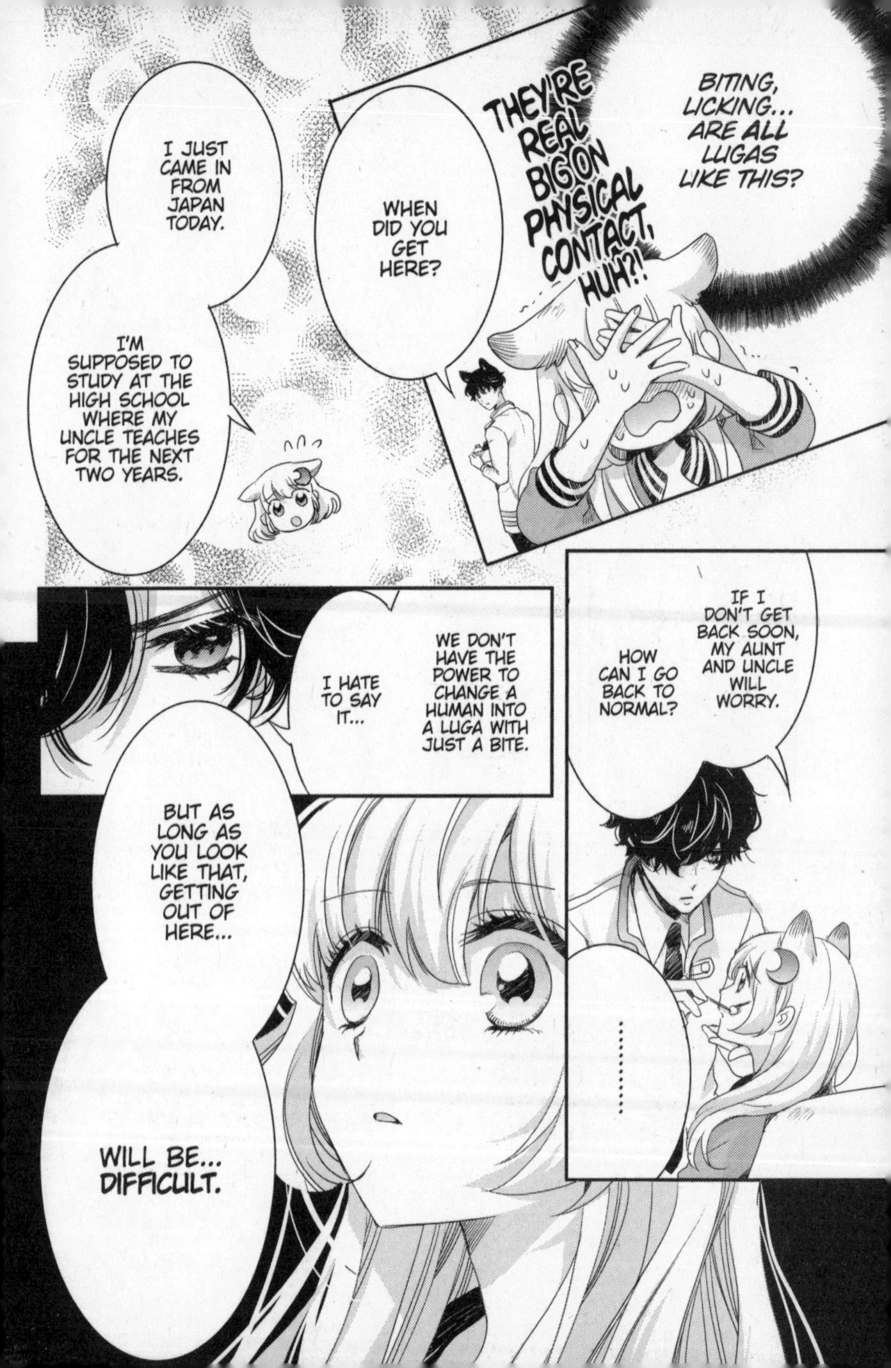
BITING, LICKING... ARE ALL LUGAS LIKE THIS?
THEY'RE REAL BIG ON PHYSICAL CONTACT, HUH?!
WHEN DID YOU GET HERE?
I JUST CAME IN FROM JAPAN TODAY.
I'M SUPPOSED TO STUDY AT THE HIGH SCHOOL WHERE MY UNCLE TEACHES FOR THE NEXT TWO YEARS.
IF I DON'T GET BACK SOON, MY AUNT AND UNCLE WILL WORRY.
HOW CAN I GO BACK TO NORMAL?
......
WE DON'T HAVE THE POWER TO CHANGE A HUMAN INTO A LUGA WITH JUST A BITE.
I HATE TO SAY IT...
BUT AS LONG AS YOU LOOK LIKE THAT, GETTING OUT OF HERE...
WILL BE... DIFFICULT.

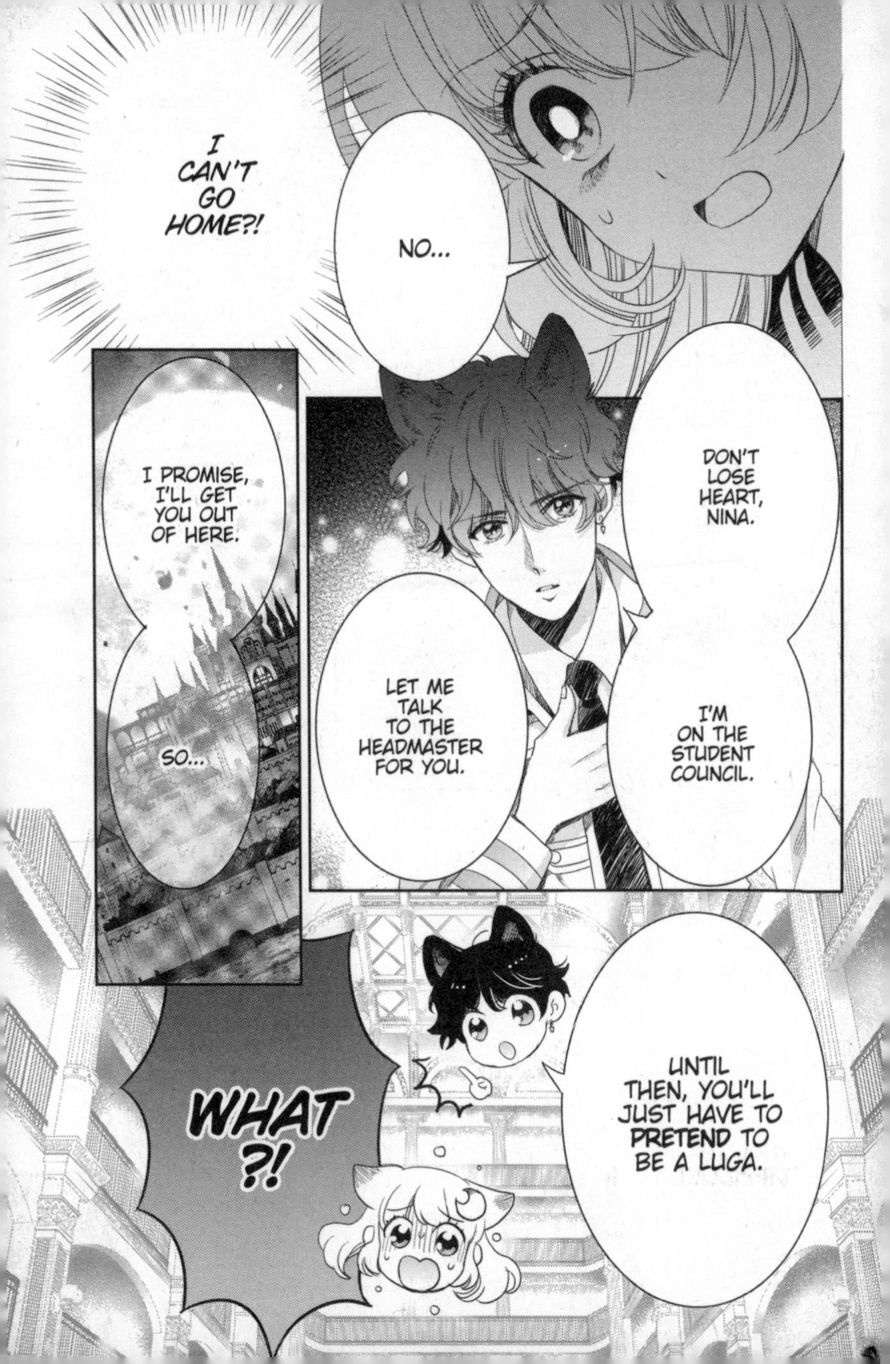
I CAN'T GO HOME?!
NO...
DON'T LOSE HEART, NINA.
I'M ON THE STUDENT COUNCIL.
LET ME TALK TO THE HEADMASTER FOR YOU.
I PROMISE, I'LL GET YOU OUT OF HERE.
SO...
UNTIL THEN, YOU'LL JUST HAVE TO **PRETEND** TO BE A LUGA.
WHAT?!

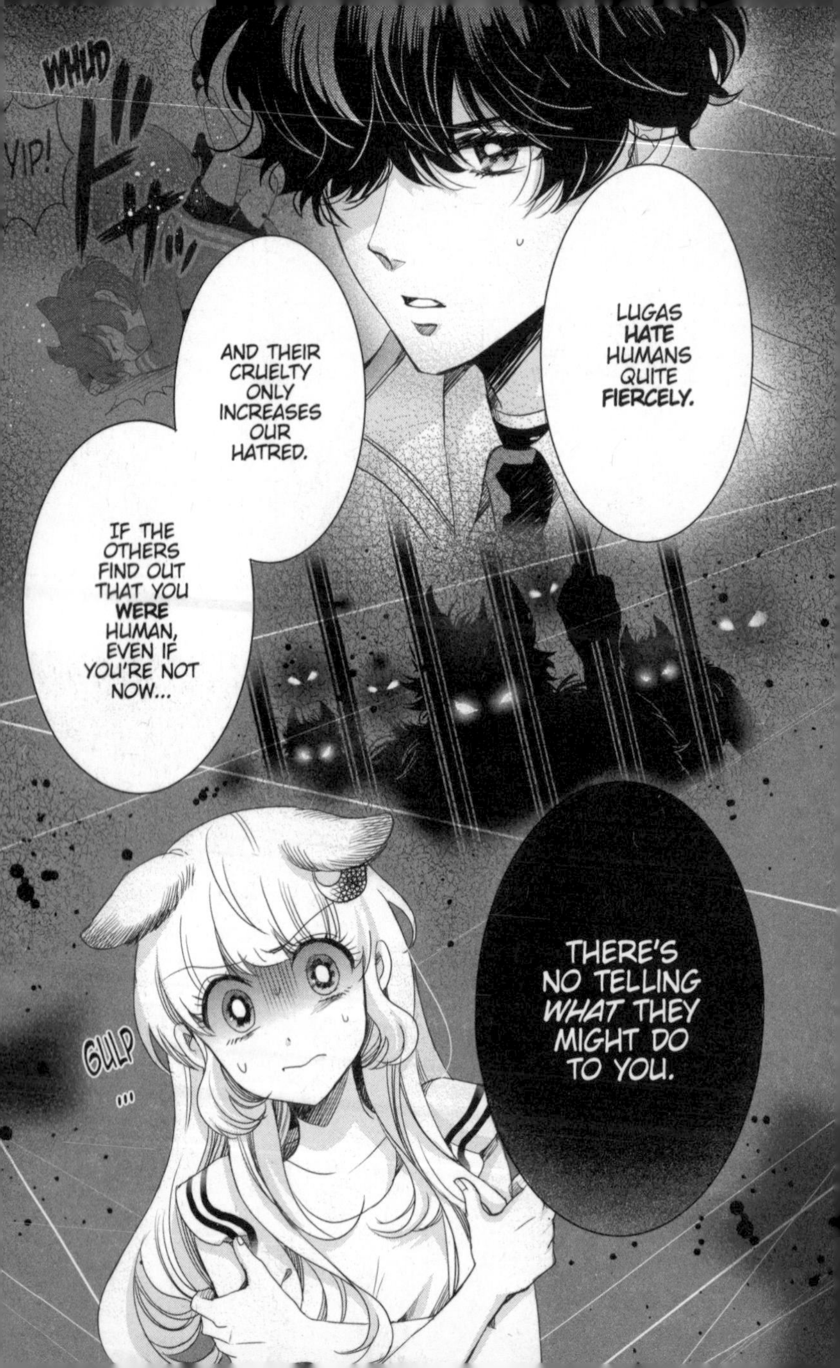
LUGAS HATE HUMANS QUITE FIERCELY.
AND THEIR CRUELTY ONLY INCREASES OUR HATRED.
WHUD
YIP!
IF THE OTHERS FIND OUT THAT YOU WERE HUMAN, EVEN IF YOU'RE NOT NOW...
THERE'S NO TELLING *WHAT* THEY MIGHT DO TO YOU.
GULP
...

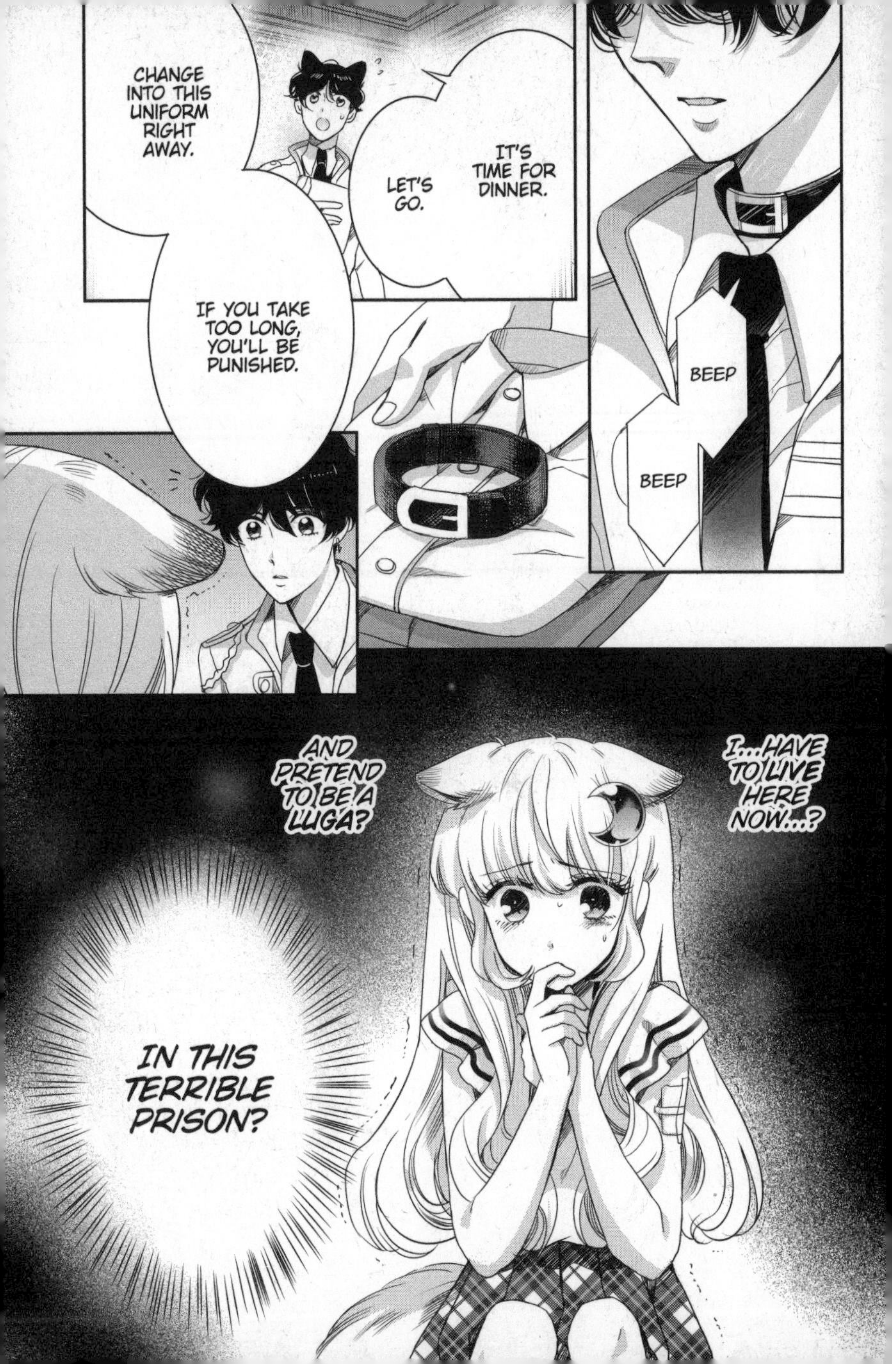
BEEP
BEEP
IT'S TIME FOR DINNER.
LET'S GO.
CHANGE INTO THIS UNIFORM RIGHT AWAY.
IF YOU TAKE TOO LONG, YOU'LL BE PUNISHED.
I...HAVE TO LIVE HERE NOW...?
AND PRETEND TO BE A LUGA?
IN THIS TERRIBLE PRISON?

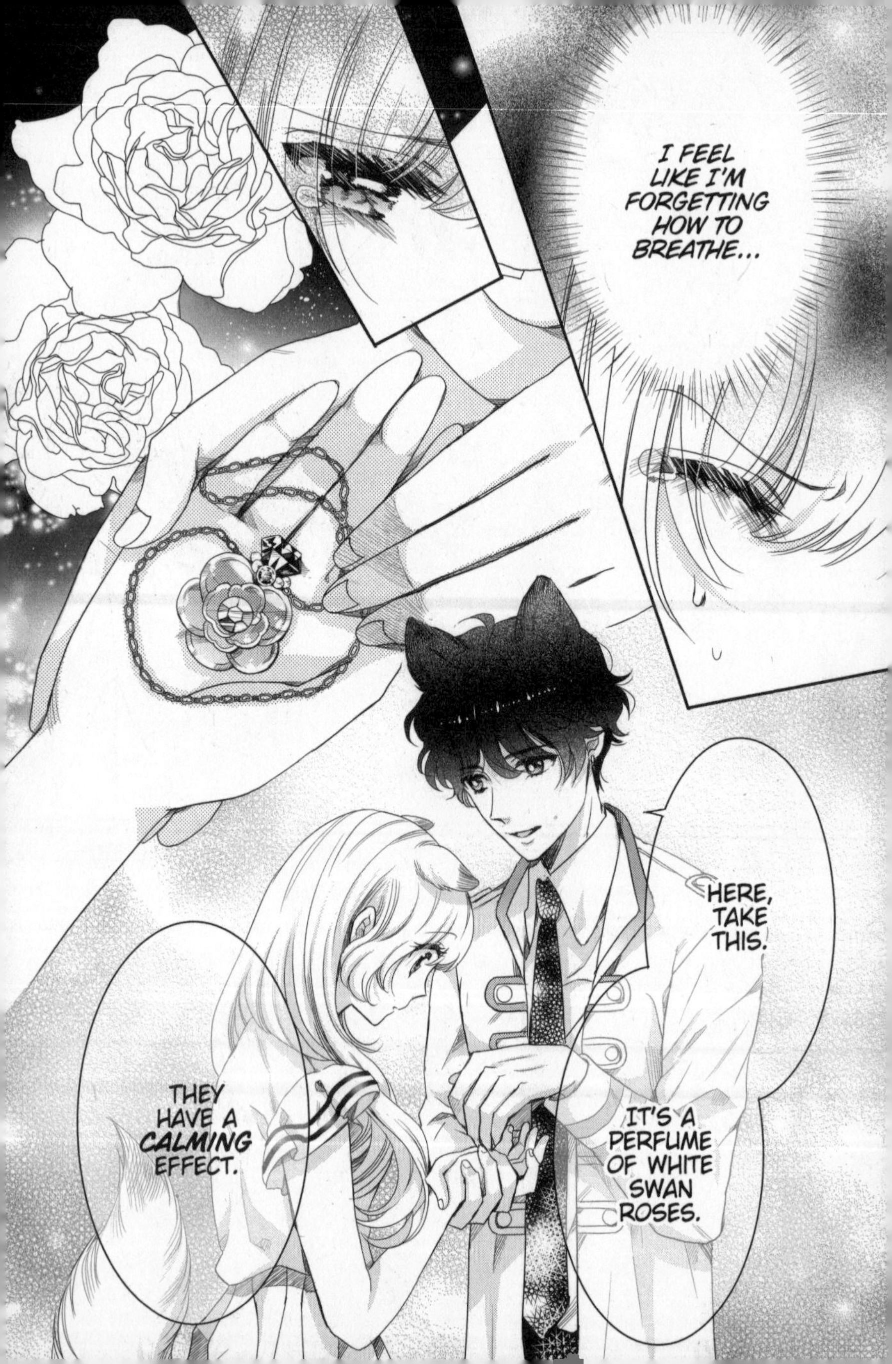
I FEEL LIKE I'M FORGETTING HOW TO BREATHE...
HERE, TAKE THIS.
IT'S A PERFUME OF WHITE SWAN ROSES.
THEY HAVE A CALMING EFFECT.

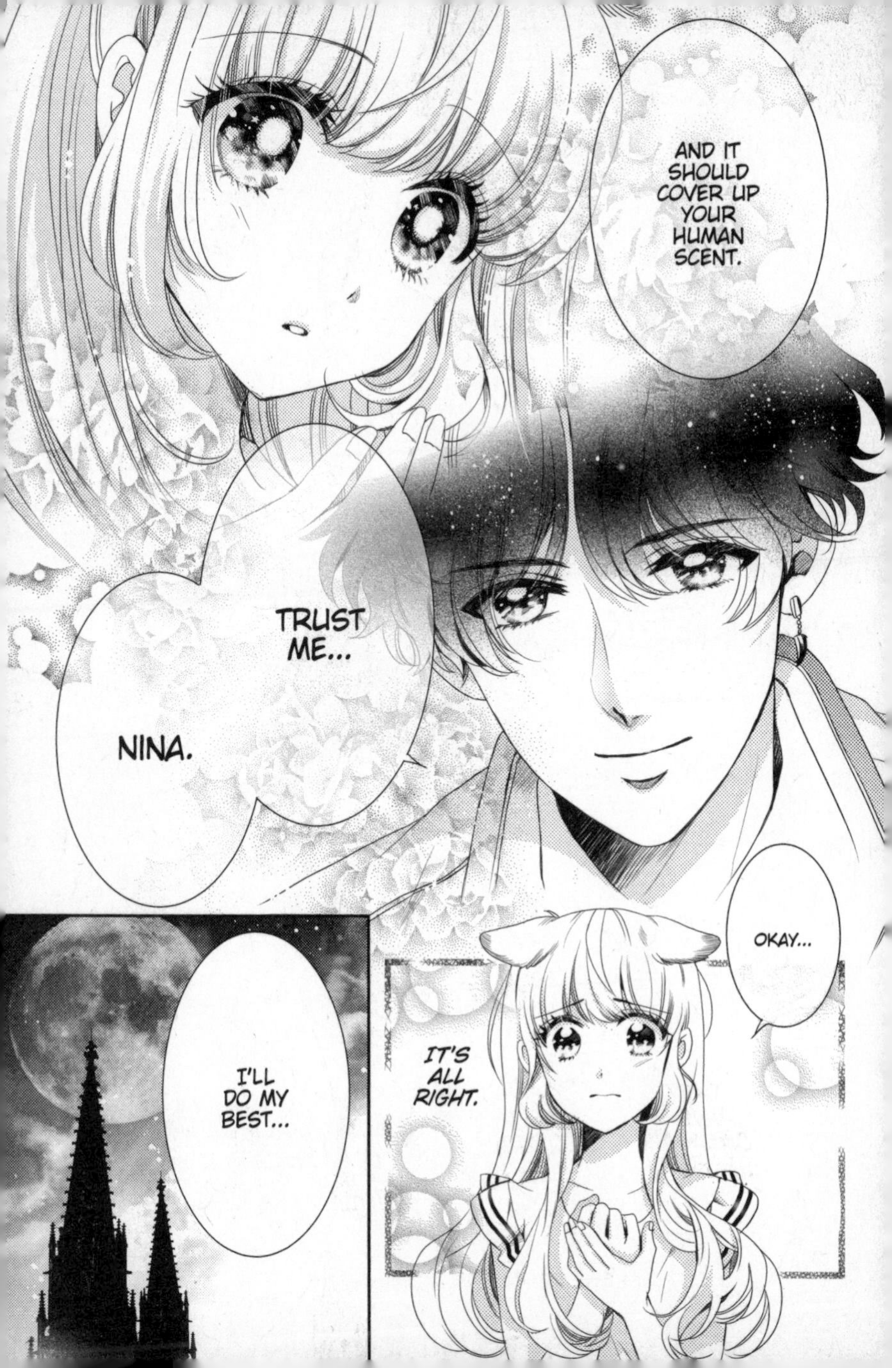
AND IT SHOULD COVER UP YOUR HUMAN SCENT.
TRUST ME...
NINA.
OKAY...
IT'S ALL RIGHT.
I'LL DO MY BEST...

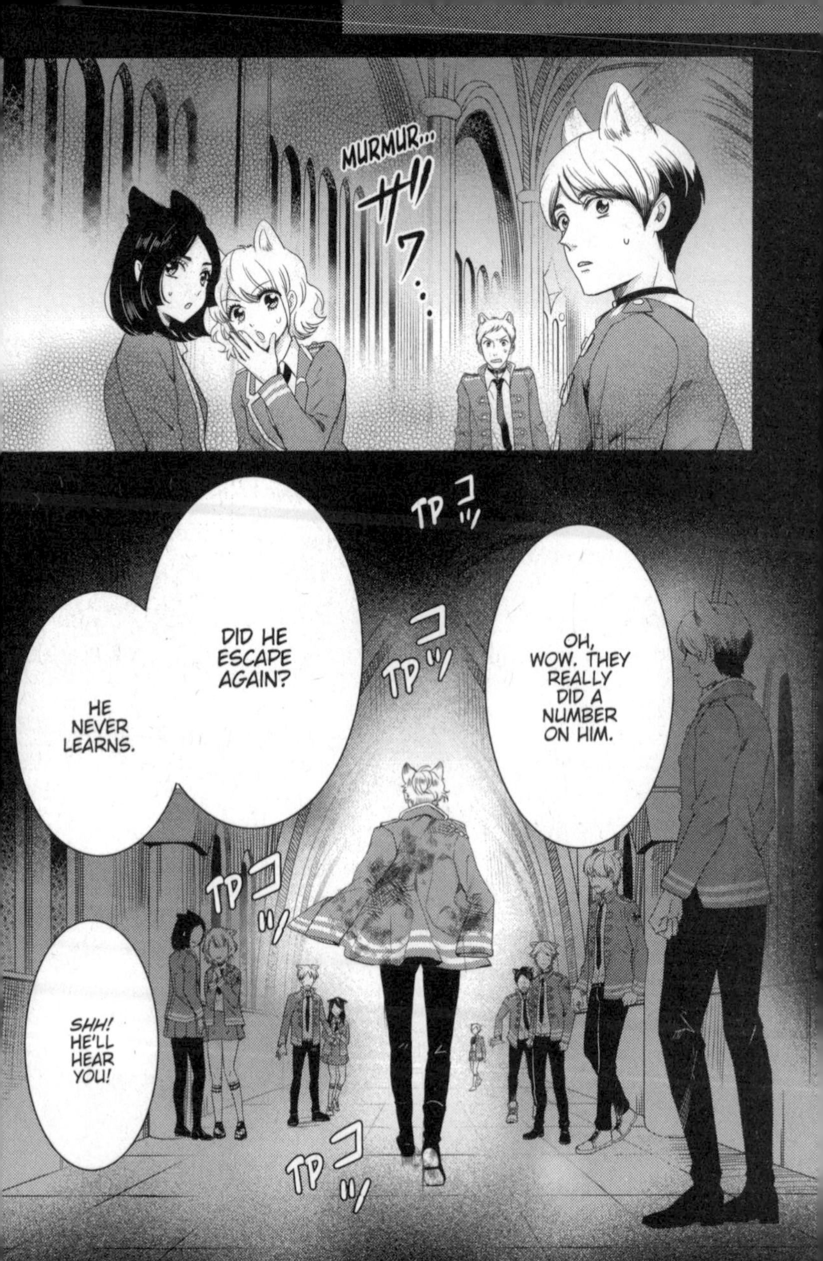
MURMUR...
ザワ…
TP コツ
OH, WOW. THEY REALLY DID A NUMBER ON HIM.
DID HE ESCAPE AGAIN?
HE NEVER LEARNS.
SHH! HE'LL HEAR YOU!

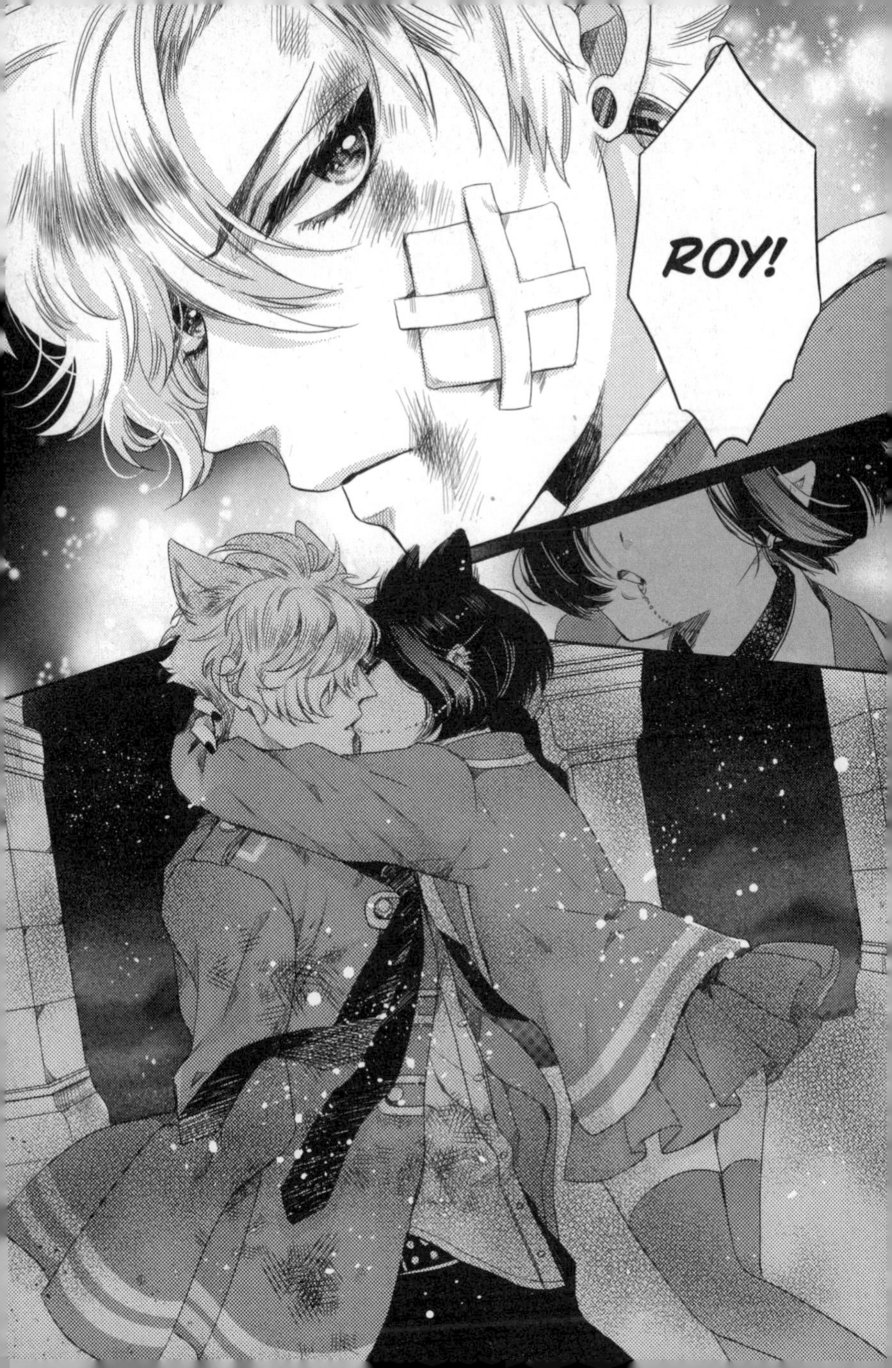
ROY!

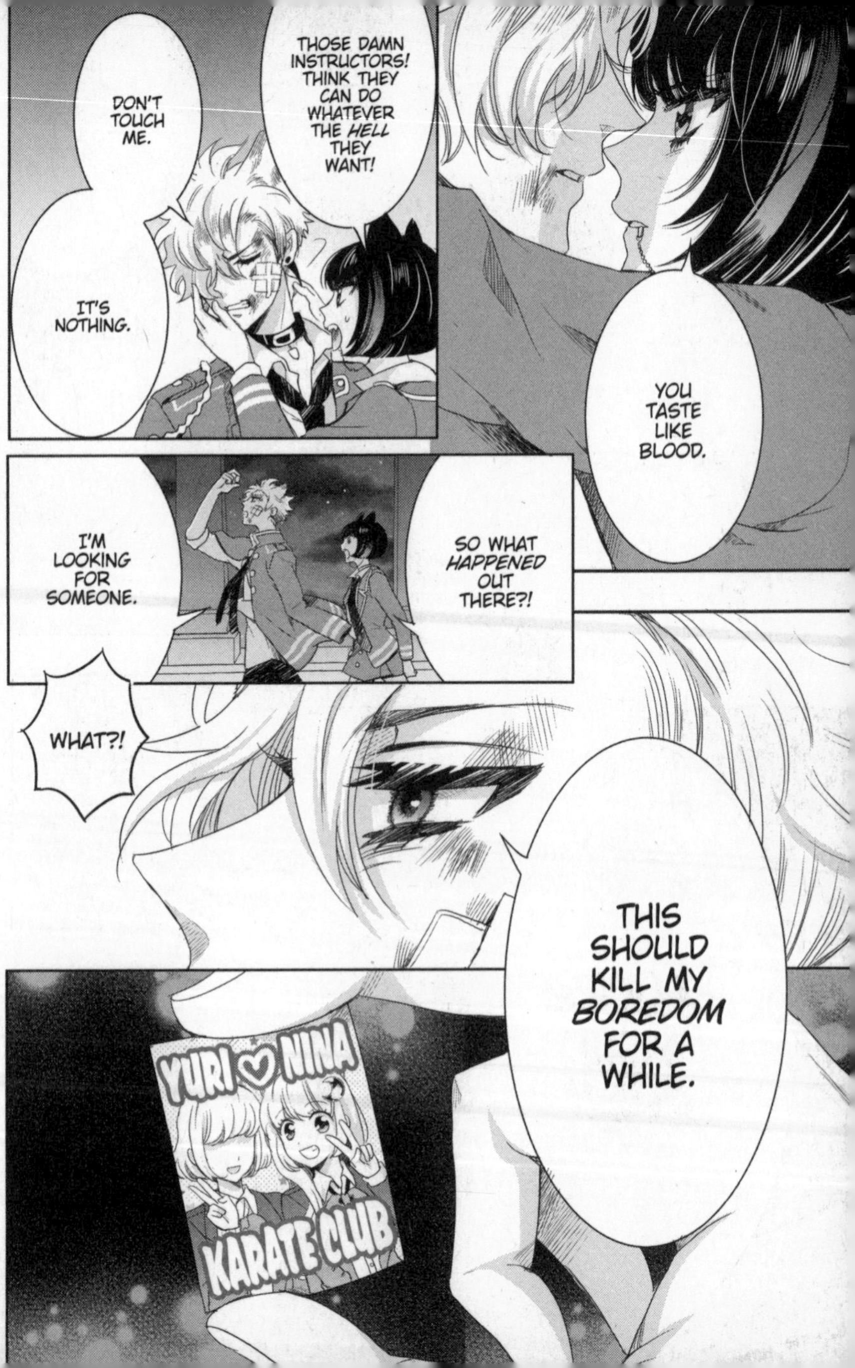
YOU TASTE LIKE BLOOD.
THOSE DAMN INSTRUCTORS! THINK THEY CAN DO WHATEVER THE *HELL* THEY WANT!
DON'T TOUCH ME.
IT'S NOTHING.
SO WHAT *HAPPENED* OUT THERE?!
I'M LOOKING FOR SOMEONE.
WHAT?!
THIS SHOULD KILL MY *BOREDOM* FOR A WHILE.
YURI ♡ NINA
KARATE CLUB

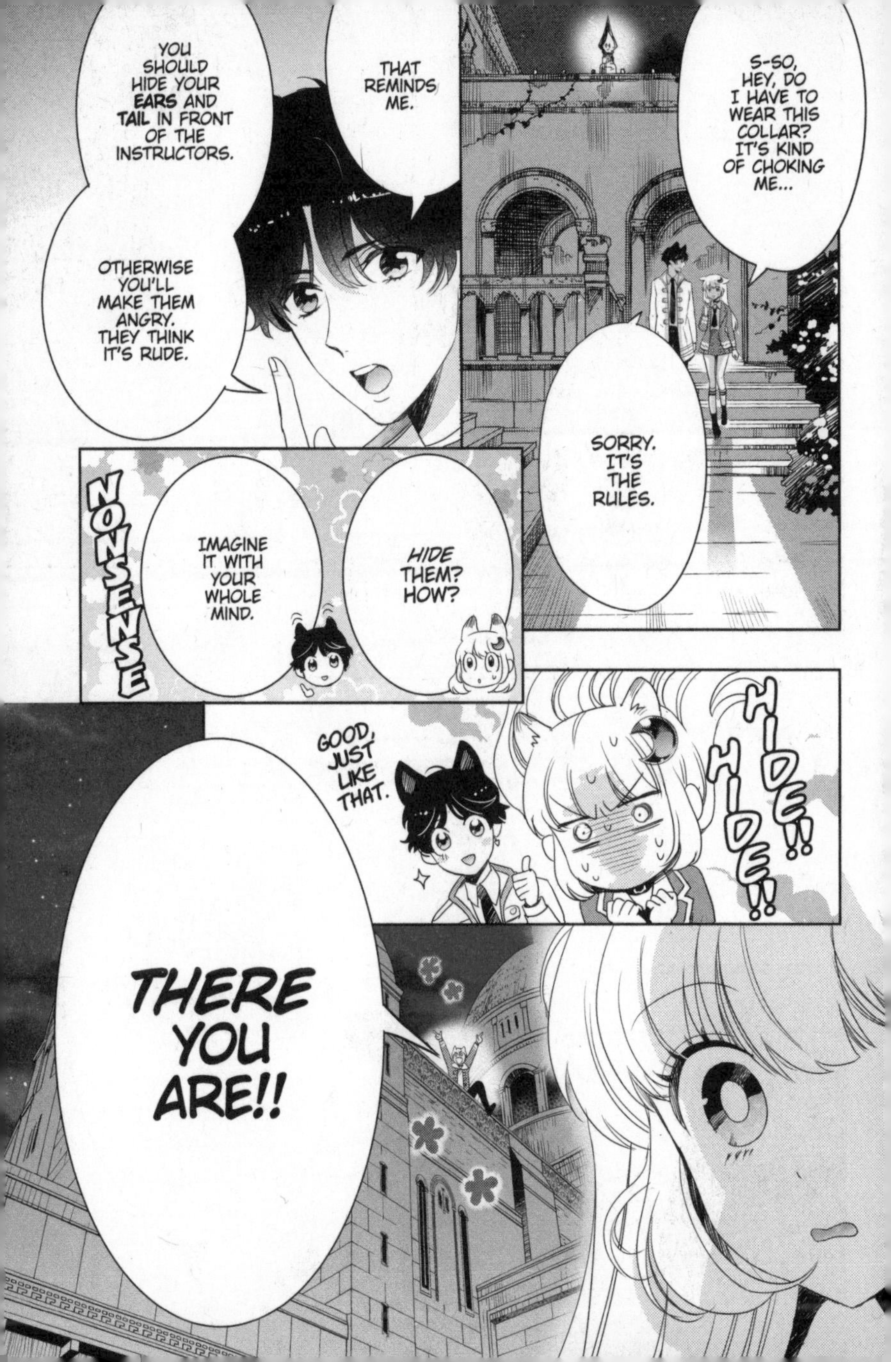
S-SO, HEY, DO I HAVE TO WEAR THIS COLLAR? IT'S KIND OF CHOKING ME...
SORRY. IT'S THE RULES.
THAT REMINDS ME.
YOU SHOULD HIDE YOUR **EARS** AND **TAIL** IN FRONT OF THE INSTRUCTORS.
OTHERWISE YOU'LL MAKE THEM ANGRY. THEY THINK IT'S RUDE.
HIDE THEM? HOW?
IMAGINE IT WITH YOUR WHOLE MIND.
NONSENSE
HIDE!! HIDE!!
GOOD, JUST LIKE THAT.
THERE YOU ARE!!

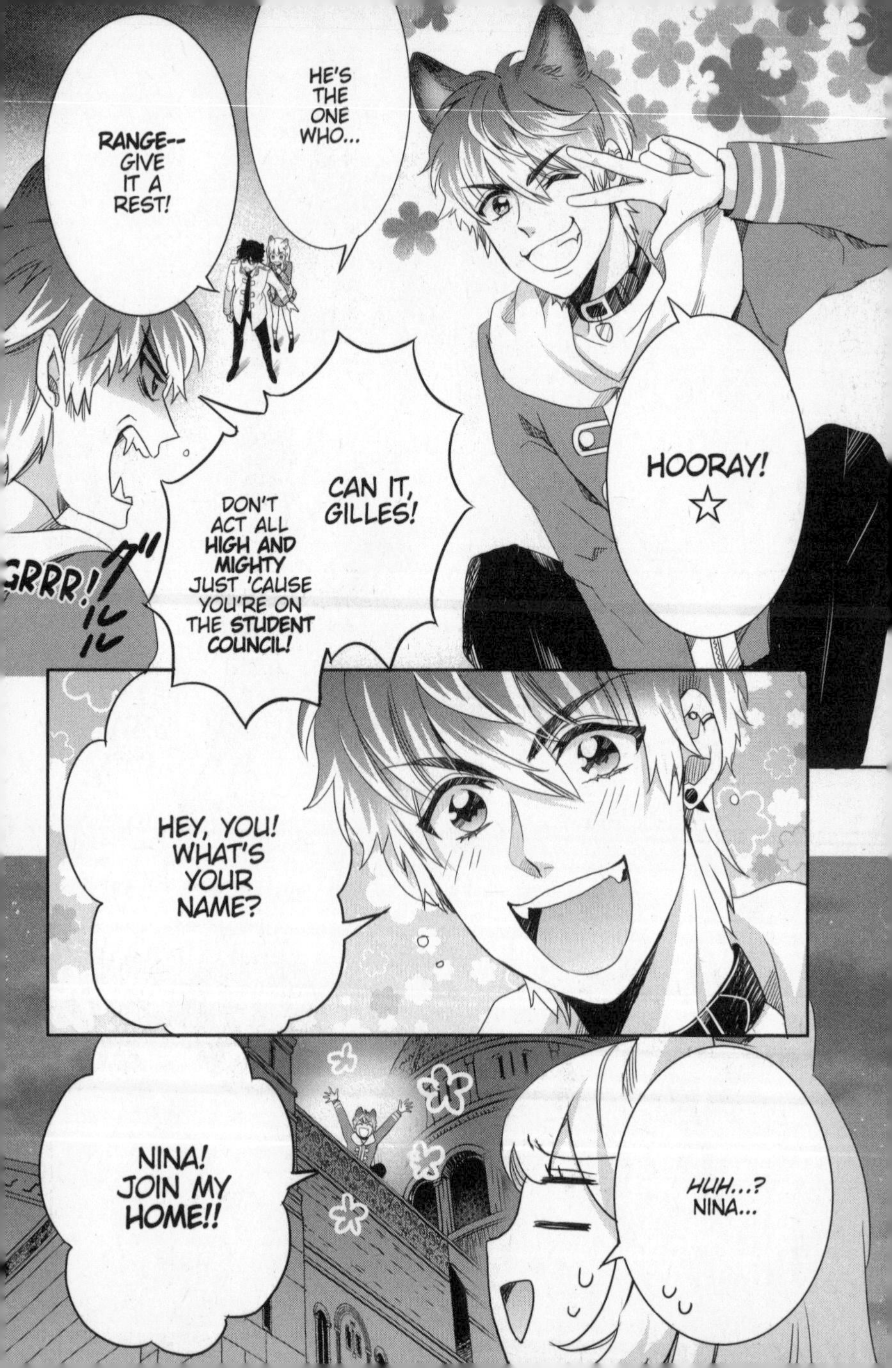
HOORAY! ☆
HE'S THE ONE WHO...
RANGE-- GIVE IT A REST!
CAN IT, GILLES!
DON'T ACT ALL **HIGH AND MIGHTY** JUST 'CAUSE YOU'RE ON THE **STUDENT COUNCIL**!
GRRR!
HEY, YOU! WHAT'S YOUR NAME?
HUH...? NINA...
NINA! JOIN MY HOME!!

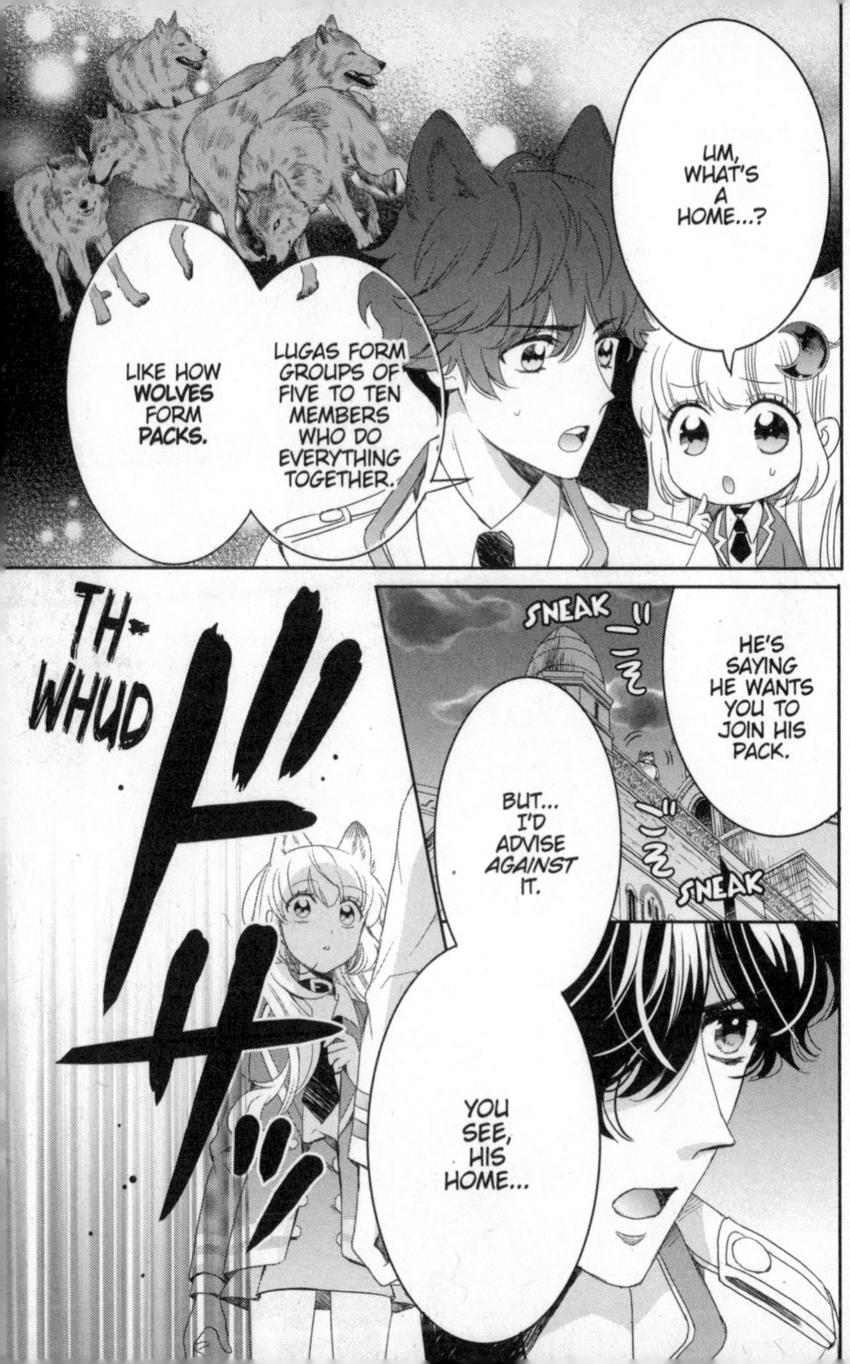
UM, WHAT'S A HOME...?
LUGAS FORM GROUPS OF FIVE TO TEN MEMBERS WHO DO EVERYTHING TOGETHER.
LIKE HOW WOLVES FORM PACKS.
HE'S SAYING HE WANTS YOU TO JOIN HIS PACK.
SNEAK
SNEAK
BUT... I'D ADVISE AGAINST IT.
YOU SEE, HIS HOME...
TH-WHUD

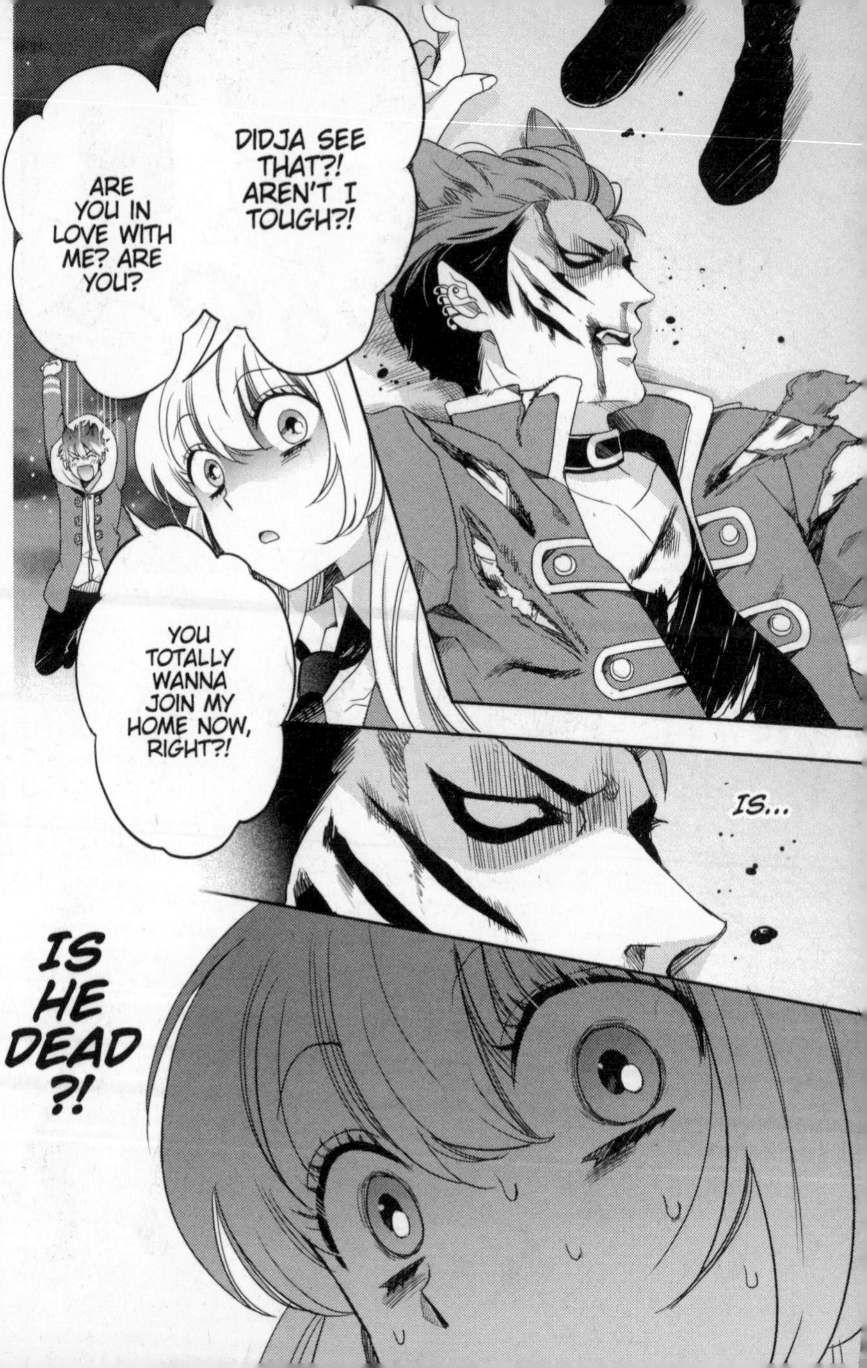
DIDJA SEE THAT?! AREN'T I TOUGH?!
ARE YOU IN LOVE WITH ME? ARE YOU?
YOU TOTALLY WANNA JOIN MY HOME NOW, RIGHT?!
IS...
IS HE DEAD ?!

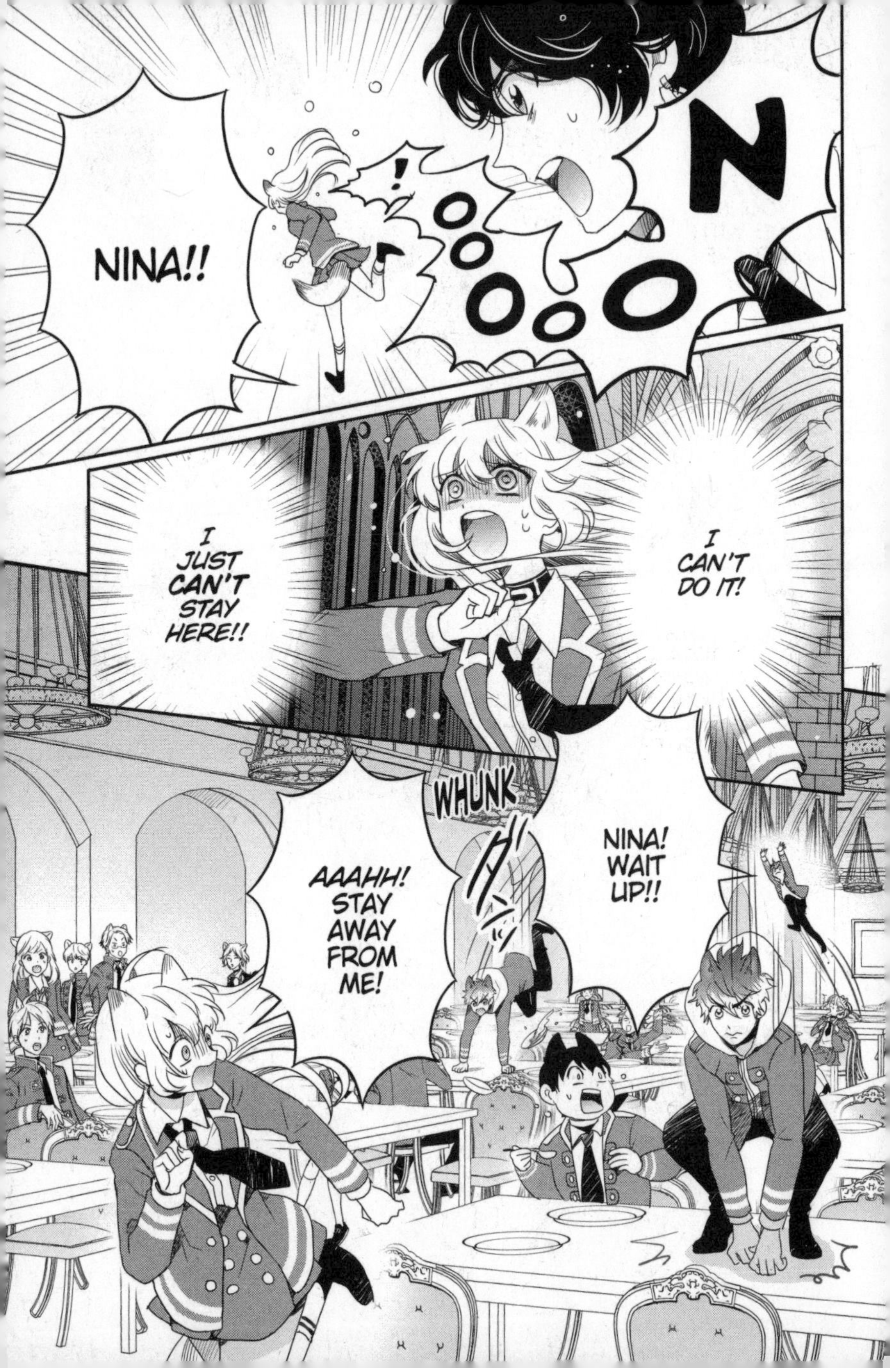

NOOOOO
!
NINA!!
I CAN'T DO IT!
I JUST CAN'T STAY HERE!!
NINA! WAIT UP!!
WHUNK
AAAHH! STAY AWAY FROM ME!

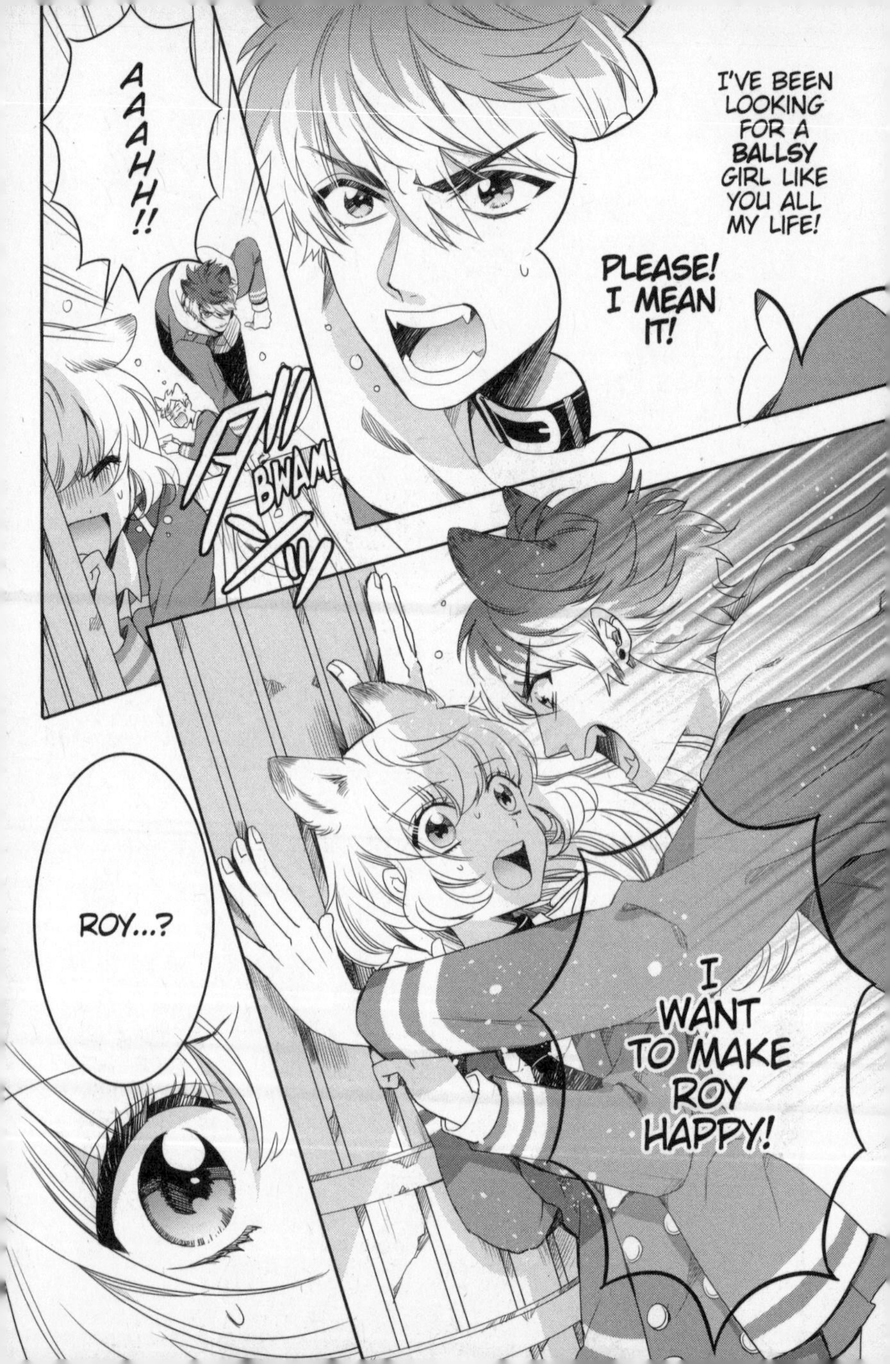
I'VE BEEN LOOKING FOR A BALLSY GIRL LIKE YOU ALL MY LIFE!
PLEASE! I MEAN IT!
AAAAHH!!
BWAM
I WANT TO MAKE ROY HAPPY!
ROY...?

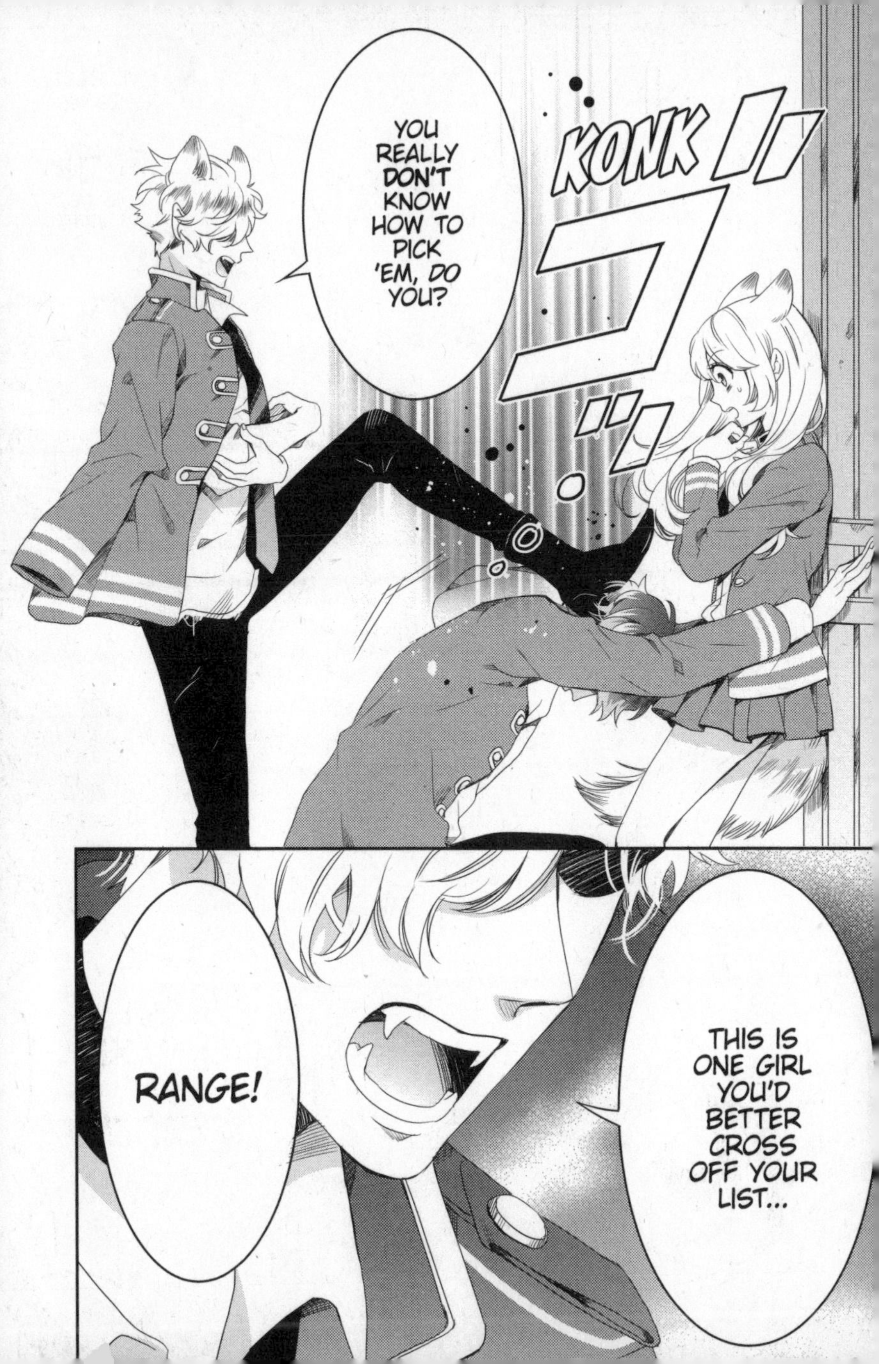
KONK
YOU REALLY DON'T KNOW HOW TO PICK 'EM, DO YOU?
THIS IS ONE GIRL YOU'D BETTER CROSS OFF YOUR LIST...
RANGE!

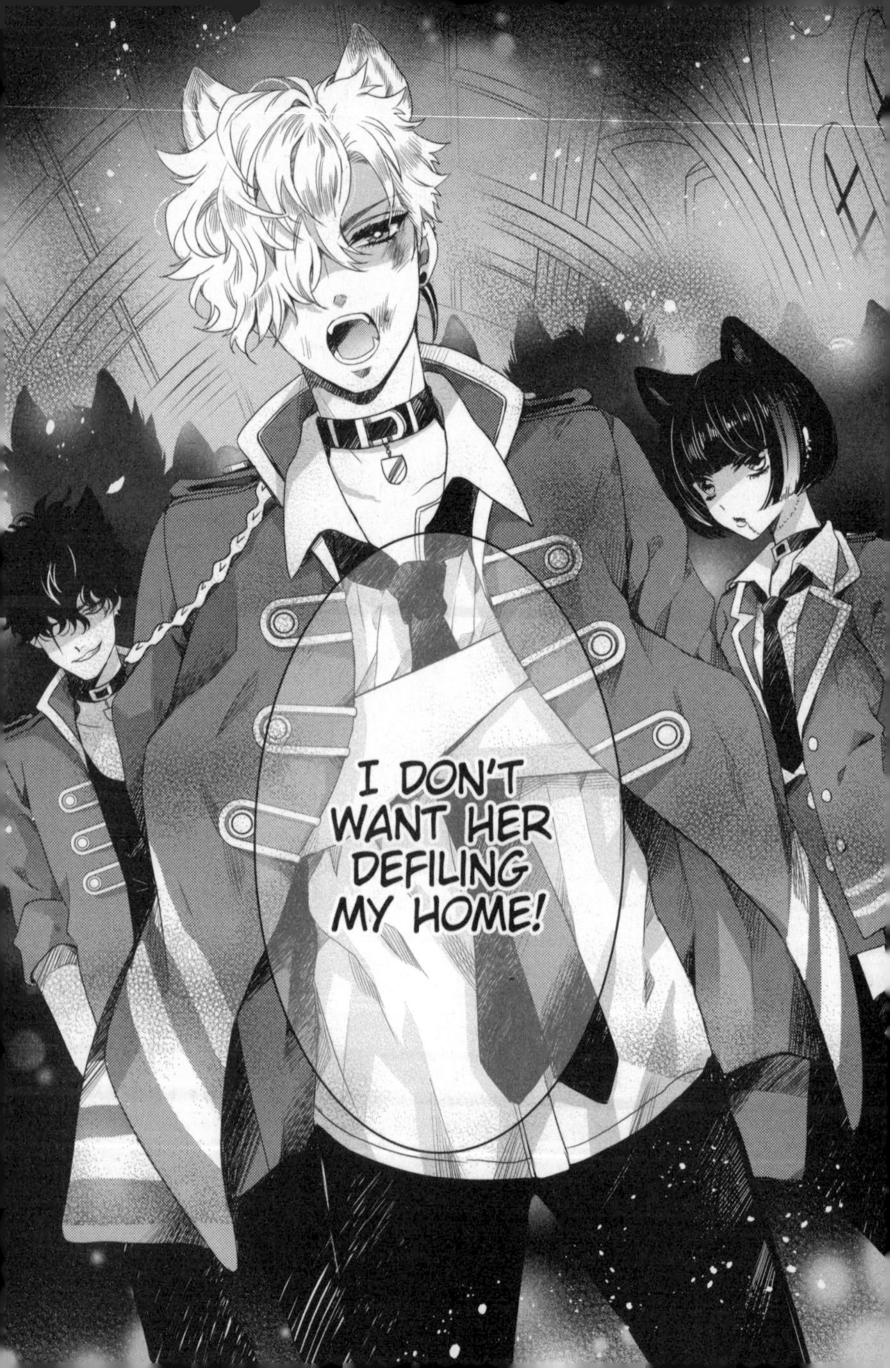
I DON'T WANT HER DEFILING MY HOME!

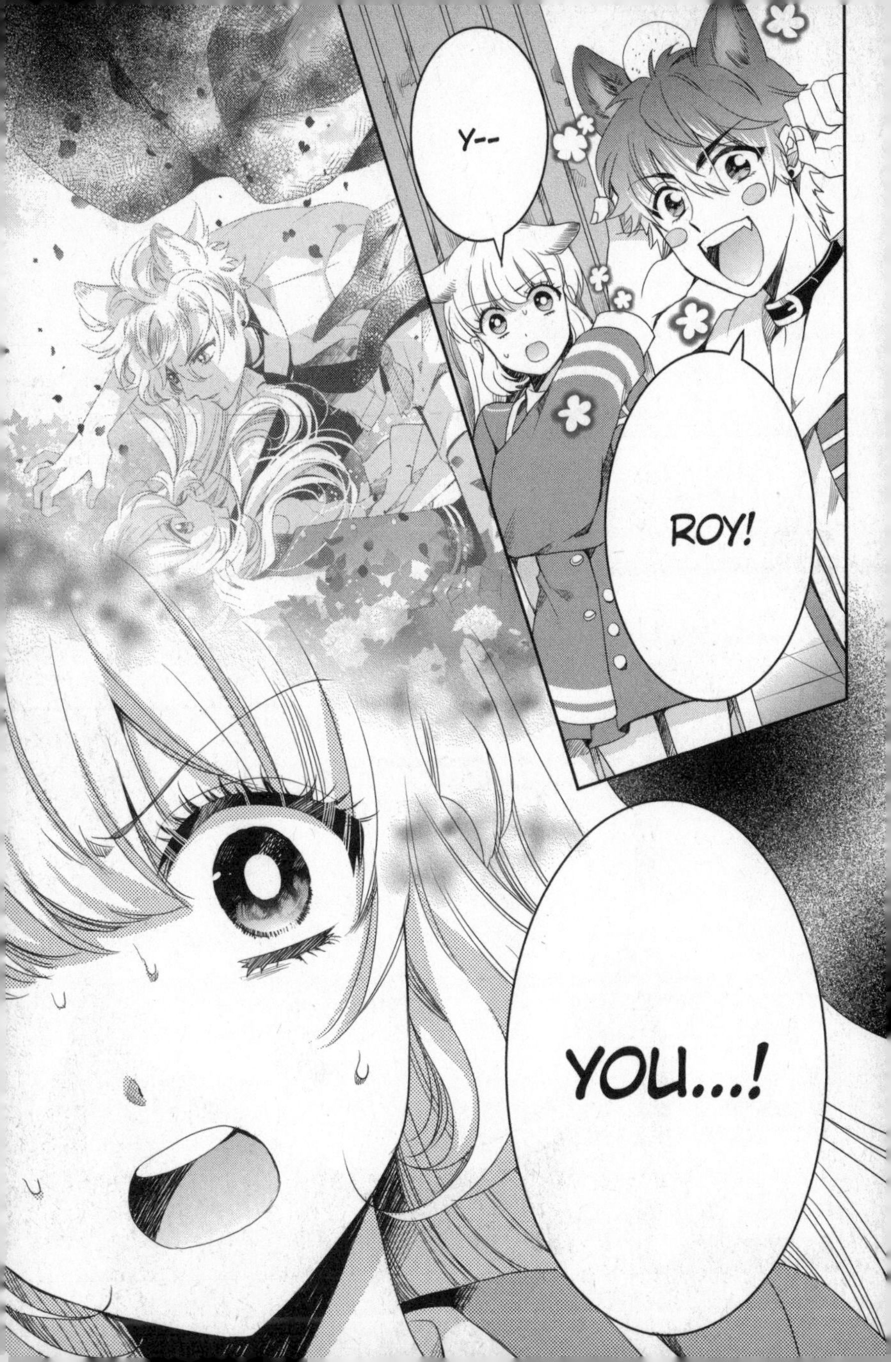
Y--
ROY!
YOU...!

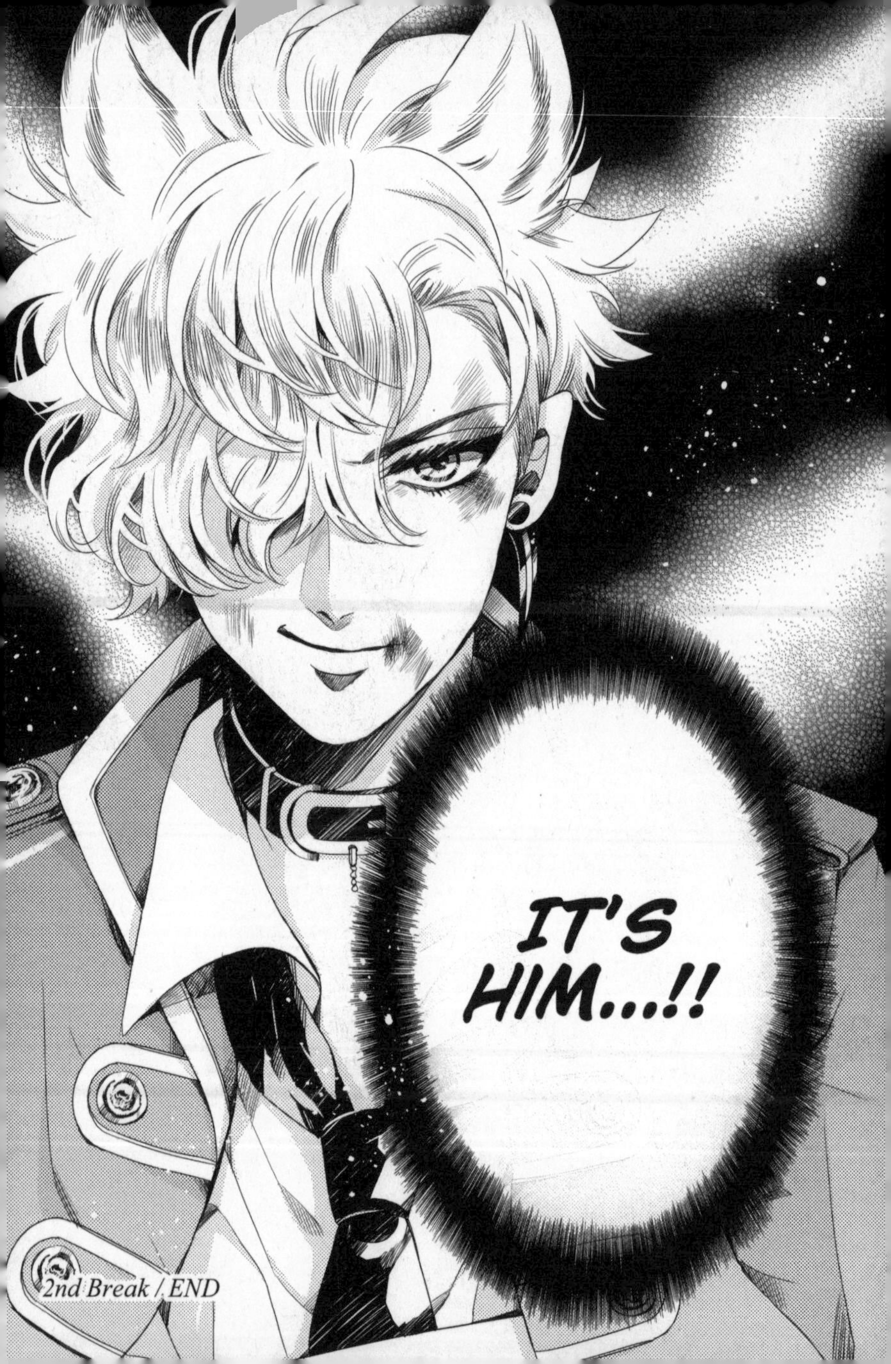
IT'S HIM...!!
2nd Break / END

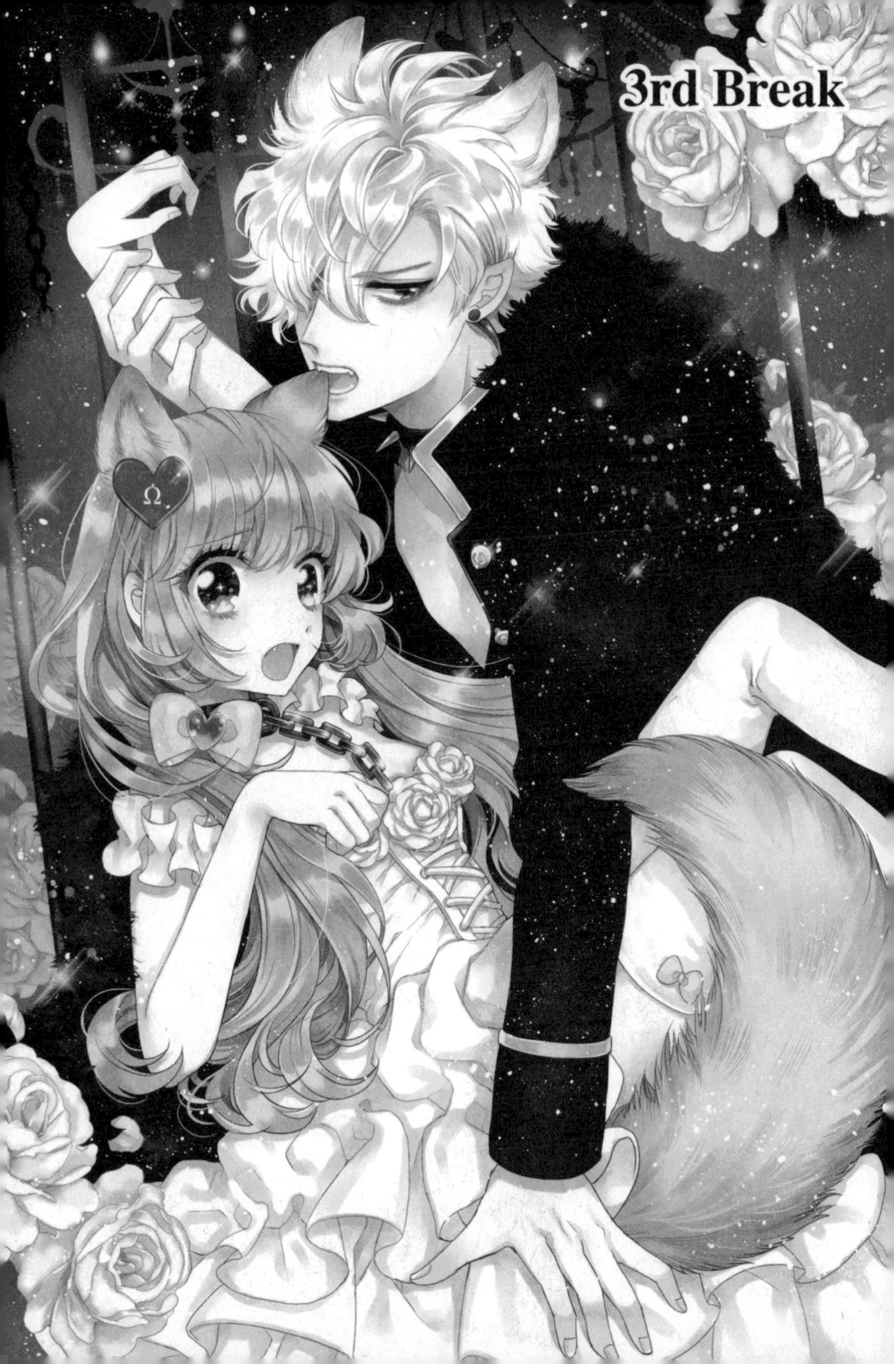
3rd Break

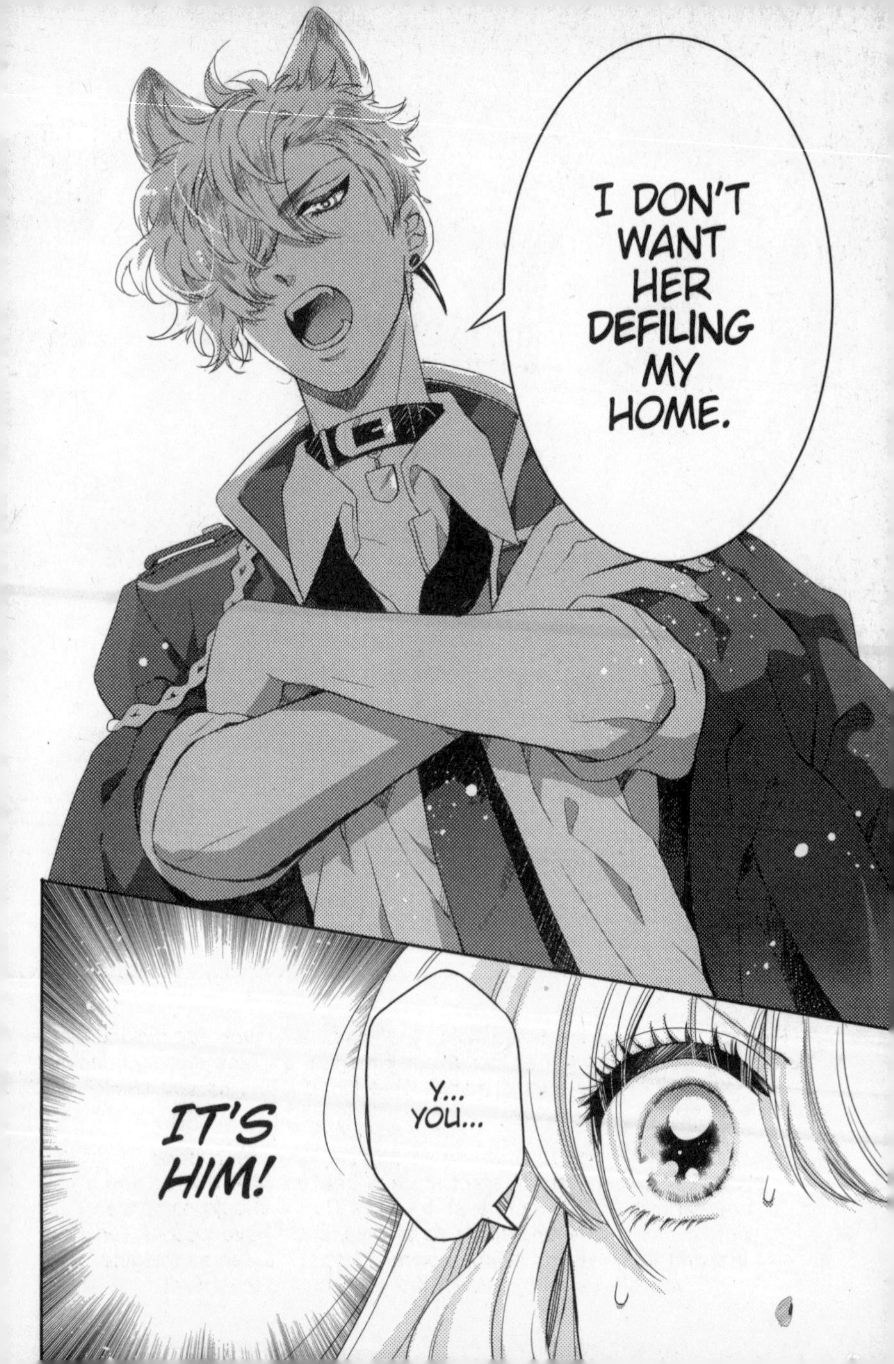
I DON'T WANT HER DEFILING MY HOME.
Y... YOU...
IT'S HIM!

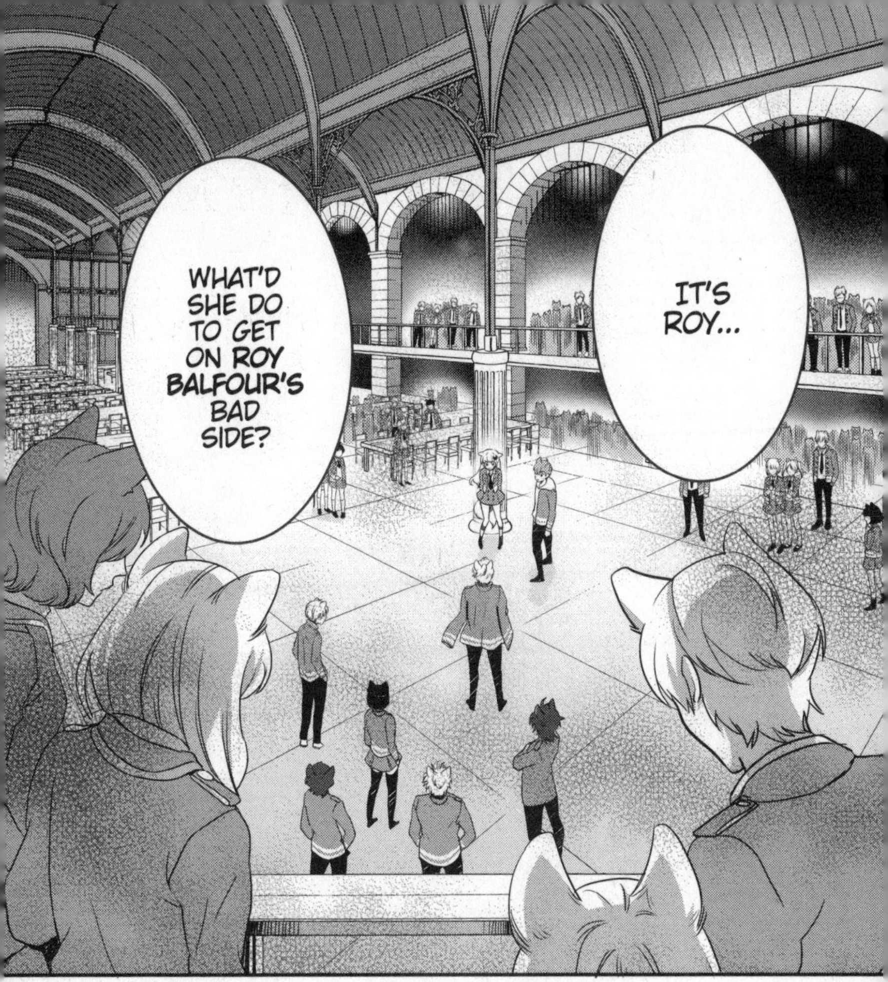
IT'S ROY...
WHAT'D SHE DO TO GET ON ROY BALFOUR'S BAD SIDE?

Nice to meet you! I'm Spica Aoki. Thank you so much for picking up *Beasts of Abigaile* Volume One! After finishing my last series, I decided to write a classic shoujo manga this time! What do you think?

....

Right in the first chapter, a little kid gets tossed around, and the main character gets beaten with a whip. *Hm*... I guess my stories can never be 100% fluffy shoujo romance. Well, my manga is the same as always, but I have lots of fun drawing and weeping every month! I hope you can all imagine yourselves as Nina-chan as you enjoy the series!

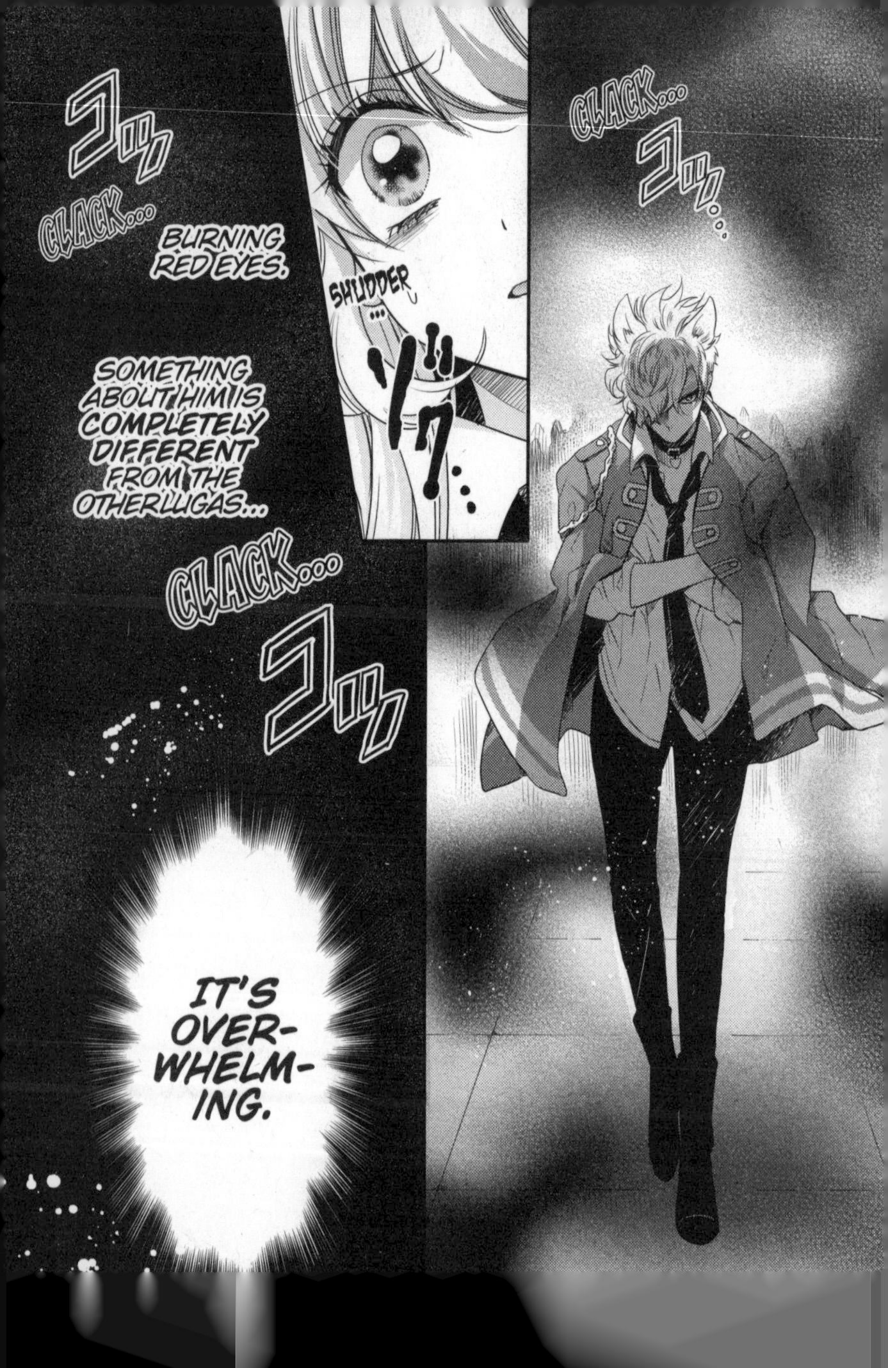
CLACK...
SHUDDER...
CLACK...
BURNING RED EYES.
SOMETHING ABOUT HIM IS COMPLETELY DIFFERENT FROM THE OTHER LUGAS...
CLACK...
IT'S OVERWHELMING.

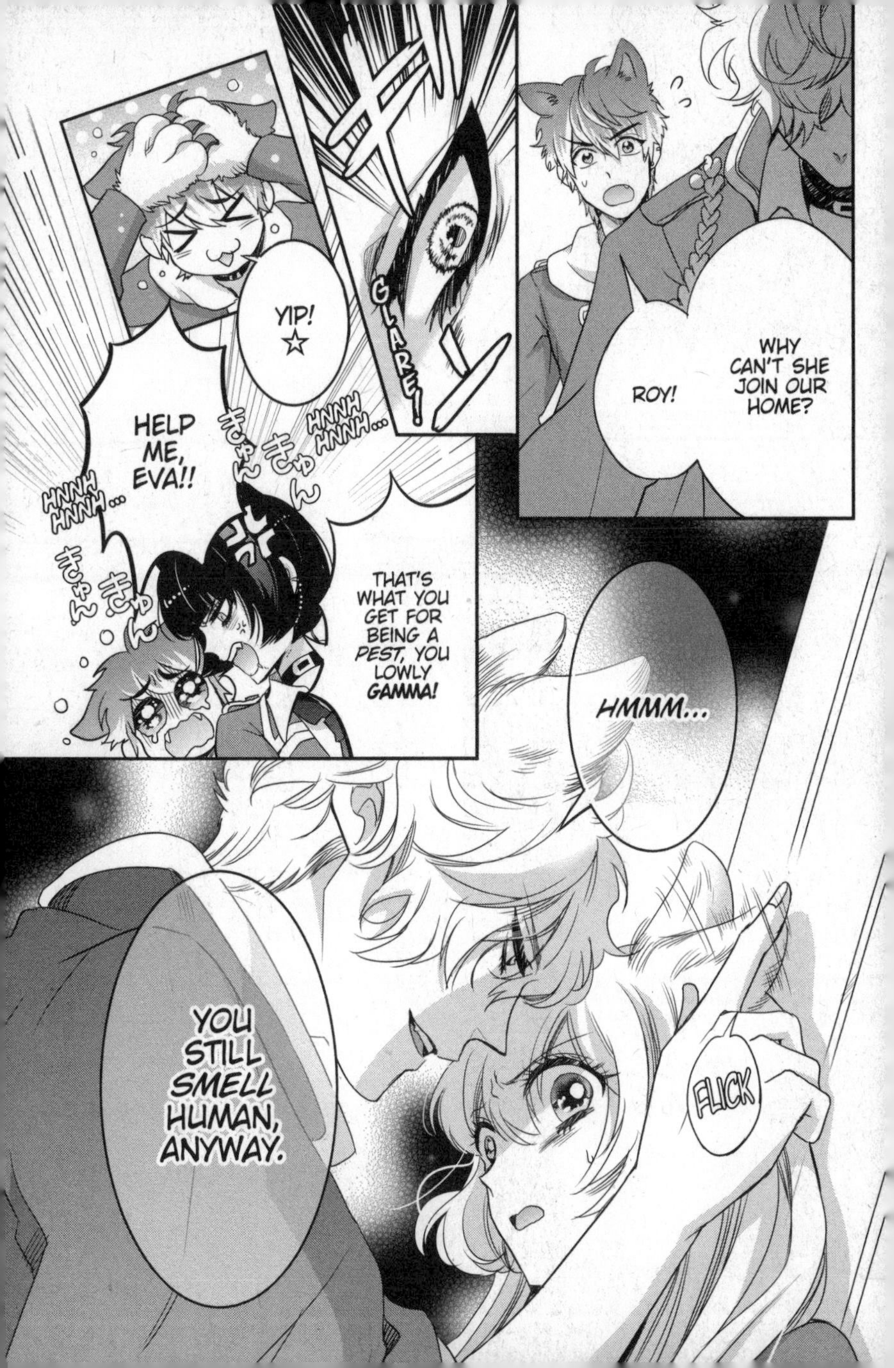
ROY! WHY CAN'T SHE JOIN OUR HOME?
GLARE!
YIP! ☆
HNNH HNNH...
きゅんきゅん
HELP ME, EVA!!
HNNH HNNH...
きゅんきゅん
THAT'S WHAT YOU GET FOR BEING A *PEST*, YOU LOWLY **GAMMA**!
HMMM...
FLICK
YOU STILL *SMELL* HUMAN, ANYWAY.

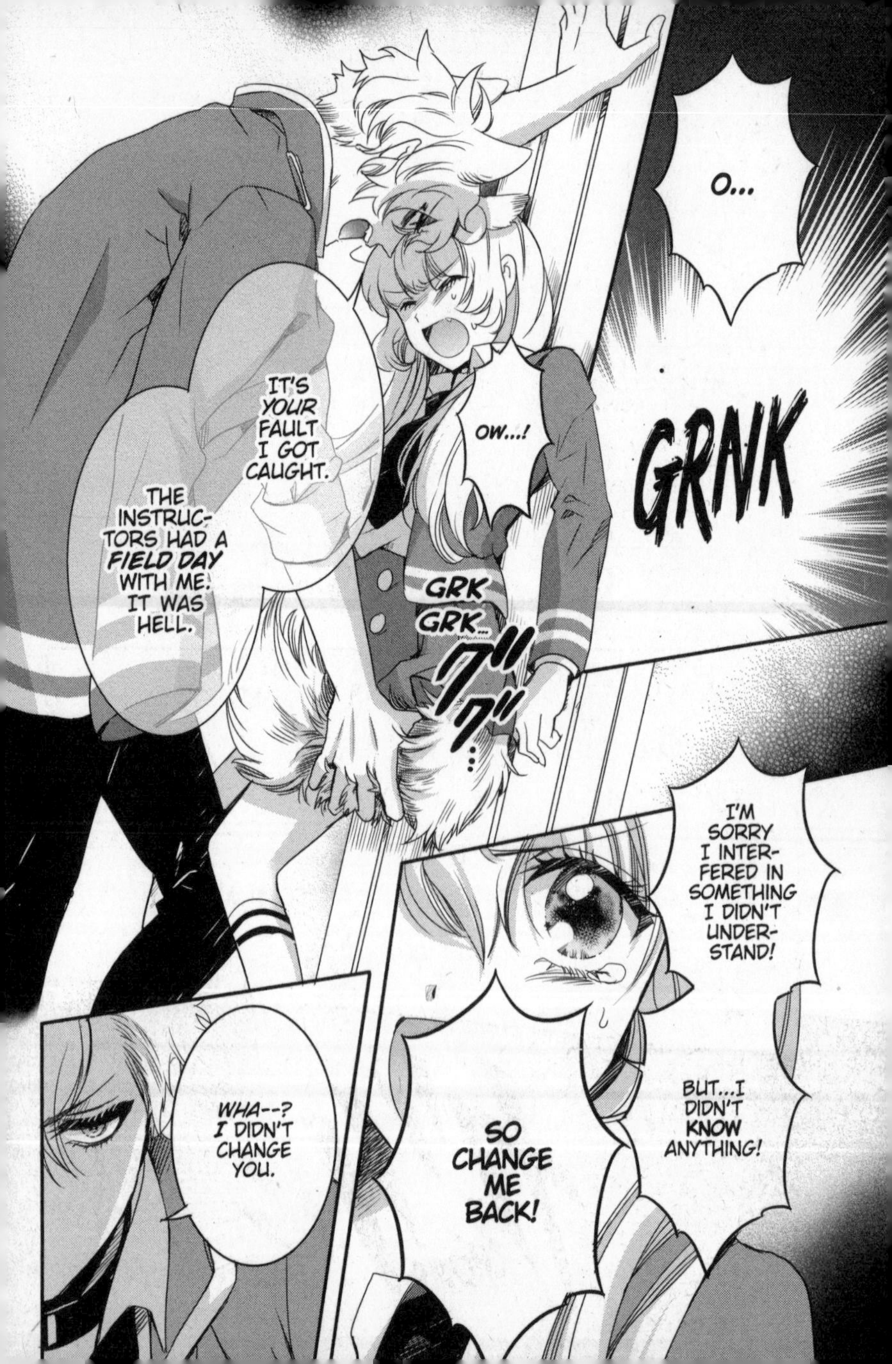
O...
GRNK
OW...!
IT'S *YOUR* FAULT I GOT CAUGHT.
THE INSTRUCTORS HAD A *FIELD DAY* WITH ME. IT WAS HELL.
GRK GRK...
グッ グッ...
I'M SORRY I INTERFERED IN SOMETHING I DIDN'T UNDERSTAND!
BUT...I DIDN'T KNOW ANYTHING!
SO CHANGE ME BACK!
WHA--? *I* DIDN'T CHANGE YOU.

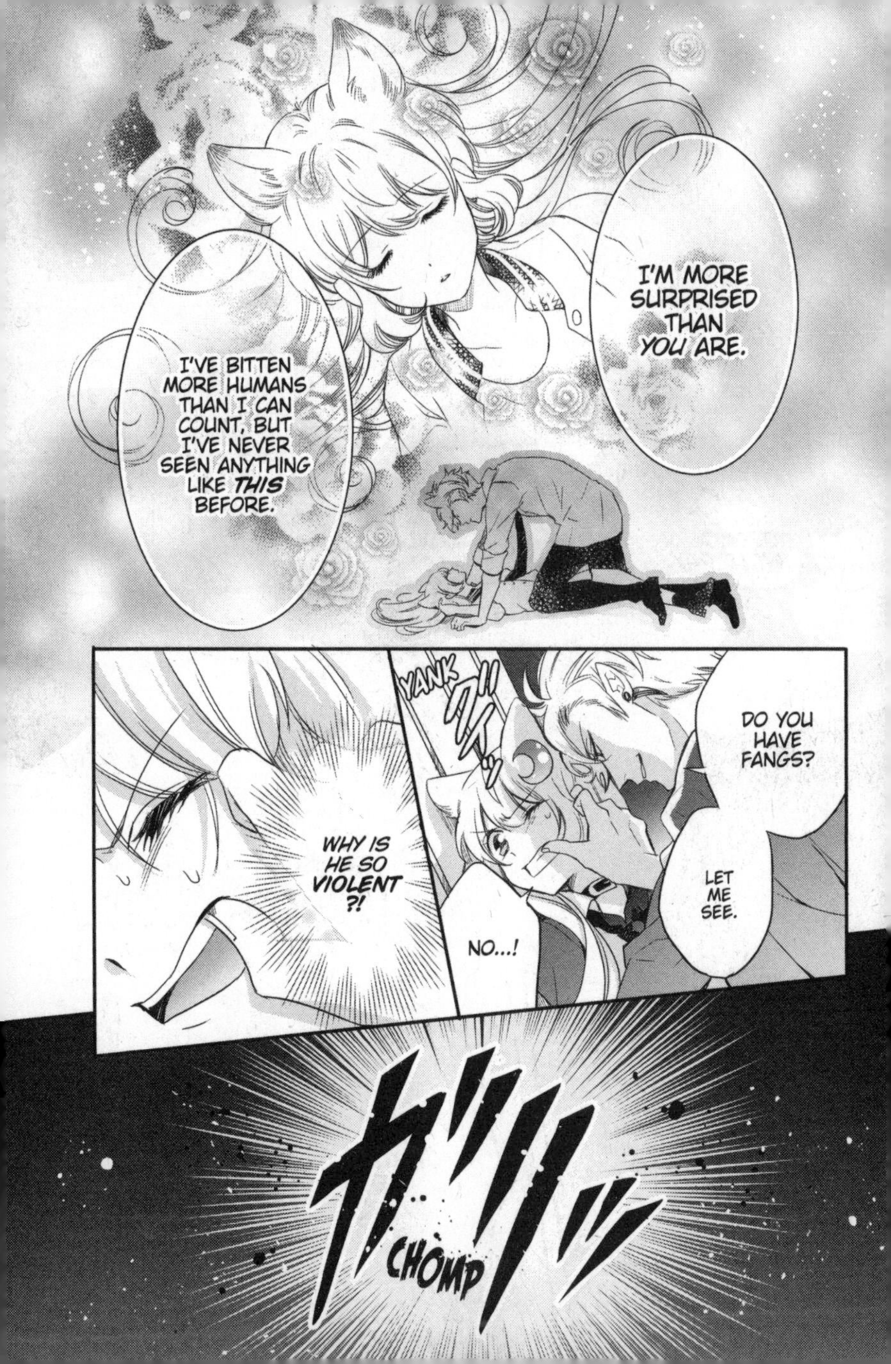
I'M MORE SURPRISED THAN YOU ARE.
I'VE BITTEN MORE HUMANS THAN I CAN COUNT, BUT I'VE NEVER SEEN ANYTHING LIKE THIS BEFORE.
YANK
DO YOU HAVE FANGS?
LET ME SEE.
NO...!
WHY IS HE SO VIOLENT?!
CHOMP

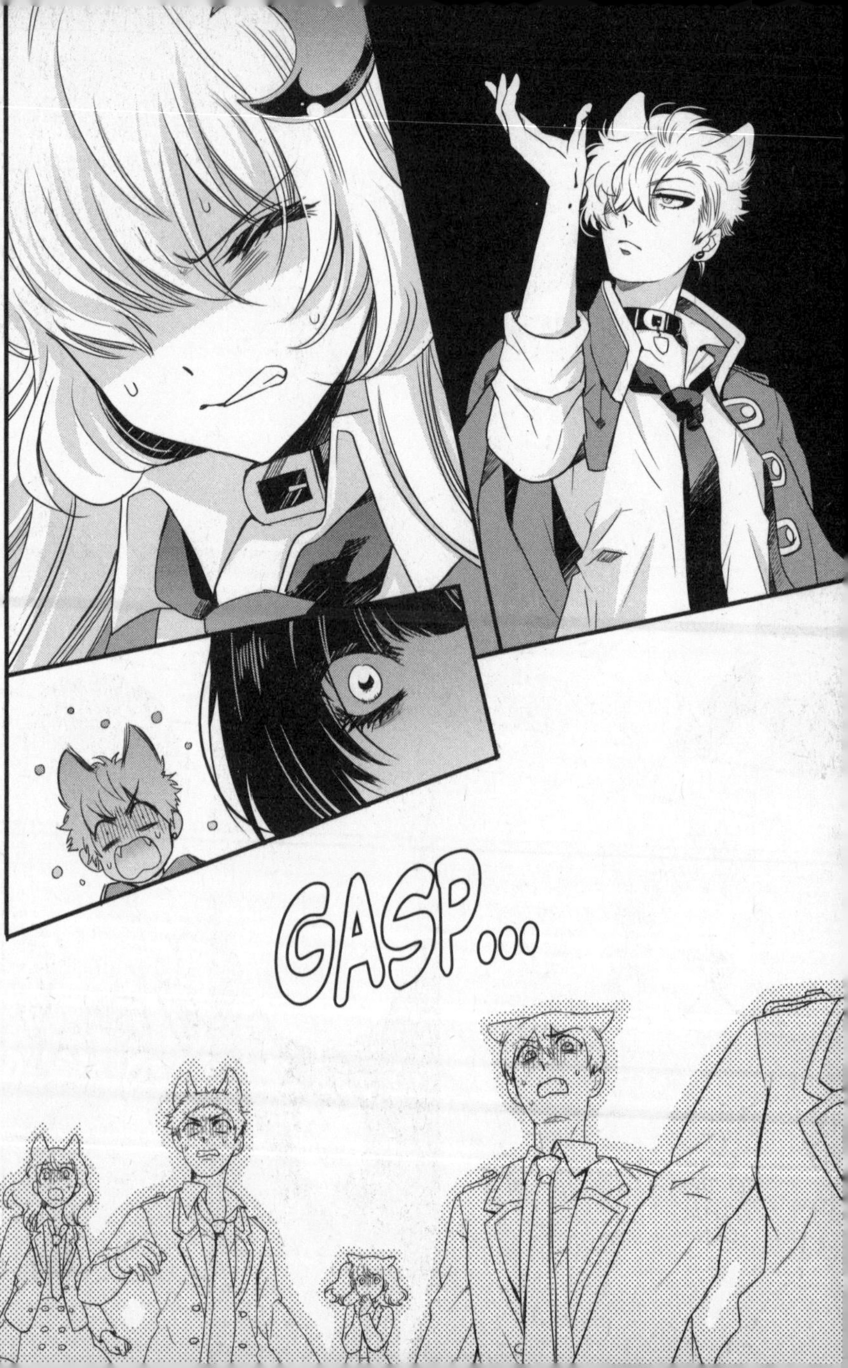
GASP...

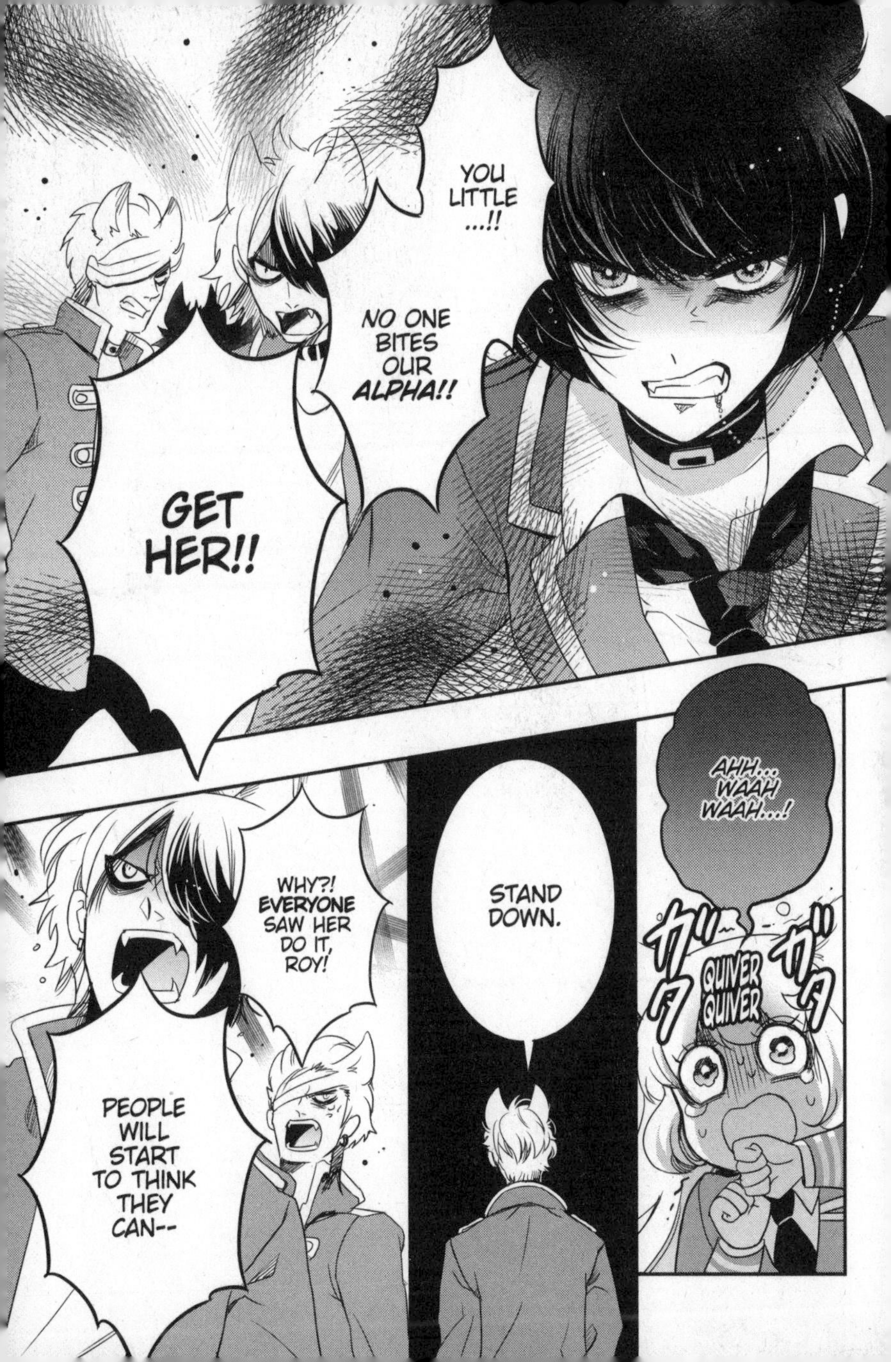
YOU LITTLE ...!!
NO ONE BITES OUR ALPHA!!
GET HER!!
AHH... WAAH WAAH...!
ガタ
QUIVER QUIVER
ガタ
STAND DOWN.
WHY?! EVERYONE SAW HER DO IT, ROY!
PEOPLE WILL START TO THINK THEY CAN--

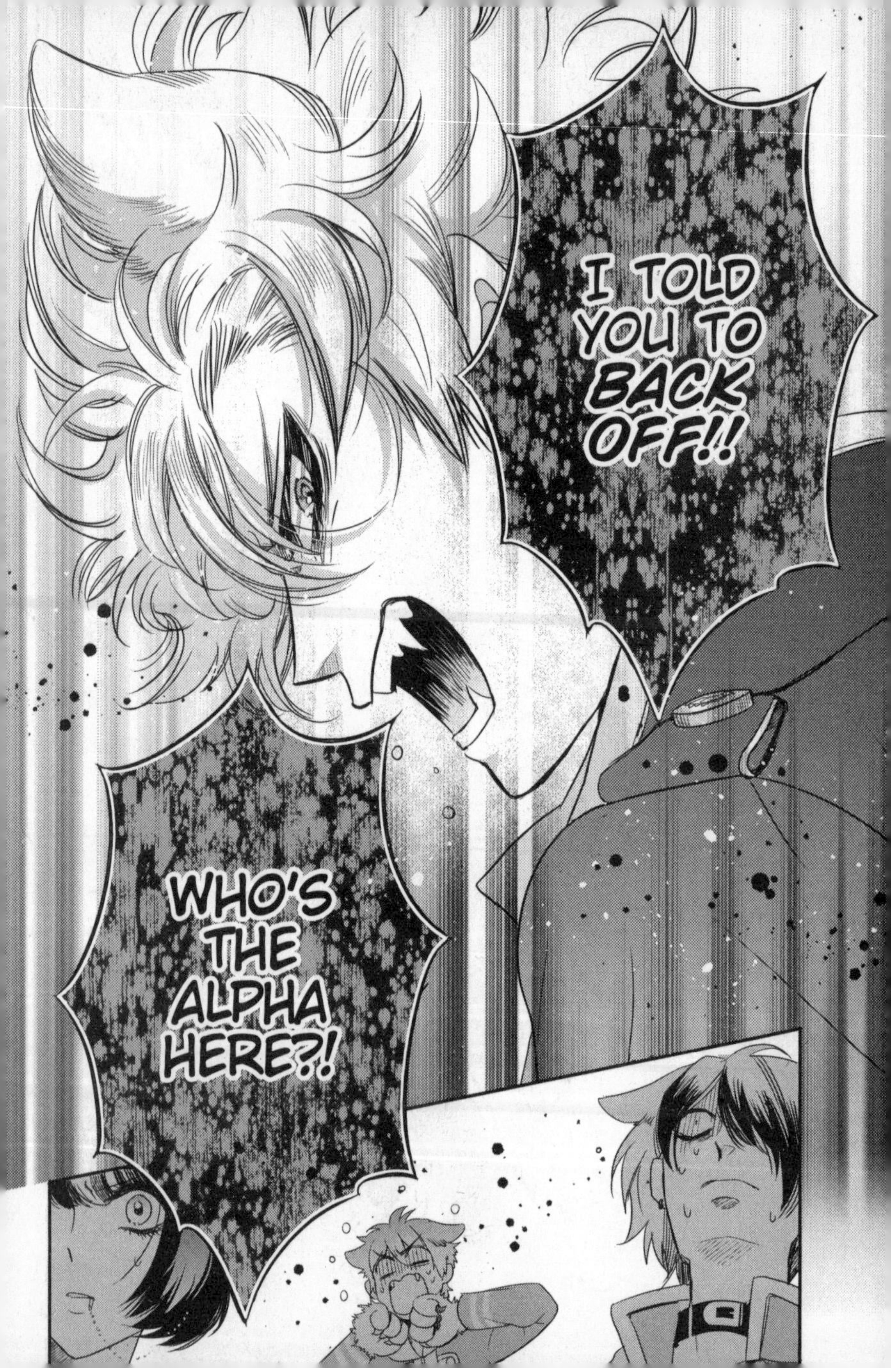
I TOLD YOU TO BACK OFF!!
WHO'S THE ALPHA HERE?!

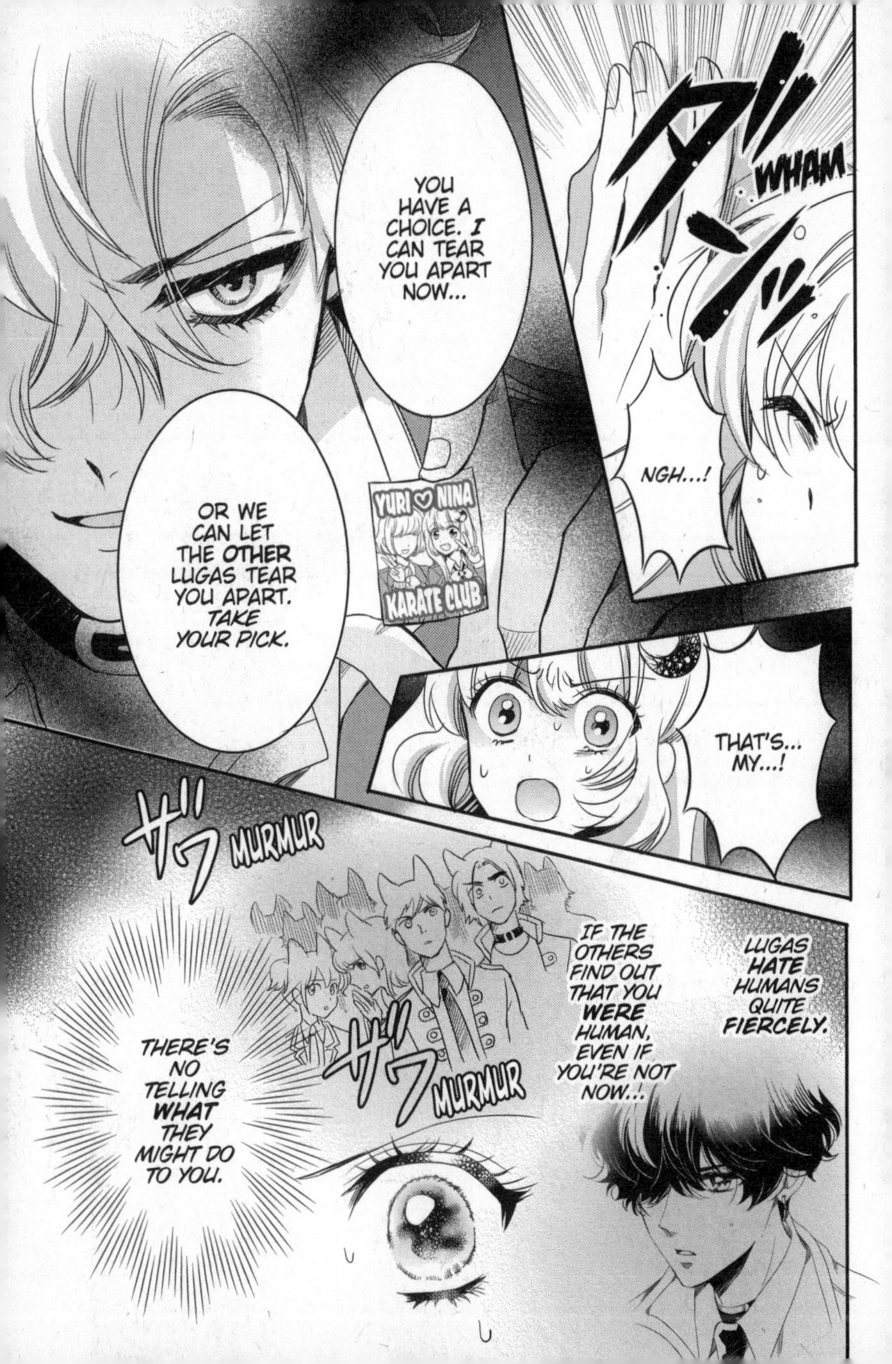
WHAM
NGH...!
YOU HAVE A CHOICE. *I* CAN TEAR YOU APART NOW...
OR WE CAN LET THE OTHER LUGAS TEAR YOU APART. *TAKE YOUR PICK.*
YURI ♡ NINA
KARATE CLUB
THAT'S... MY...!
MURMUR
LUGAS **HATE** HUMANS QUITE **FIERCELY.**
IF THE OTHERS FIND OUT THAT YOU **WERE** HUMAN, EVEN IF YOU'RE NOT NOW...
THERE'S NO TELLING **WHAT** THEY MIGHT DO TO YOU.
MURMUR

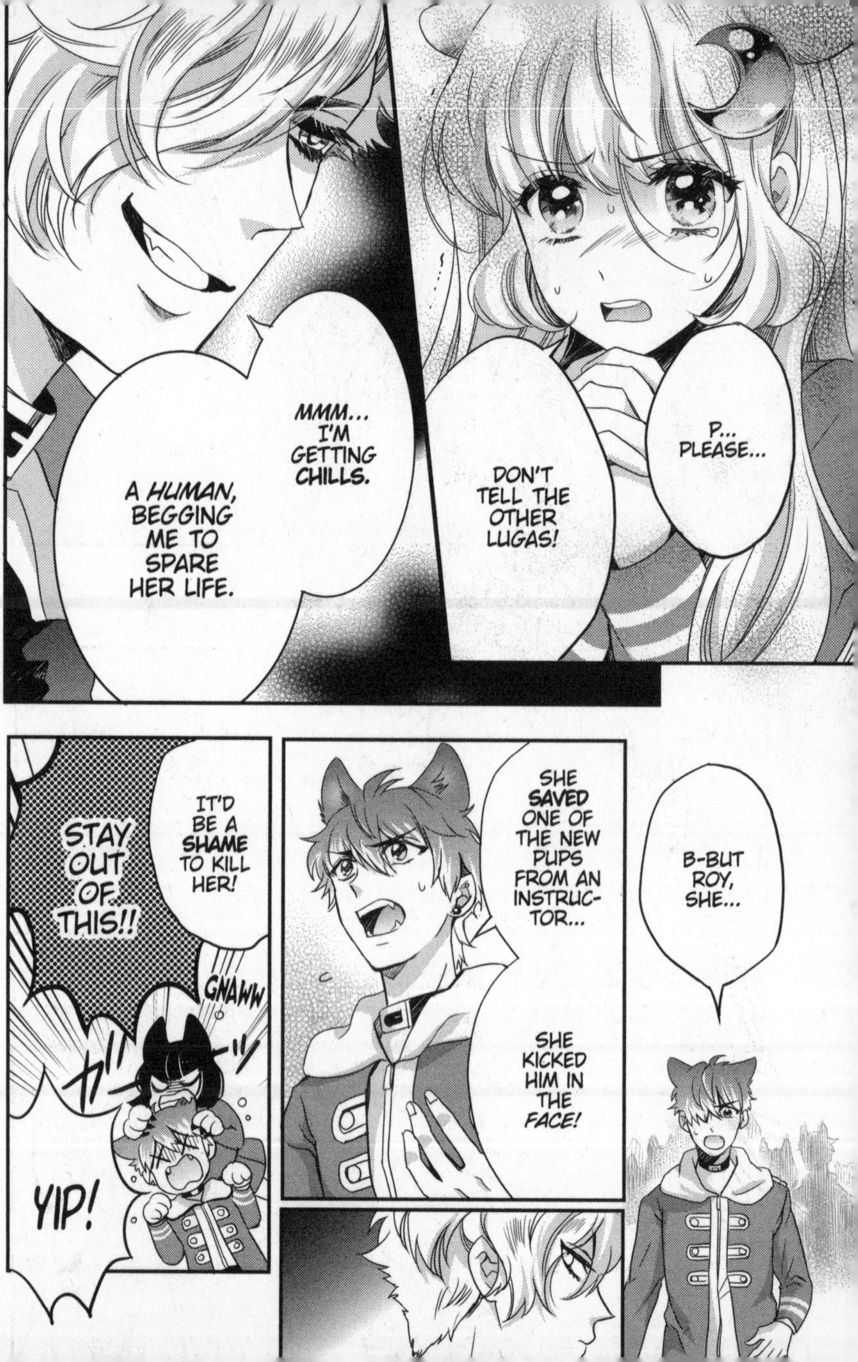
P... PLEASE...
DON'T TELL THE OTHER LUGAS!
MMM... I'M GETTING CHILLS.
A *HUMAN*, BEGGING ME TO SPARE HER LIFE.
B-BUT ROY, SHE...
SHE **SAVED** ONE OF THE NEW PUPS FROM AN INSTRUC-TOR...
SHE KICKED HIM IN THE *FACE!*
IT'D BE A **SHAME** TO KILL HER!
STAY OUT OF THIS!!
GNAWW
YIP!

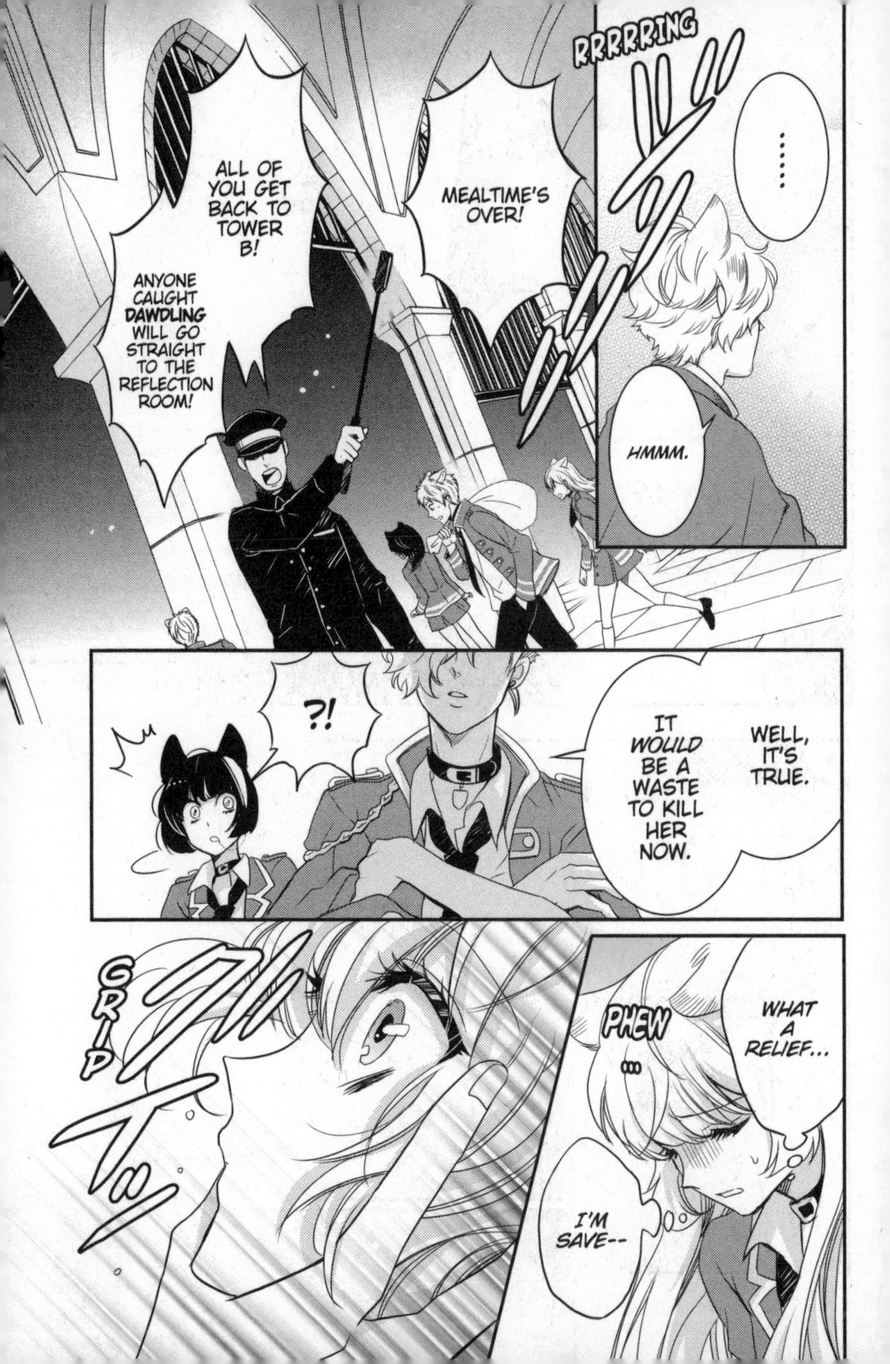
RRRRRING
......
HMMM.
MEALTIME'S OVER!
ALL OF YOU GET BACK TO TOWER B!
ANYONE CAUGHT DAWDLING WILL GO STRAIGHT TO THE REFLECTION ROOM!
WELL, IT'S TRUE.
IT WOULD BE A WASTE TO KILL HER NOW.
?!
WHAT A RELIEF...
PHEW
...
I'M SAVE--
GRIP

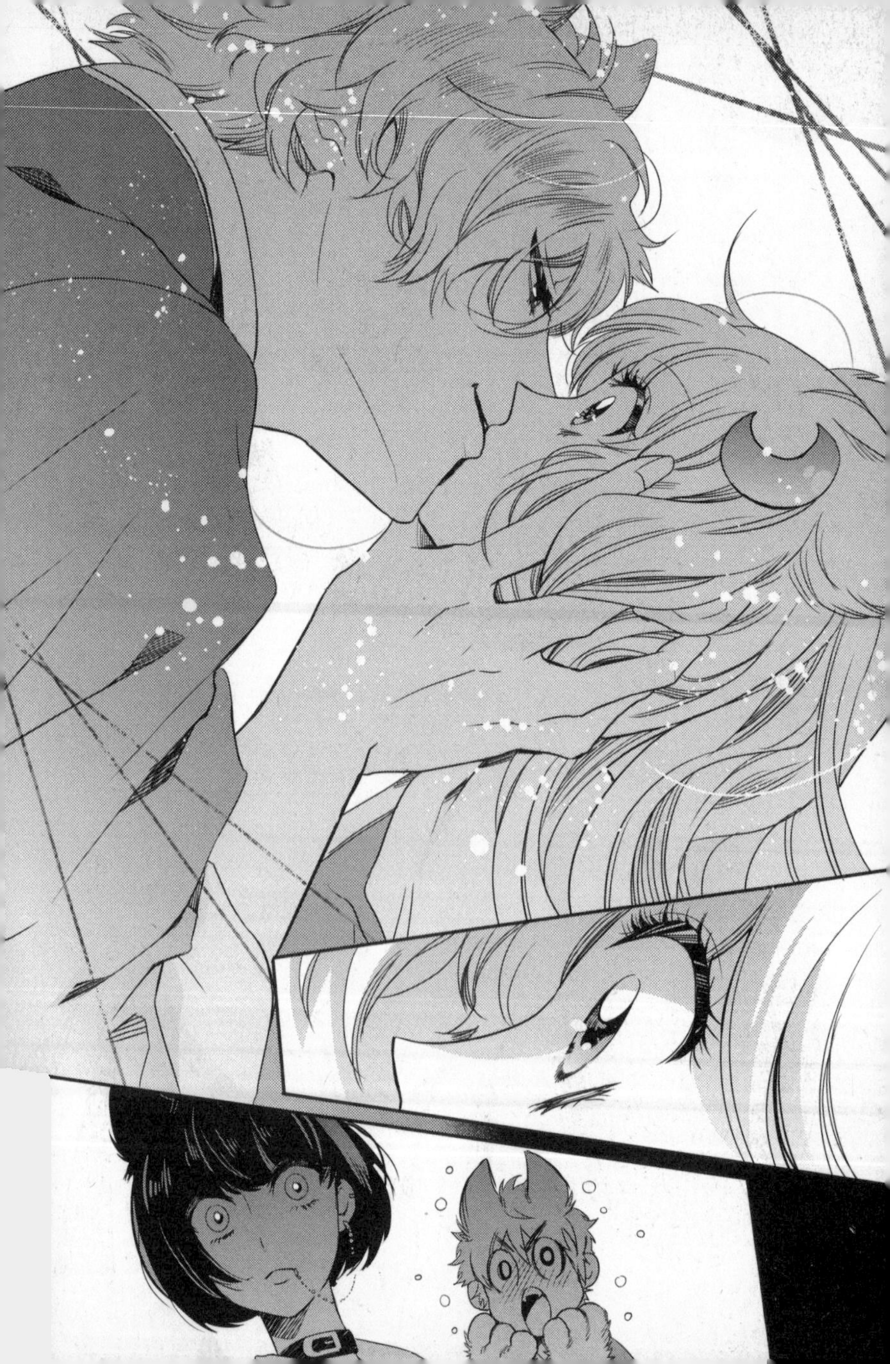

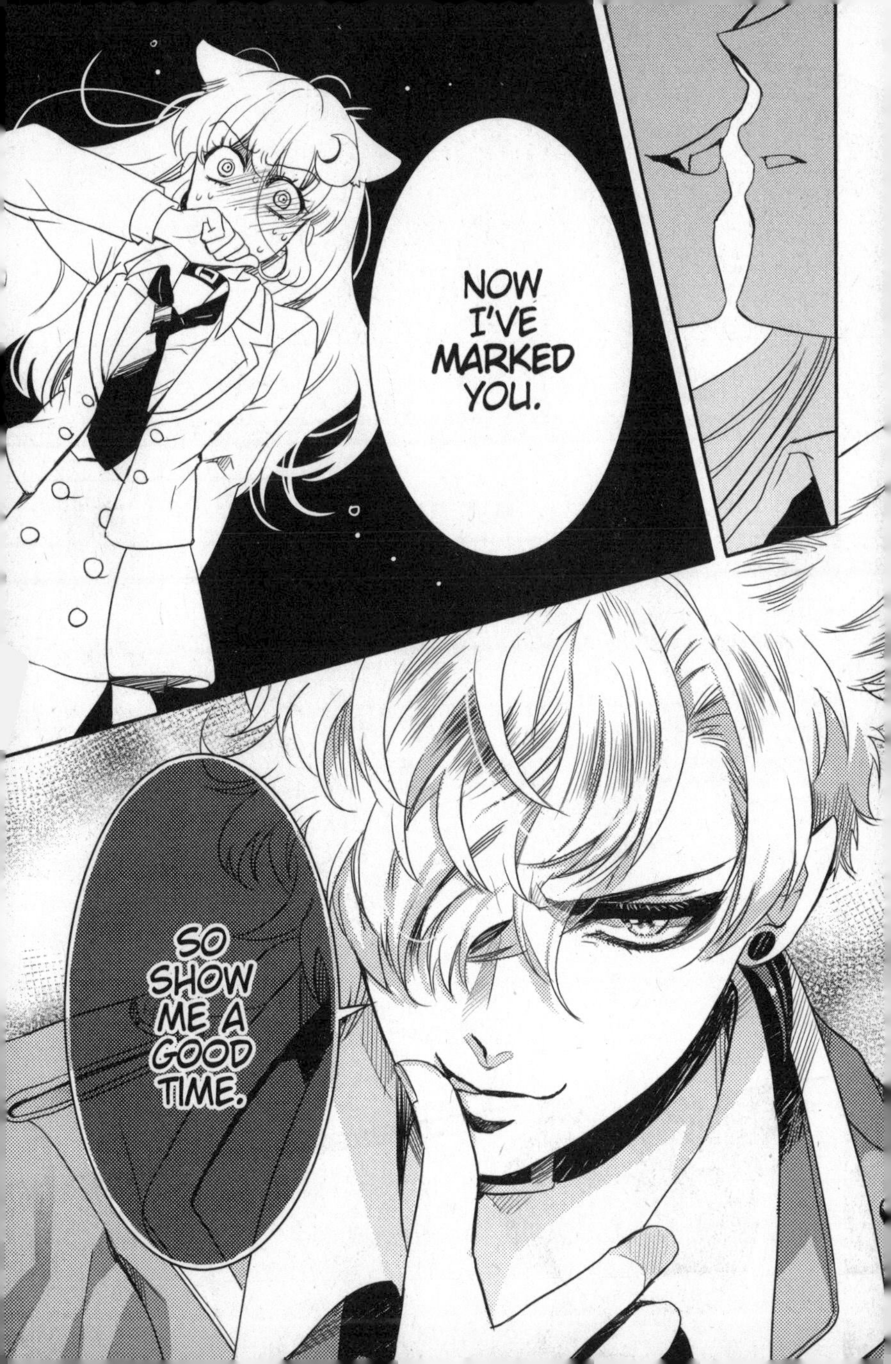
NOW I'VE MARKED YOU.
SO SHOW ME A GOOD TIME.

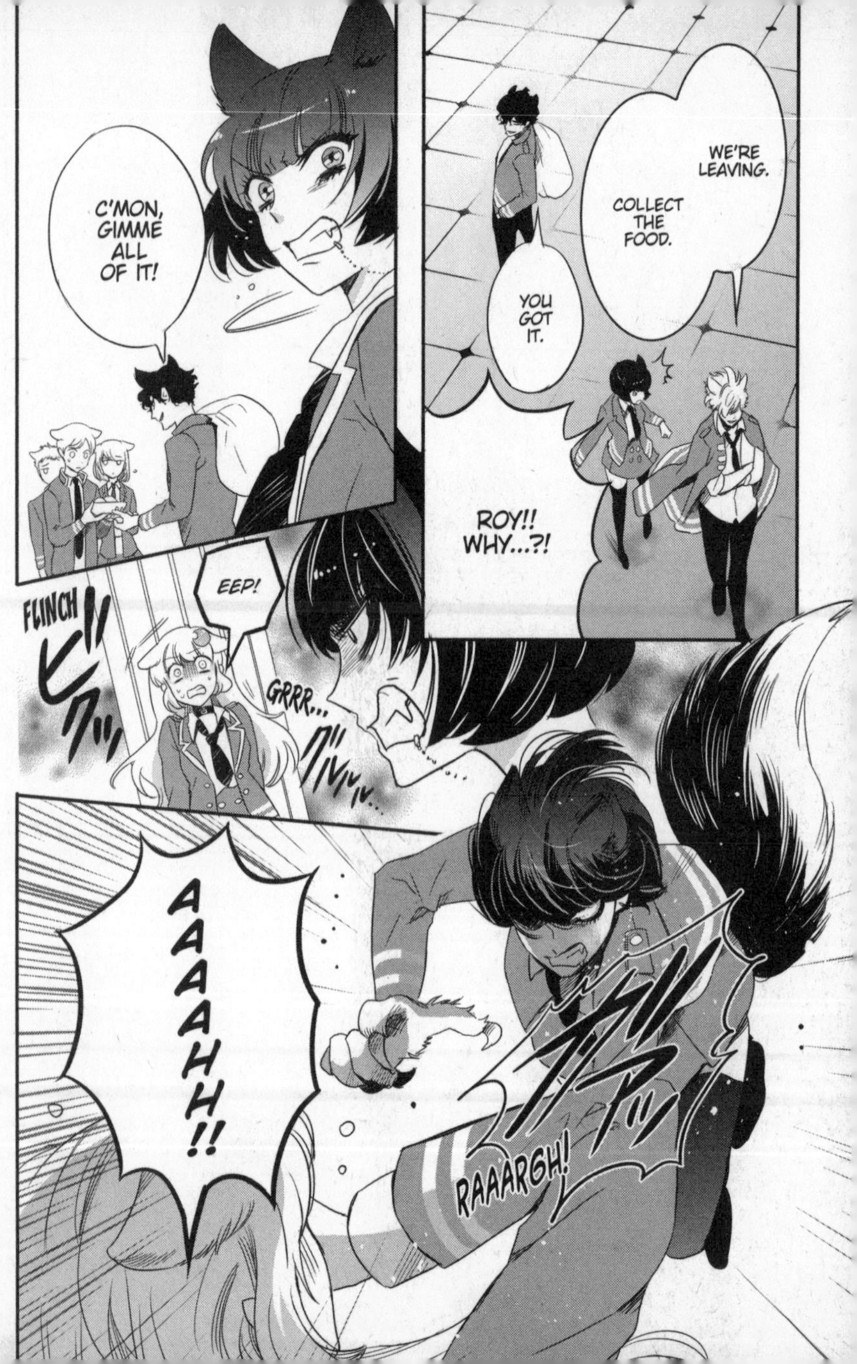
WE'RE LEAVING.
COLLECT THE FOOD.
YOU GOT IT.
ROY!! WHY...?!
C'MON, GIMME ALL OF IT!
GRRR...
EEP!
FLINCH
AAAAHH!!
RAAARGH!

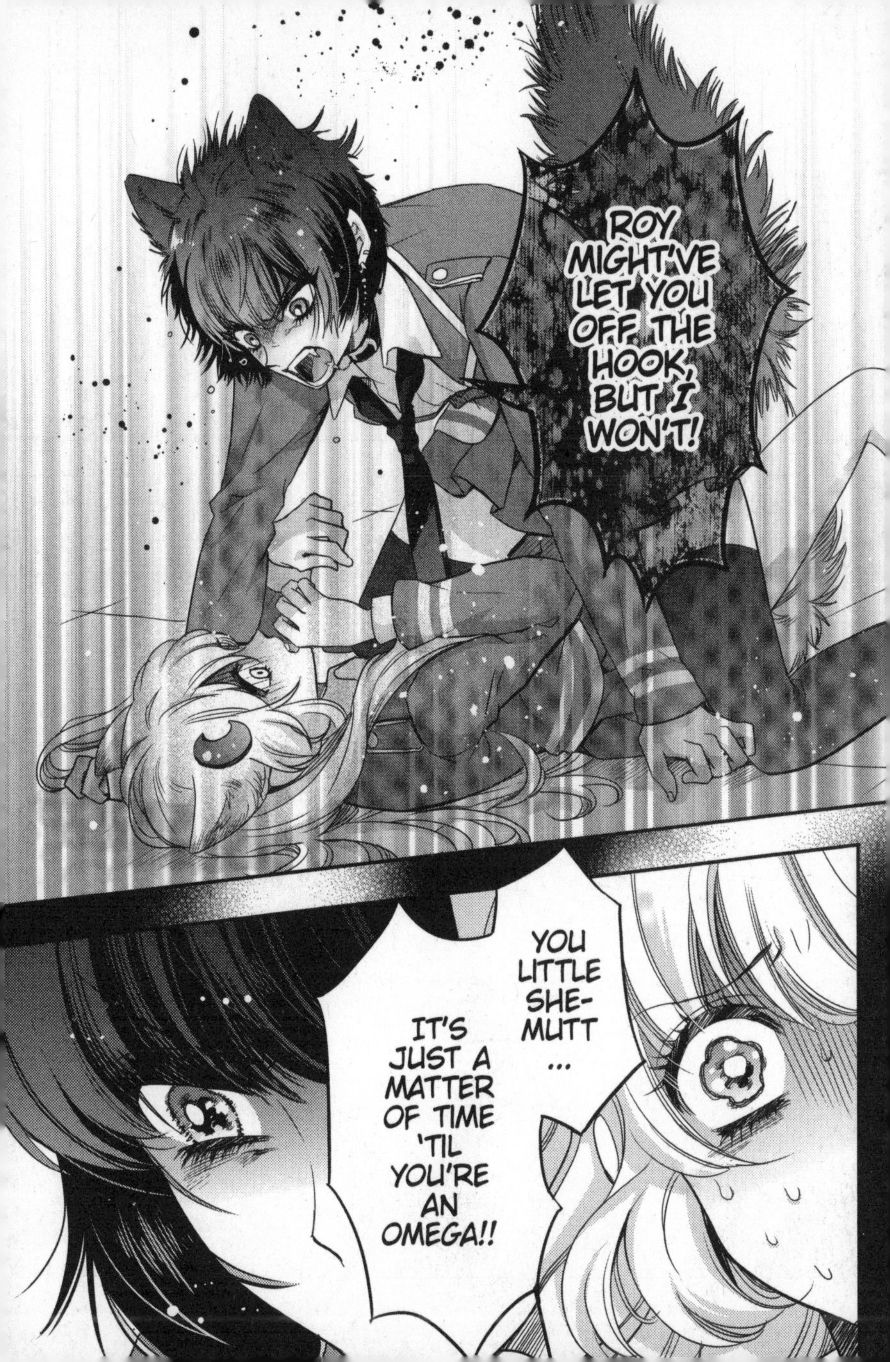
ROY MIGHT'VE LET YOU OFF THE HOOK, BUT I WON'T!
YOU LITTLE SHE-MUTT ...
IT'S JUST A MATTER OF TIME 'TIL YOU'RE AN OMEGA!!

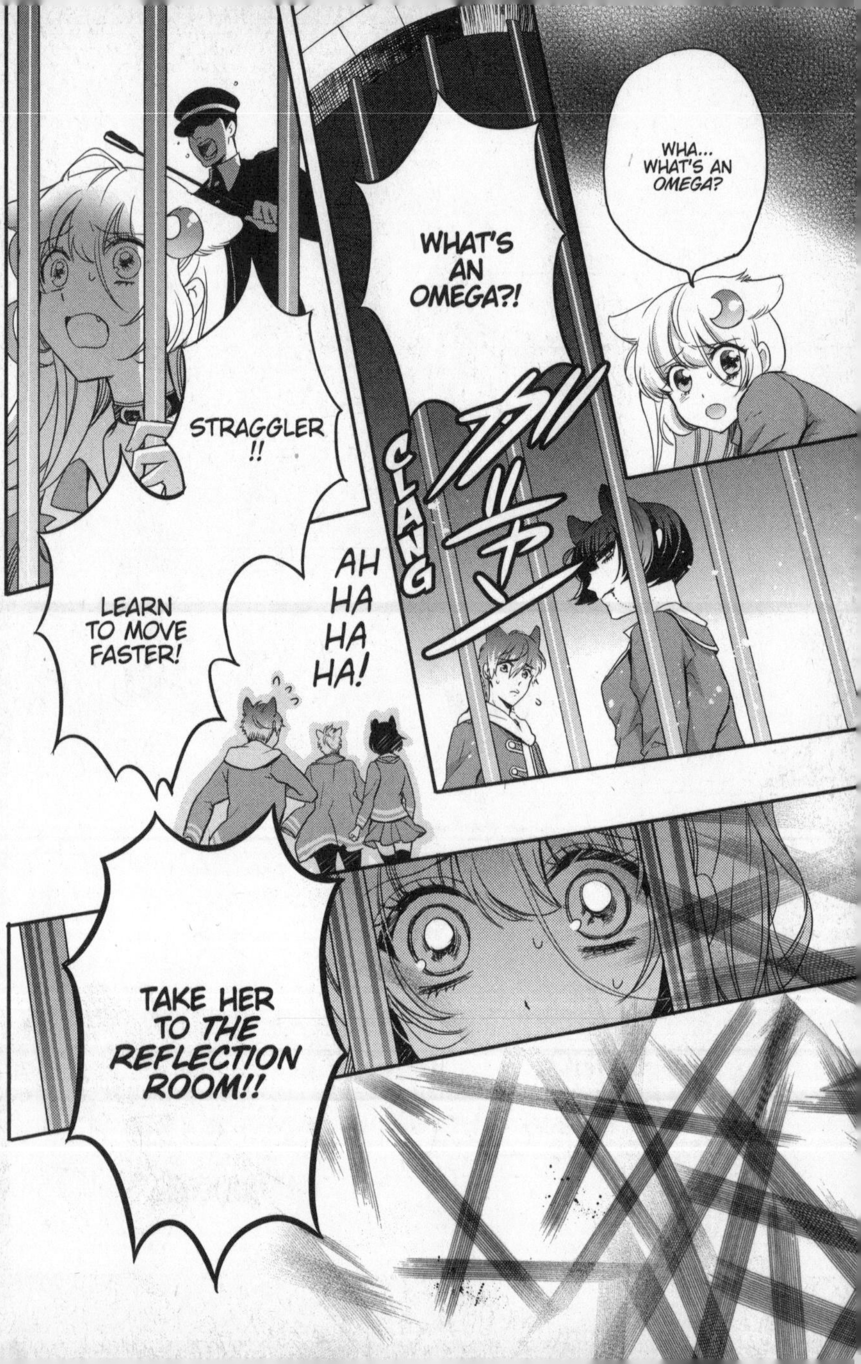
WHA... WHAT'S AN OMEGA?
WHAT'S AN OMEGA?!
CLANG
STRAGGLER!!
LEARN TO MOVE FASTER!
AH HA HA HA!
TAKE HER TO THE REFLECTION ROOM!!

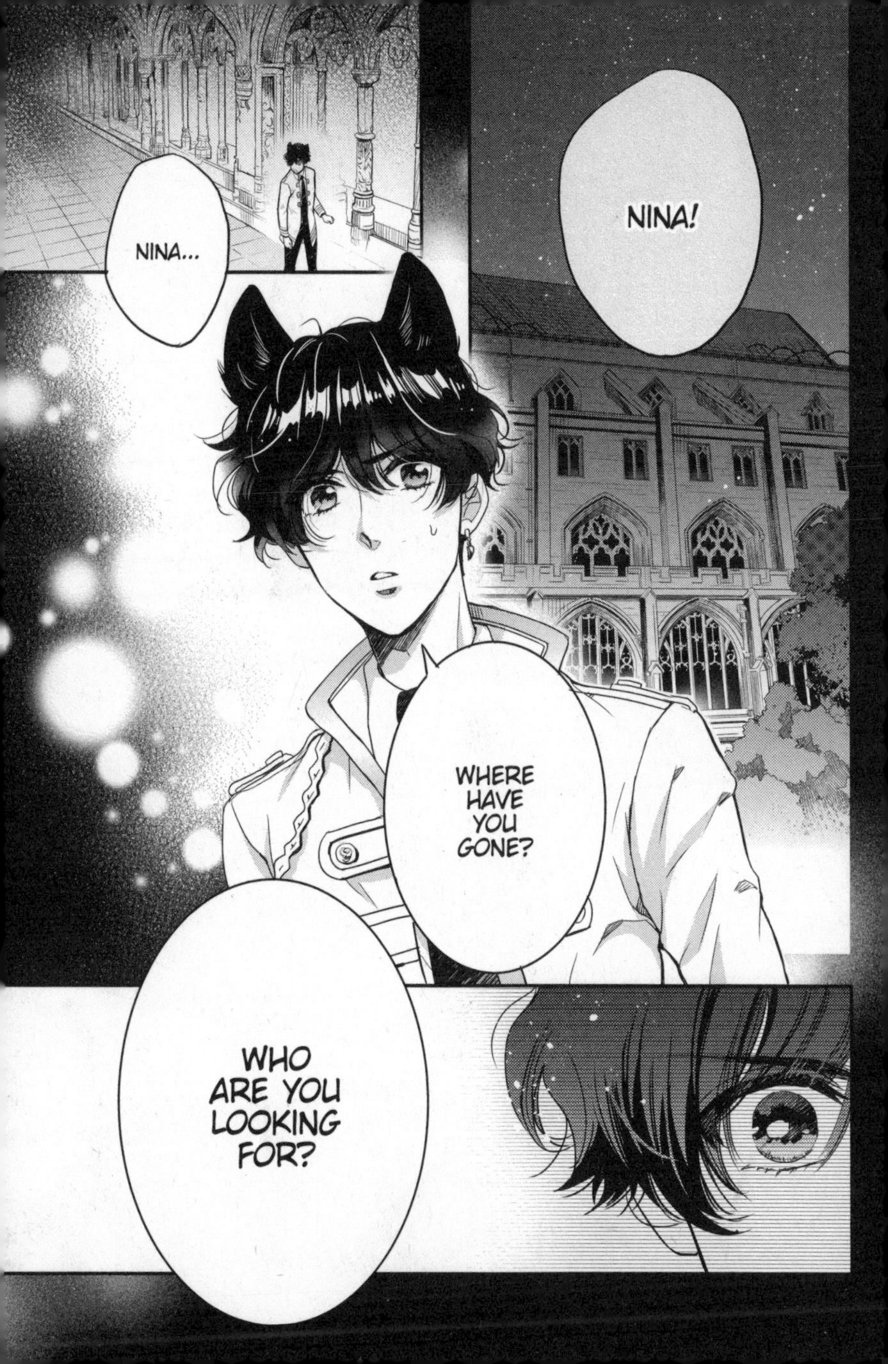
NINA!
NINA...
WHERE HAVE YOU GONE?
WHO ARE YOU LOOKING FOR?

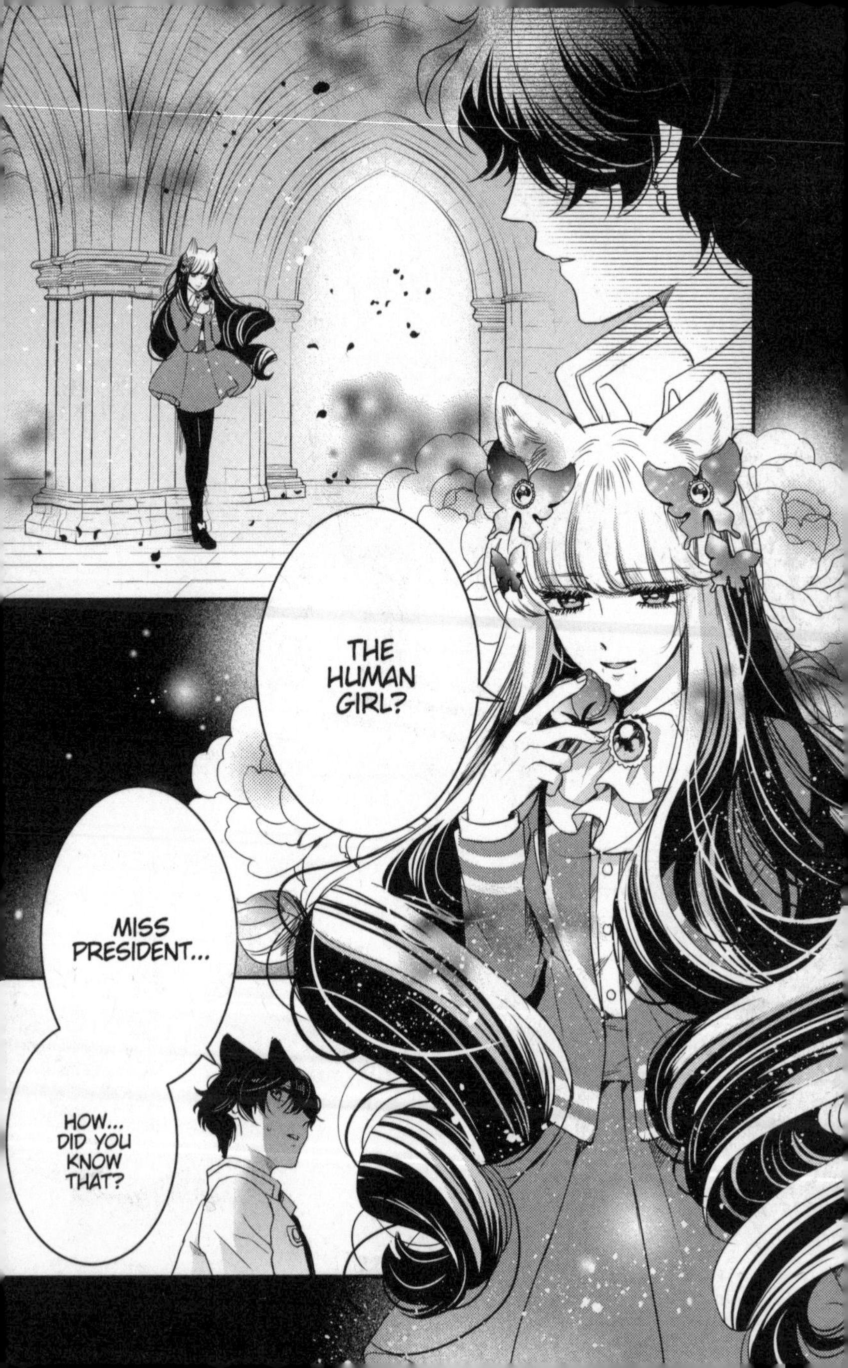
THE HUMAN GIRL?
MISS PRESIDENT...
HOW... DID YOU KNOW THAT?

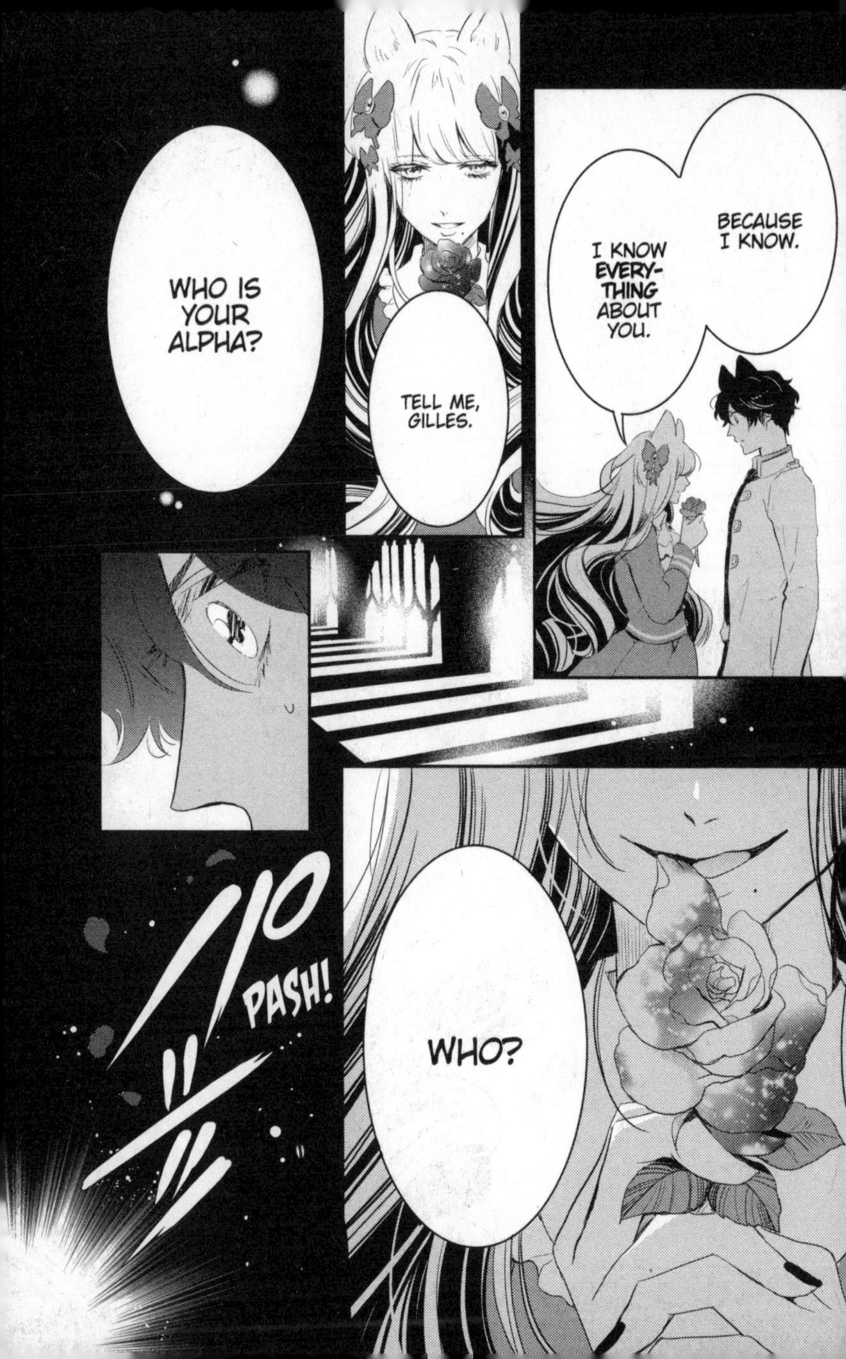
BECAUSE I KNOW.
I KNOW EVERY-THING ABOUT YOU.
TELL ME, GILLES.
WHO IS YOUR ALPHA?
WHO?
PASH!

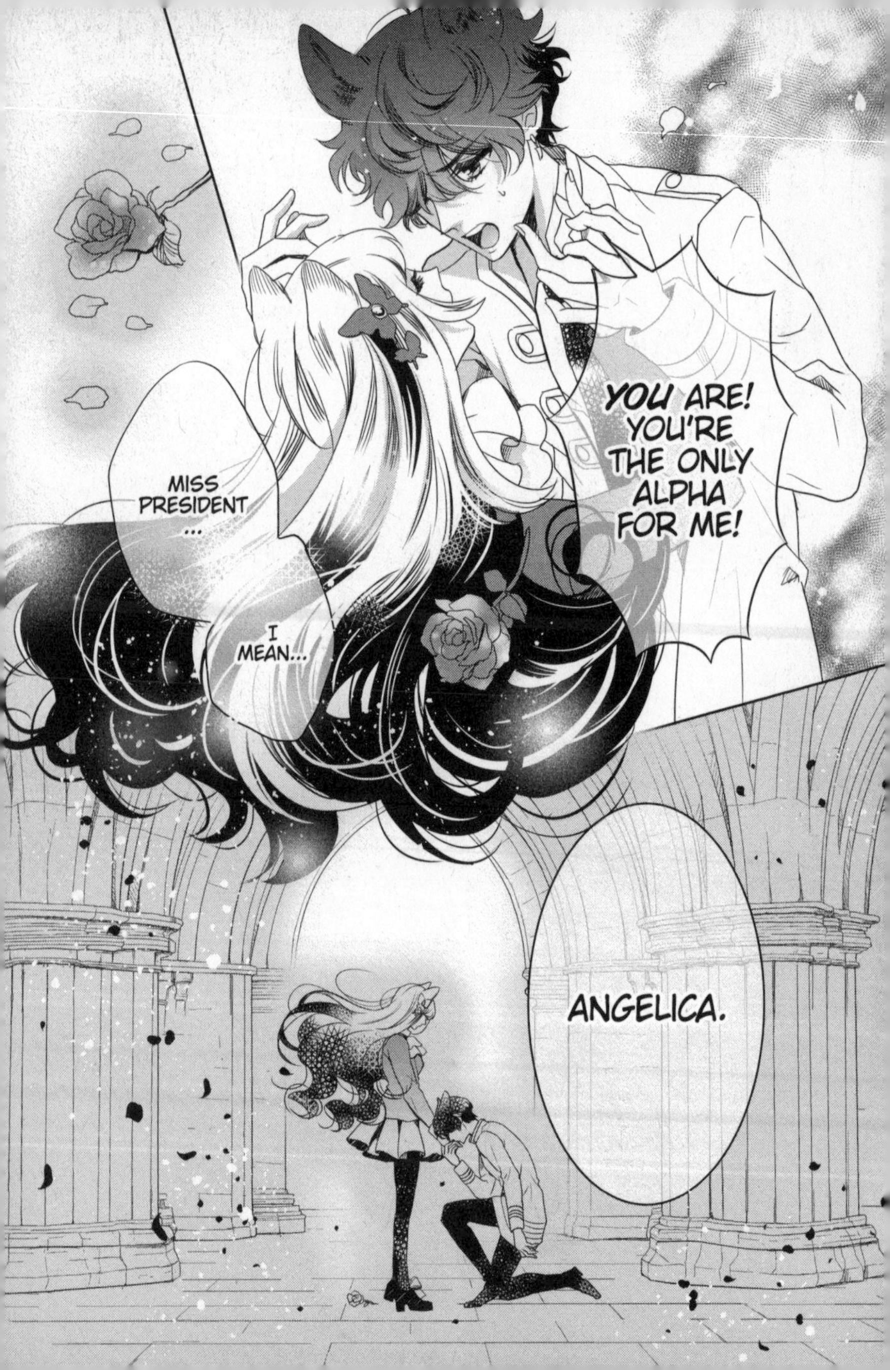
YOU ARE! YOU'RE THE ONLY ALPHA FOR ME!
MISS PRESIDENT ...
I MEAN...
ANGELICA.

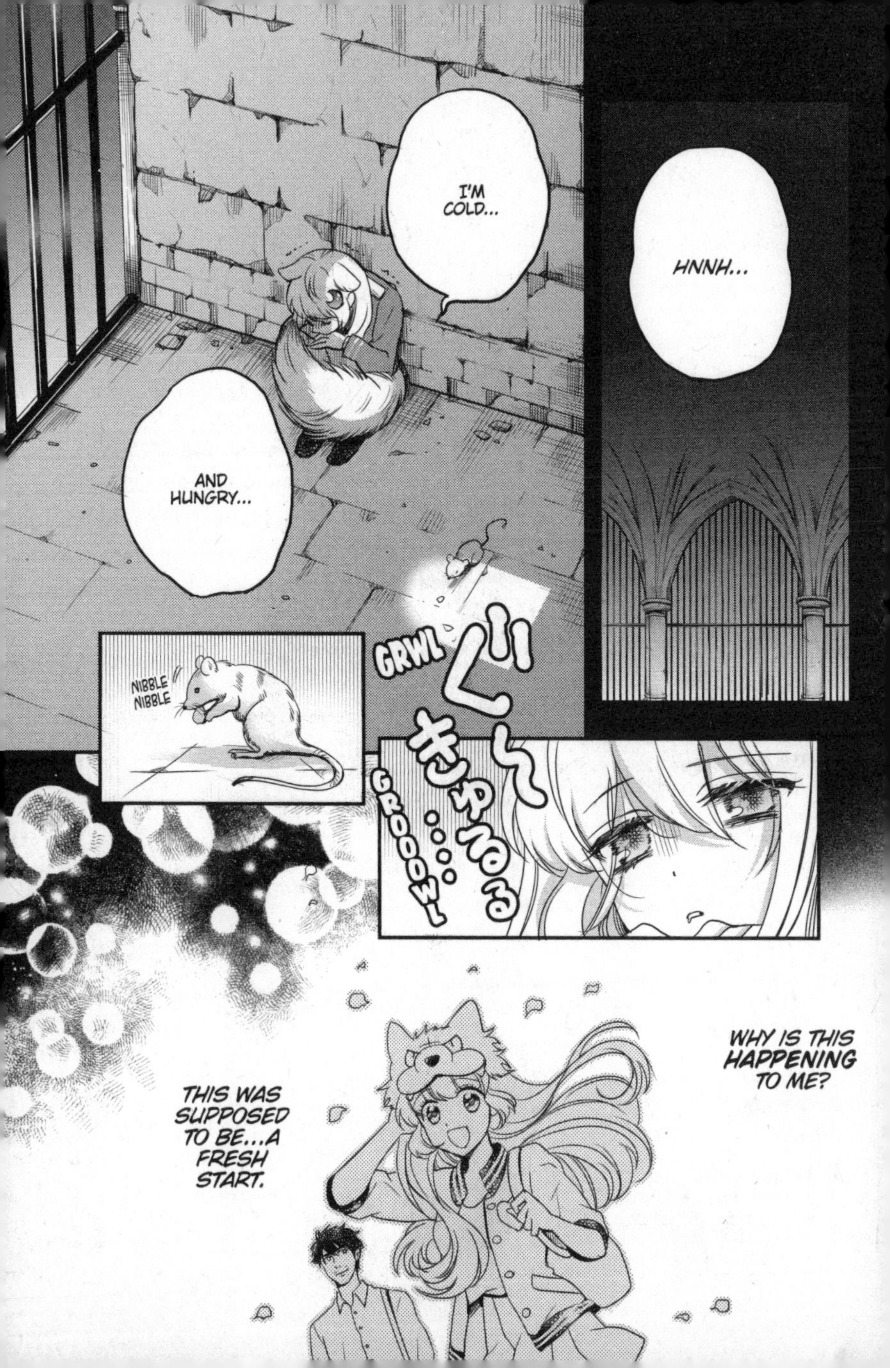

HNNH...
I'M COLD...
AND HUNGRY...
GRWL
GROOOWL
NIBBLE NIBBLE
WHY IS THIS HAPPENING TO ME?
THIS WAS SUPPOSED TO BE...A FRESH START.

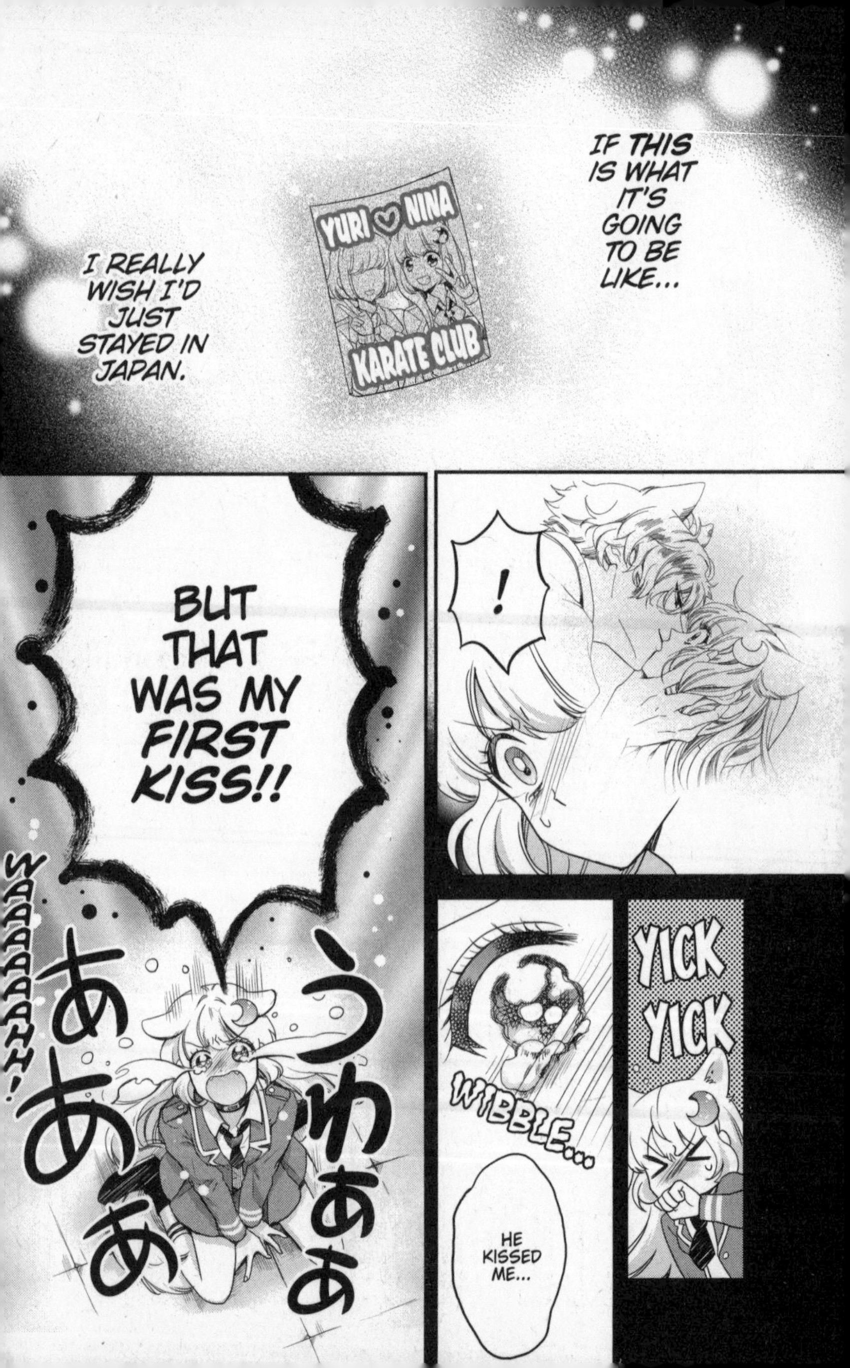
IF THIS IS WHAT IT'S GOING TO BE LIKE...
YURI ♡ NINA
KARATE CLUB
I REALLY WISH I'D JUST STAYED IN JAPAN.
!
YICK YICK
WIBBLE...
HE KISSED ME...
BUT THAT WAS MY FIRST KISS!!
うわあああああ
WAAAAAAAAH!

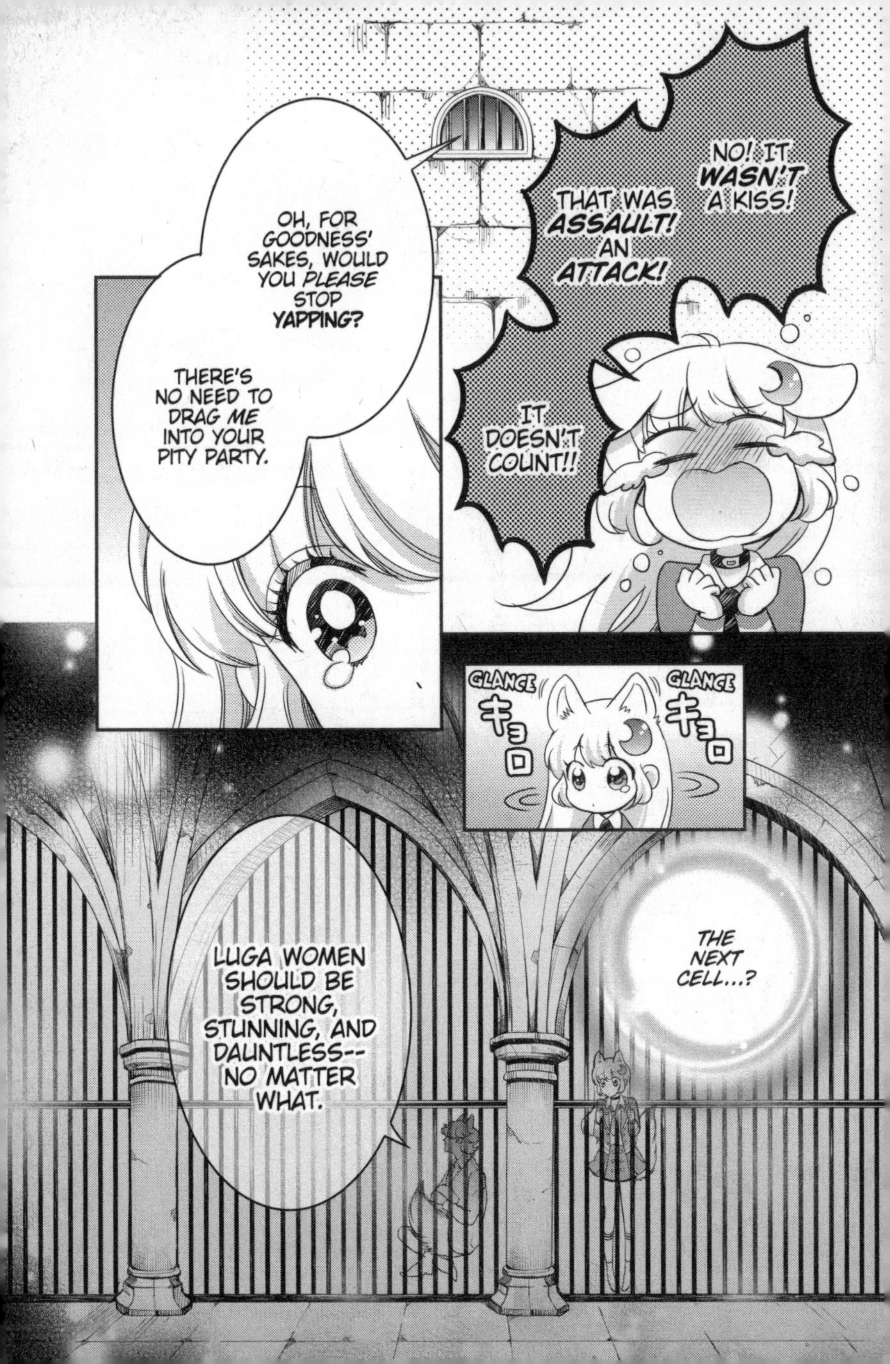
NO! IT WASN'T A KISS!
THAT WAS ASSAULT! AN ATTACK!
IT DOESN'T COUNT!!
OH, FOR GOODNESS' SAKES, WOULD YOU PLEASE STOP YAPPING?
THERE'S NO NEED TO DRAG ME INTO YOUR PITY PARTY.
GLANCE
キョロ
GLANCE
キョロ
THE NEXT CELL...?
LUGA WOMEN SHOULD BE STRONG, STUNNING, AND DAUNTLESS-- NO MATTER WHAT.

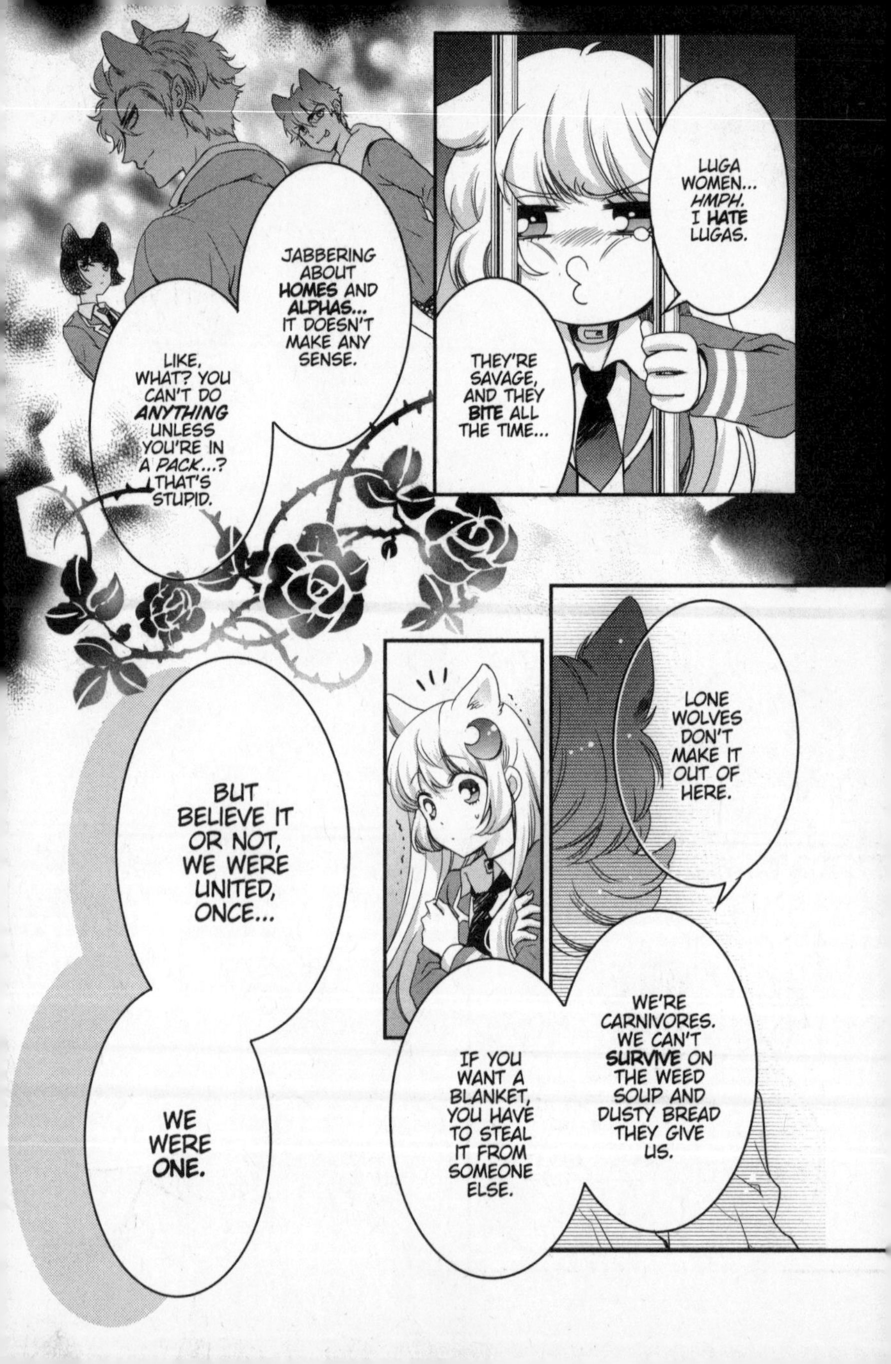

LUGA WOMEN... *HMPH.* I **HATE** LUGAS.
THEY'RE SAVAGE, AND THEY **BITE** ALL THE TIME...
JABBERING ABOUT **HOMES** AND **ALPHAS...** IT DOESN'T MAKE ANY SENSE.
LIKE, WHAT? YOU CAN'T DO ***ANYTHING*** UNLESS YOU'RE IN A *PACK*...? THAT'S STUPID.
LONE WOLVES DON'T MAKE IT OUT OF HERE.
WE'RE CARNIVORES. WE CAN'T **SURVIVE** ON THE WEED SOUP AND DUSTY BREAD THEY GIVE US.
IF YOU WANT A BLANKET, YOU HAVE TO STEAL IT FROM SOMEONE ELSE.
BUT BELIEVE IT OR NOT, WE WERE UNITED, ONCE...
WE WERE **ONE.**

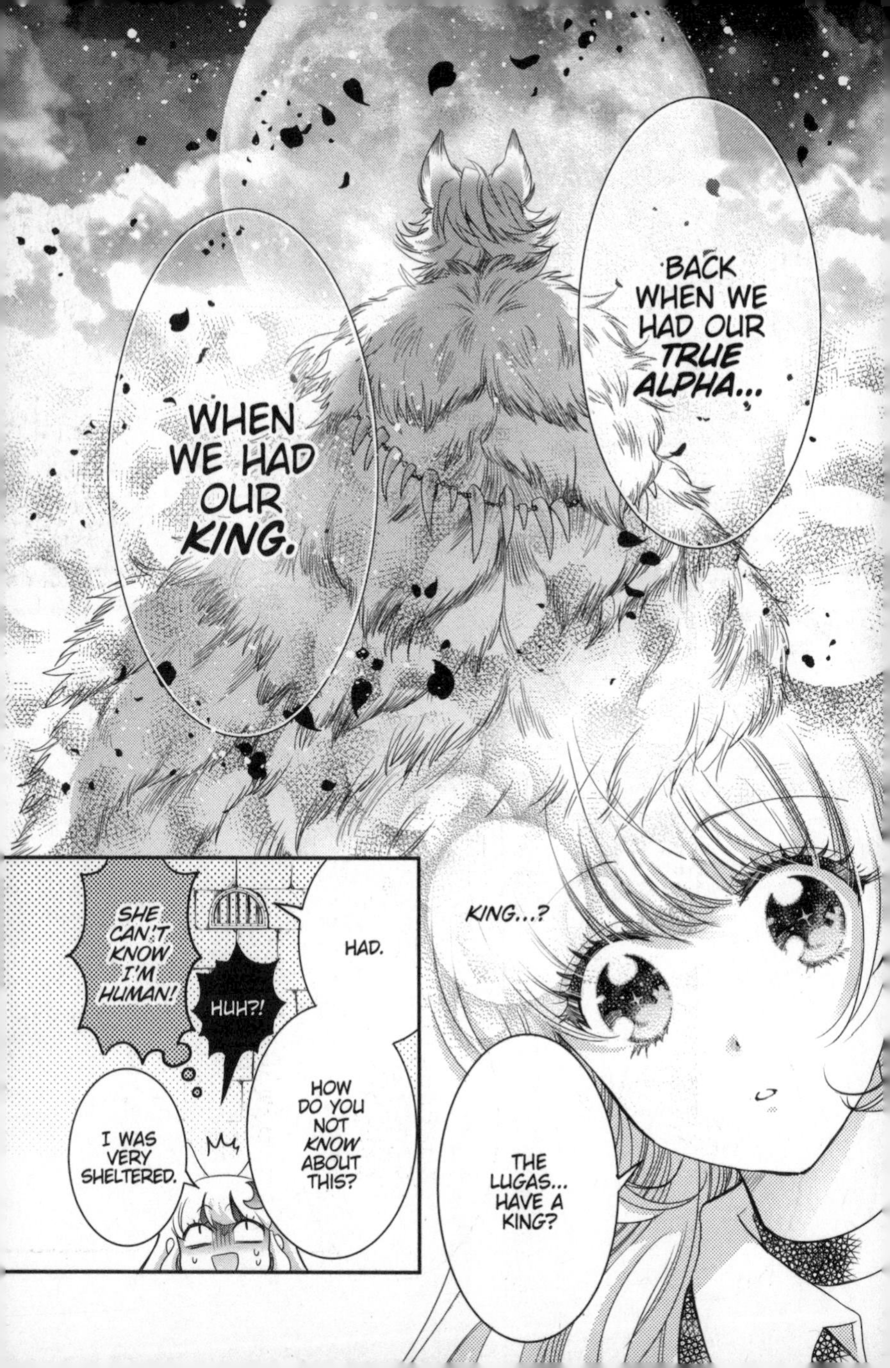
BACK WHEN WE HAD OUR TRUE ALPHA...
WHEN WE HAD OUR KING.
KING...?
THE LUGAS... HAVE A KING?
HAD.
HUH?!
SHE CAN'T KNOW I'M HUMAN!
HOW DO YOU NOT KNOW ABOUT THIS?
I WAS VERY SHELTERED.

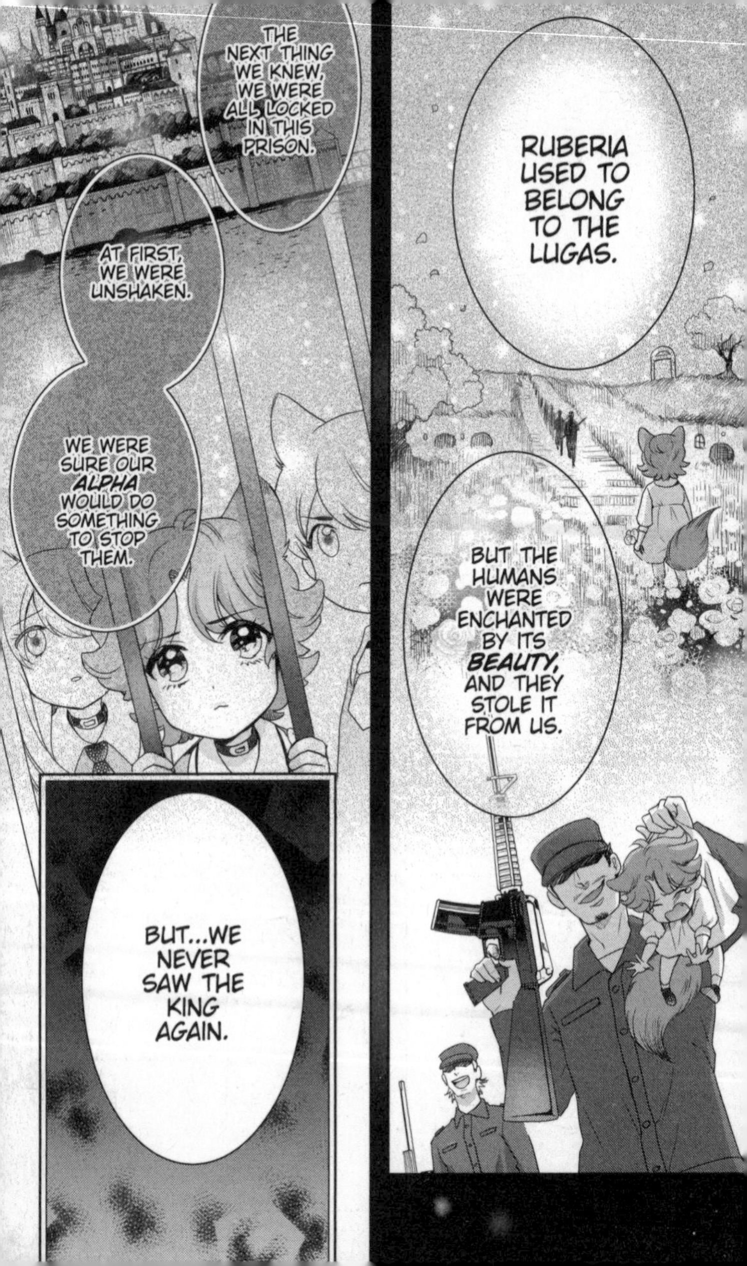
RUBERIA USED TO BELONG TO THE LUGAS.
BUT THE HUMANS WERE ENCHANTED BY ITS *BEAUTY,* AND THEY STOLE IT FROM US.
THE NEXT THING WE KNEW, WE WERE ALL LOCKED IN THIS PRISON.
AT FIRST, WE WERE UNSHAKEN.
WE WERE SURE OUR *ALPHA* WOULD DO SOMETHING TO STOP THEM.
BUT...WE NEVER SAW THE KING AGAIN.

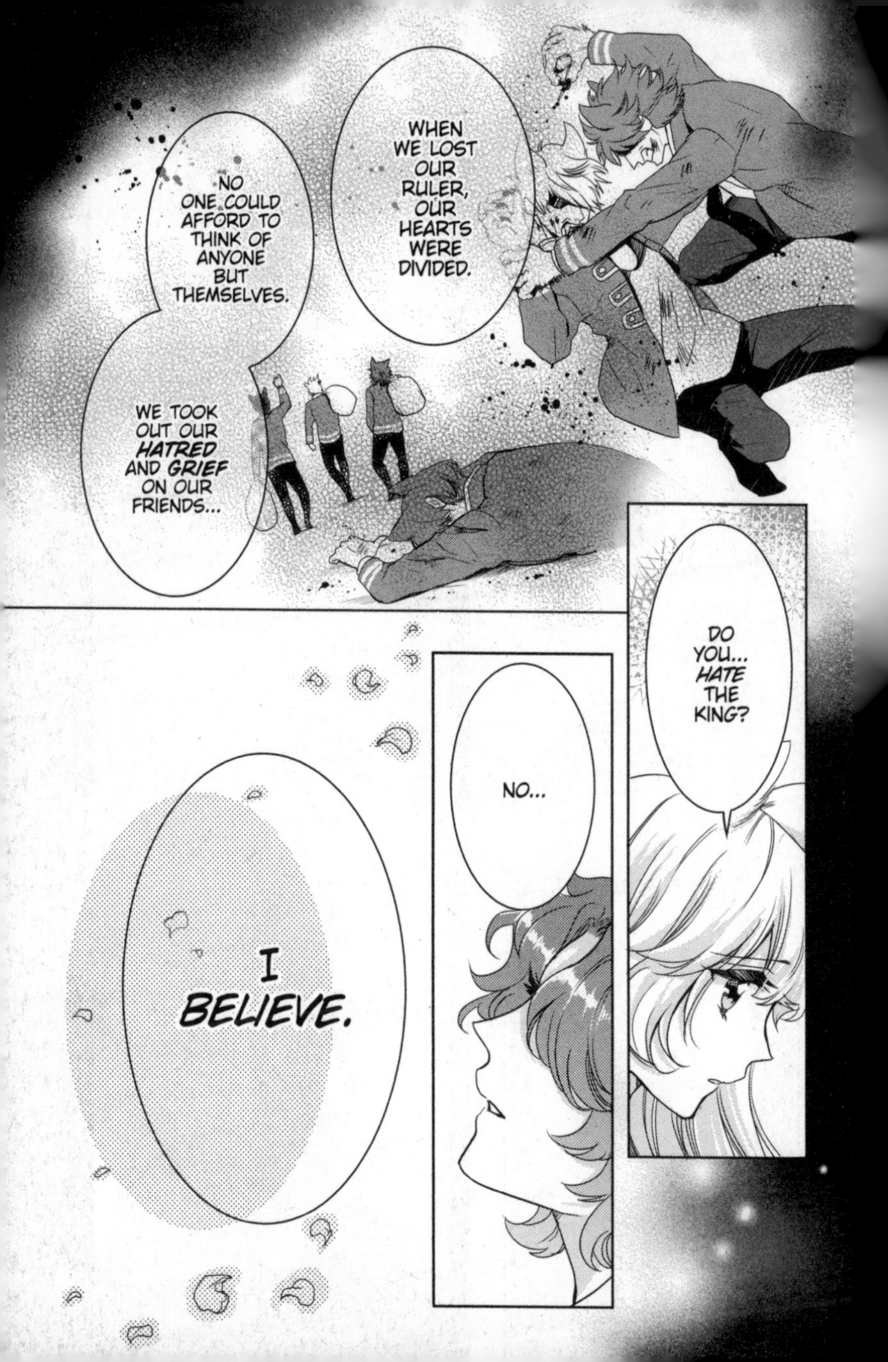
WHEN WE LOST OUR RULER, OUR HEARTS WERE DIVIDED.
NO ONE COULD AFFORD TO THINK OF ANYONE BUT THEMSELVES.
WE TOOK OUT OUR *HATRED* AND *GRIEF* ON OUR FRIENDS...
DO YOU... *HATE* THE KING?
NO...
I *BELIEVE.*

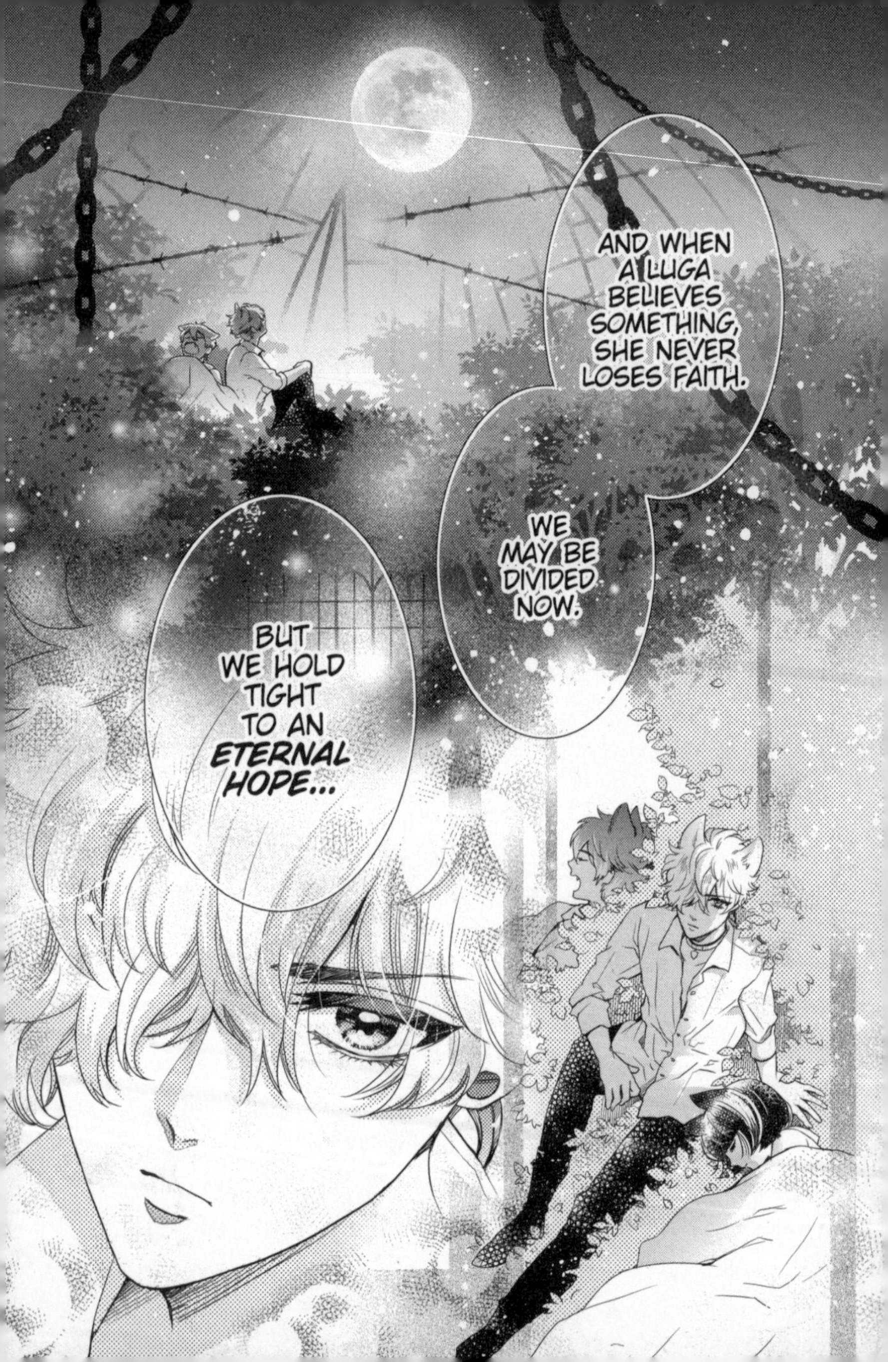
AND WHEN A LUGA BELIEVES SOMETHING, SHE NEVER LOSES FAITH.
WE MAY BE DIVIDED NOW.
BUT WE HOLD TIGHT TO AN *ETERNAL HOPE...*

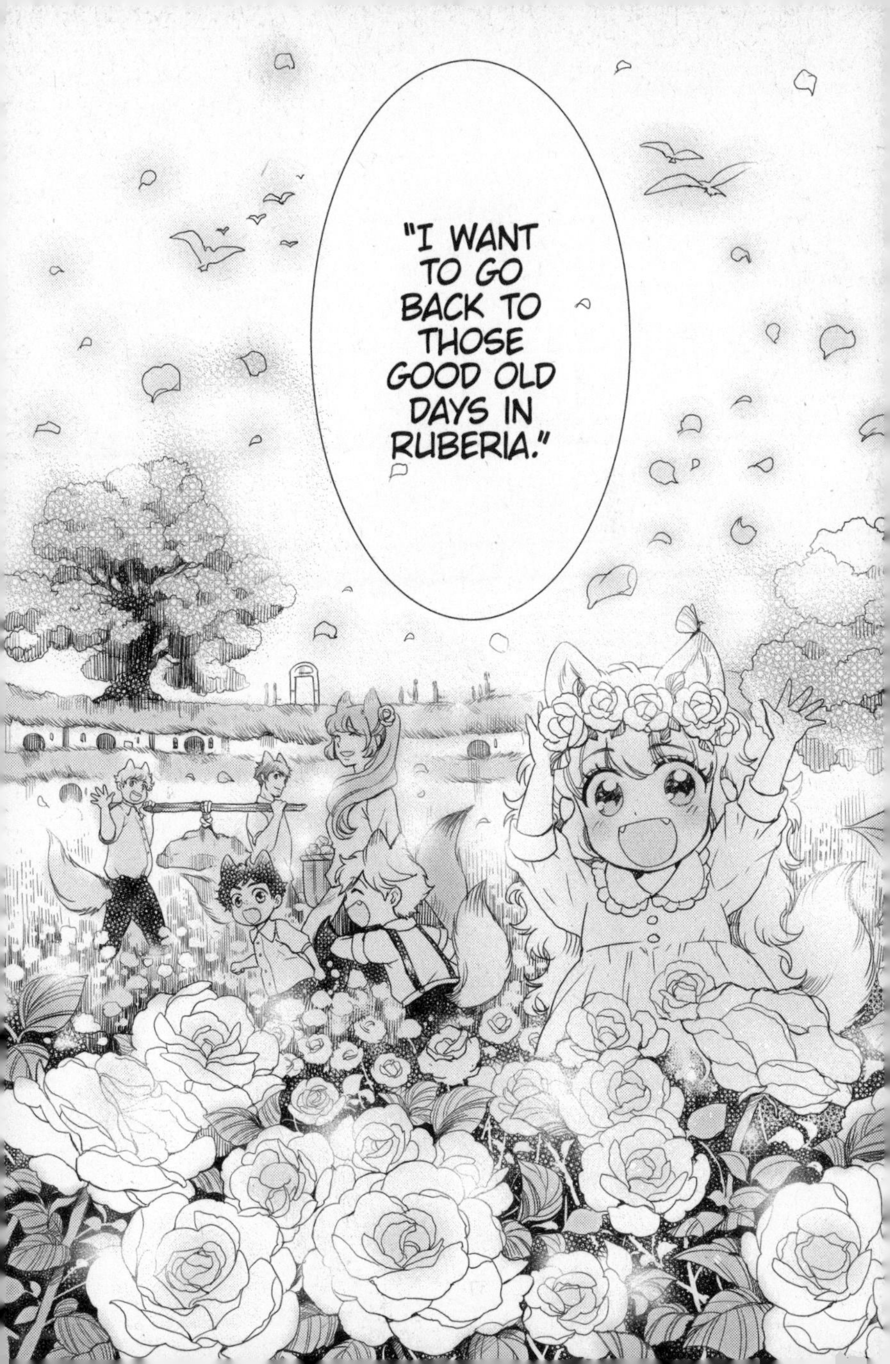
"I WANT TO GO BACK TO THOSE GOOD OLD DAYS IN RUBERIA."

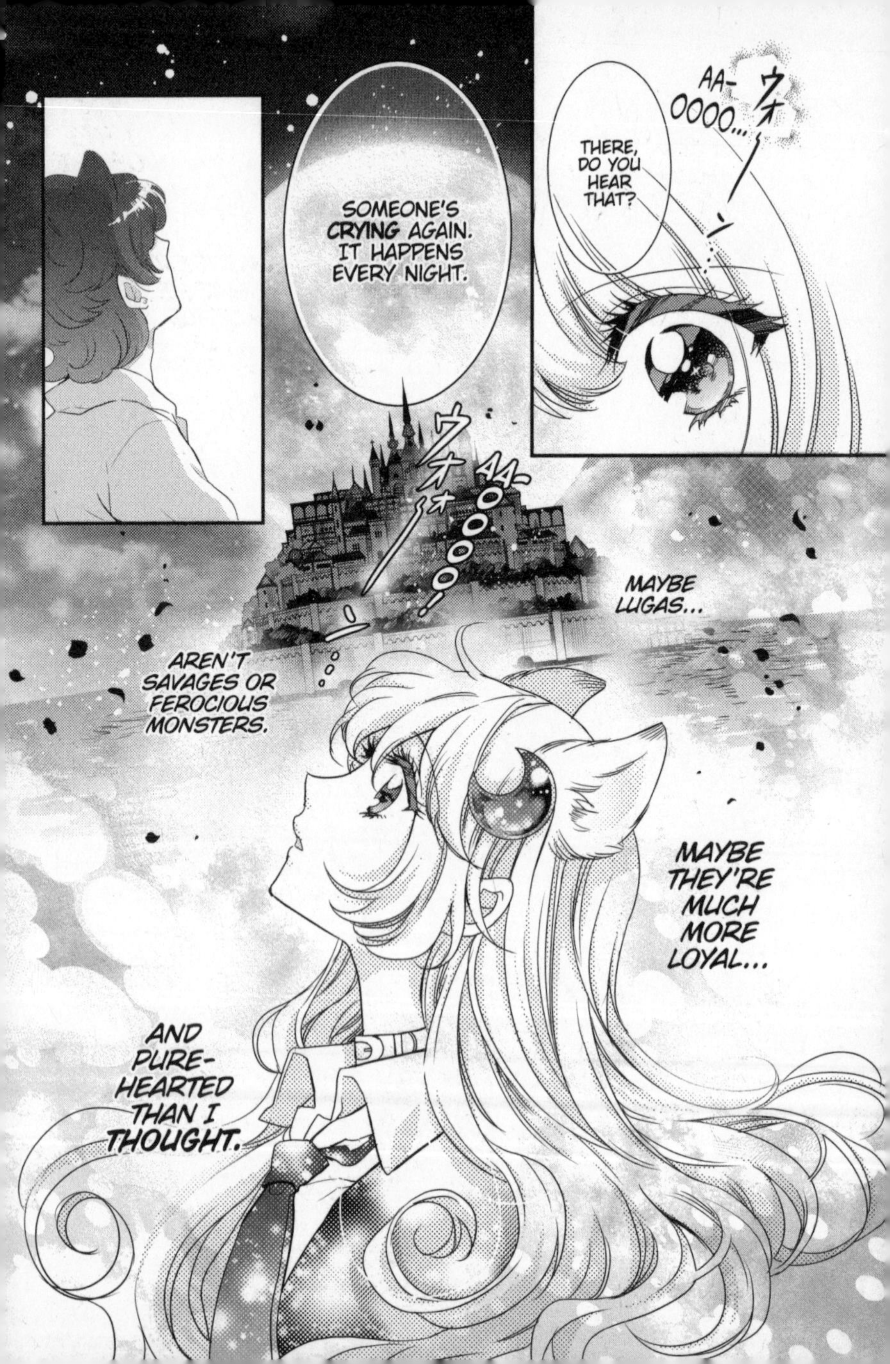

AA-OOOO...
THERE, DO YOU HEAR THAT?
SOMEONE'S CRYING AGAIN. IT HAPPENS EVERY NIGHT.
AA-OOOOOO!
MAYBE LUGAS...
AREN'T SAVAGES OR FEROCIOUS MONSTERS.
MAYBE THEY'RE MUCH MORE LOYAL...
AND PURE-HEARTED THAN I THOUGHT.

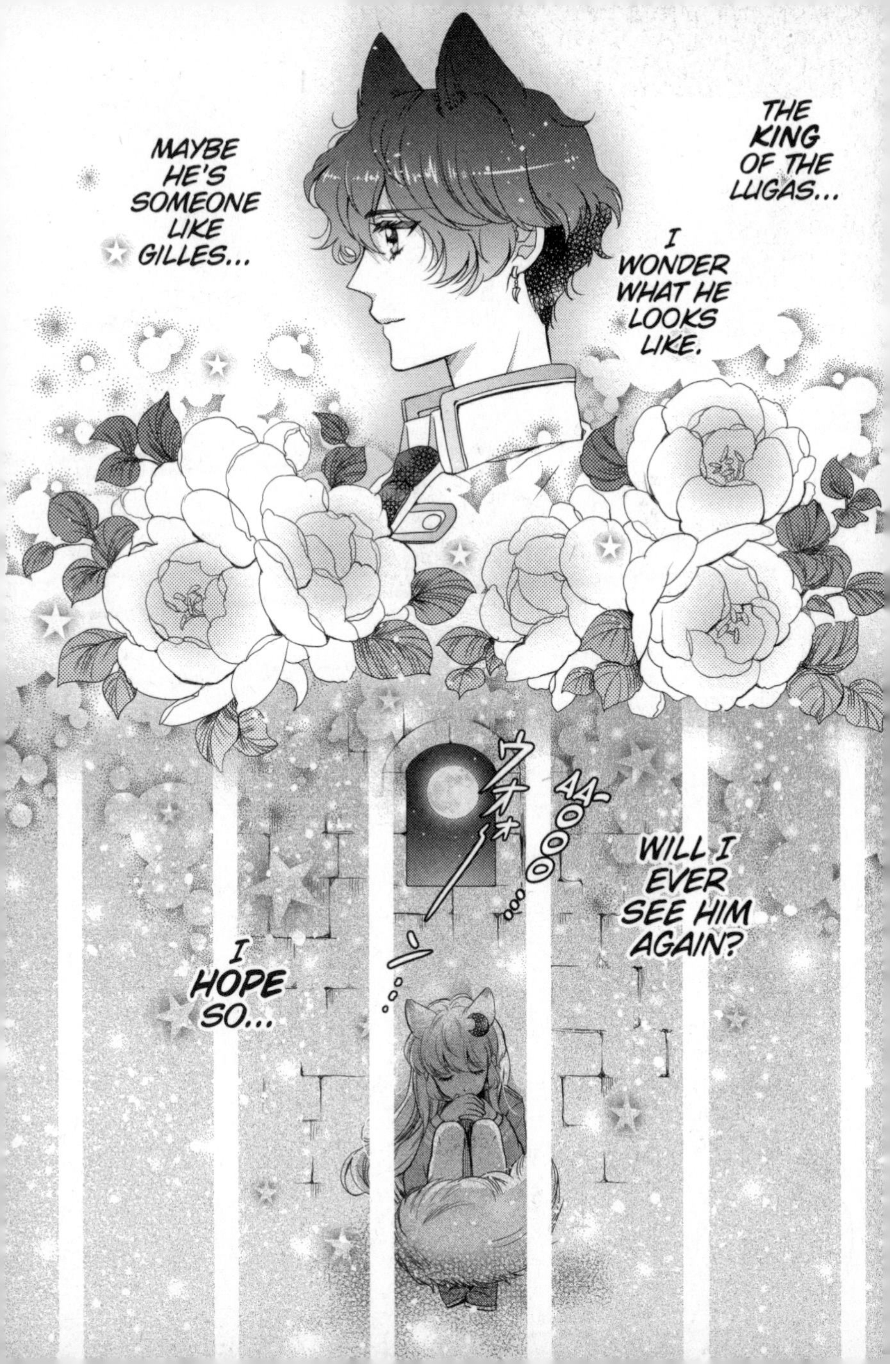

THE KING OF THE LUGAS...
I WONDER WHAT HE LOOKS LIKE.
MAYBE HE'S SOMEONE LIKE GILLES...
AA-OOOO...
WILL I EVER SEE HIM AGAIN?
I HOPE SO...

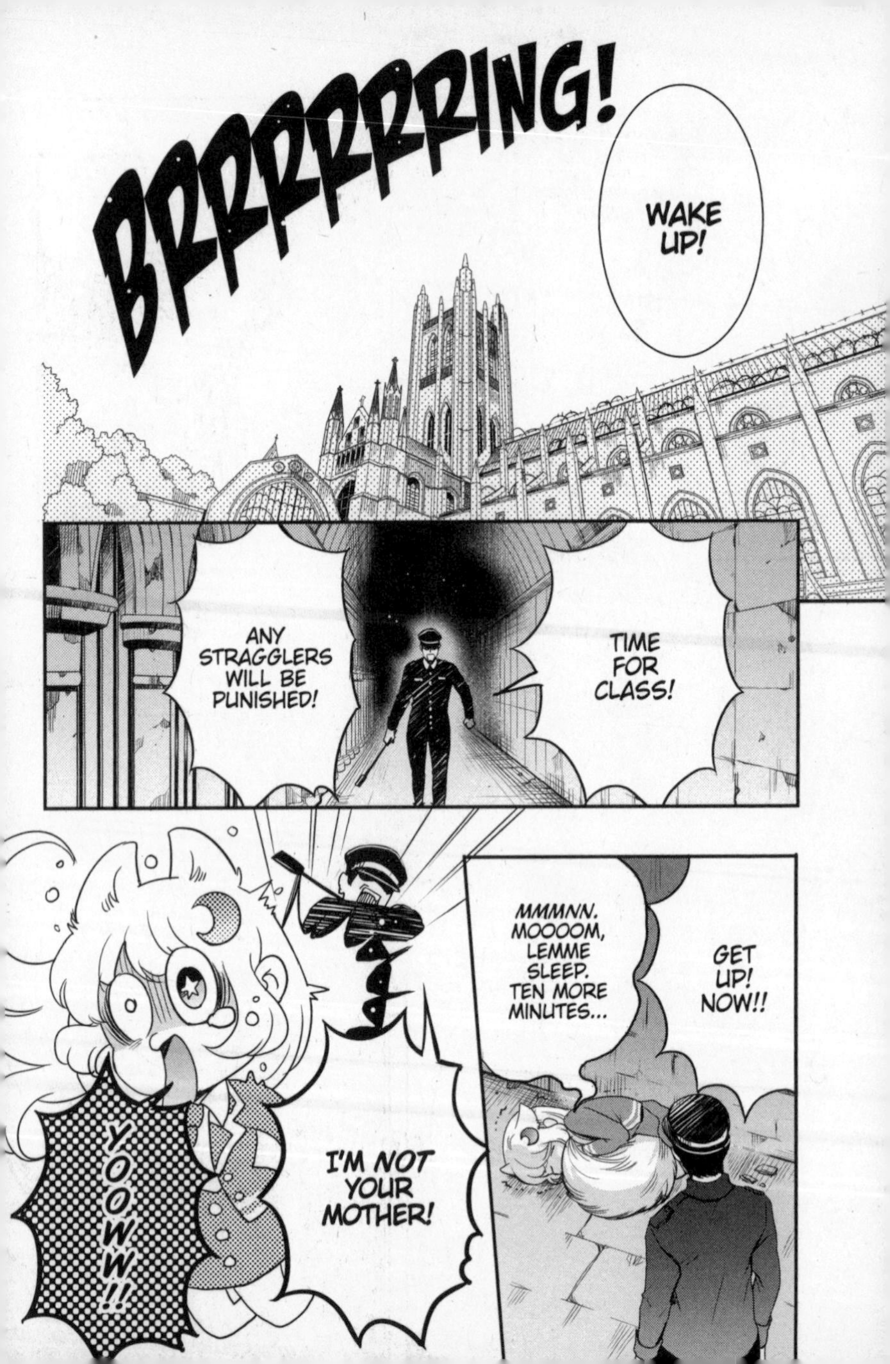
BRRRRRING!
WAKE UP!
TIME FOR CLASS!
ANY STRAGGLERS WILL BE PUNISHED!
GET UP! NOW!!
MMMNN. MOOOOM, LEMME SLEEP. TEN MORE MINUTES...
I'M NOT YOUR MOTHER!
YOOWW!!

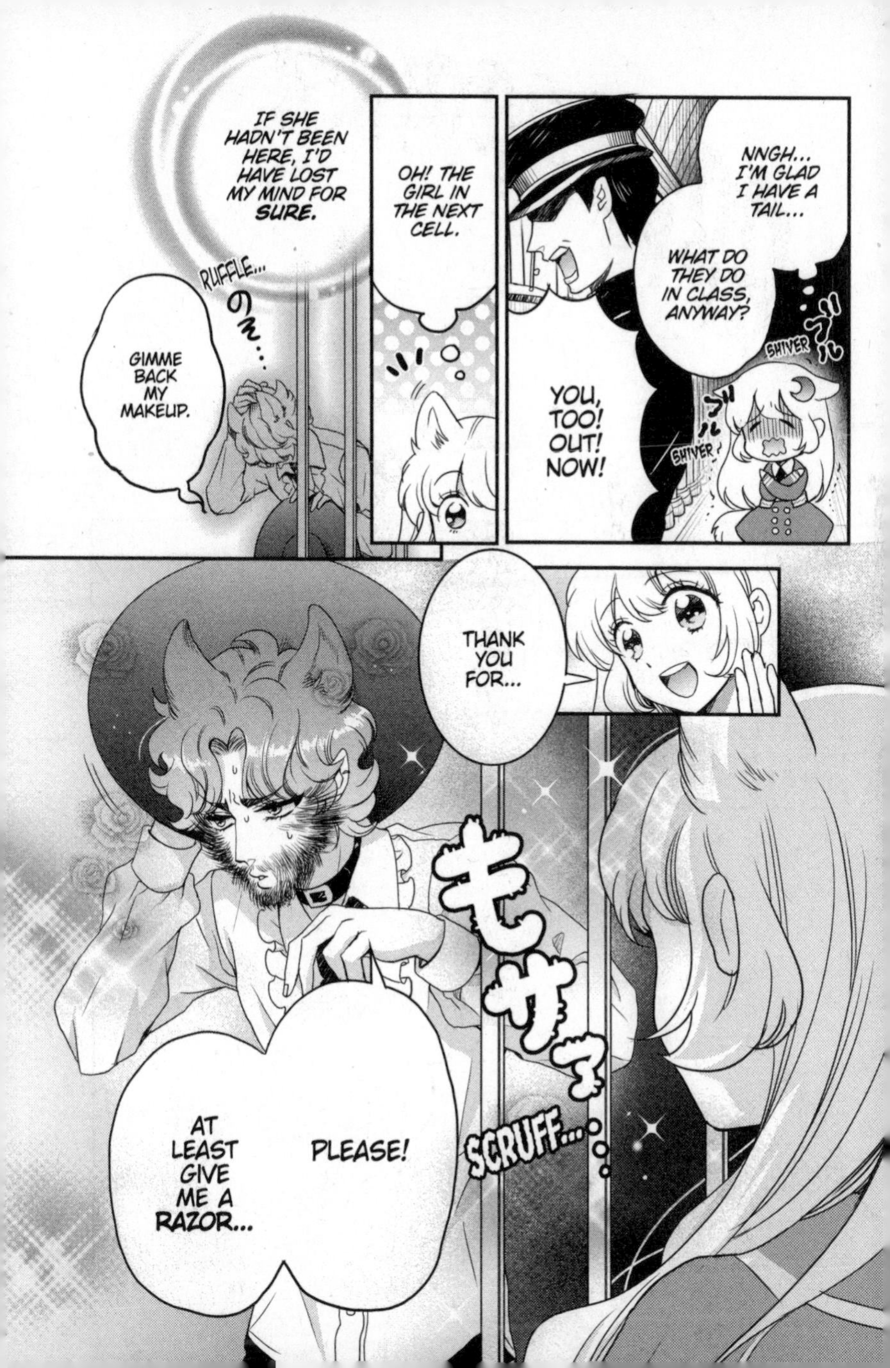
NNGH... I'M GLAD I HAVE A TAIL...
WHAT DO THEY DO IN CLASS, ANYWAY?
SHIVER
YOU, TOO! OUT! NOW!
SHIVER
OH! THE GIRL IN THE NEXT CELL.
IF SHE HADN'T BEEN HERE, I'D HAVE LOST MY MIND FOR SURE.
RUFFLE...
GIMME BACK MY MAKEUP.
THANK YOU FOR...
SCRUFF...
AT LEAST GIVE ME A RAZOR... PLEASE!

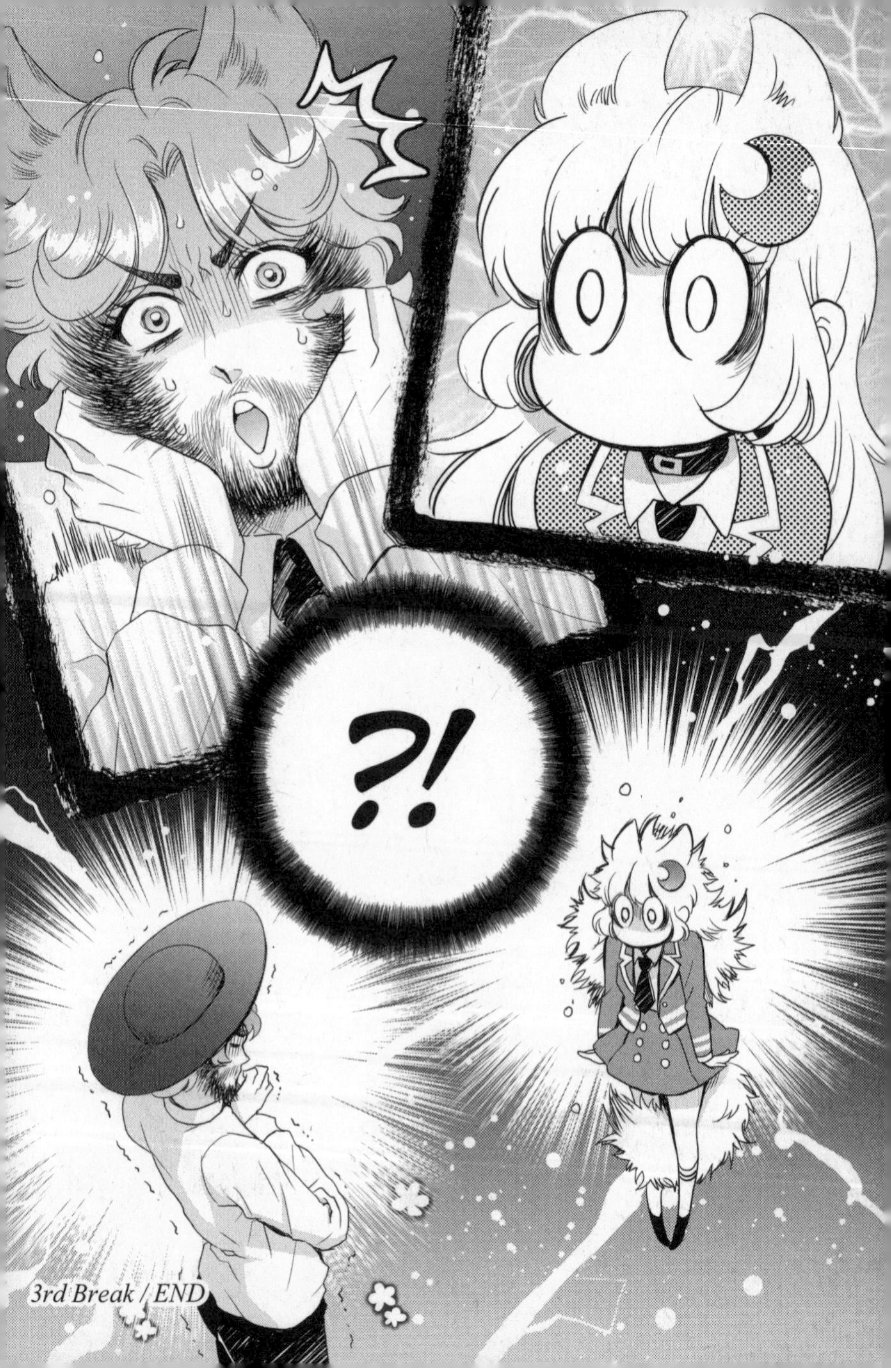
?!
3rd Break / END

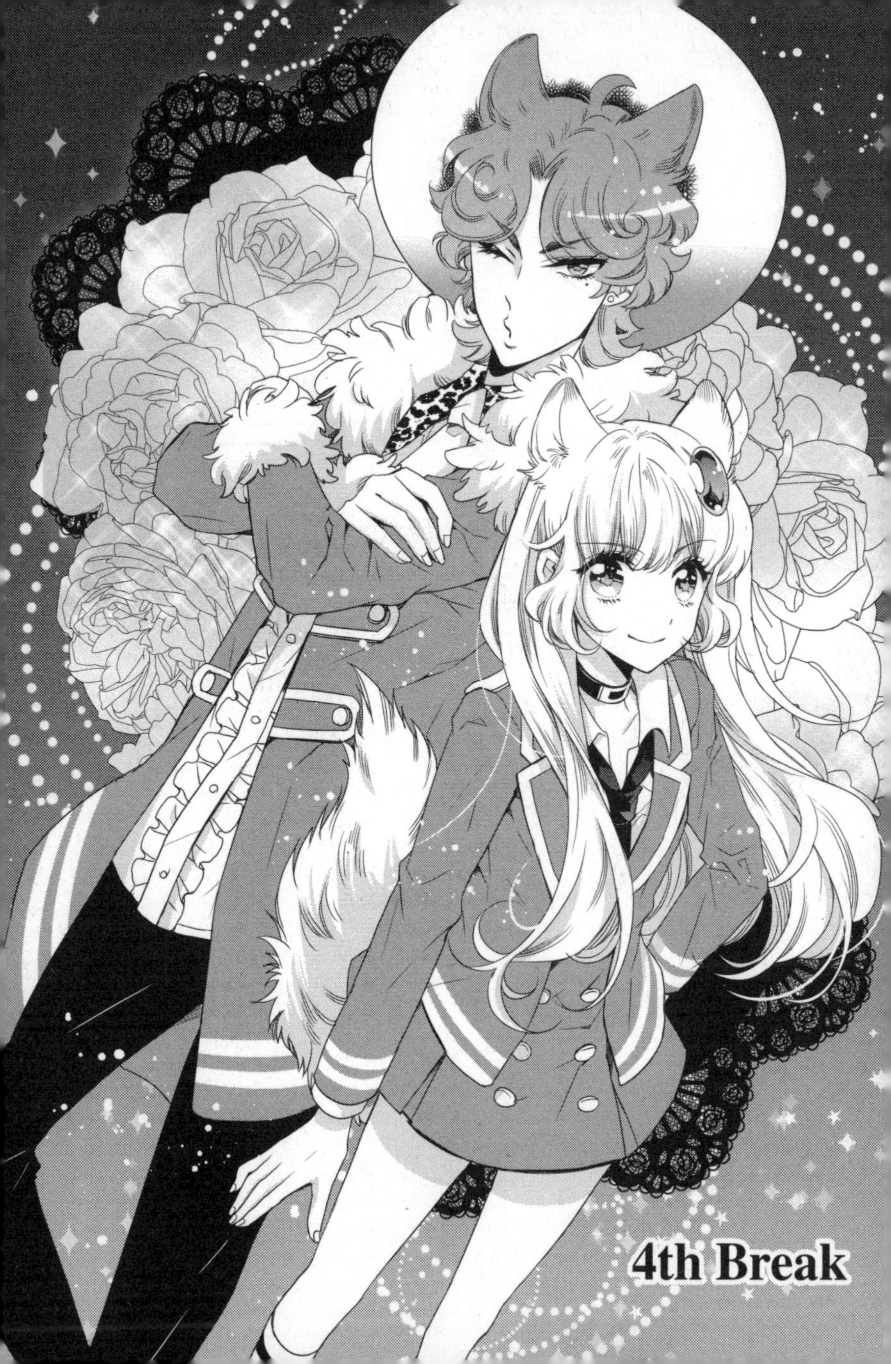
4th Break

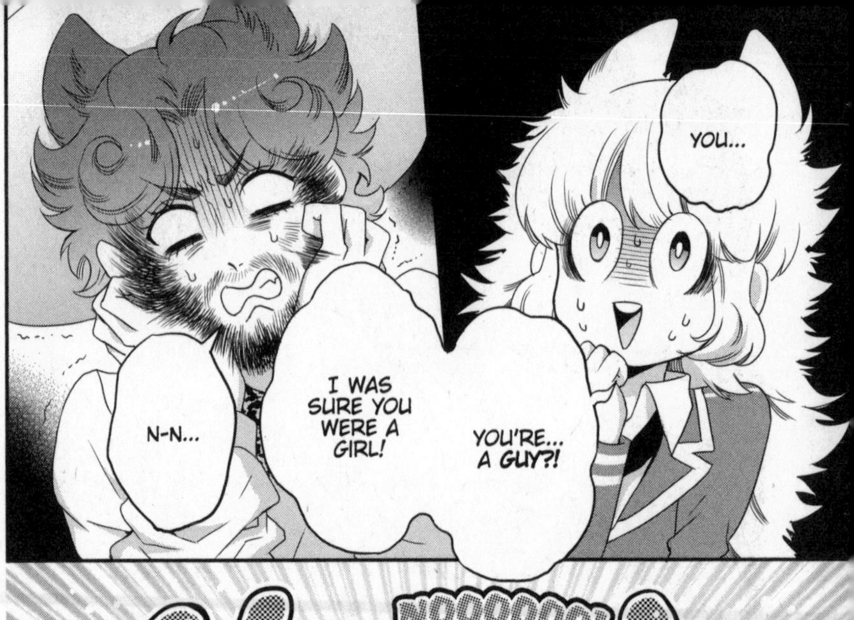
YOU...
YOU'RE... A GUY?!
I WAS SURE YOU WERE A GIRL!
N-N...
NOOOOOO!

ABIGAILE TRIVIA

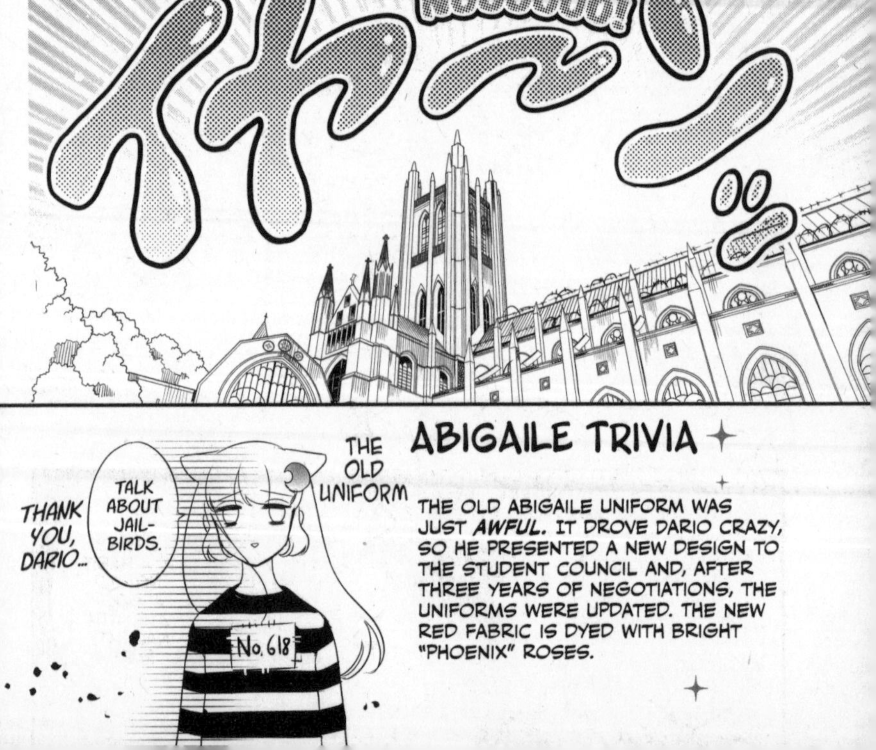
THE OLD UNIFORM
TALK ABOUT JAIL-BIRDS.
THANK YOU, DARIO...
No. 618

THE OLD ABIGAILE UNIFORM WAS JUST ***AWFUL.*** IT DROVE DARIO CRAZY, SO HE PRESENTED A NEW DESIGN TO THE STUDENT COUNCIL AND, AFTER THREE YEARS OF NEGOTIATIONS, THE UNIFORMS WERE UPDATED. THE NEW RED FABRIC IS DYED WITH BRIGHT "PHOENIX" ROSES.

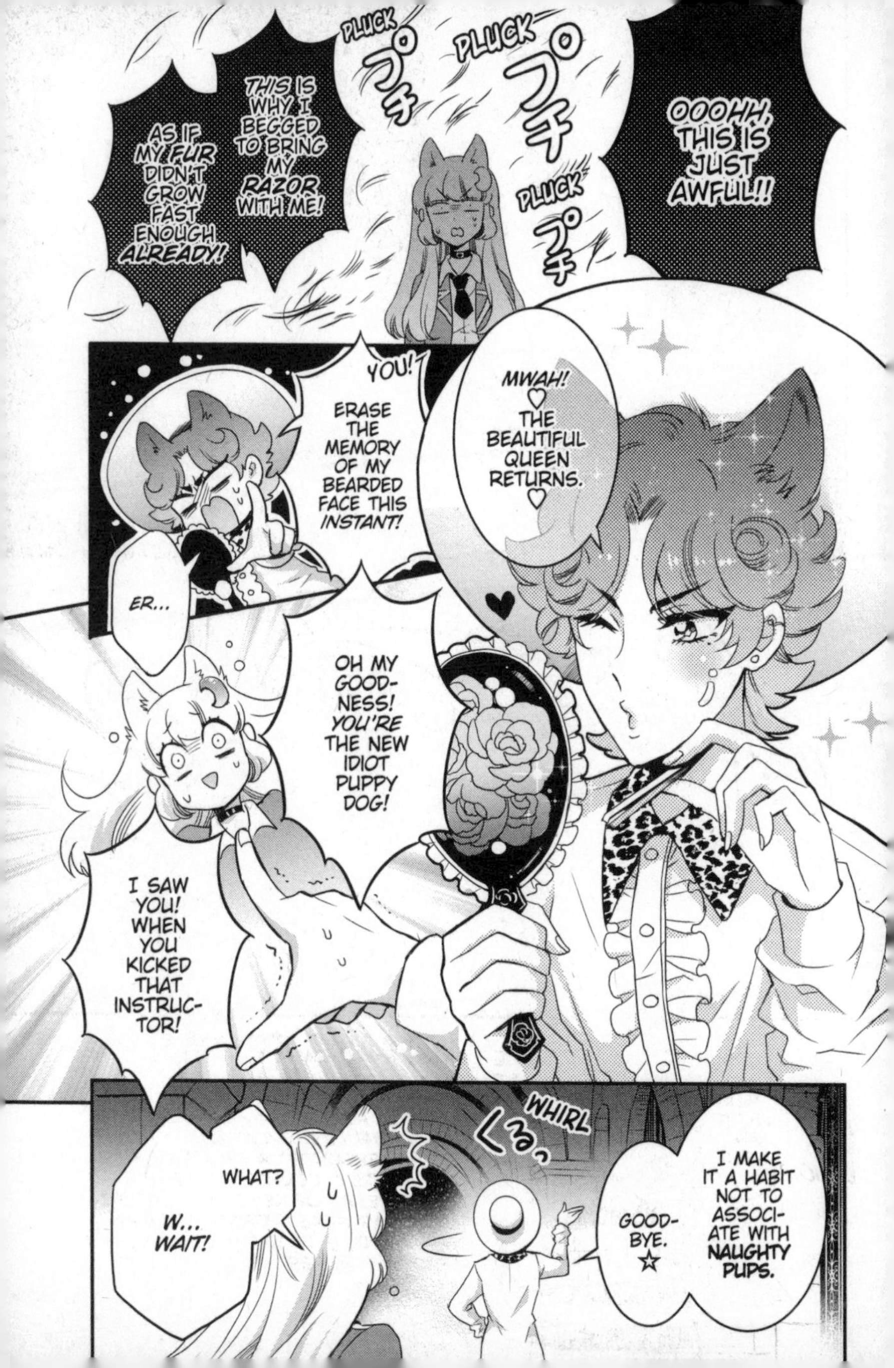
OOOHH, THIS IS JUST AWFUL!!
PLUCK プチ
PLUCK プチ
PLUCK プチ
THIS IS WHY I BEGGED TO BRING MY RAZOR WITH ME!
AS IF MY FUR DIDN'T GROW FAST ENOUGH ALREADY!
MWAH! ♡ THE BEAUTIFUL QUEEN RETURNS. ♡
YOU! ERASE THE MEMORY OF MY BEARDED FACE THIS INSTANT!
ER...
OH MY GOODNESS! YOU'RE THE NEW IDIOT PUPPY DOG!
I SAW YOU! WHEN YOU KICKED THAT INSTRUCTOR!
WHIRL くるっ
I MAKE IT A HABIT NOT TO ASSOCIATE WITH NAUGHTY PUPS.
GOOD-BYE. ☆
WHAT?
W... WAIT!

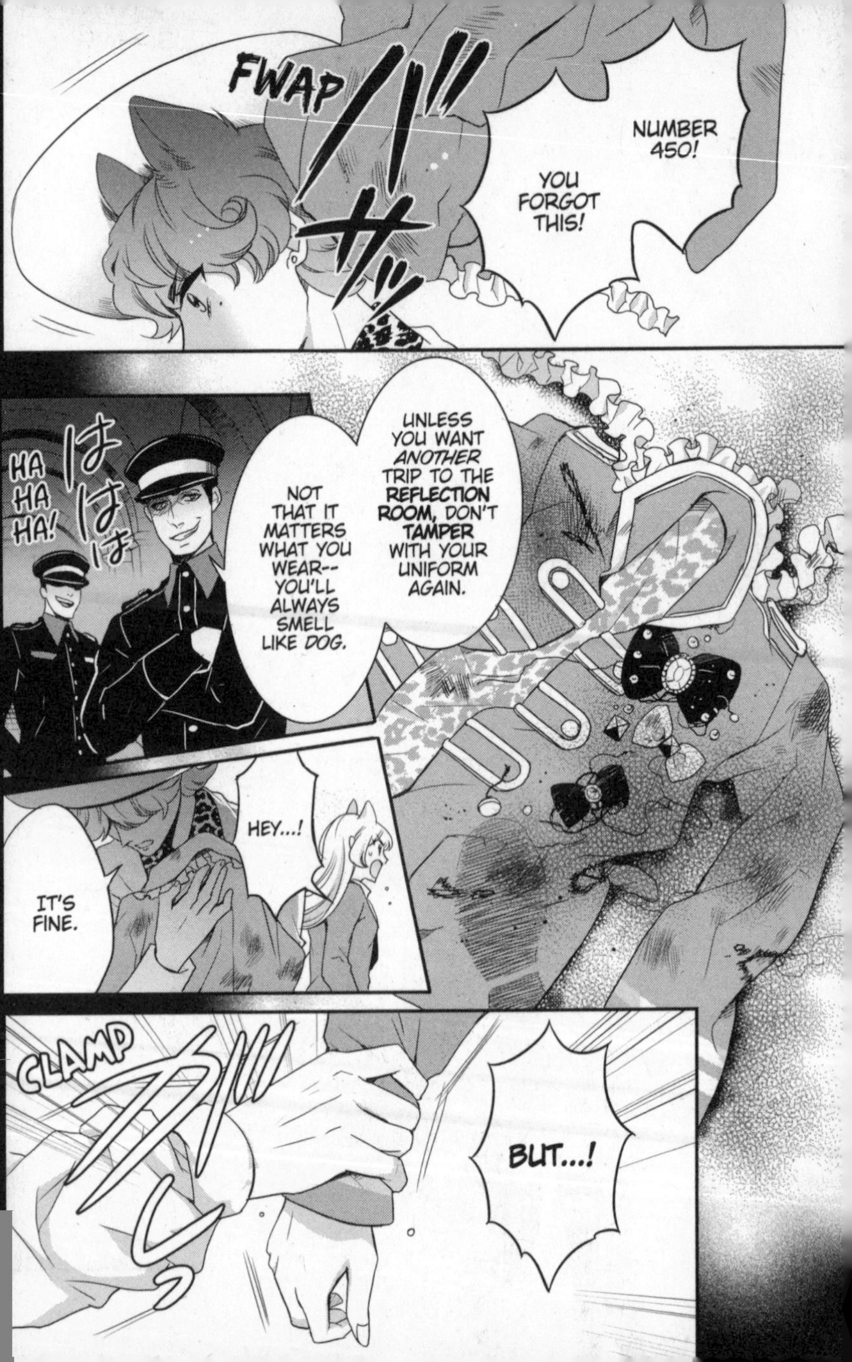
NUMBER 450!
YOU FORGOT THIS!
FWAP
UNLESS YOU WANT *ANOTHER* TRIP TO THE **REFLECTION ROOM**, DON'T **TAMPER** WITH YOUR UNIFORM AGAIN.
NOT THAT IT MATTERS WHAT YOU WEAR-- YOU'LL ALWAYS SMELL LIKE *DOG*.
ははは
HA HA HA!
HEY...!
IT'S FINE.
BUT...!
CLAMP

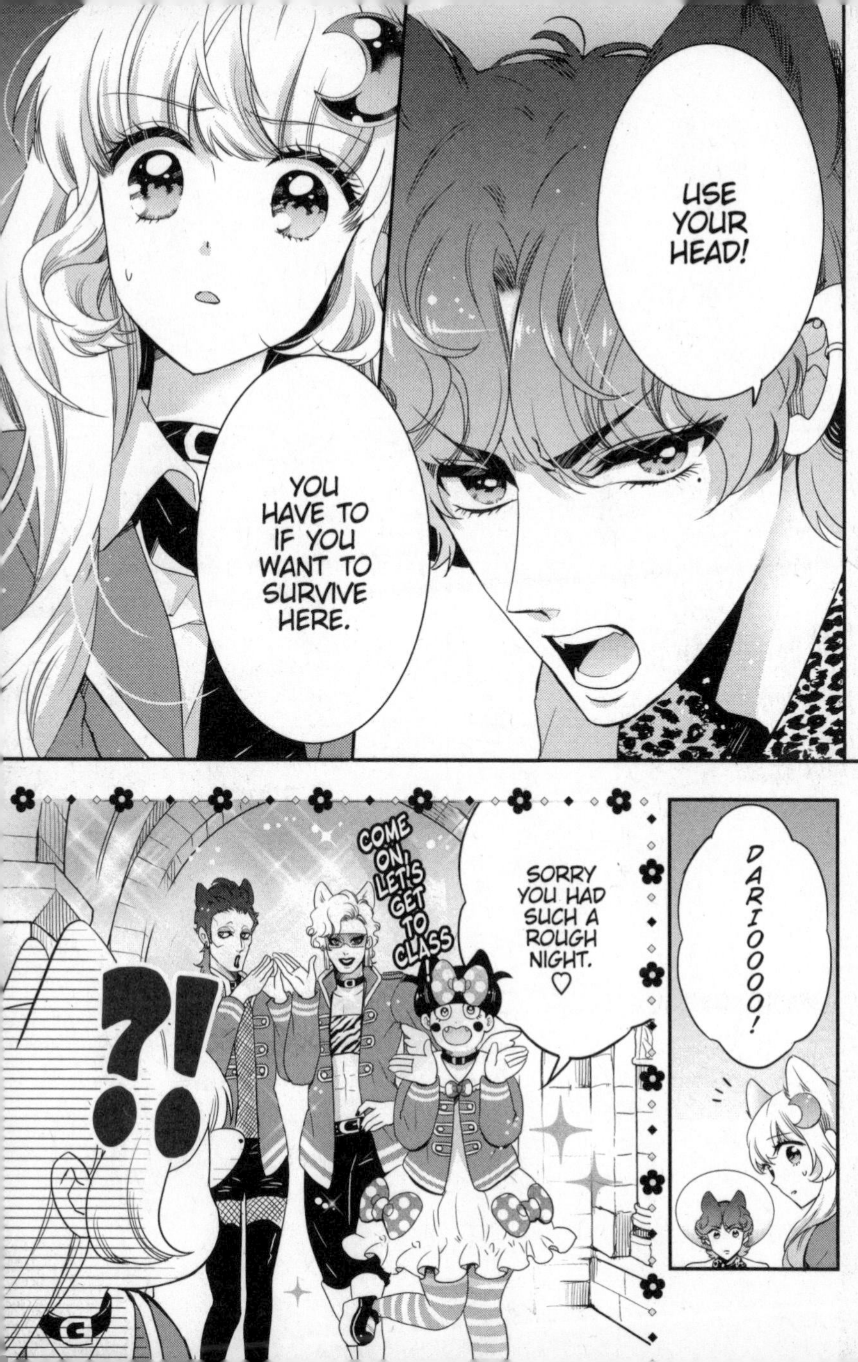
USE YOUR HEAD!
YOU HAVE TO IF YOU WANT TO SURVIVE HERE.
DARIOOOOO!
SORRY YOU HAD SUCH A ROUGH NIGHT. ♡
COME ON, LET'S GET TO CLASS!
?!

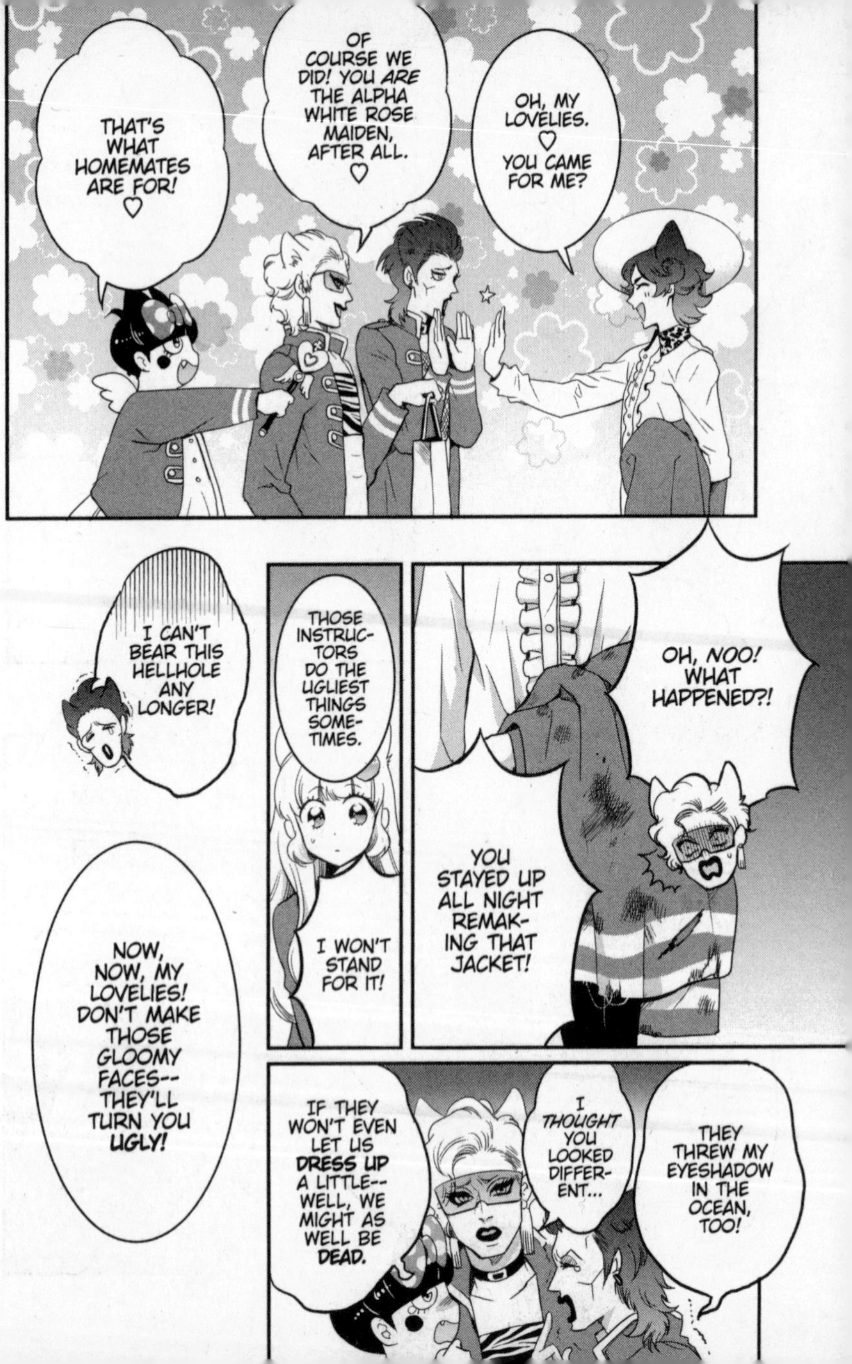
OH, MY LOVELIES. ♡ YOU CAME FOR ME?
OF COURSE WE DID! YOU *ARE* THE ALPHA WHITE ROSE MAIDEN, AFTER ALL. ♡
THAT'S WHAT HOMEMATES ARE FOR! ♡
OH, *NOO!* WHAT HAPPENED?!
YOU STAYED UP ALL NIGHT REMAKING THAT JACKET!
THOSE INSTRUCTORS DO THE UGLIEST THINGS SOMETIMES.
I WON'T STAND FOR IT!
I CAN'T BEAR THIS HELLHOLE ANY LONGER!
THEY THREW MY EYESHADOW IN THE OCEAN, TOO!
I *THOUGHT* YOU LOOKED DIFFERENT...
IF THEY WON'T EVEN LET US **DRESS UP** A LITTLE-- WELL, WE MIGHT AS WELL BE **DEAD.**
NOW, NOW, MY LOVELIES! DON'T MAKE THOSE GLOOMY FACES-- THEY'LL TURN YOU **UGLY!**

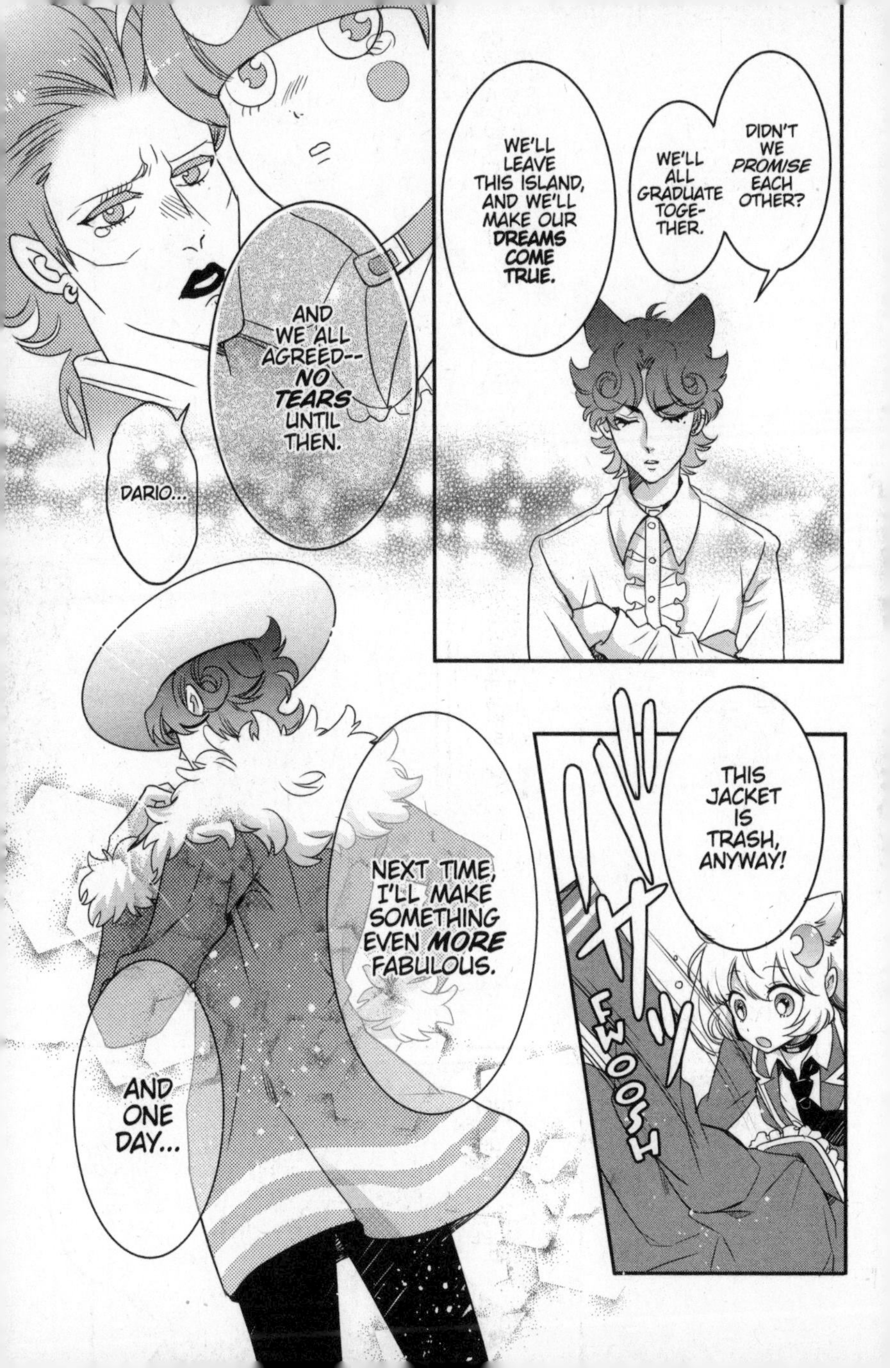
DIDN'T WE PROMISE EACH OTHER?
WE'LL ALL GRADUATE TOGE-THER.
WE'LL LEAVE THIS ISLAND, AND WE'LL MAKE OUR DREAMS COME TRUE.
AND WE ALL AGREED-- NO TEARS UNTIL THEN.
DARIO...
THIS JACKET IS TRASH, ANYWAY!
FWOOSH
NEXT TIME, I'LL MAKE SOMETHING EVEN MORE FABULOUS.
AND ONE DAY...

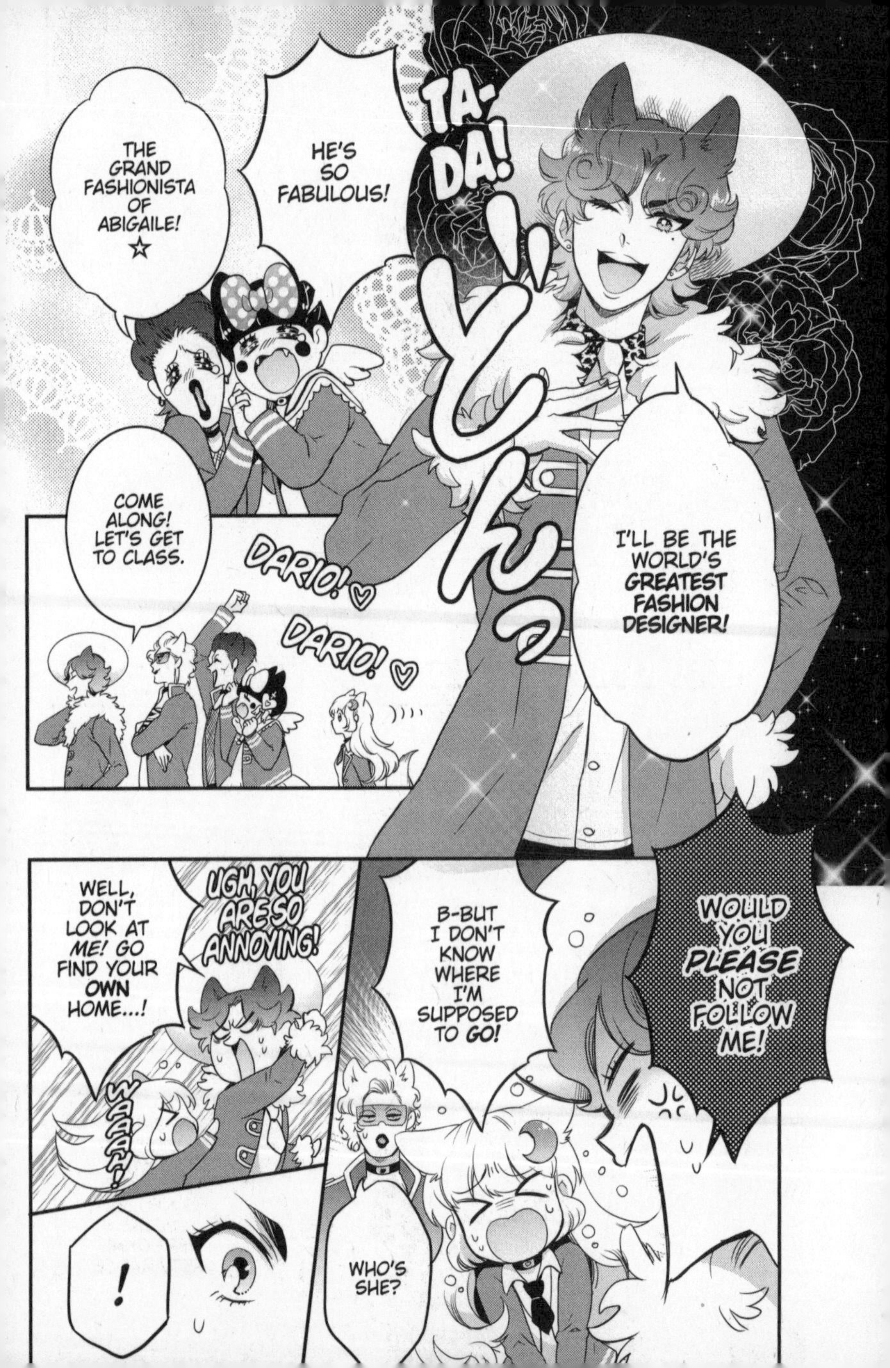
TA-DA!
どんっ
I'LL BE THE WORLD'S GREATEST FASHION DESIGNER!
HE'S SO FABULOUS!
THE GRAND FASHIONISTA OF ABIGAILE! ☆
COME ALONG! LET'S GET TO CLASS.
DARIO! ♡
DARIO! ♡
WOULD YOU PLEASE NOT FOLLOW ME!
B-BUT I DON'T KNOW WHERE I'M SUPPOSED TO GO!
UGH YOU ARE SO ANNOYING!
WELL, DON'T LOOK AT ME! GO FIND YOUR OWN HOME...!
WAAAH!
WHO'S SHE?
!

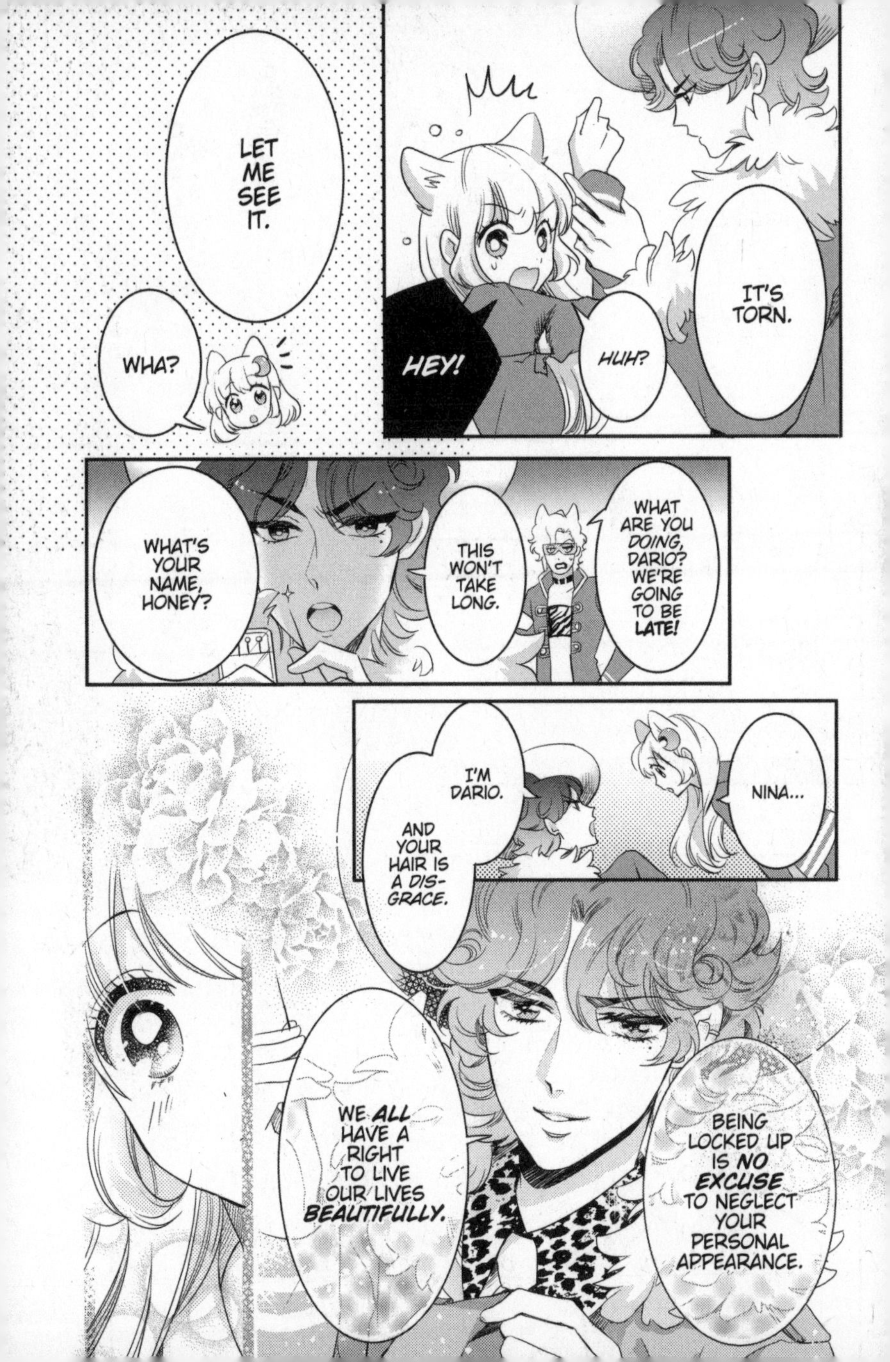
Mu
IT'S TORN.
HUH?
HEY!
LET ME SEE IT.
WHA?
WHAT ARE YOU DOING, DARIO? WE'RE GOING TO BE LATE!
THIS WON'T TAKE LONG.
WHAT'S YOUR NAME, HONEY?
NINA...
I'M DARIO.
AND YOUR HAIR IS A DIS-GRACE.
BEING LOCKED UP IS NO EXCUSE TO NEGLECT YOUR PERSONAL APPEARANCE.
WE ALL HAVE A RIGHT TO LIVE OUR LIVES BEAUTIFULLY.

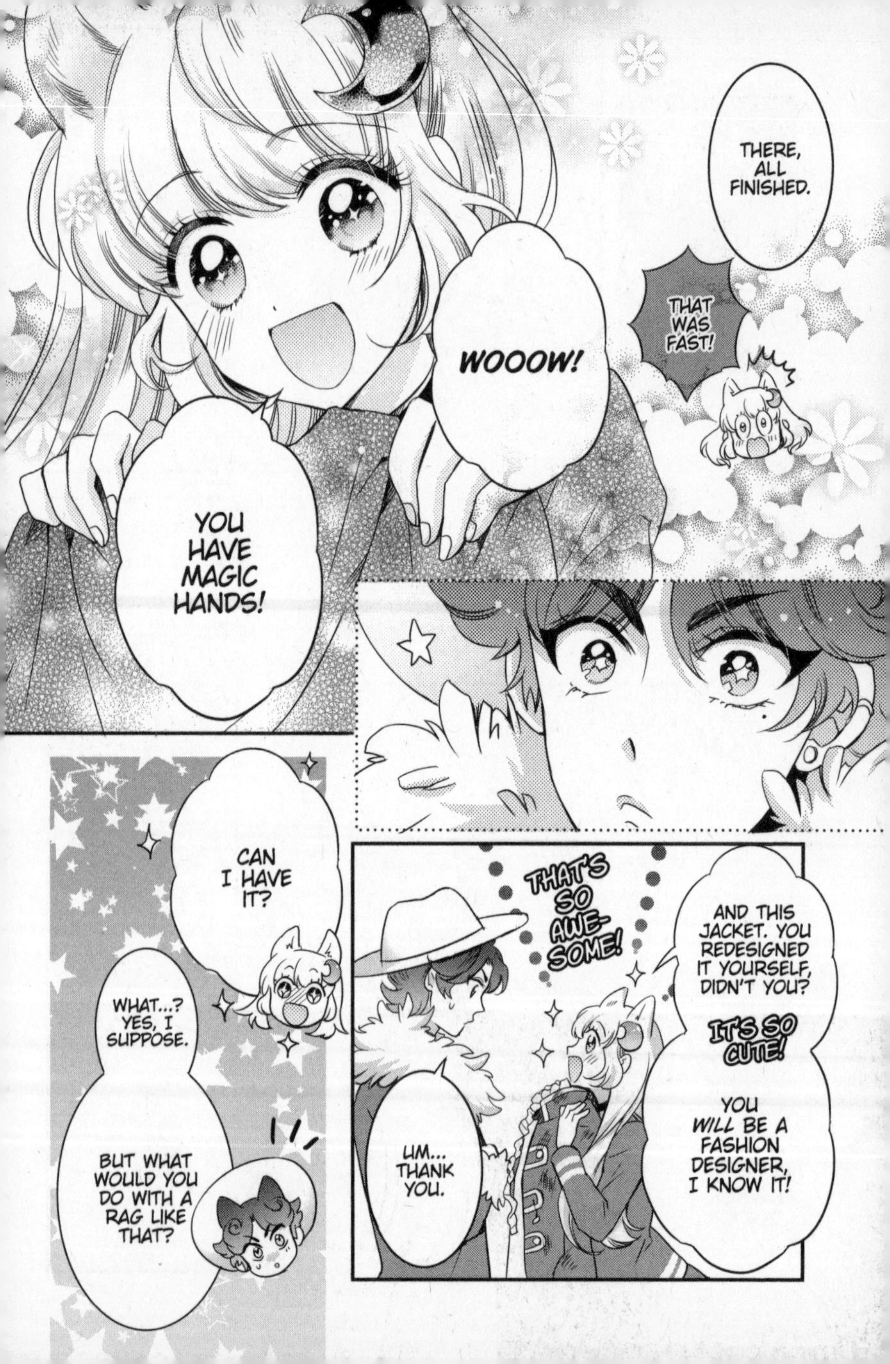
THERE, ALL FINISHED.
THAT WAS FAST!
WOOOW!
YOU HAVE MAGIC HANDS!
AND THIS JACKET. YOU REDESIGNED IT YOURSELF, DIDN'T YOU?
THAT'S SO AWE-SOME!
IT'S SO CUTE!
YOU WILL BE A FASHION DESIGNER, I KNOW IT!
UM... THANK YOU.
CAN I HAVE IT?
WHAT...? YES, I SUPPOSE.
BUT WHAT WOULD YOU DO WITH A RAG LIKE THAT?

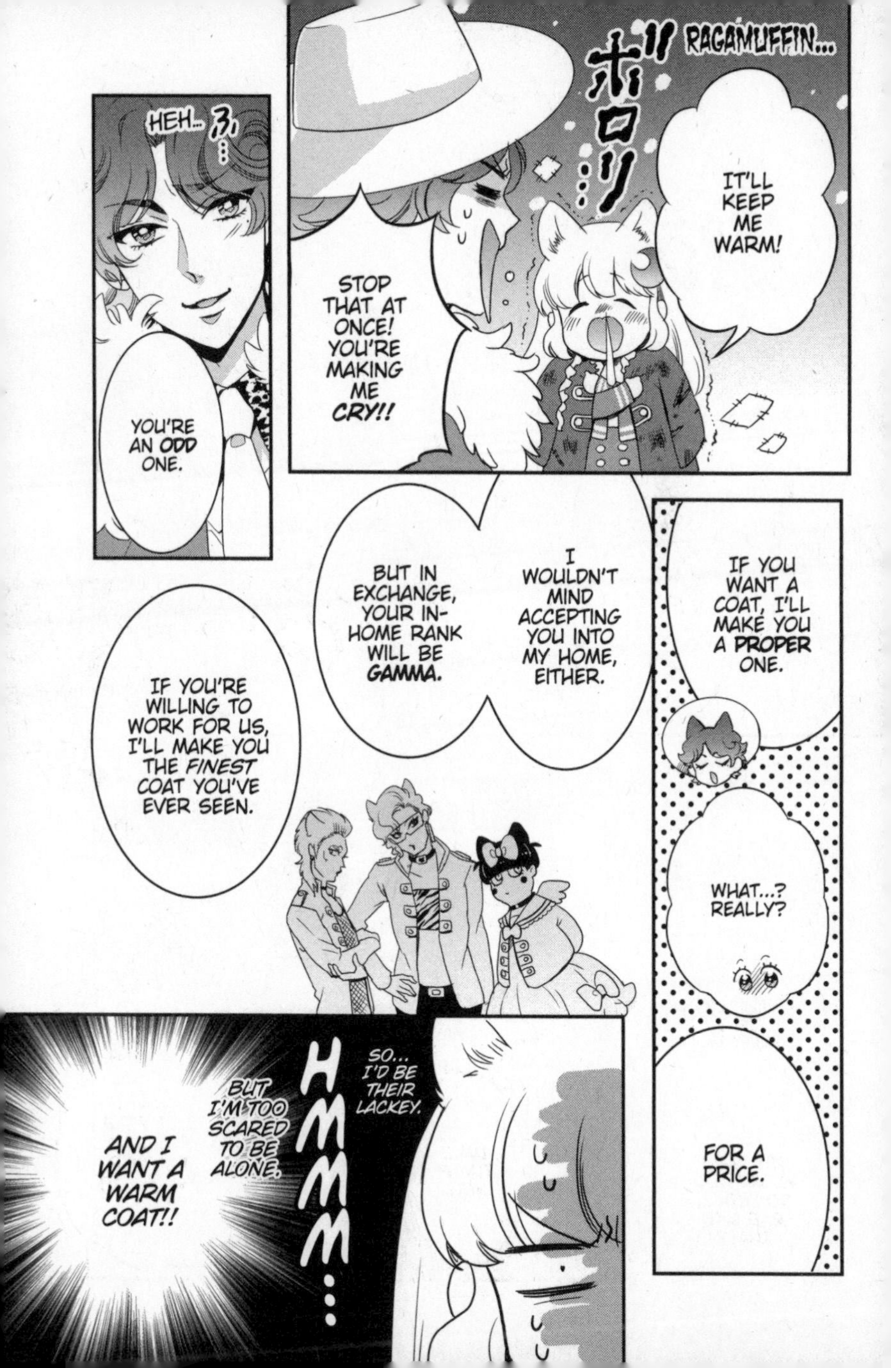
RAGAMUFFIN...
ホロリ…
IT'LL KEEP ME WARM!
STOP THAT AT ONCE! YOU'RE MAKING ME CRY!!
HEH... ふ…
YOU'RE AN ODD ONE.
IF YOU WANT A COAT, I'LL MAKE YOU A PROPER ONE.
WHAT...? REALLY?
FOR A PRICE.
I WOULDN'T MIND ACCEPTING YOU INTO MY HOME, EITHER.
BUT IN EXCHANGE, YOUR IN-HOME RANK WILL BE GAMMA.
IF YOU'RE WILLING TO WORK FOR US, I'LL MAKE YOU THE FINEST COAT YOU'VE EVER SEEN.
HMMM...
SO... I'D BE THEIR LACKEY.
BUT I'M TOO SCARED TO BE ALONE.
AND I WANT A WARM COAT!!

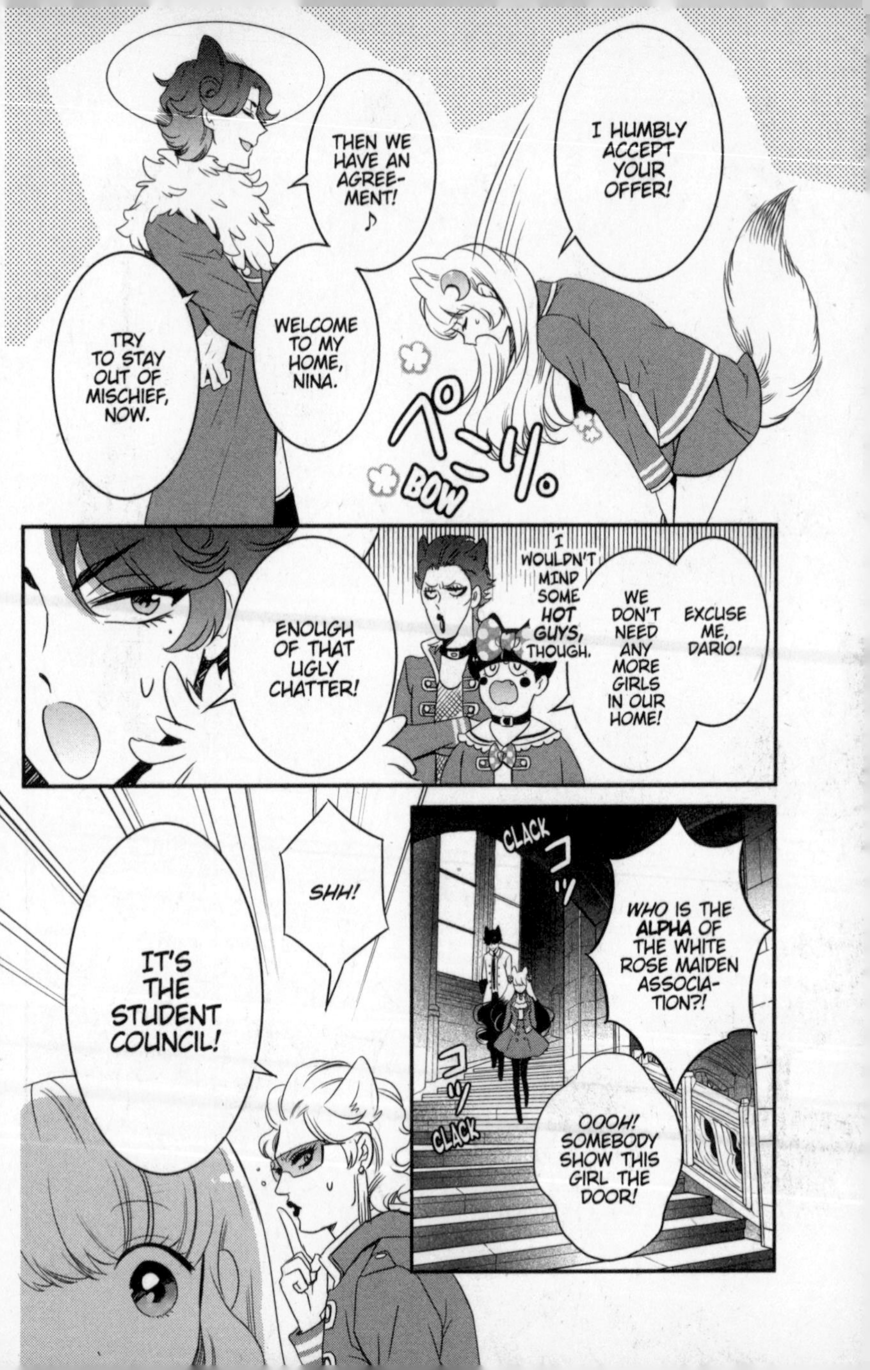
I HUMBLY ACCEPT YOUR OFFER!
BOW
THEN WE HAVE AN AGREEMENT! ♪
WELCOME TO MY HOME, NINA.
TRY TO STAY OUT OF MISCHIEF, NOW.
EXCUSE ME, DARIO!
WE DON'T NEED ANY MORE GIRLS IN OUR HOME!
I WOULDN'T MIND SOME **HOT GUYS**, THOUGH.
ENOUGH OF THAT UGLY CHATTER!
CLACK
WHO IS THE **ALPHA** OF THE WHITE ROSE MAIDEN ASSOCIATION?!
CLACK
OOOH! SOMEBODY SHOW THIS GIRL THE DOOR!
SHH!
IT'S THE STUDENT COUNCIL!

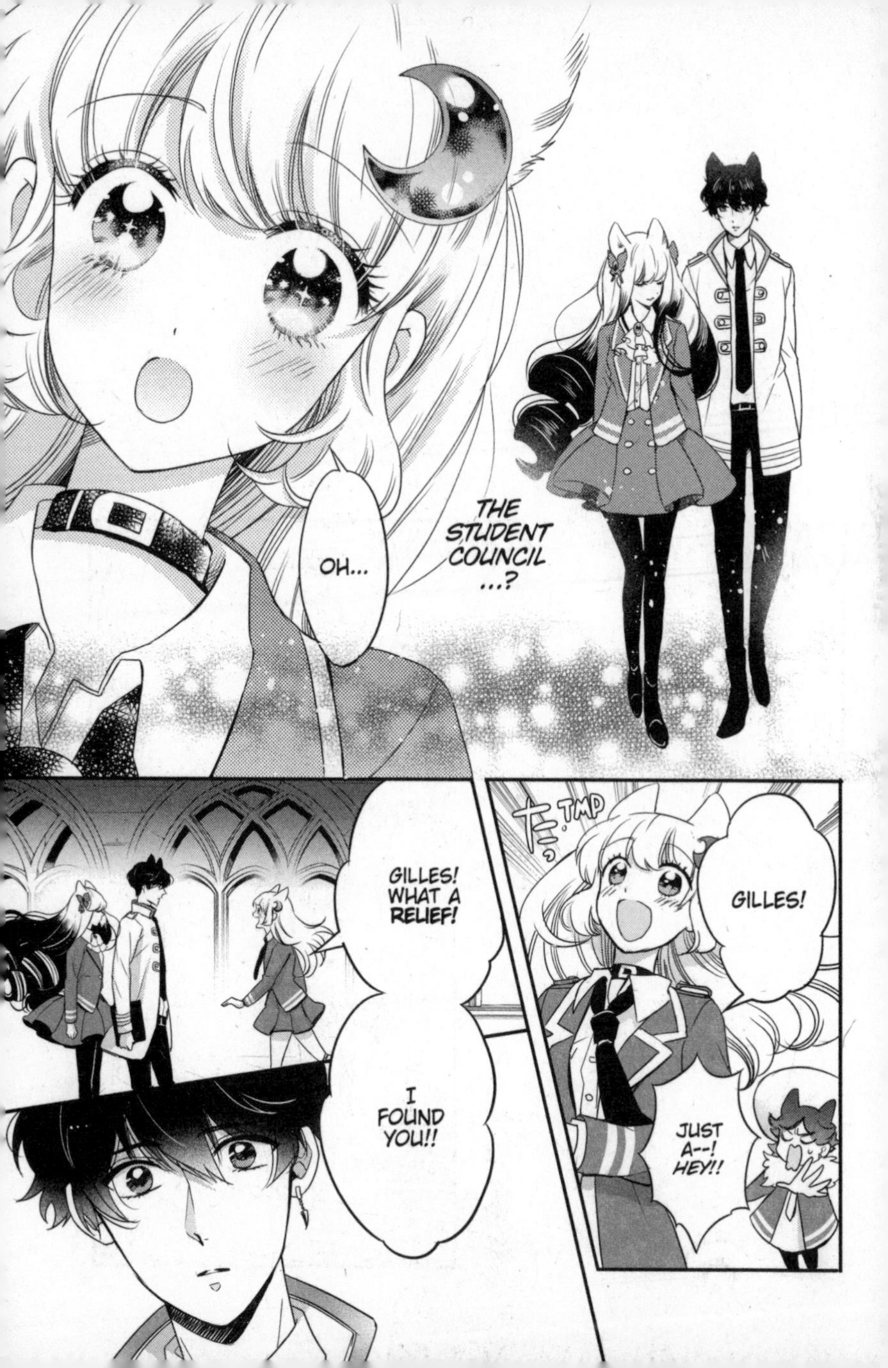
THE STUDENT COUNCIL ...?
OH...
TMP
GILLES!
JUST A--! HEY!!
GILLES! WHAT A RELIEF!
I FOUND YOU!!

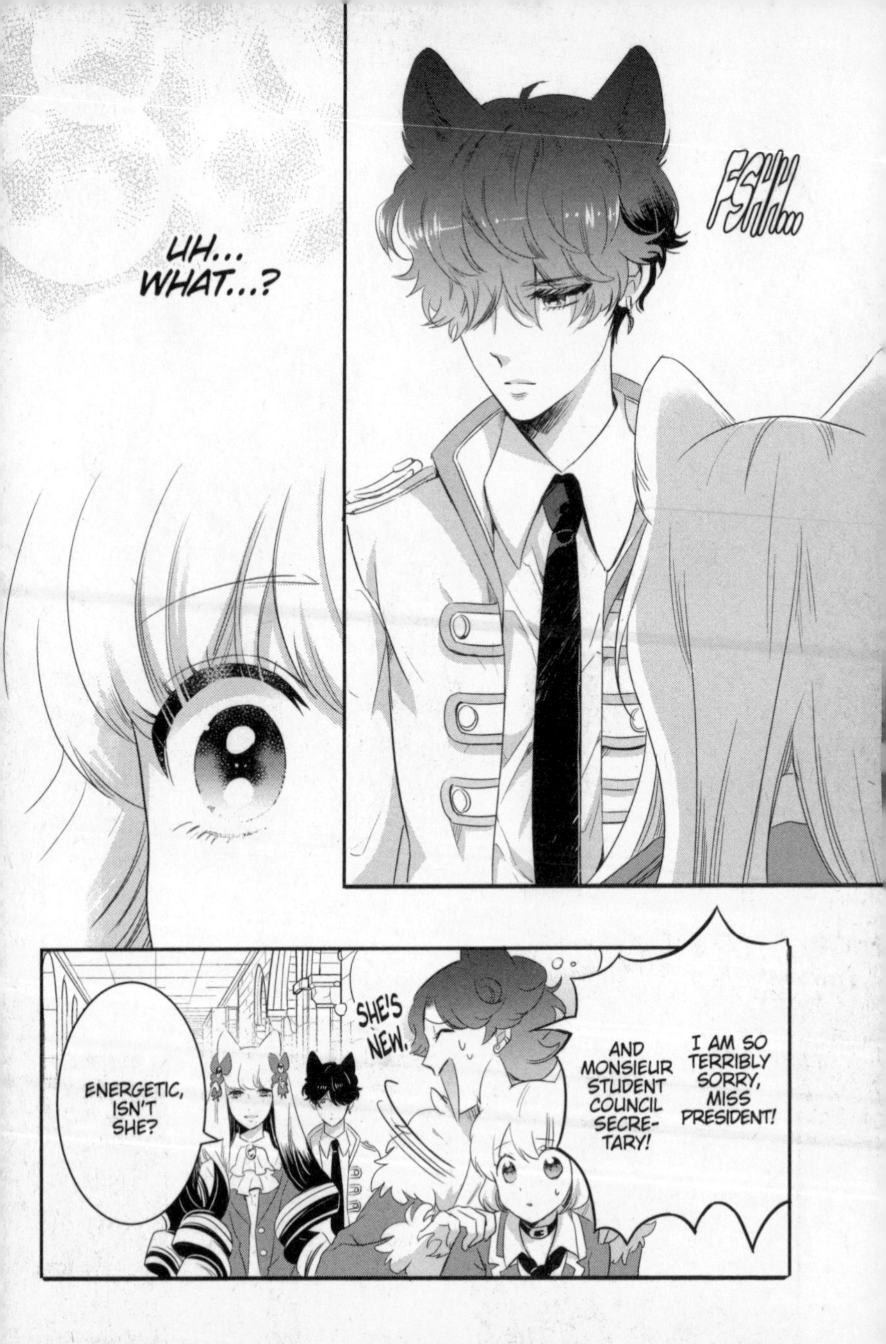
FSHH...
UH... WHAT...?
I AM SO TERRIBLY SORRY, MISS PRESIDENT!
AND MONSIEUR STUDENT COUNCIL SECRETARY!
SHE'S NEW.
ENERGETIC, ISN'T SHE?

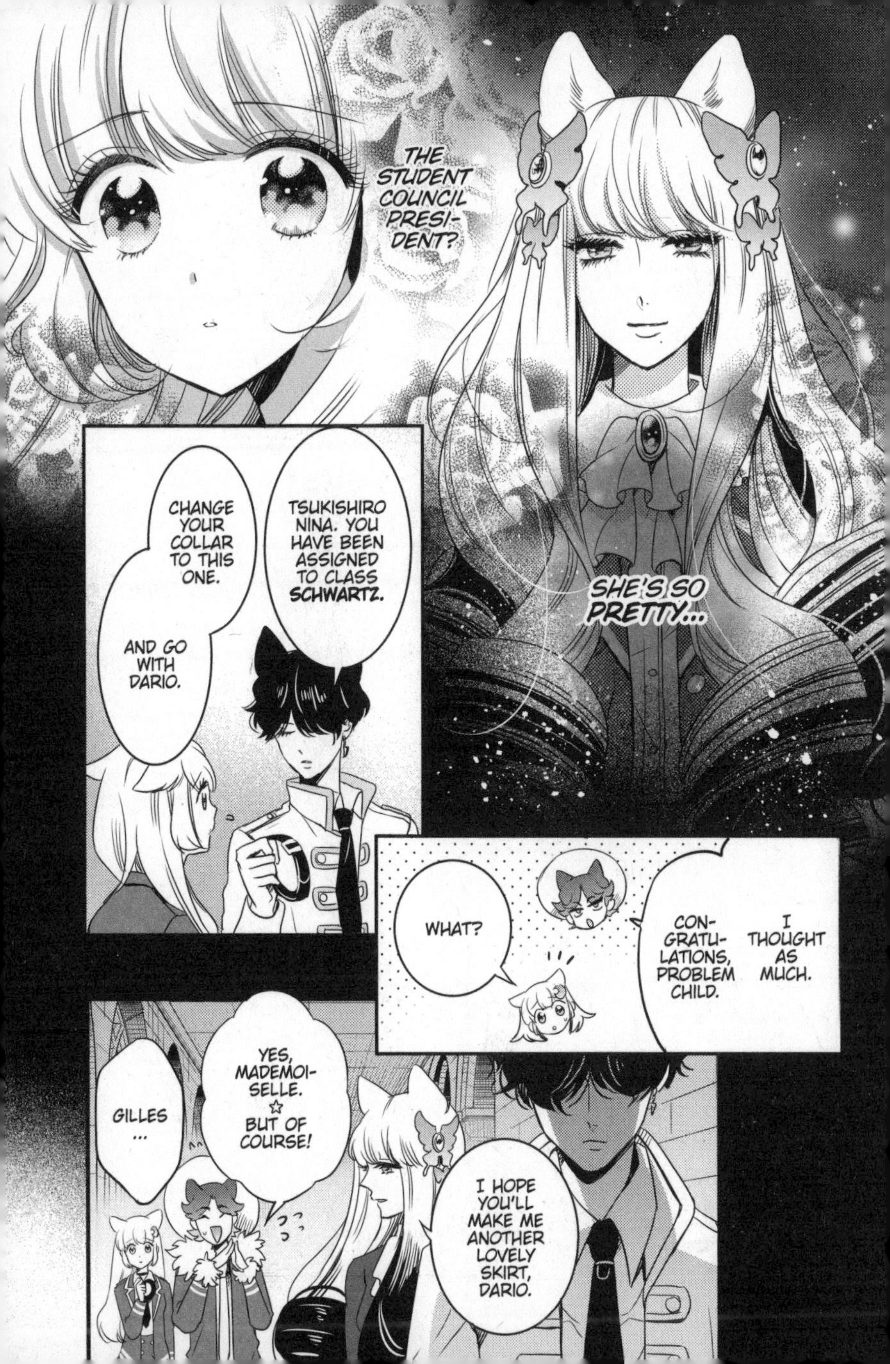
THE STUDENT COUNCIL PRESIDENT?
SHE'S SO PRETTY...
TSUKISHIRO NINA. YOU HAVE BEEN ASSIGNED TO CLASS SCHWARTZ.
CHANGE YOUR COLLAR TO THIS ONE.
AND GO WITH DARIO.
I THOUGHT AS MUCH.
CONGRATULATIONS, PROBLEM CHILD.
WHAT?
I HOPE YOU'LL MAKE ME ANOTHER LOVELY SKIRT, DARIO.
YES, MADEMOISELLE. ☆ BUT OF COURSE!
GILLES...

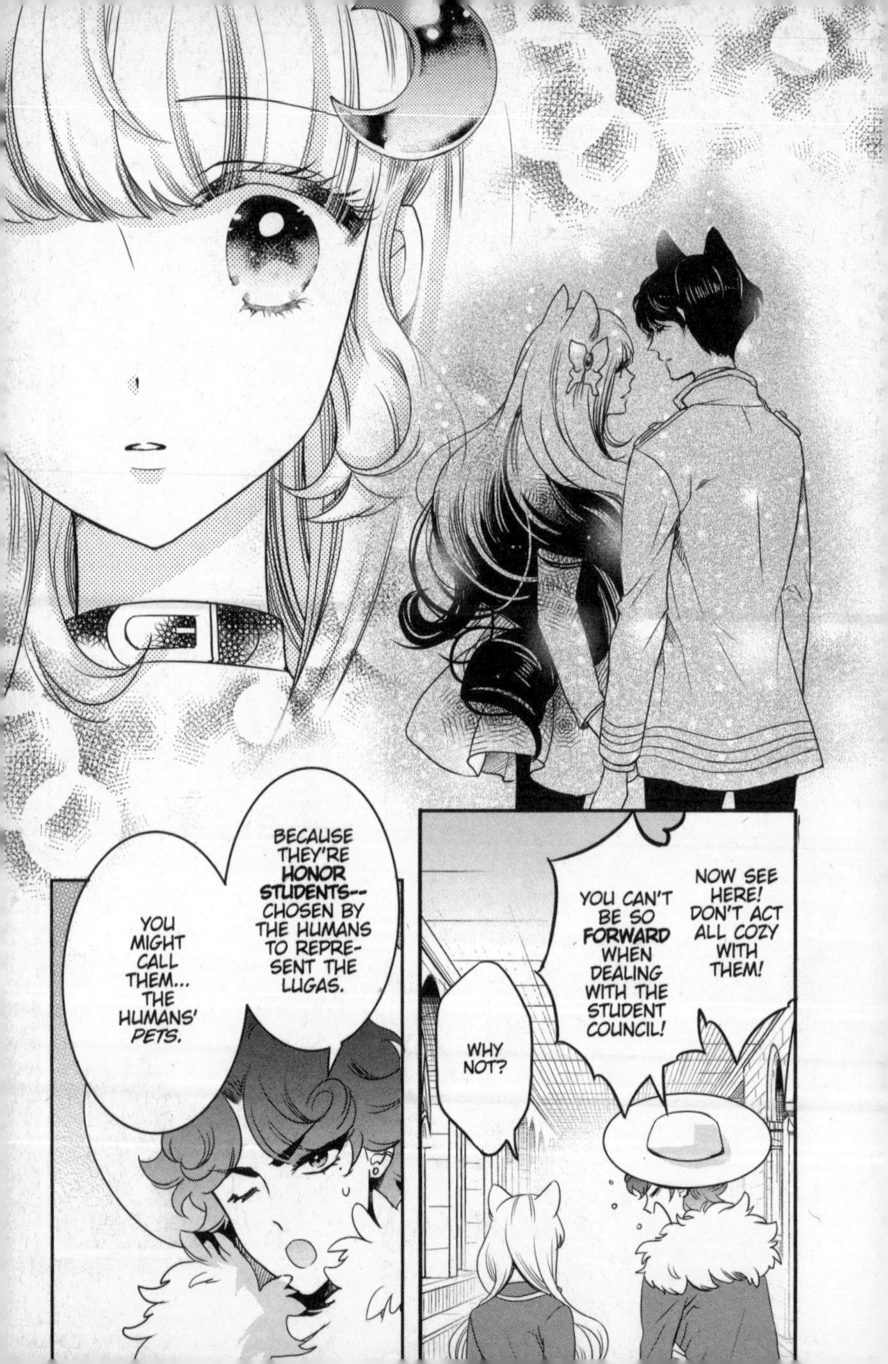
NOW SEE HERE! DON'T ACT ALL COZY WITH THEM!
YOU CAN'T BE SO FORWARD WHEN DEALING WITH THE STUDENT COUNCIL!
WHY NOT?
BECAUSE THEY'RE HONOR STUDENTS-- CHOSEN BY THE HUMANS TO REPRE-SENT THE LUGAS.
YOU MIGHT CALL THEM... THE HUMANS' PETS.

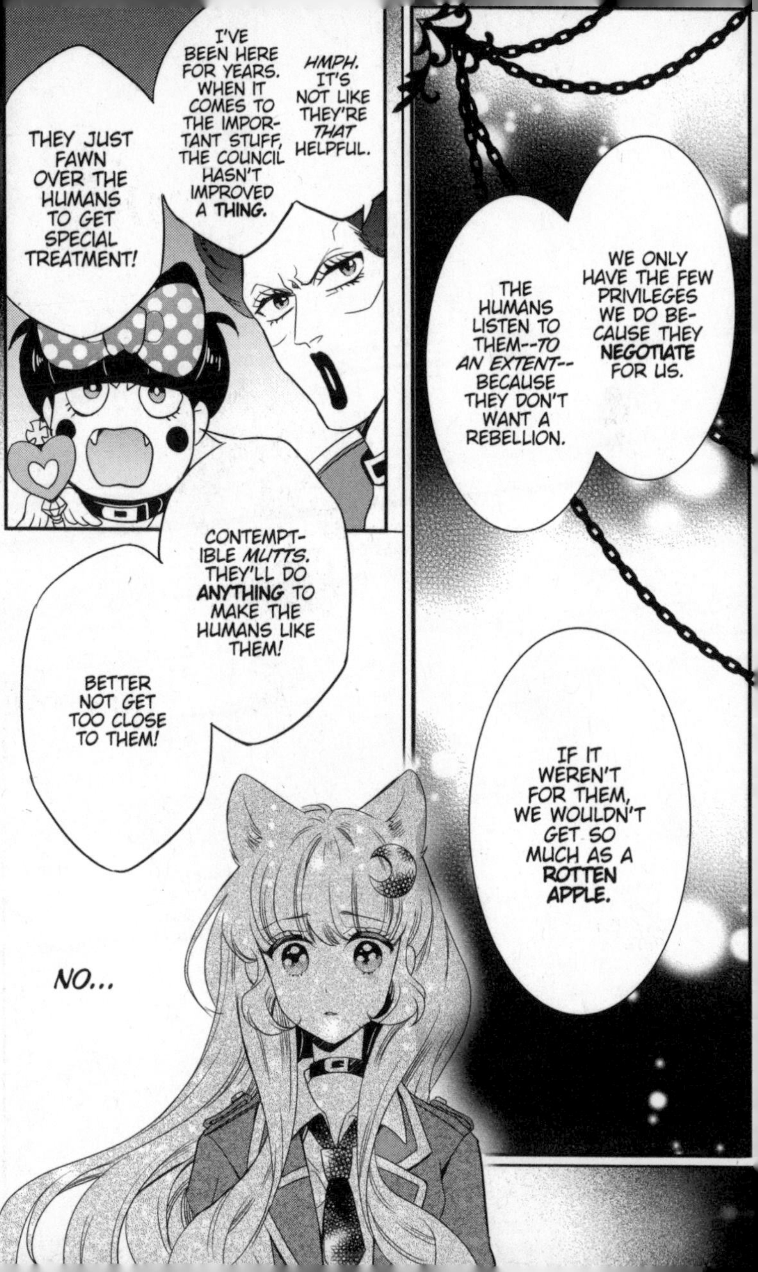
WE ONLY HAVE THE FEW PRIVILEGES WE DO BE-CAUSE THEY **NEGOTIATE** FOR US.
THE HUMANS LISTEN TO THEM--*TO AN EXTENT*--BECAUSE THEY DON'T WANT A REBELLION.
IF IT WEREN'T FOR THEM, WE WOULDN'T GET SO MUCH AS A **ROTTEN APPLE.**
HMPH. IT'S NOT LIKE THEY'RE *THAT* HELPFUL.
I'VE BEEN HERE FOR YEARS. WHEN IT COMES TO THE IMPOR-TANT STUFF, THE COUNCIL HASN'T IMPROVED A **THING.**
THEY JUST FAWN OVER THE HUMANS TO GET SPECIAL TREATMENT!
CONTEMPT-IBLE *MUTTS.* THEY'LL DO **ANYTHING** TO MAKE THE HUMANS LIKE THEM!
BETTER NOT GET TOO CLOSE TO THEM!
NO...

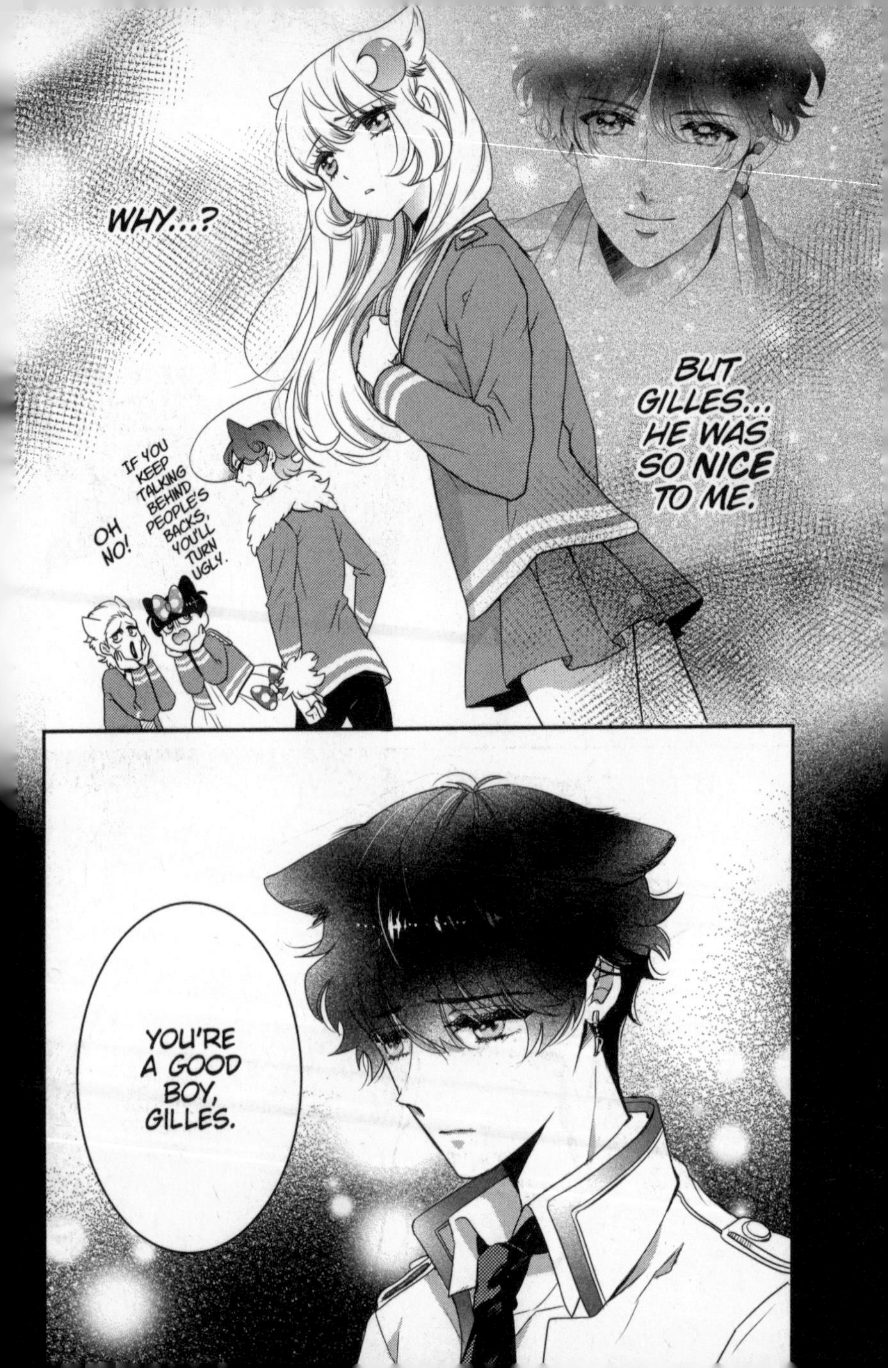
BUT GILLES... HE WAS SO NICE TO ME.
WHY...?
IF YOU KEEP TALKING BEHIND PEOPLE'S BACKS, YOU'LL TURN UGLY.
OH NO!
YOU'RE A GOOD BOY, GILLES.

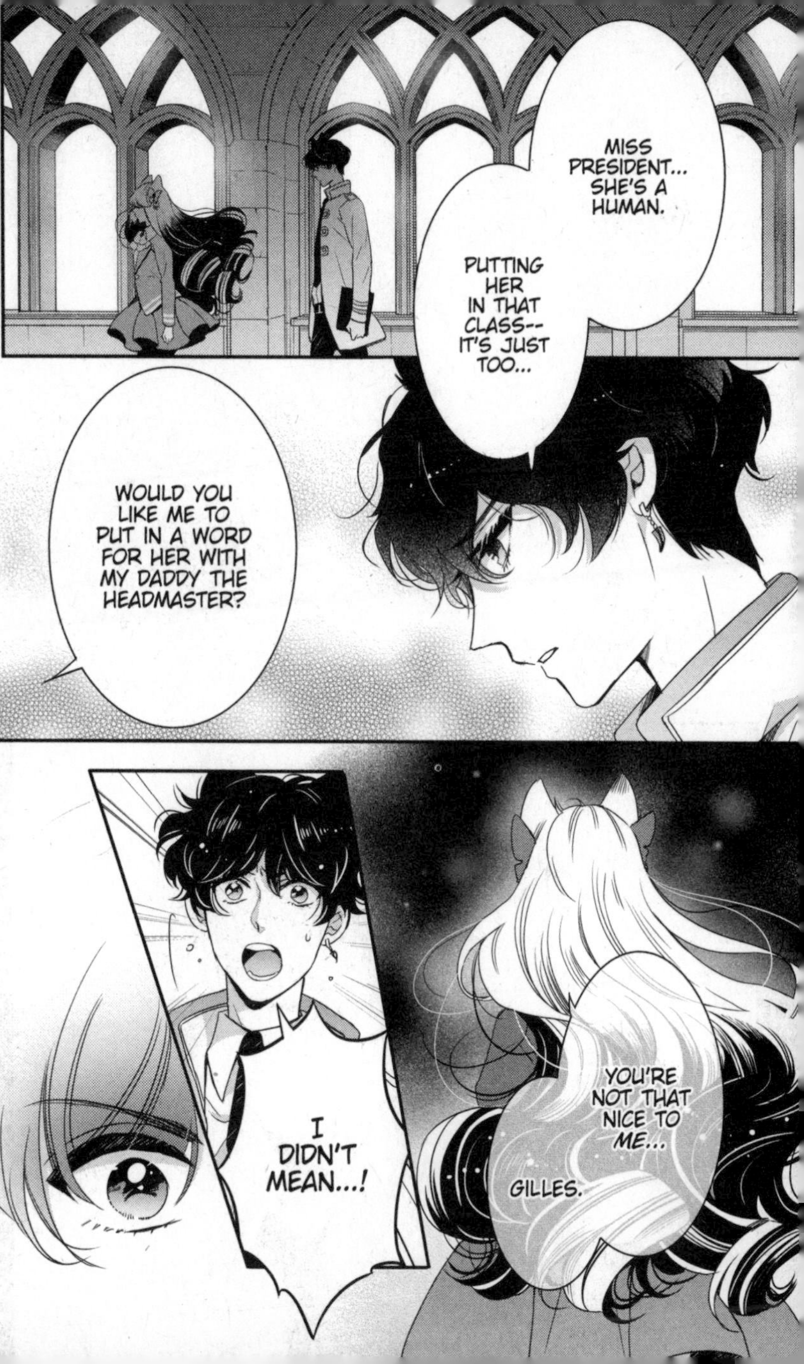
MISS PRESIDENT... SHE'S A HUMAN.
PUTTING HER IN THAT CLASS-- IT'S JUST TOO...
WOULD YOU LIKE ME TO PUT IN A WORD FOR HER WITH MY DADDY THE HEADMASTER?
YOU'RE NOT THAT NICE TO ME...
GILLES.
I DIDN'T MEAN...!

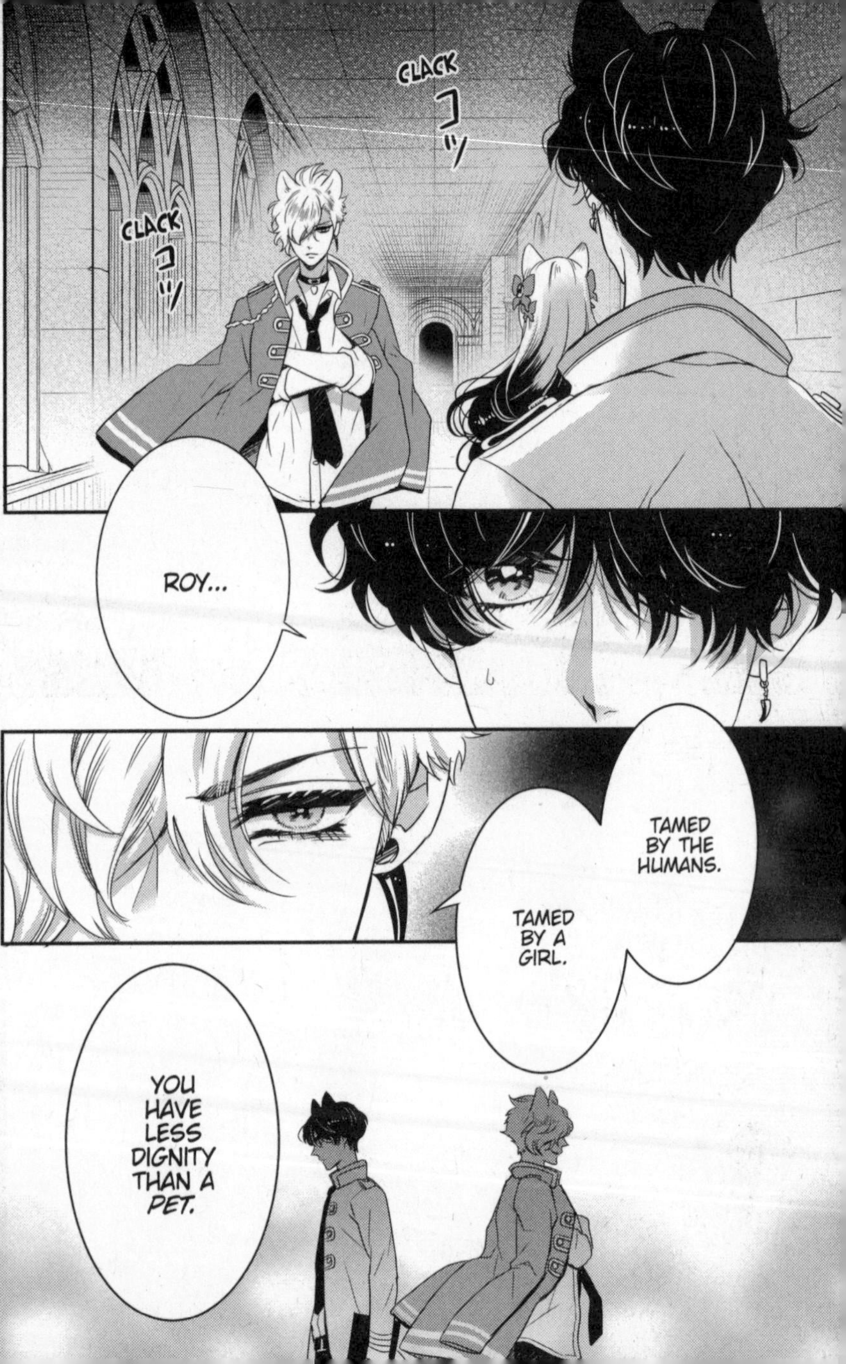
CLACK
コツ
CLACK
コツ
ROY...
TAMED BY THE HUMANS.
TAMED BY A GIRL.
YOU HAVE LESS DIGNITY THAN A PET.

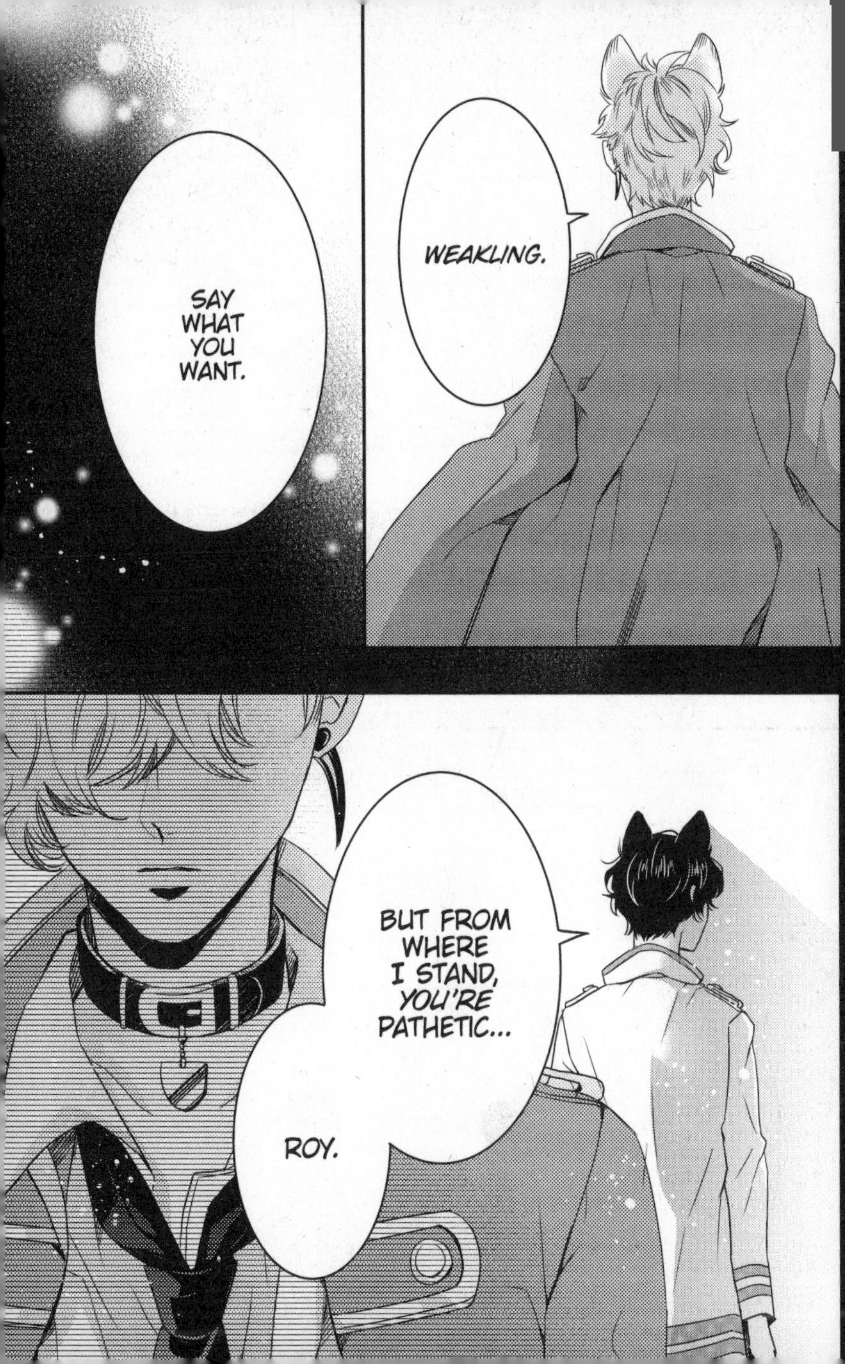
WEAKLING.
SAY WHAT YOU WANT.
BUT FROM WHERE I STAND, YOU'RE PATHETIC...
ROY.

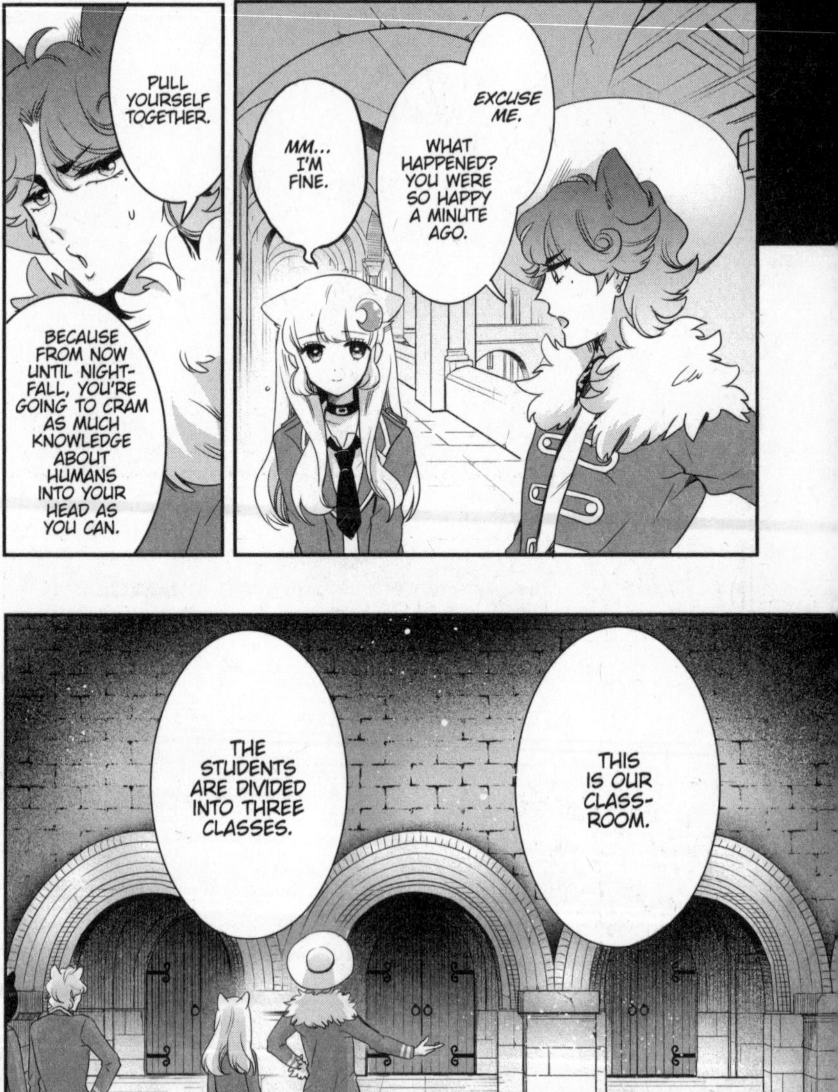
EXCUSE ME.
WHAT HAPPENED? YOU WERE SO HAPPY A MINUTE AGO.
MM... I'M FINE.
PULL YOURSELF TOGETHER.
BECAUSE FROM NOW UNTIL NIGHT-FALL, YOU'RE GOING TO CRAM AS MUCH KNOWLEDGE ABOUT HUMANS INTO YOUR HEAD AS YOU CAN.
THIS IS OUR CLASS-ROOM.
THE STUDENTS ARE DIVIDED INTO THREE CLASSES.

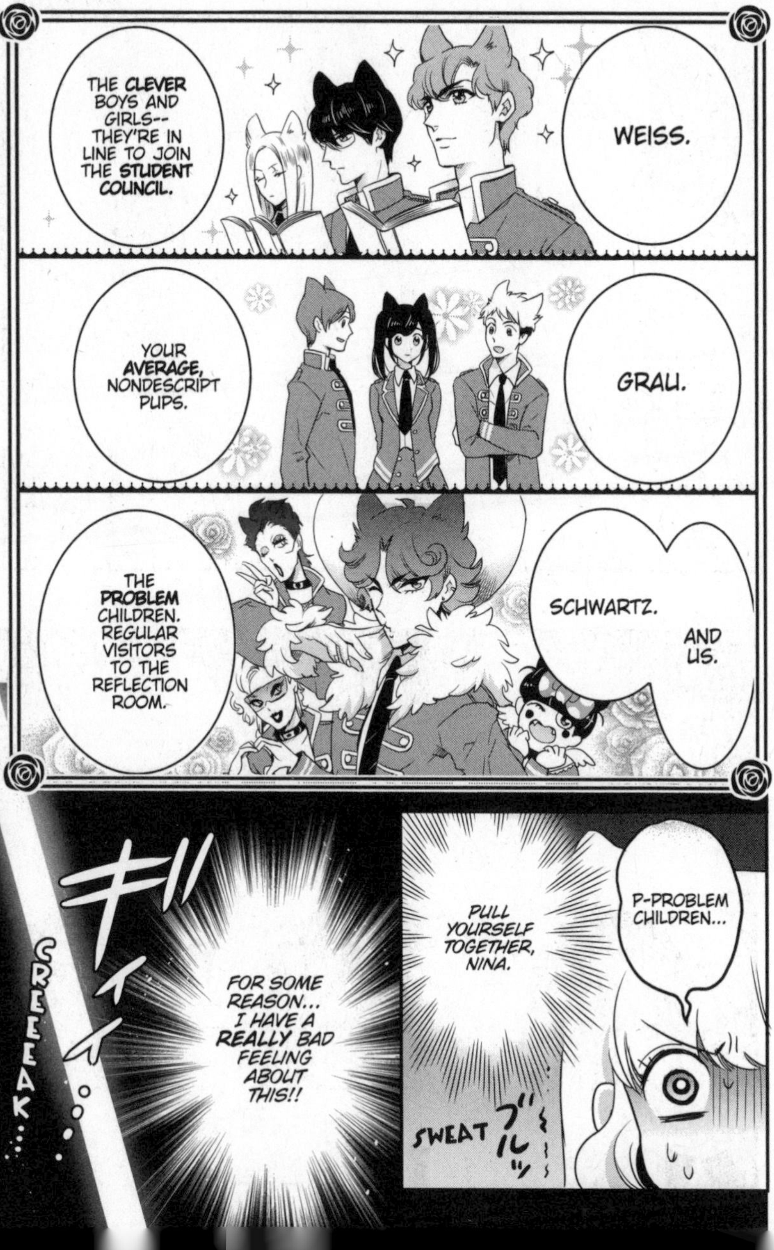
WEISS.
THE CLEVER BOYS AND GIRLS-- THEY'RE IN LINE TO JOIN THE STUDENT COUNCIL.
GRAU.
YOUR AVERAGE, NONDESCRIPT PUPS.
SCHWARTZ.
AND US.
THE PROBLEM CHILDREN. REGULAR VISITORS TO THE REFLECTION ROOM.
P-PROBLEM CHILDREN...
PULL YOURSELF TOGETHER, NINA.
ブルッ
SWEAT
FOR SOME REASON... I HAVE A REALLY BAD FEELING ABOUT THIS!!
キィィ
CREEEAK...

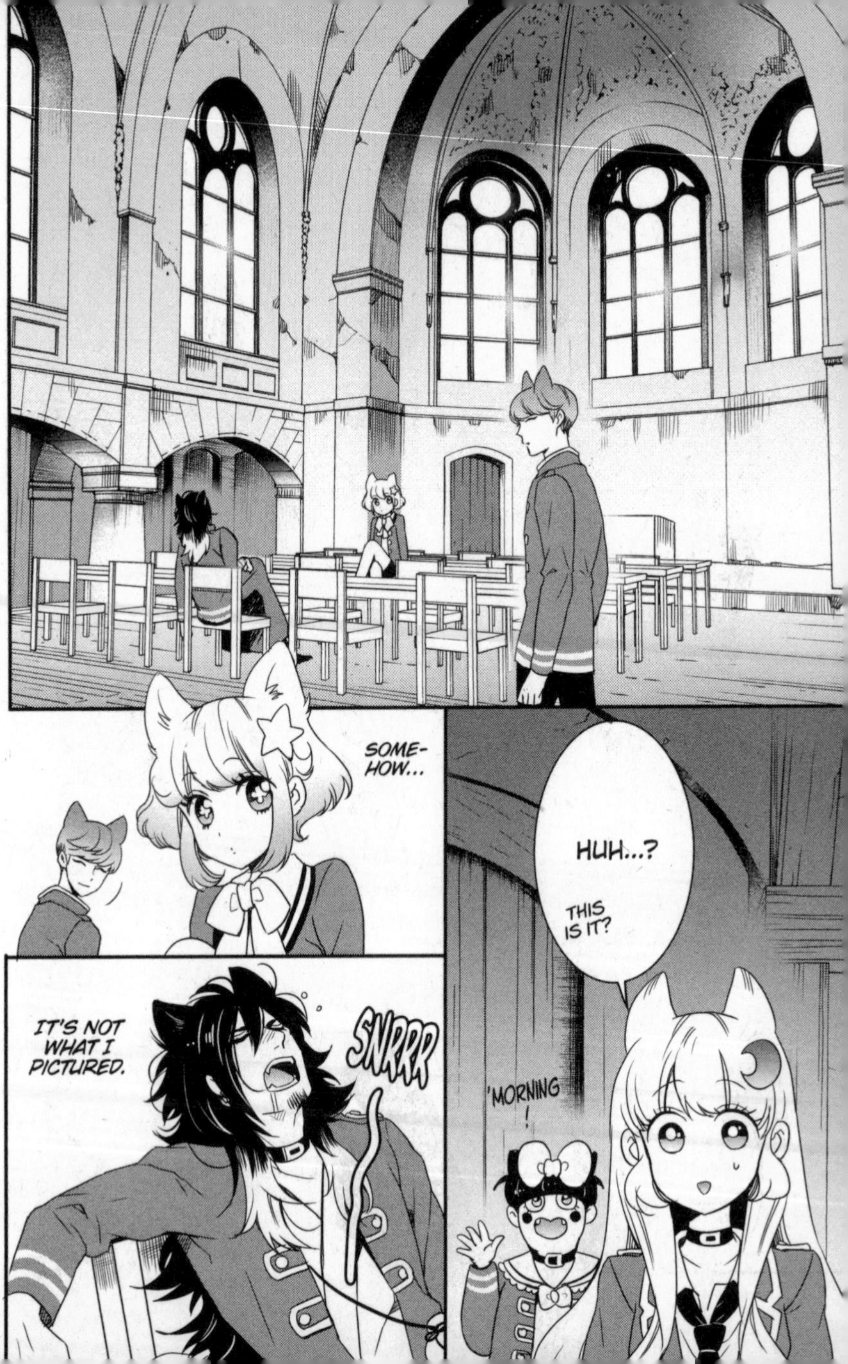
HUH...?
THIS IS IT?
'MORNING!
SOME-HOW...
IT'S NOT WHAT I PICTURED.
SNRRR

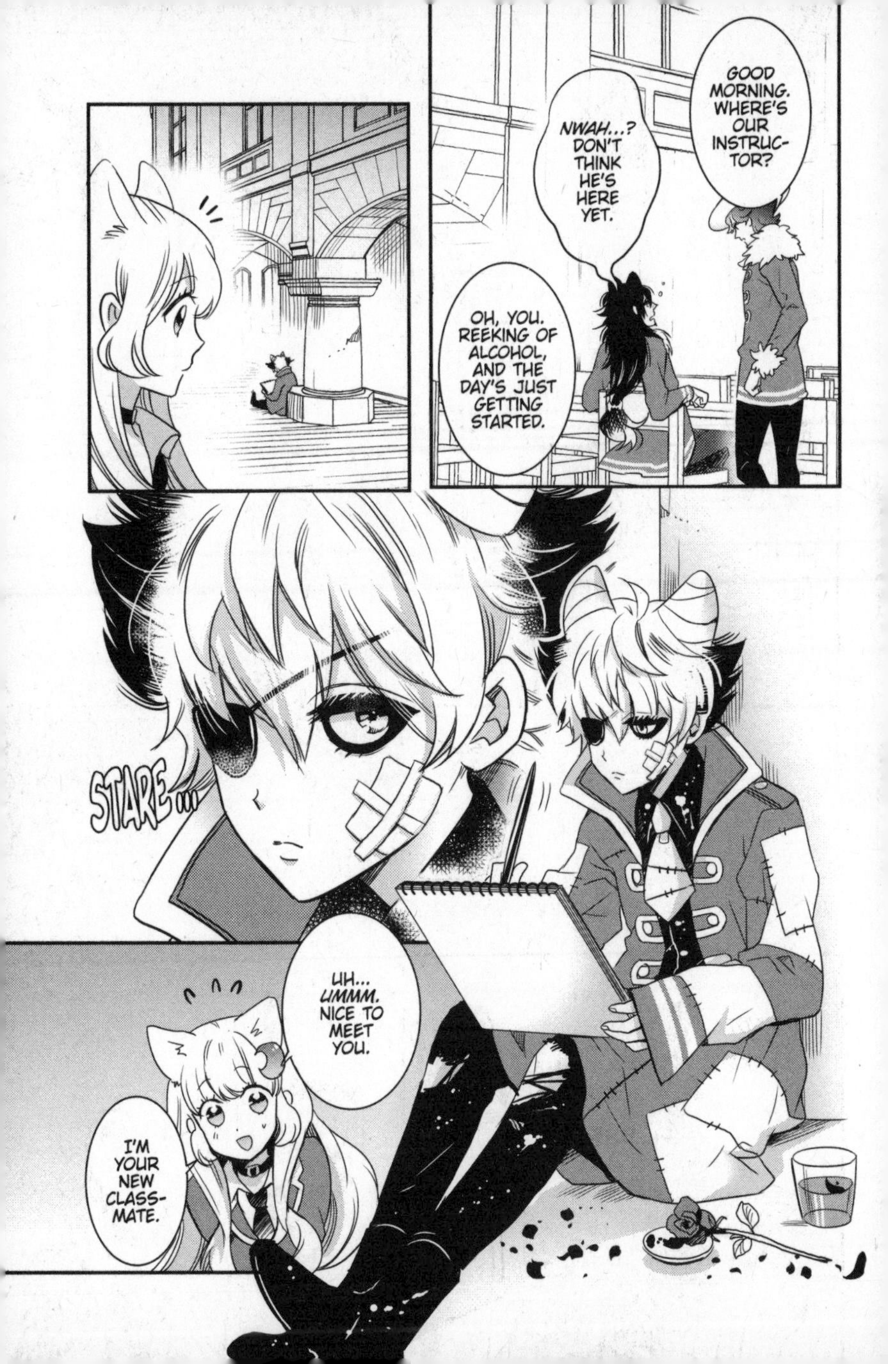
GOOD MORNING. WHERE'S OUR INSTRUCTOR?
NWAH...? DON'T THINK HE'S HERE YET.
OH, YOU. REEKING OF ALCOHOL, AND THE DAY'S JUST GETTING STARTED.
STARE...
UH... UMMM. NICE TO MEET YOU.
I'M YOUR NEW CLASSMATE.

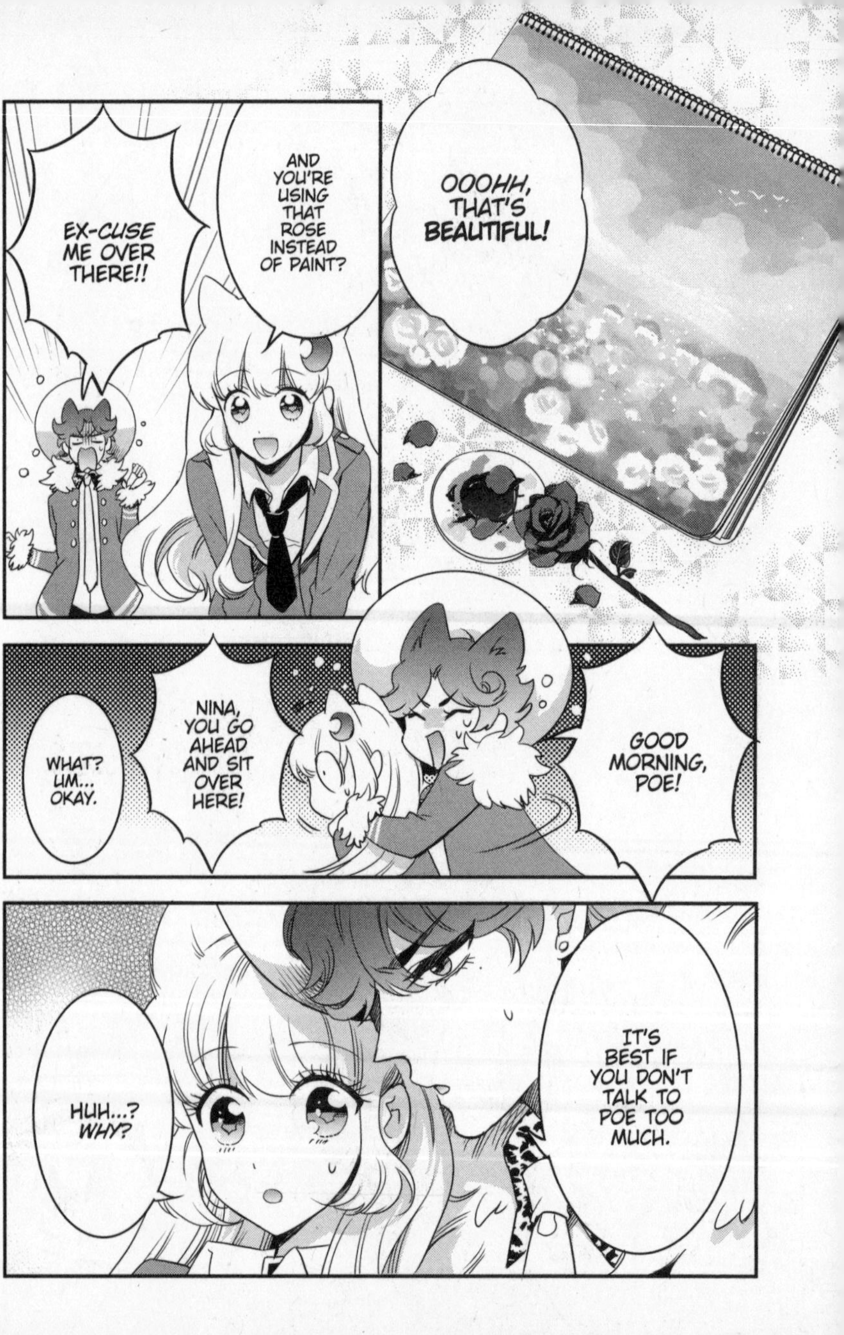
OOOHH, THAT'S BEAUTIFUL!
AND YOU'RE USING THAT ROSE INSTEAD OF PAINT?
EX-CUSE ME OVER THERE!!
GOOD MORNING, POE!
NINA, YOU GO AHEAD AND SIT OVER HERE!
WHAT? UM... OKAY.
IT'S BEST IF YOU DON'T TALK TO POE TOO MUCH.
HUH...? WHY?

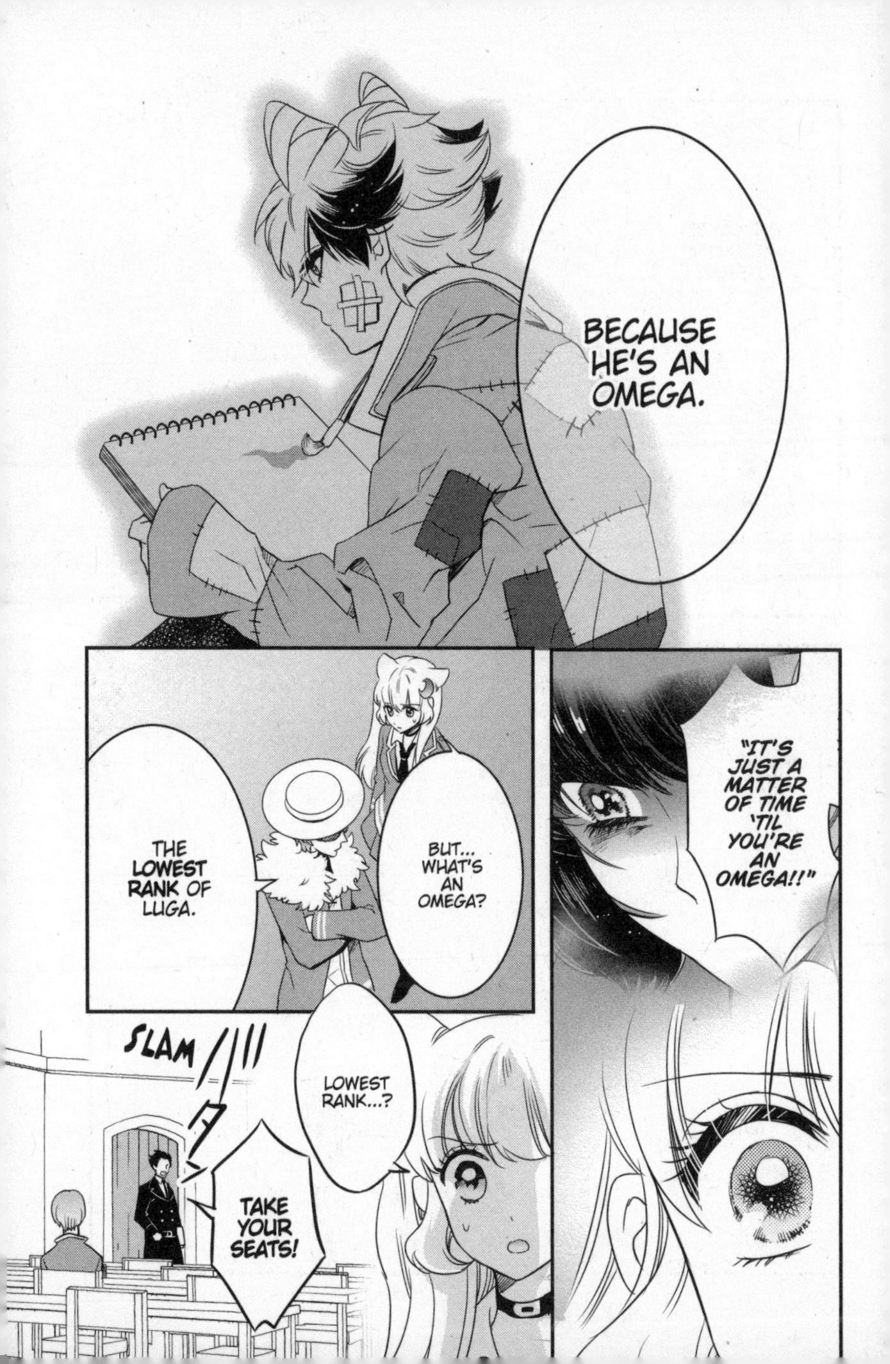
BECAUSE HE'S AN OMEGA.
"IT'S JUST A MATTER OF TIME 'TIL YOU'RE AN OMEGA!!"
BUT... WHAT'S AN OMEGA?
THE LOWEST RANK OF LUGA.
LOWEST RANK...?
SLAM
TAKE YOUR SEATS!

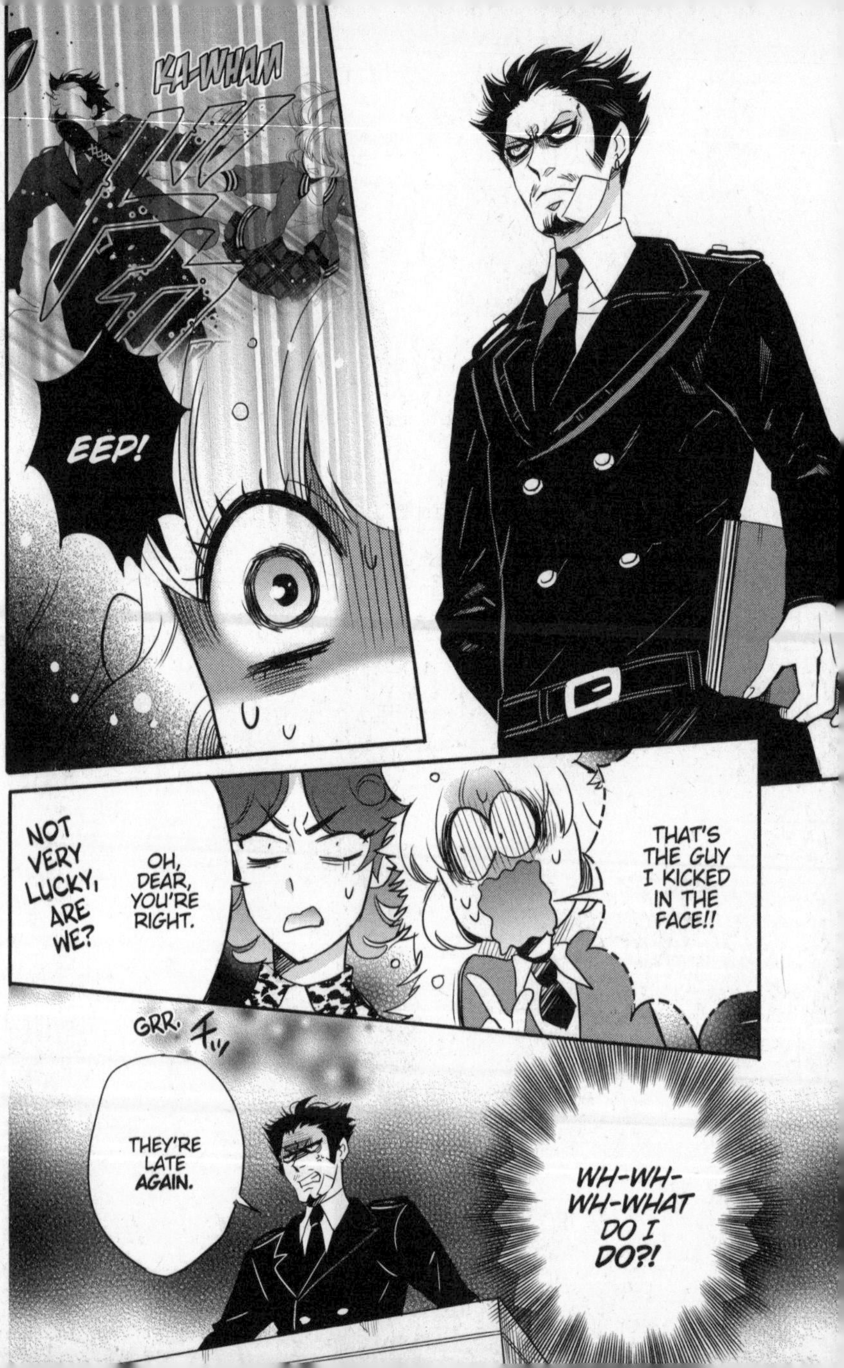
KA-WHAM
EEP!
THAT'S THE GUY I KICKED IN THE FACE!!
OH, DEAR, YOU'RE RIGHT.
NOT VERY LUCKY, ARE WE?
WH-WH-WH-WHAT DO I DO?!
GRR. チッ
THEY'RE LATE AGAIN.

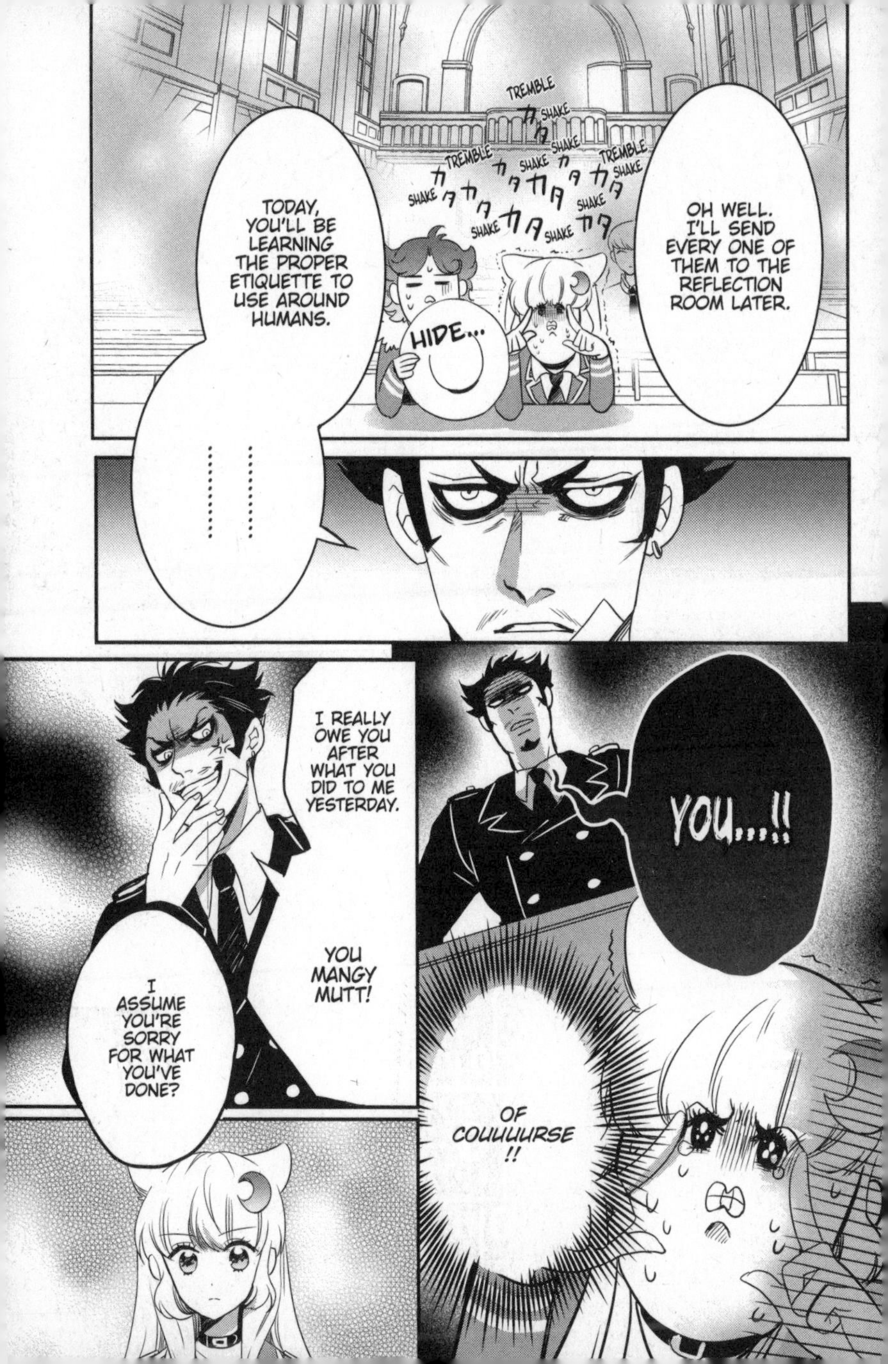
OH WELL. I'LL SEND EVERY ONE OF THEM TO THE REFLECTION ROOM LATER.
TREMBLE SHAKE SHAKE SHAKE TREMBLE TREMBLE SHAKE SHAKE SHAKE SHAKE SHAKE SHAKE SHAKE
TODAY, YOU'LL BE LEARNING THE PROPER ETIQUETTE TO USE AROUND HUMANS.
HIDE...
......
YOU...!!
I REALLY OWE YOU AFTER WHAT YOU DID TO ME YESTERDAY.
YOU MANGY MUTT!
I ASSUME YOU'RE SORRY FOR WHAT YOU'VE DONE?
OF COUUUURSE !!

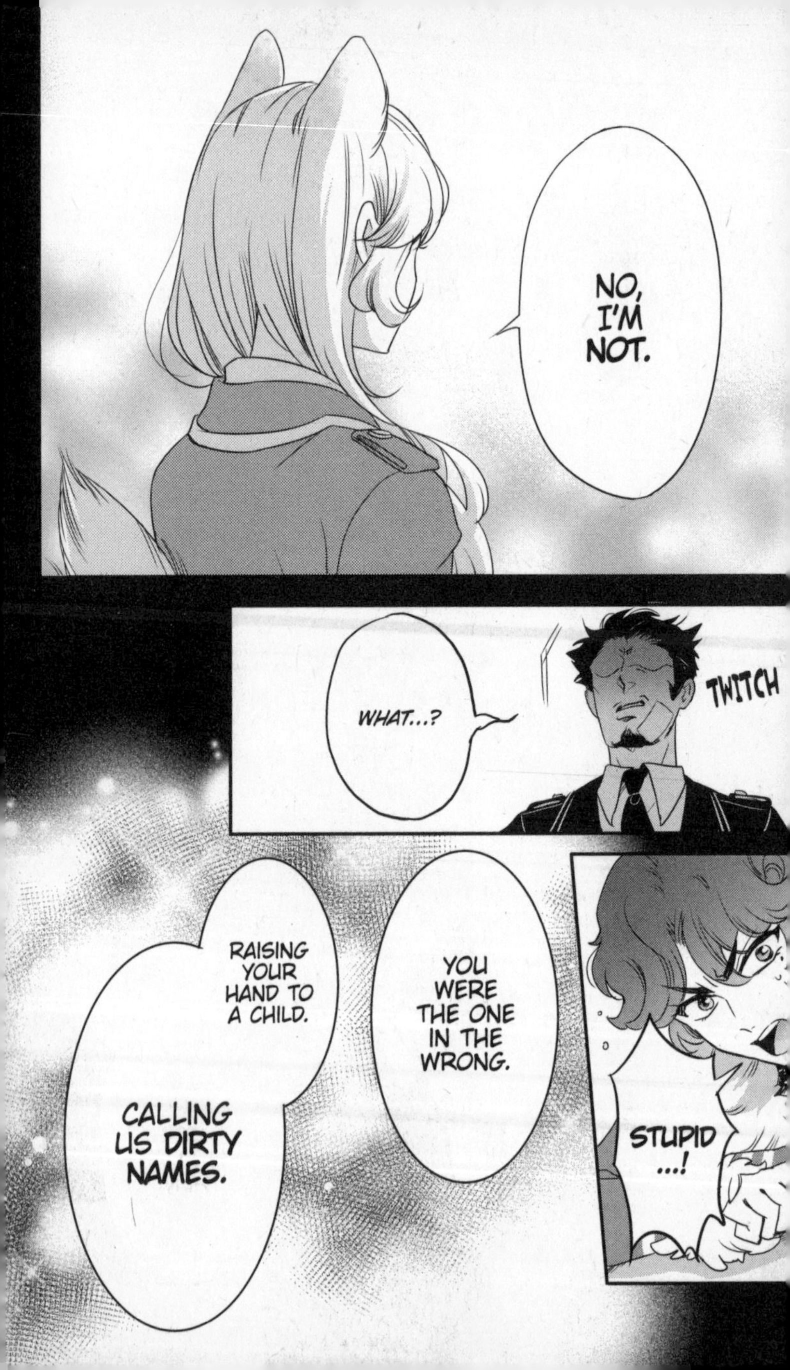
NO, I'M NOT.
TWITCH
WHAT...?
STUPID ...!
YOU WERE THE ONE IN THE WRONG.
RAISING YOUR HAND TO A CHILD.
CALLING US DIRTY NAMES.

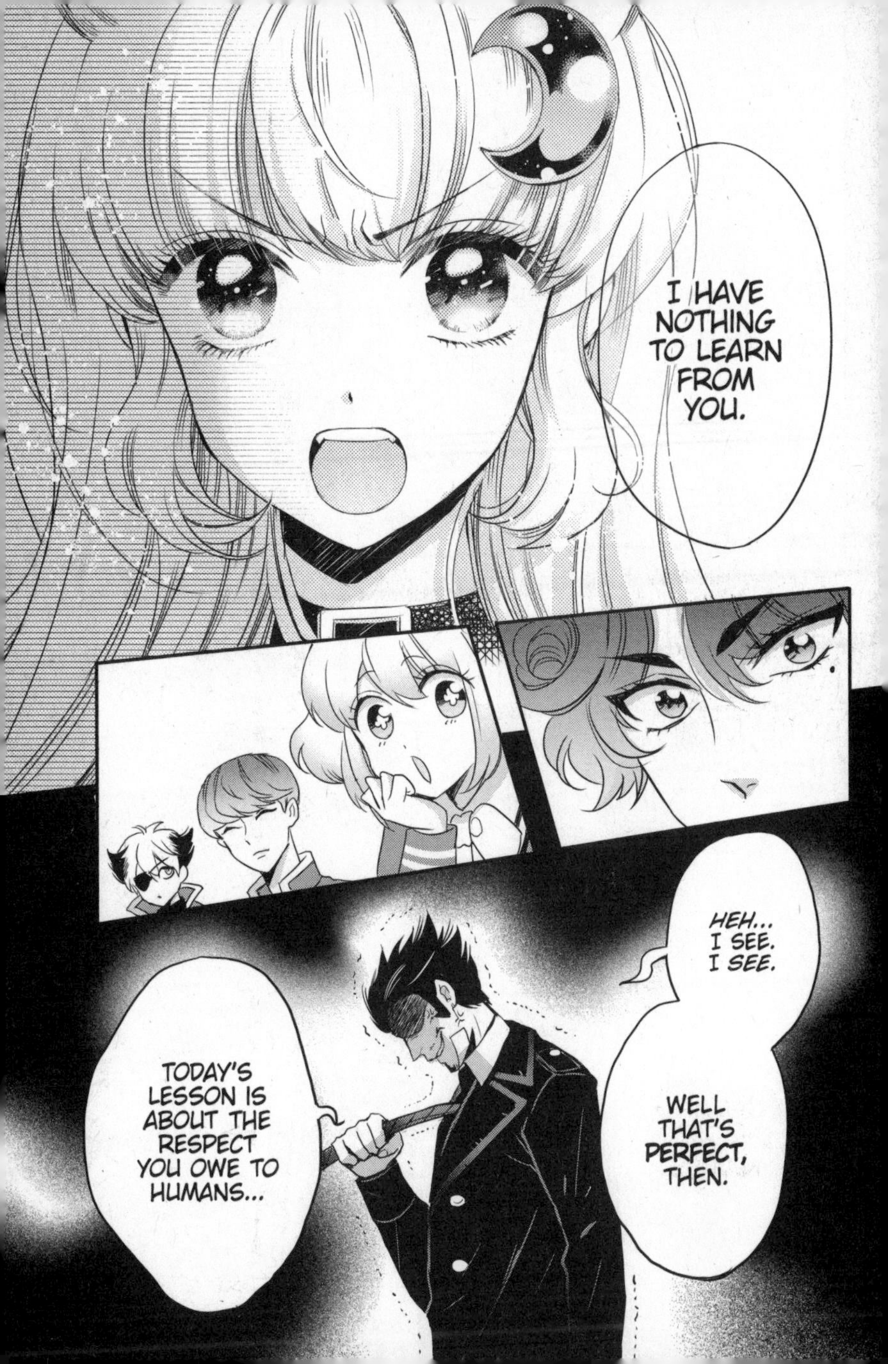
I HAVE NOTHING TO LEARN FROM YOU.
HEH... I SEE. I SEE.
WELL THAT'S PERFECT, THEN.
TODAY'S LESSON IS ABOUT THE RESPECT YOU OWE TO HUMANS...

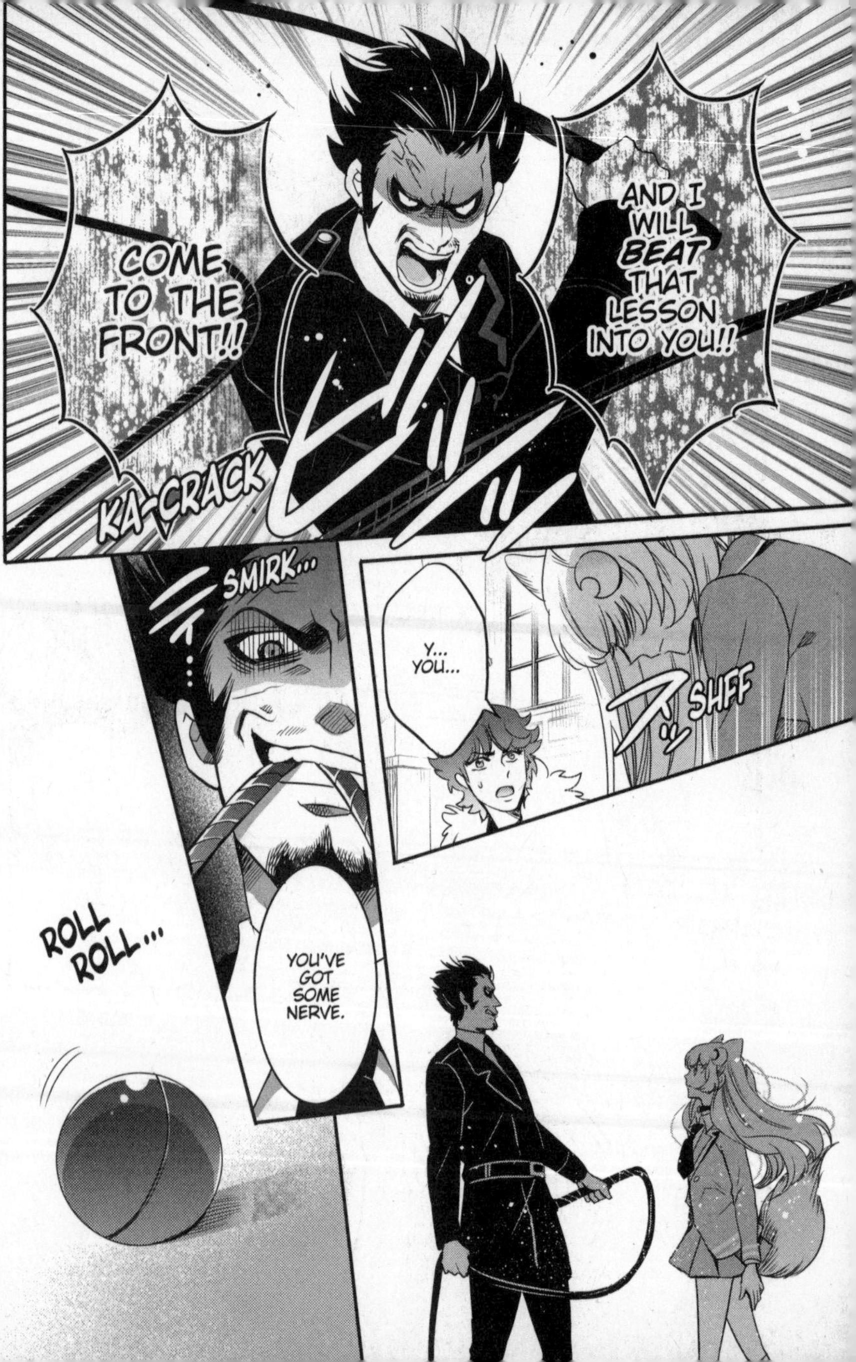
AND I WILL BEAT THAT LESSON INTO YOU!!
COME TO THE FRONT!!
KA-CRACK
SHFF
Y... YOU...
SMIRK...
YOU'VE GOT SOME NERVE.
ROLL ROLL...

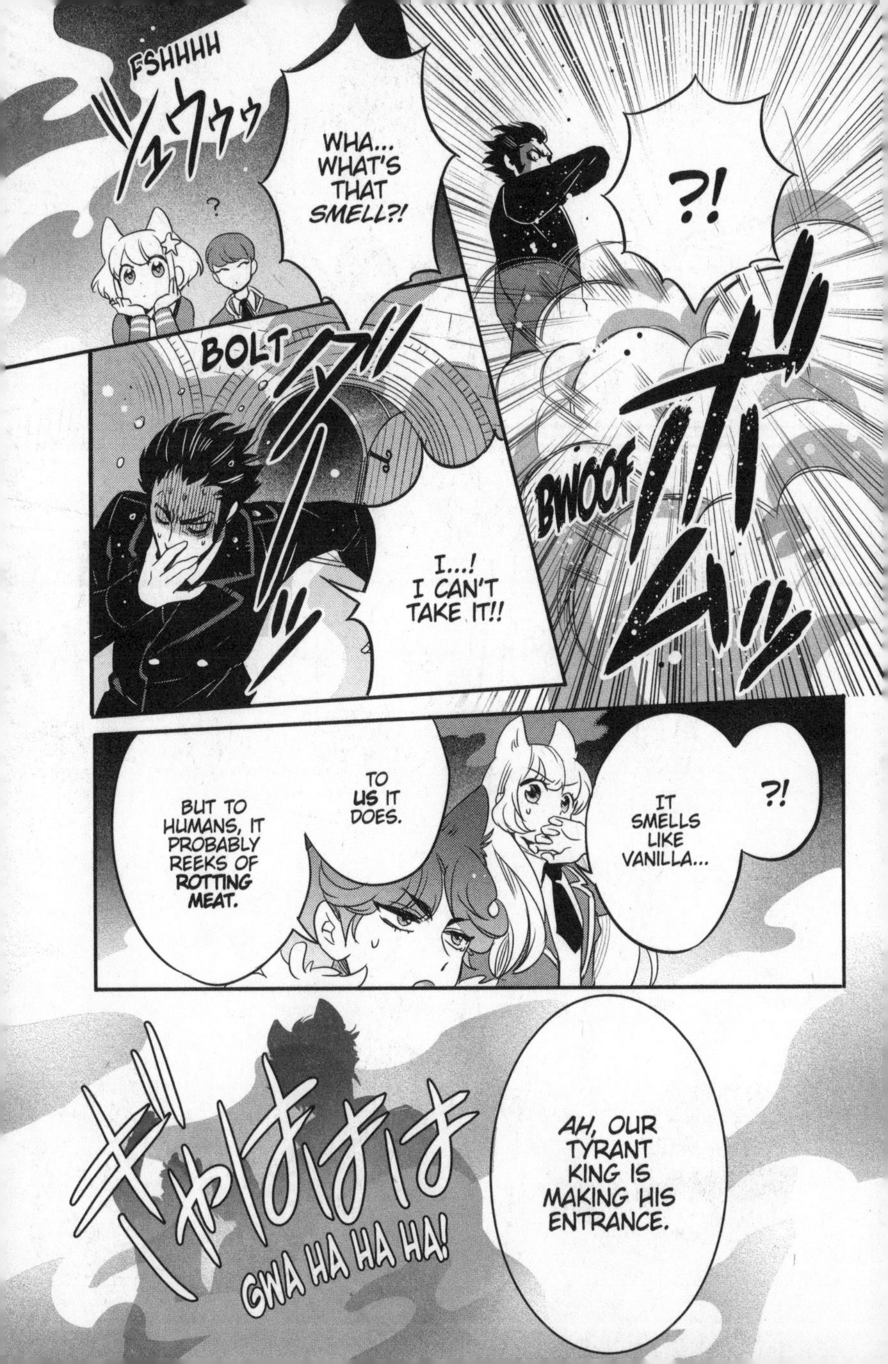
?!
ザムッ
BWOOF
FSHHHH
シュウウゥ
?
WHA... WHAT'S THAT SMELL?!
BOLT
ダッ
I...! I CAN'T TAKE IT!!
?!
IT SMELLS LIKE VANILLA...
TO US IT DOES.
BUT TO HUMANS, IT PROBABLY REEKS OF ROTTING MEAT.
AH, OUR TYRANT KING IS MAKING HIS ENTRANCE.
ぎゃははは
GWA HA HA HA!

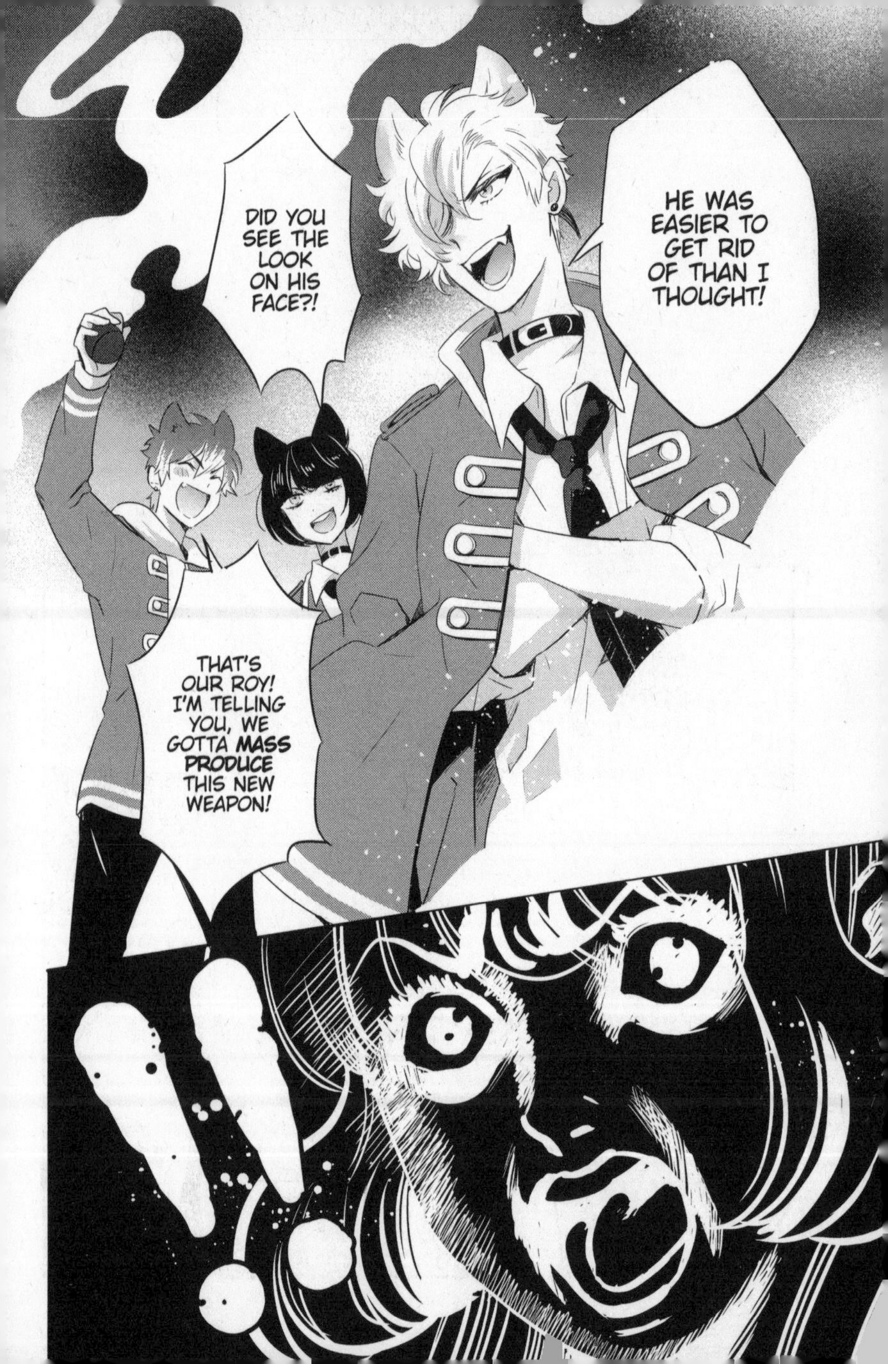
HE WAS EASIER TO GET RID OF THAN I THOUGHT!
DID YOU SEE THE LOOK ON HIS FACE?!
THAT'S OUR ROY! I'M TELLING YOU, WE GOTTA **MASS PRODUCE** THIS NEW WEAPON!

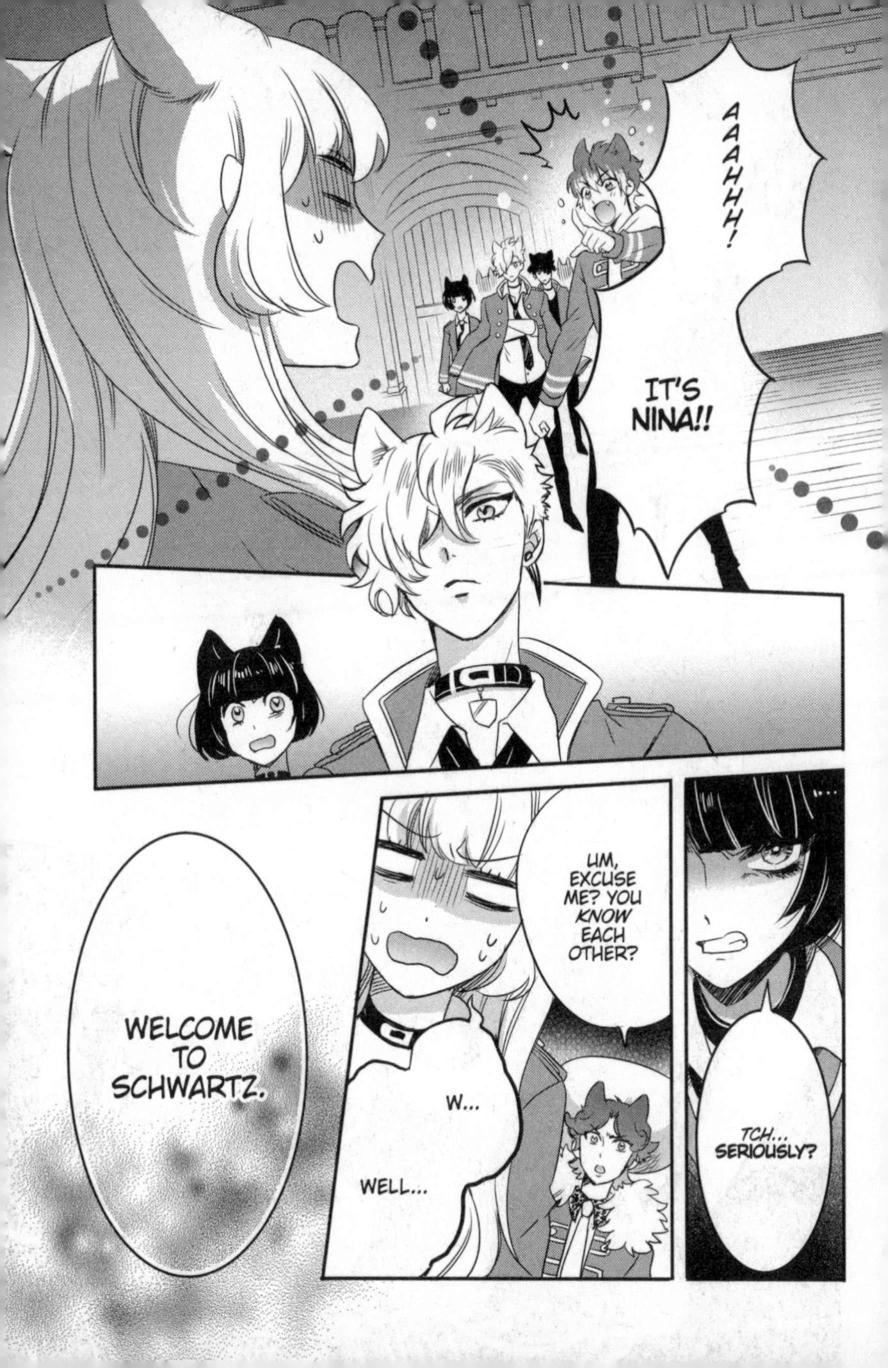
AAAHHH!
IT'S NINA!!
...
TCH... SERIOUSLY?
UM, EXCUSE ME? YOU KNOW EACH OTHER?
W...
WELL...
WELCOME TO SCHWARTZ.

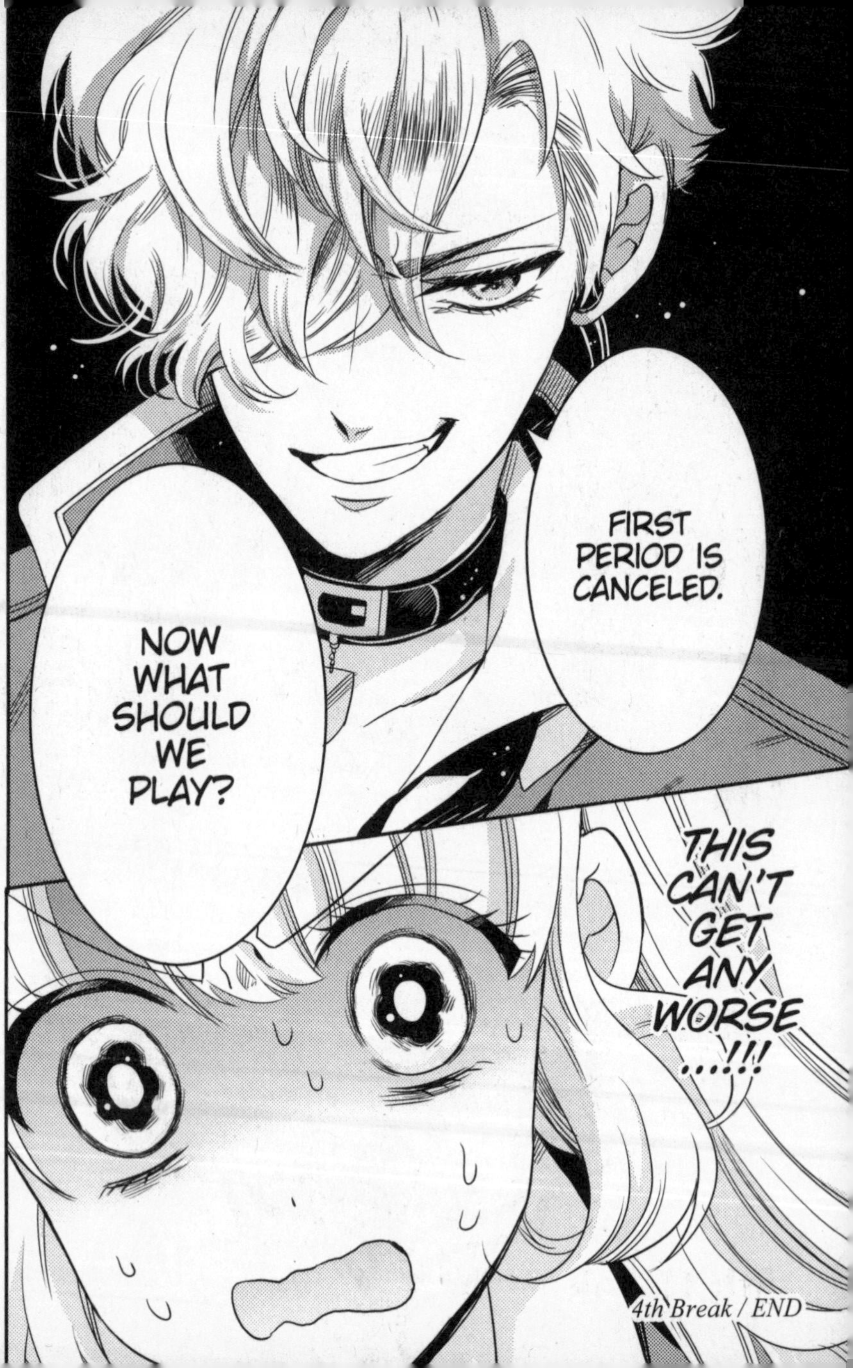
FIRST PERIOD IS CANCELED.
NOW WHAT SHOULD WE PLAY?
THIS CAN'T GET ANY WORSE ...!!!
4th Break / END

5th Break

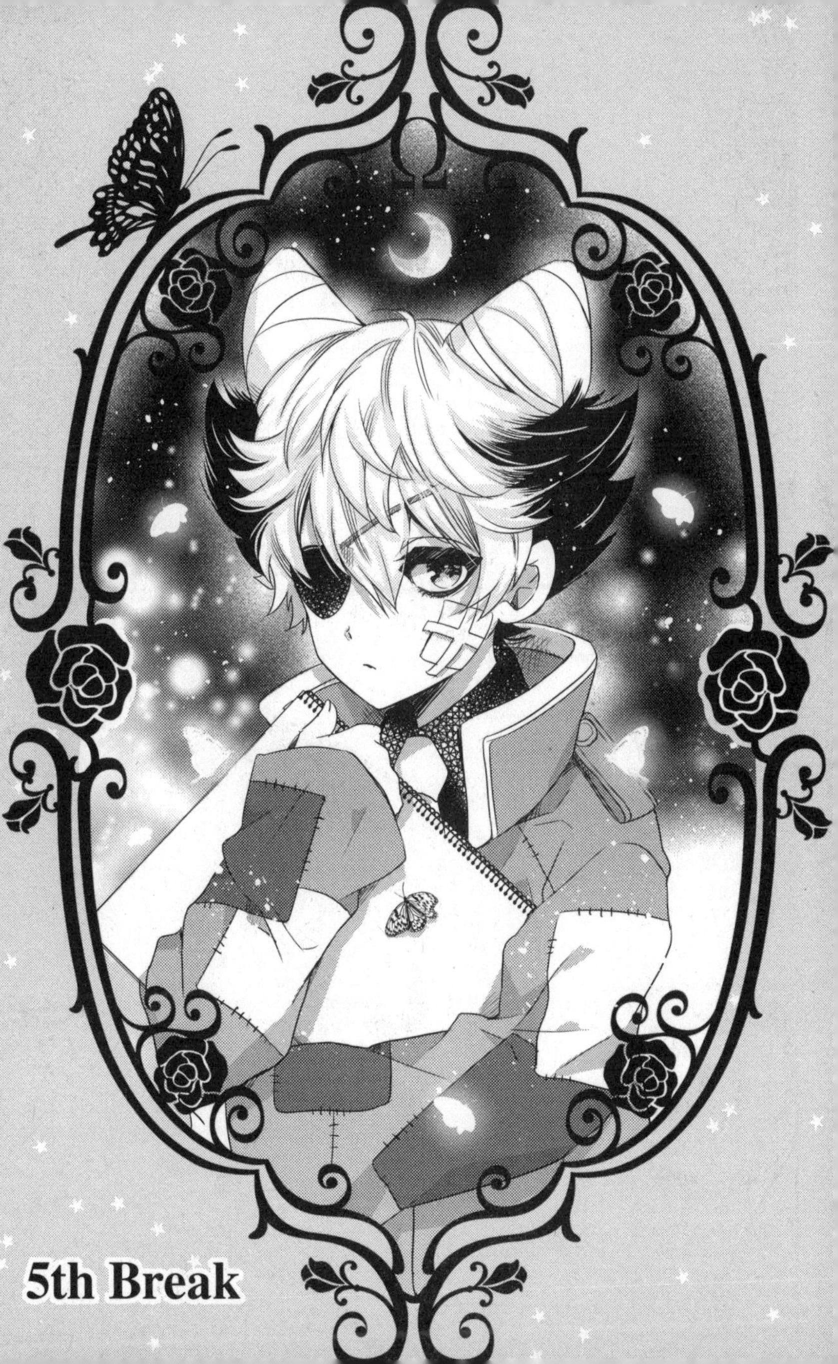

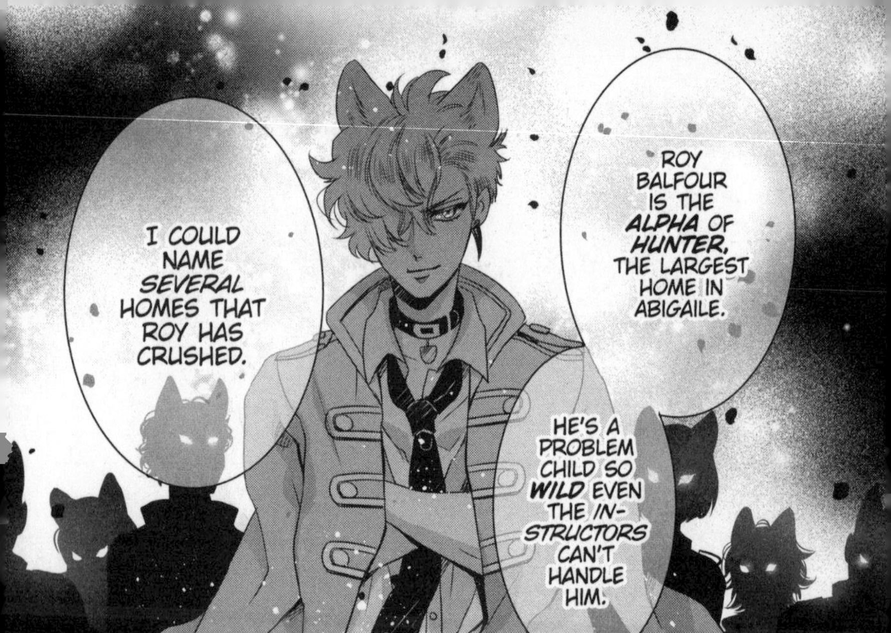
ROY BALFOUR IS THE ALPHA OF HUNTER, THE LARGEST HOME IN ABIGAILE.
HE'S A PROBLEM CHILD SO WILD EVEN THE IN-STRUCTORS CAN'T HANDLE HIM.
I COULD NAME SEVERAL HOMES THAT ROY HAS CRUSHED.

I hope we'll meet again in Volume Two! I'll be waiting to hear what you think! Sometimes I post sketches and manga of the lugas on Twitter (@nakiringo), so check it out if you're interested.

Thank you so much to the team who's always supported me--my editor, the editorial department, and my assistants!

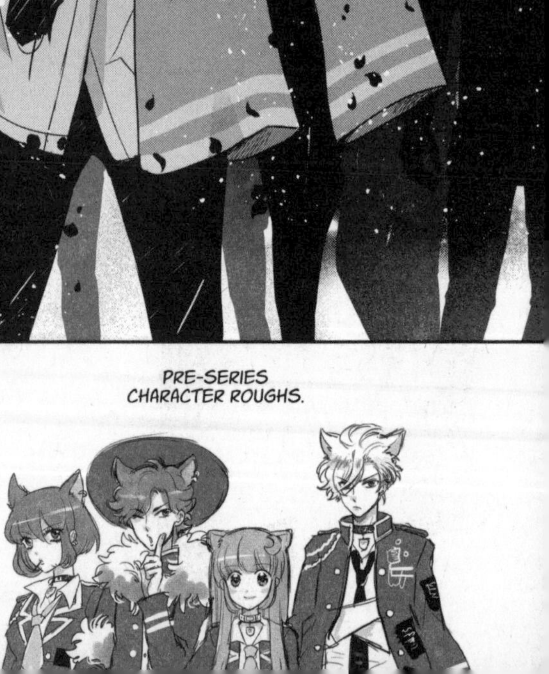

PRE-SERIES CHARACTER ROUGHS.

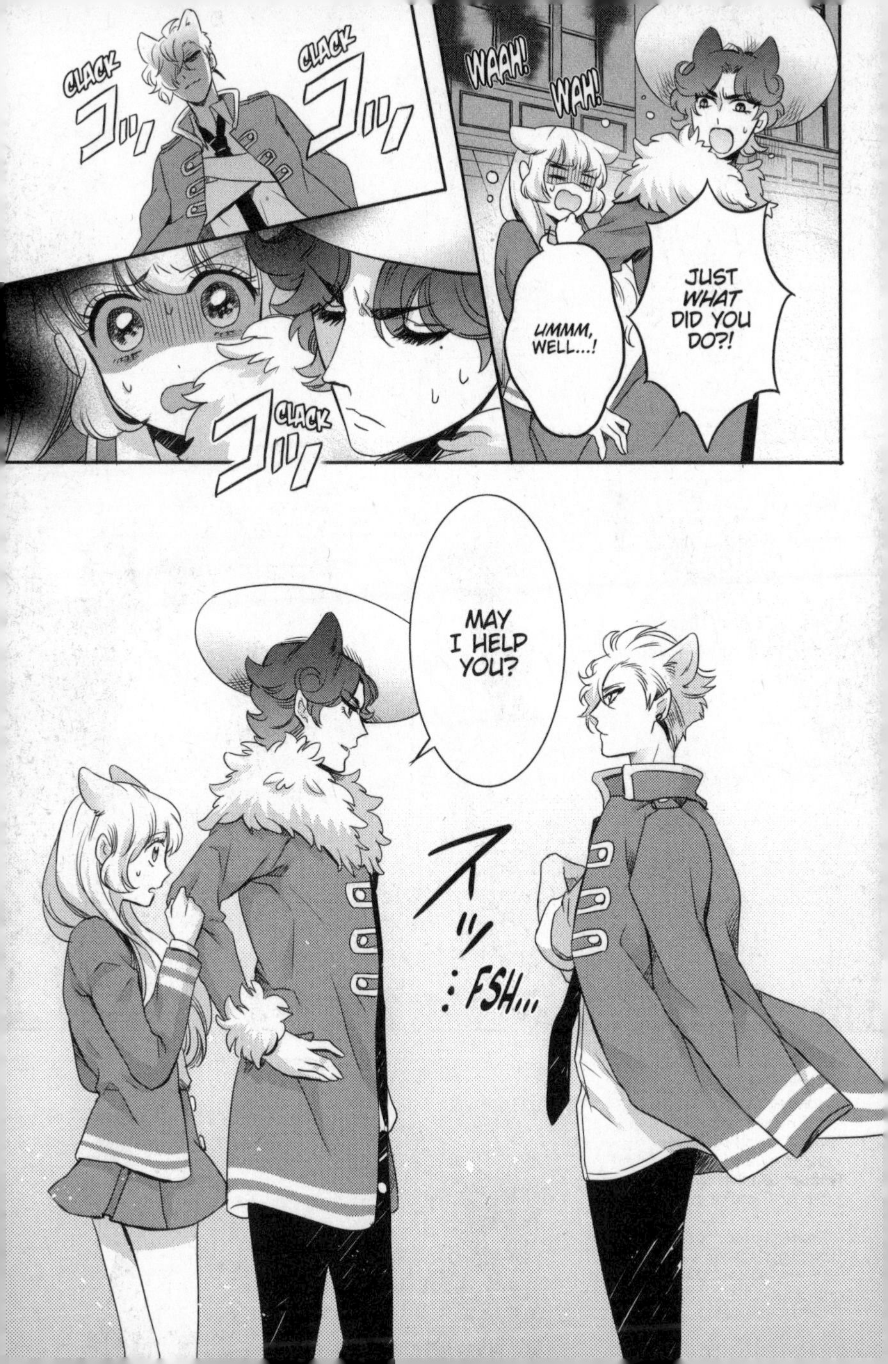
WAAH!
WAH!
JUST WHAT DID YOU DO?!
UMMM, WELL...!
CLACK
CLACK
CLACK
MAY I HELP YOU?
FSH...

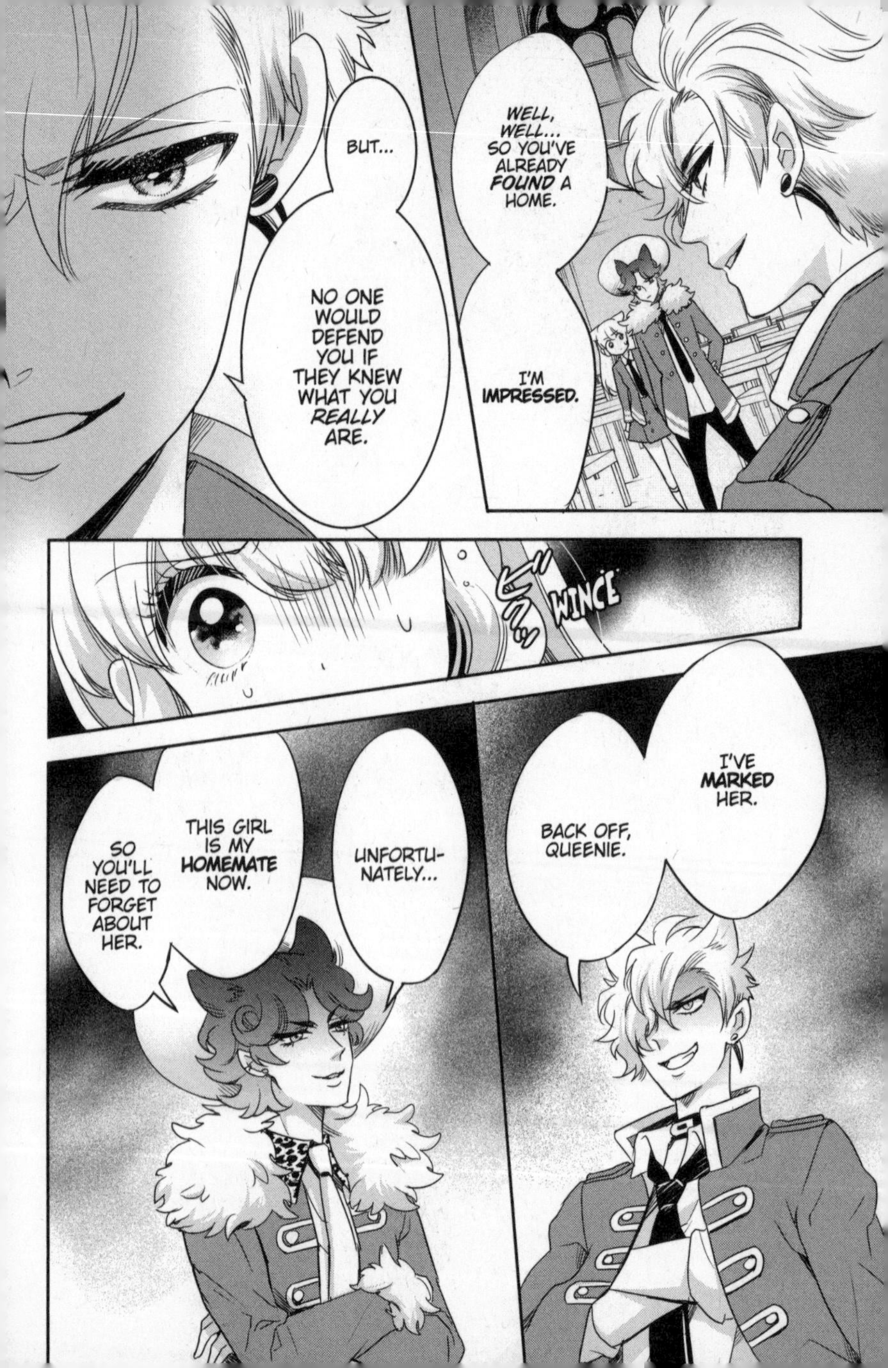
WELL, WELL... SO YOU'VE ALREADY FOUND A HOME.
I'M IMPRESSED.
BUT...
NO ONE WOULD DEFEND YOU IF THEY KNEW WHAT YOU REALLY ARE.
WINCE
I'VE MARKED HER.
BACK OFF, QUEENIE.
UNFORTU-NATELY...
THIS GIRL IS MY HOMEMATE NOW.
SO YOU'LL NEED TO FORGET ABOUT HER.

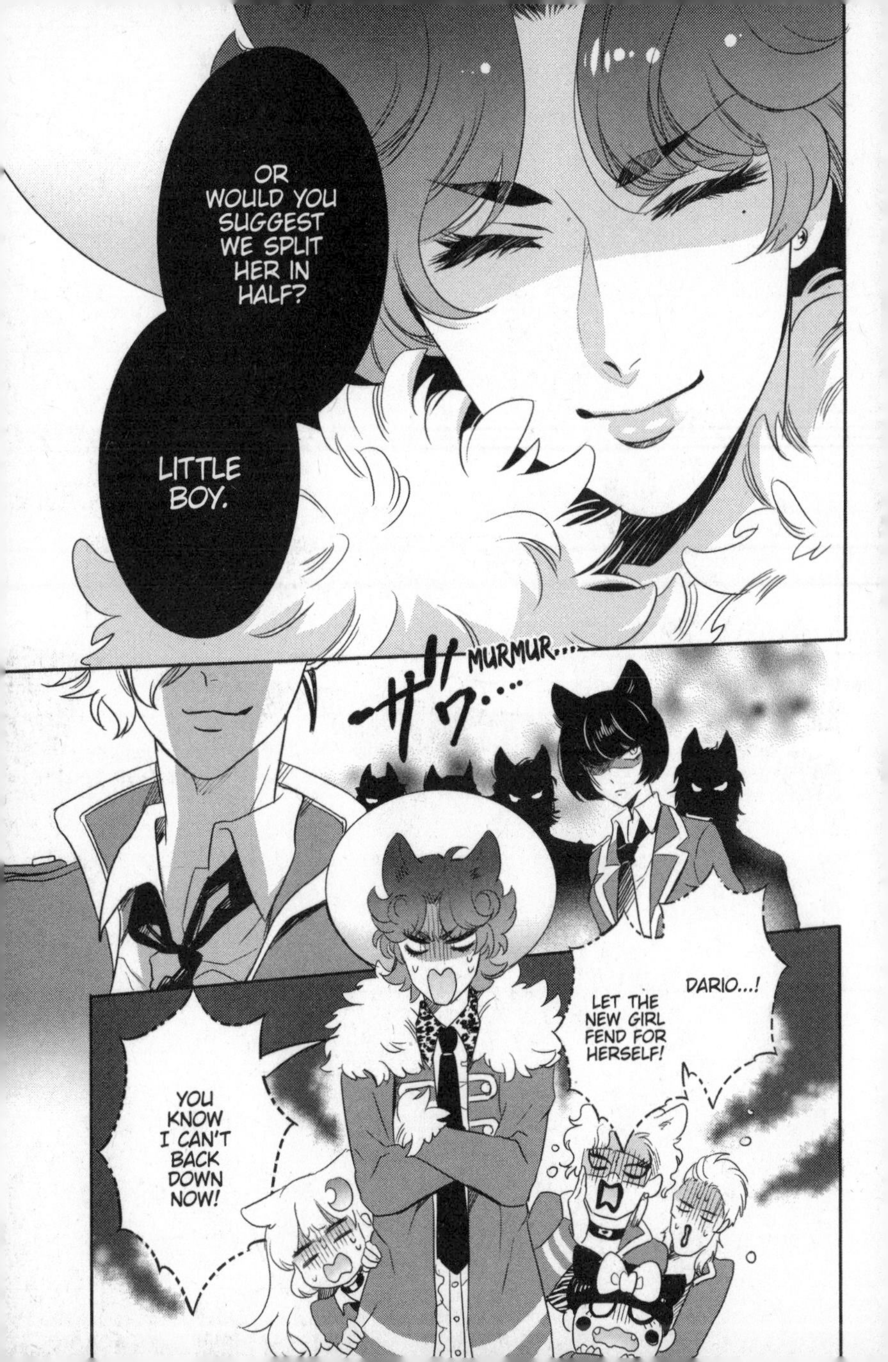
OR WOULD YOU SUGGEST WE SPLIT HER IN HALF?
LITTLE BOY.
MURMUR...
ザワ...
DARIO...!
LET THE NEW GIRL FEND FOR HERSELF!
YOU KNOW I CAN'T BACK DOWN NOW!

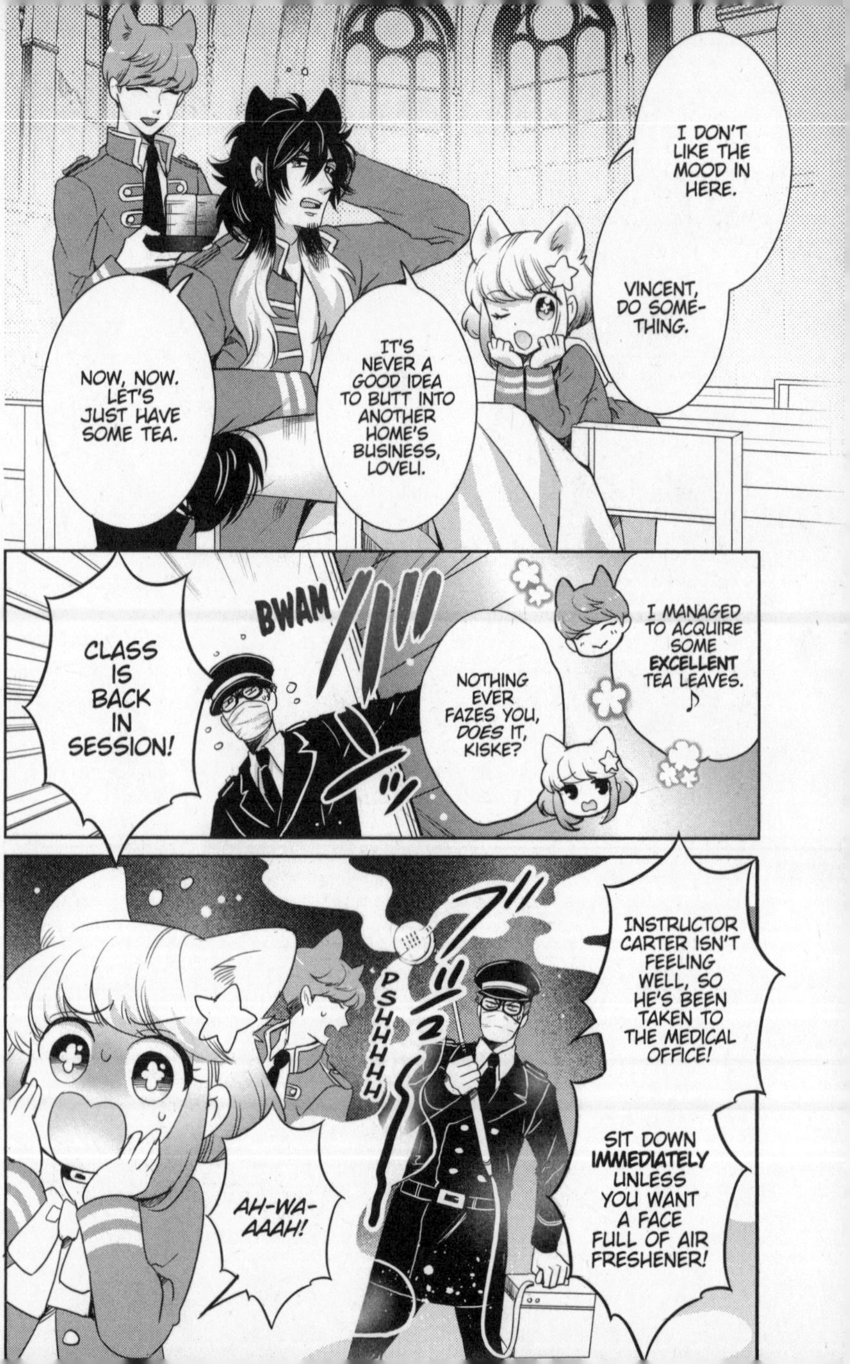
I DON'T LIKE THE MOOD IN HERE.
VINCENT, DO SOME-THING.
IT'S NEVER A GOOD IDEA TO BUTT INTO ANOTHER HOME'S BUSINESS, LOVELI.
NOW, NOW. LET'S JUST HAVE SOME TEA.
I MANAGED TO ACQUIRE SOME **EXCELLENT** TEA LEAVES. ♪
NOTHING EVER FAZES YOU, *DOES* IT, KISKE?
BWAM
CLASS IS BACK IN SESSION!
INSTRUCTOR CARTER ISN'T FEELING WELL, SO HE'S BEEN TAKEN TO THE MEDICAL OFFICE!
SIT DOWN **IMMEDIATELY** UNLESS YOU WANT A FACE FULL OF AIR FRESHENER!
PSHHHHH
AH-WA-AAAH!

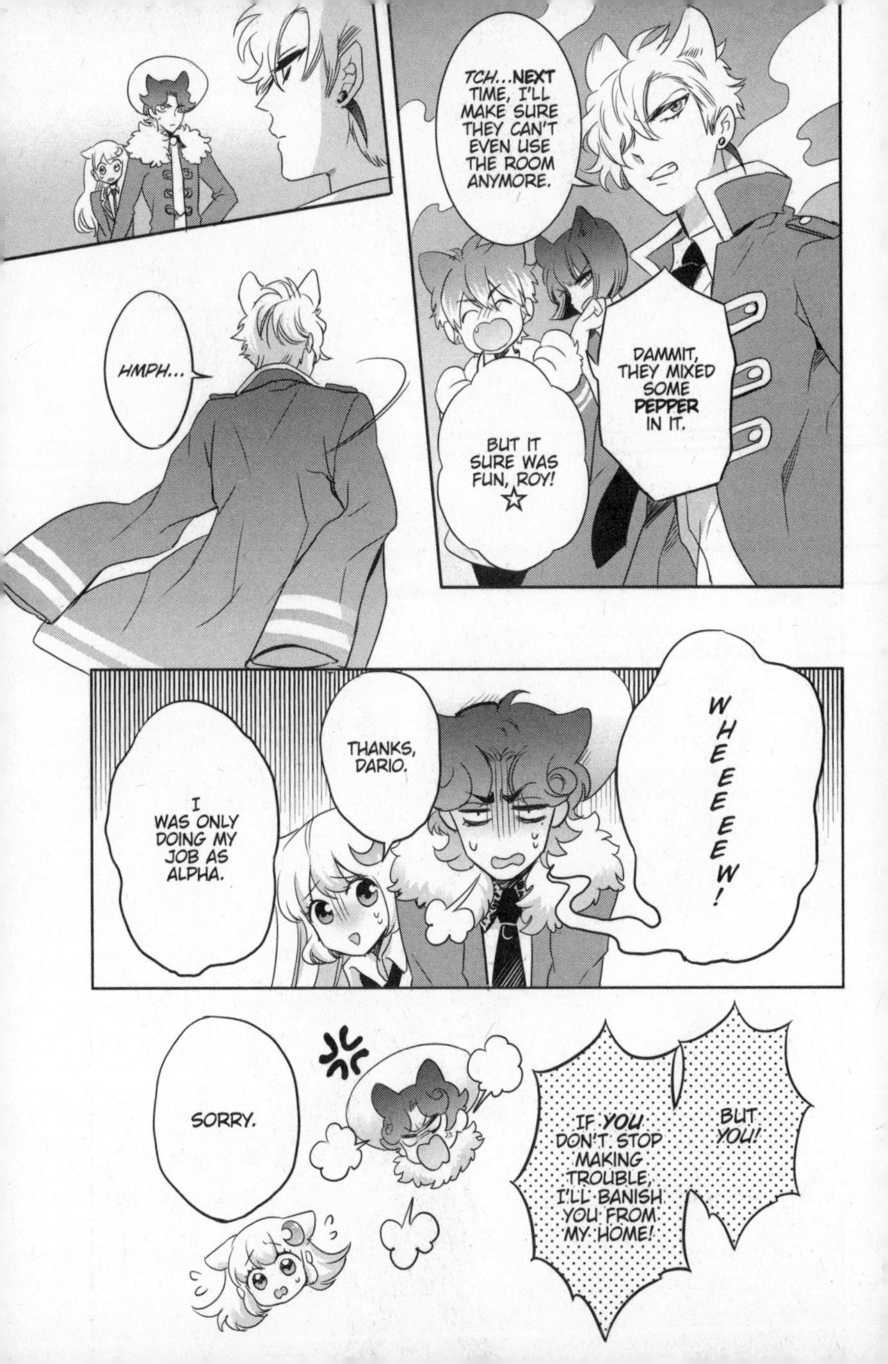
TCH...NEXT TIME, I'LL MAKE SURE THEY CAN'T EVEN USE THE ROOM ANYMORE.
DAMMIT, THEY MIXED SOME PEPPER IN IT.
BUT IT SURE WAS FUN, ROY! ☆
HMPH...
WHEEEEEEW!
THANKS, DARIO.
I WAS ONLY DOING MY JOB AS ALPHA.
BUT YOU!
IF YOU DON'T STOP MAKING TROUBLE, I'LL BANISH YOU FROM MY HOME!
SORRY.

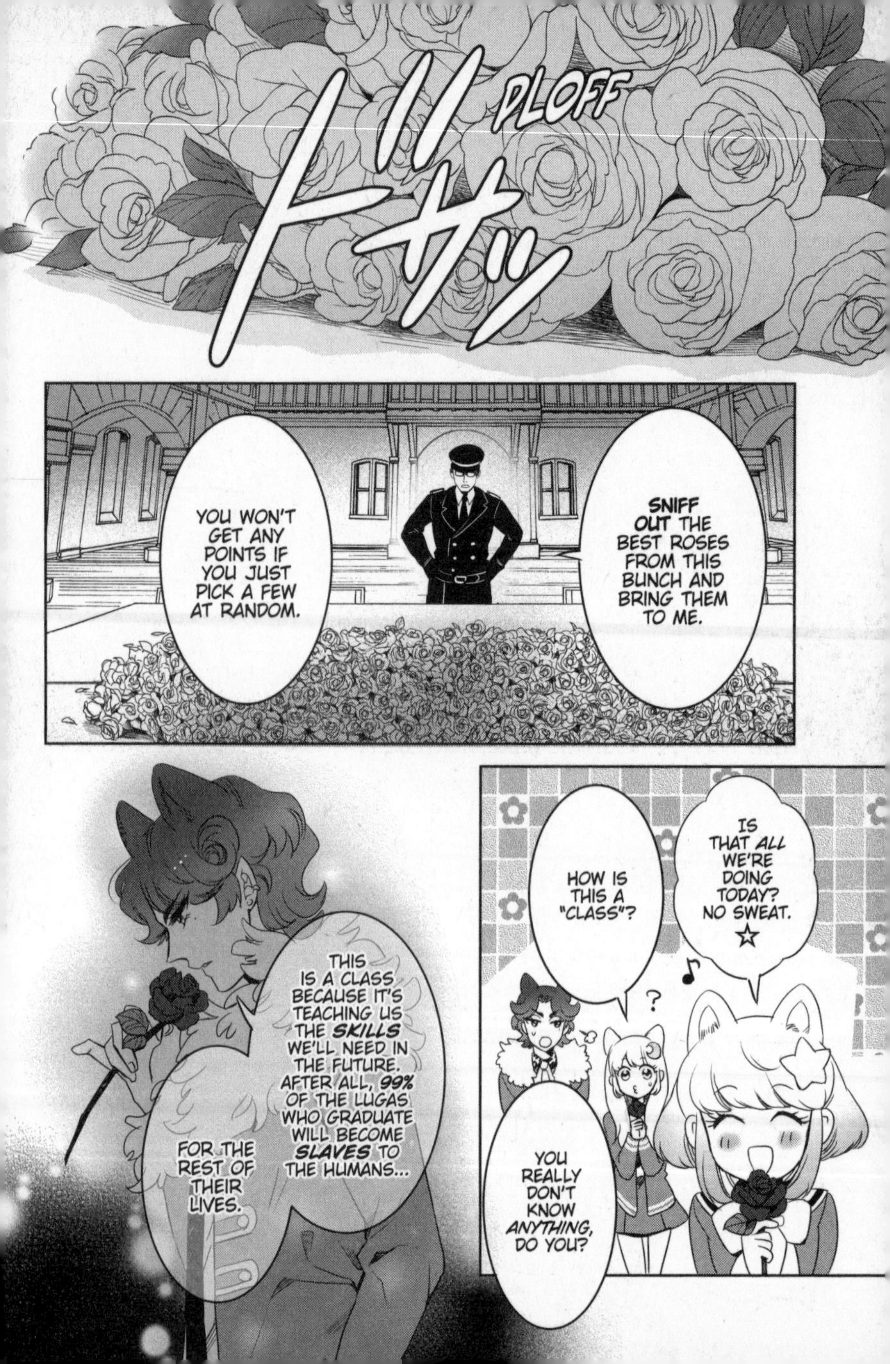
ドサッ
PLOFF
SNIFF OUT THE BEST ROSES FROM THIS BUNCH AND BRING THEM TO ME.
YOU WON'T GET ANY POINTS IF YOU JUST PICK A FEW AT RANDOM.
IS THAT ALL WE'RE DOING TODAY? NO SWEAT. ☆
HOW IS THIS A "CLASS"?
YOU REALLY DON'T KNOW ANYTHING, DO YOU?
THIS IS A CLASS BECAUSE IT'S TEACHING US THE SKILLS WE'LL NEED IN THE FUTURE. AFTER ALL, 99% OF THE LUGAS WHO GRADUATE WILL BECOME SLAVES TO THE HUMANS...
FOR THE REST OF THEIR LIVES.

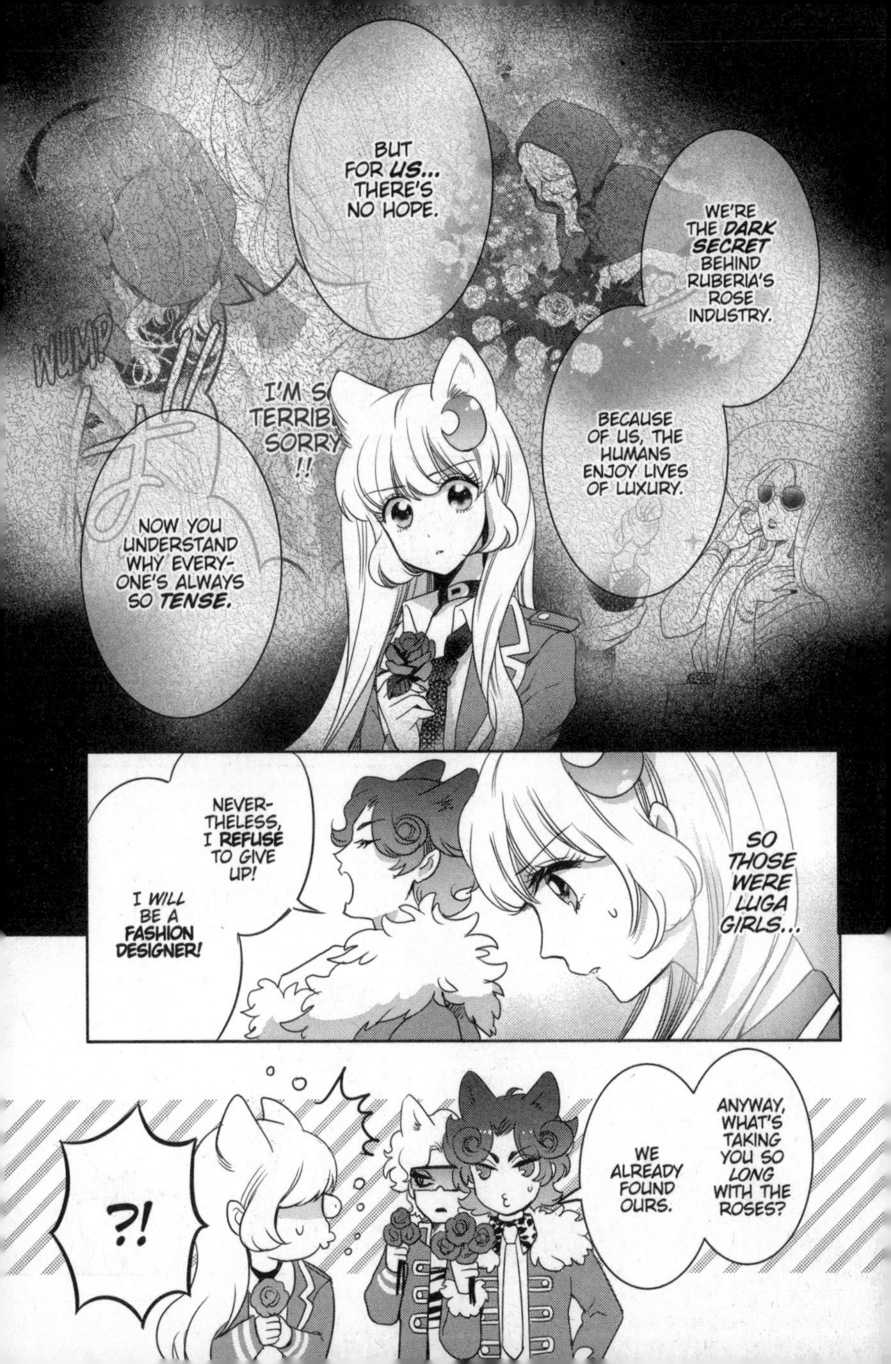
WE'RE THE DARK SECRET BEHIND RUBERIA'S ROSE INDUSTRY.
BECAUSE OF US, THE HUMANS ENJOY LIVES OF LUXURY.
BUT FOR US... THERE'S NO HOPE.
I'M S TERRIBL SORRY !!
WUMP
NOW YOU UNDERSTAND WHY EVERY-ONE'S ALWAYS SO TENSE.
SO THOSE WERE LUGA GIRLS...
NEVER-THELESS, I REFUSE TO GIVE UP!
I WILL BE A FASHION DESIGNER!
ANYWAY, WHAT'S TAKING YOU SO LONG WITH THE ROSES?
WE ALREADY FOUND OURS.
?!

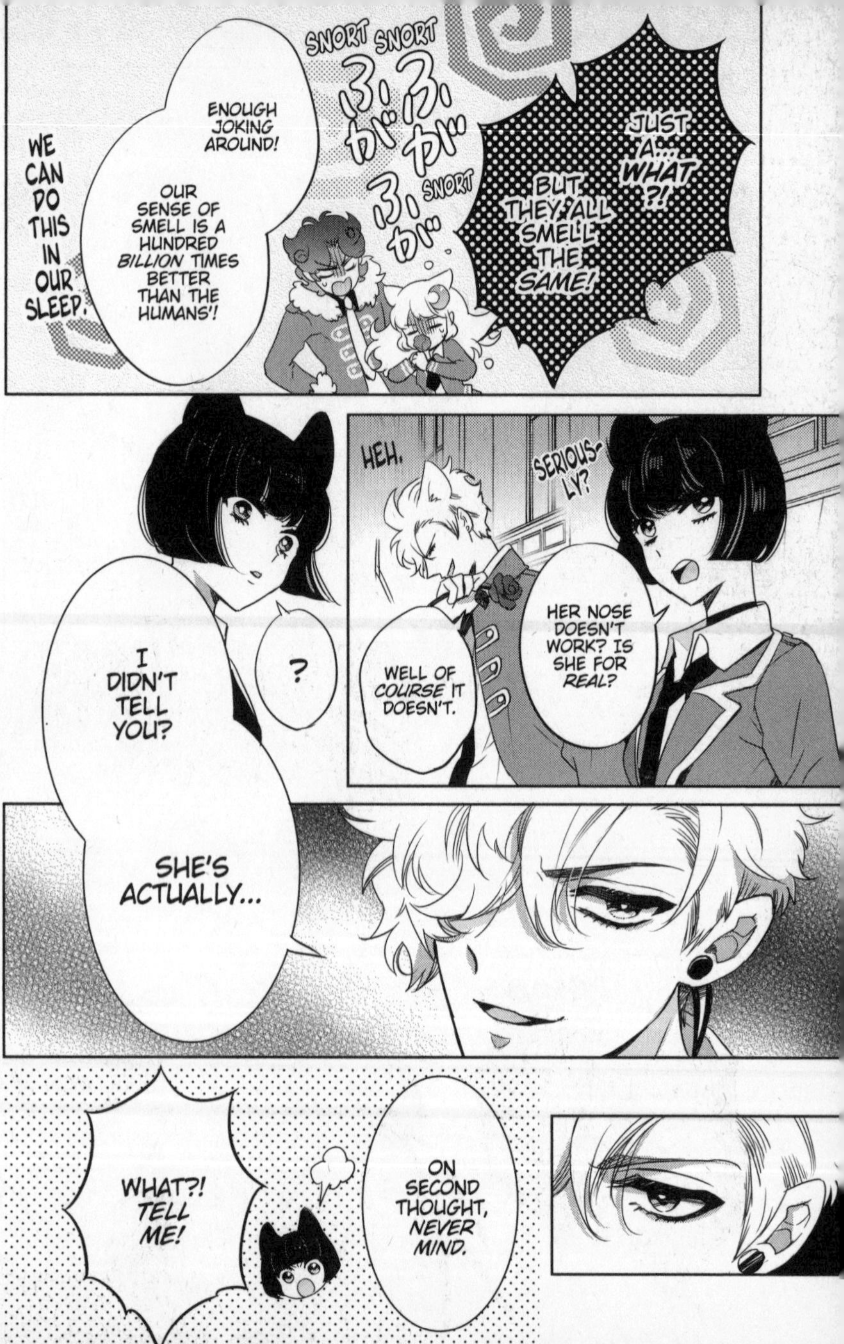
JUST A... WHAT?!
BUT THEY ALL SMELL THE SAME!
SNORT SNORT
ふが ふが
SNORT
ふが
ENOUGH JOKING AROUND!
OUR SENSE OF SMELL IS A HUNDRED *BILLION* TIMES BETTER THAN THE HUMANS'!
WE CAN DO THIS IN OUR SLEEP.
SERIOUS-LY?
HER NOSE DOESN'T WORK? IS SHE FOR *REAL*?
HEH.
WELL OF *COURSE* IT DOESN'T.
?
I DIDN'T TELL YOU?
SHE'S ACTUALLY...
ON SECOND THOUGHT, *NEVER MIND.*
WHAT?! *TELL ME!*

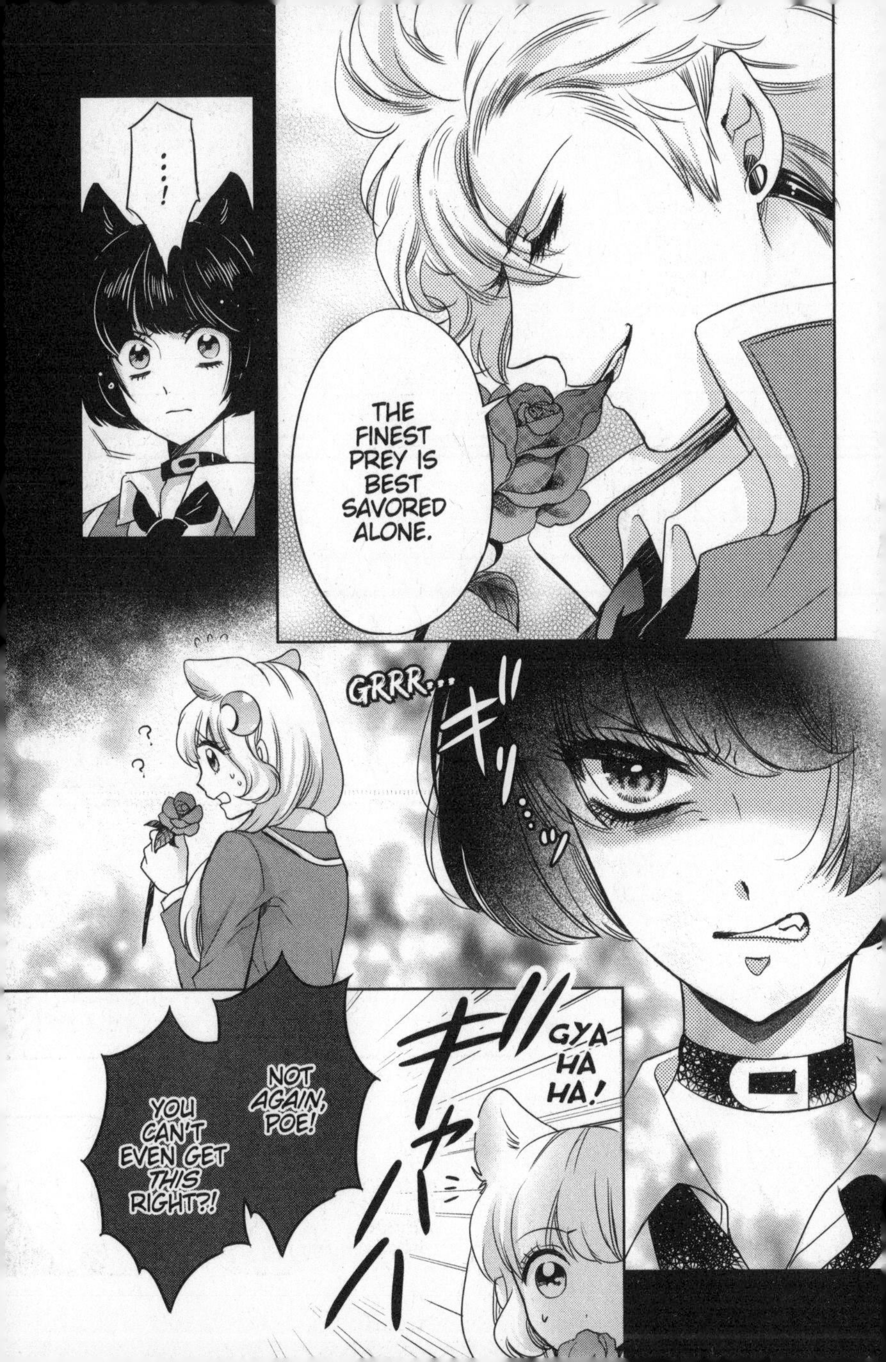
THE FINEST PREY IS BEST SAVORED ALONE.
...!
GRRR...
...!
??
GYA HA HA HA!
NOT AGAIN, POE!
YOU CAN'T EVEN GET THIS RIGHT?!

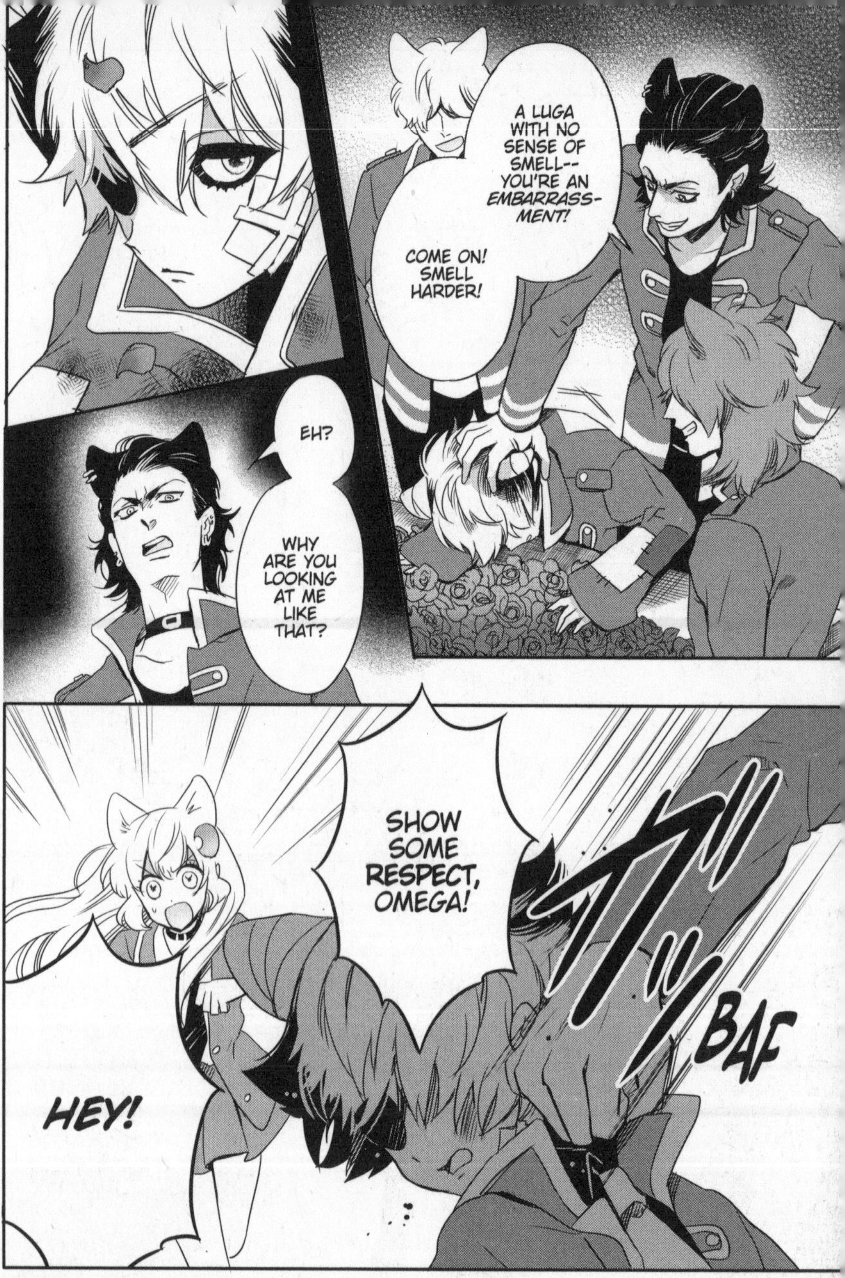
A LUGA WITH NO SENSE OF SMELL-- YOU'RE AN EMBARRASS-MENT!
COME ON! SMELL HARDER!
EH?
WHY ARE YOU LOOKING AT ME LIKE THAT?
SHOW SOME RESPECT, OMEGA!
BAF
HEY!

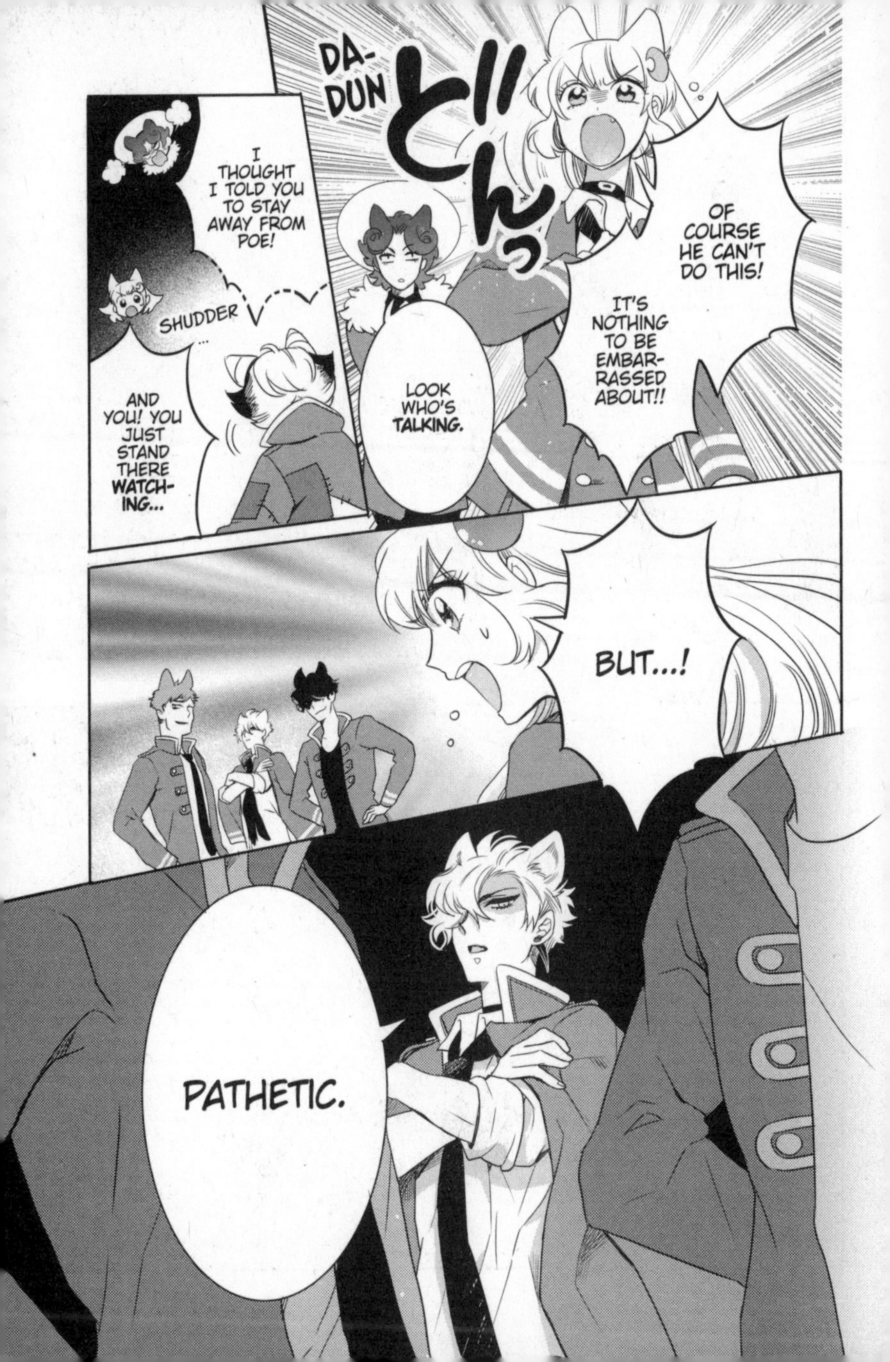
DA-DUN
とんっ
OF COURSE HE CAN'T DO THIS!
IT'S NOTHING TO BE EMBARRASSED ABOUT!!
LOOK WHO'S TALKING.
I THOUGHT I TOLD YOU TO STAY AWAY FROM POE!
SHUDDER...
AND YOU! YOU JUST STAND THERE WATCHING...
BUT...!
PATHETIC.

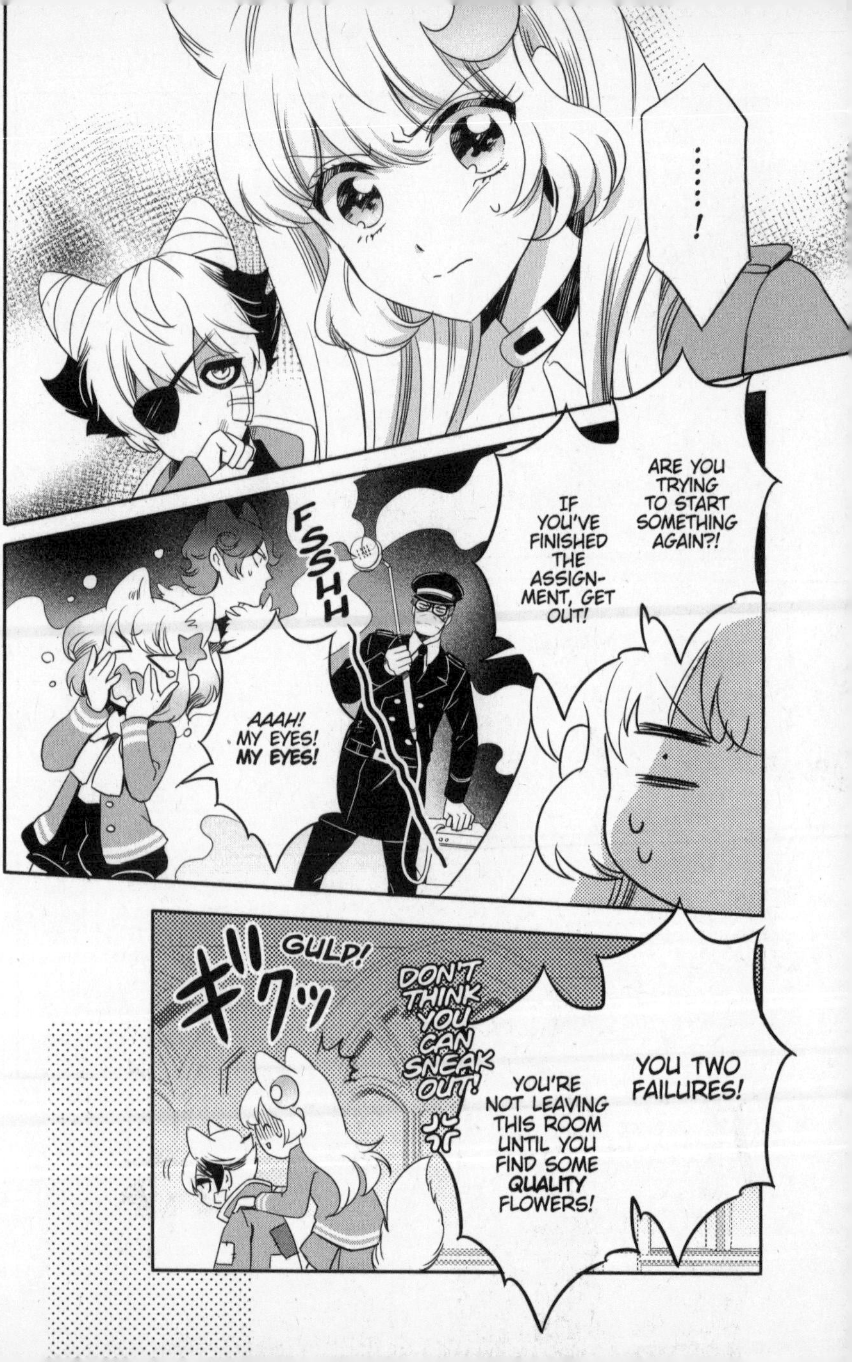
……!
ARE YOU TRYING TO START SOMETHING AGAIN?!
IF YOU'VE FINISHED THE ASSIGNMENT, GET OUT!
FSSHH
AAAH! MY EYES! MY EYES!
YOU TWO FAILURES!
YOU'RE NOT LEAVING THIS ROOM UNTIL YOU FIND SOME QUALITY FLOWERS!
DON'T THINK YOU CAN SNEAK OUT!
GULP!
ギクッ

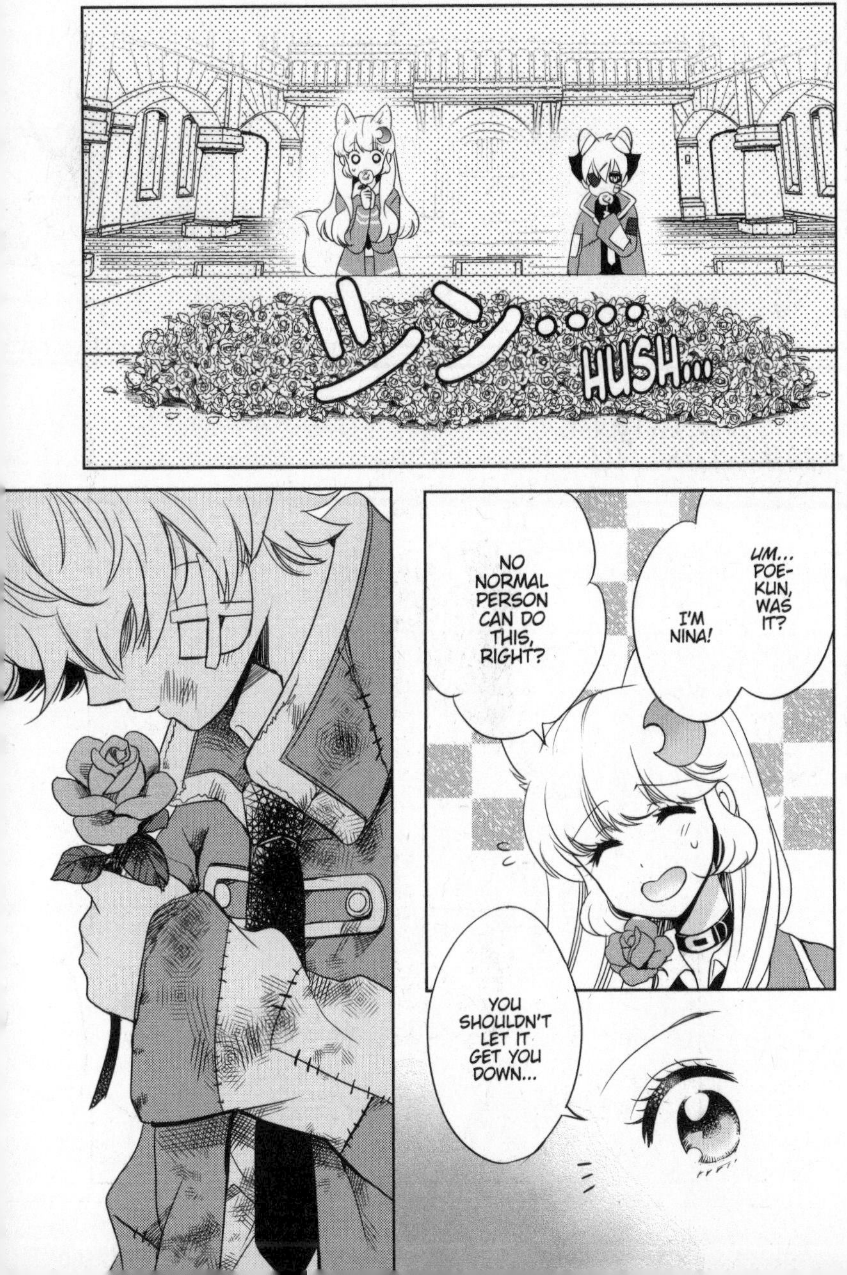
HUSH...
UM... POE-KUN, WAS IT?
I'M NINA!
NO NORMAL PERSON CAN DO THIS, RIGHT?
YOU SHOULDN'T LET IT GET YOU DOWN...

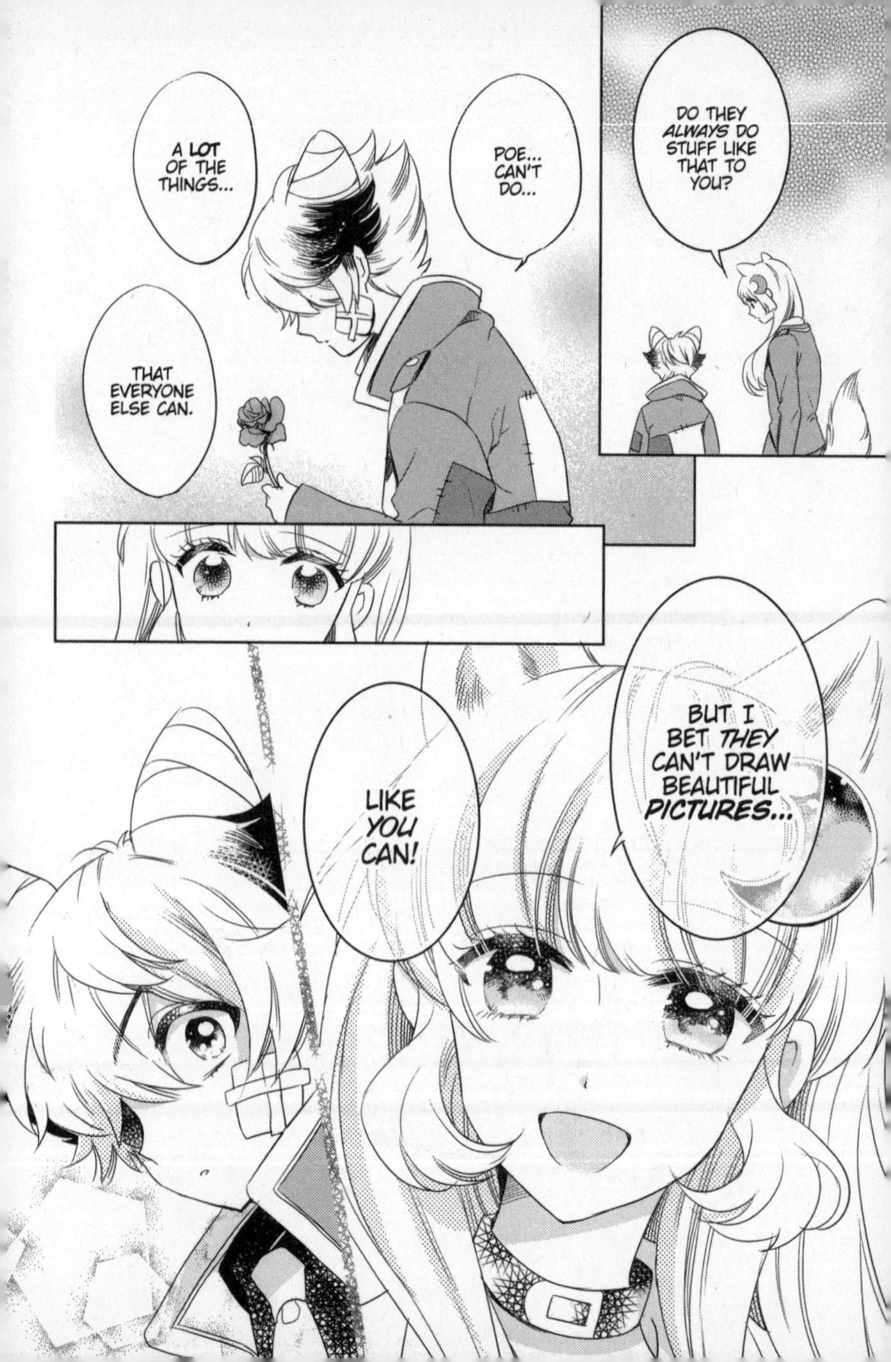
DO THEY *ALWAYS* DO STUFF LIKE THAT TO YOU?
POE... CAN'T DO...
A LOT OF THE THINGS...
THAT EVERYONE ELSE CAN.
BUT I BET *THEY* CAN'T DRAW BEAUTIFUL ***PICTURES...***
LIKE *YOU* CAN!

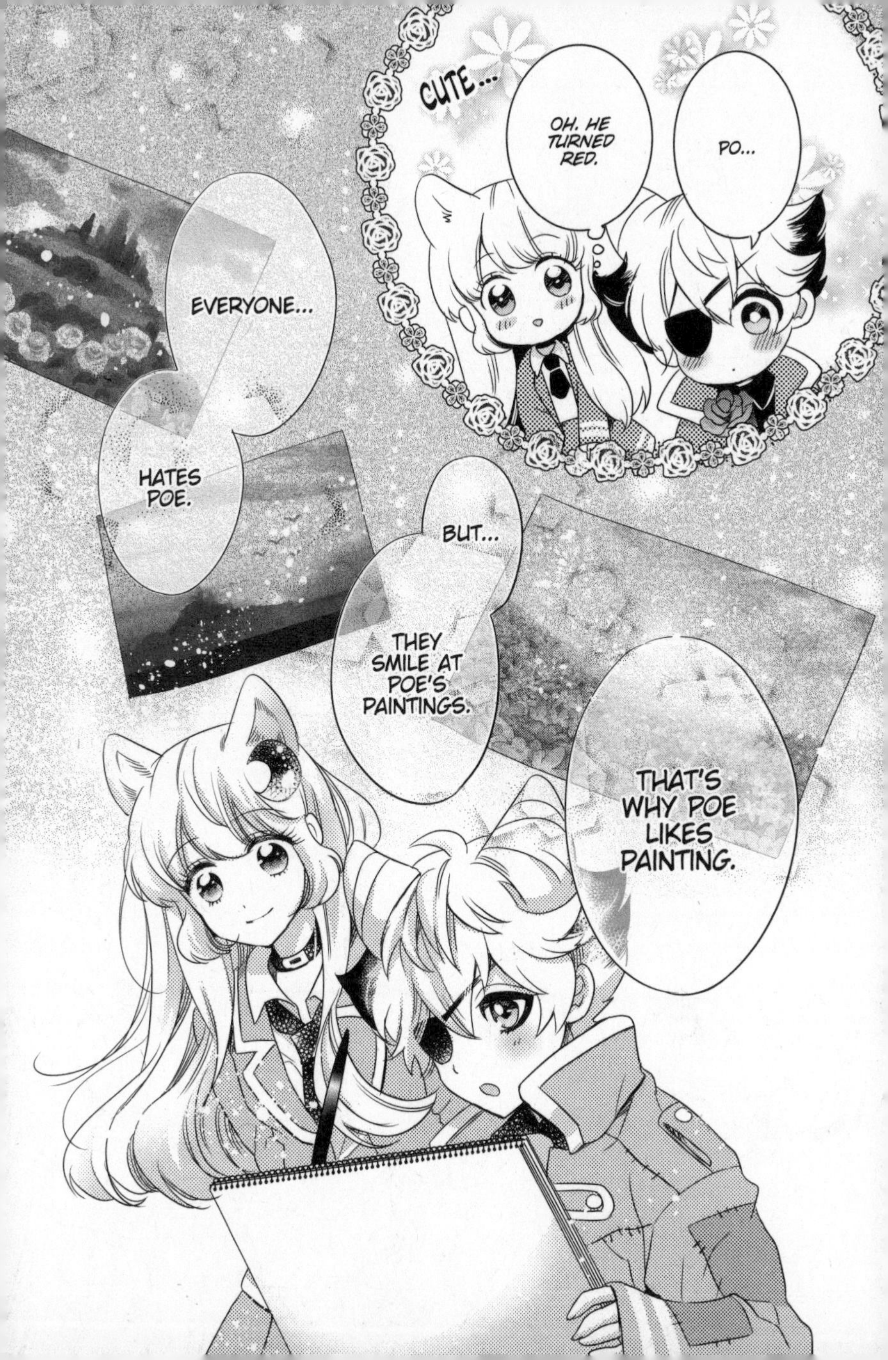
PO...
OH. HE TURNED RED.
CUTE...
EVERYONE...
HATES POE.
BUT...
THEY SMILE AT POE'S PAINTINGS.
THAT'S WHY POE LIKES PAINTING.

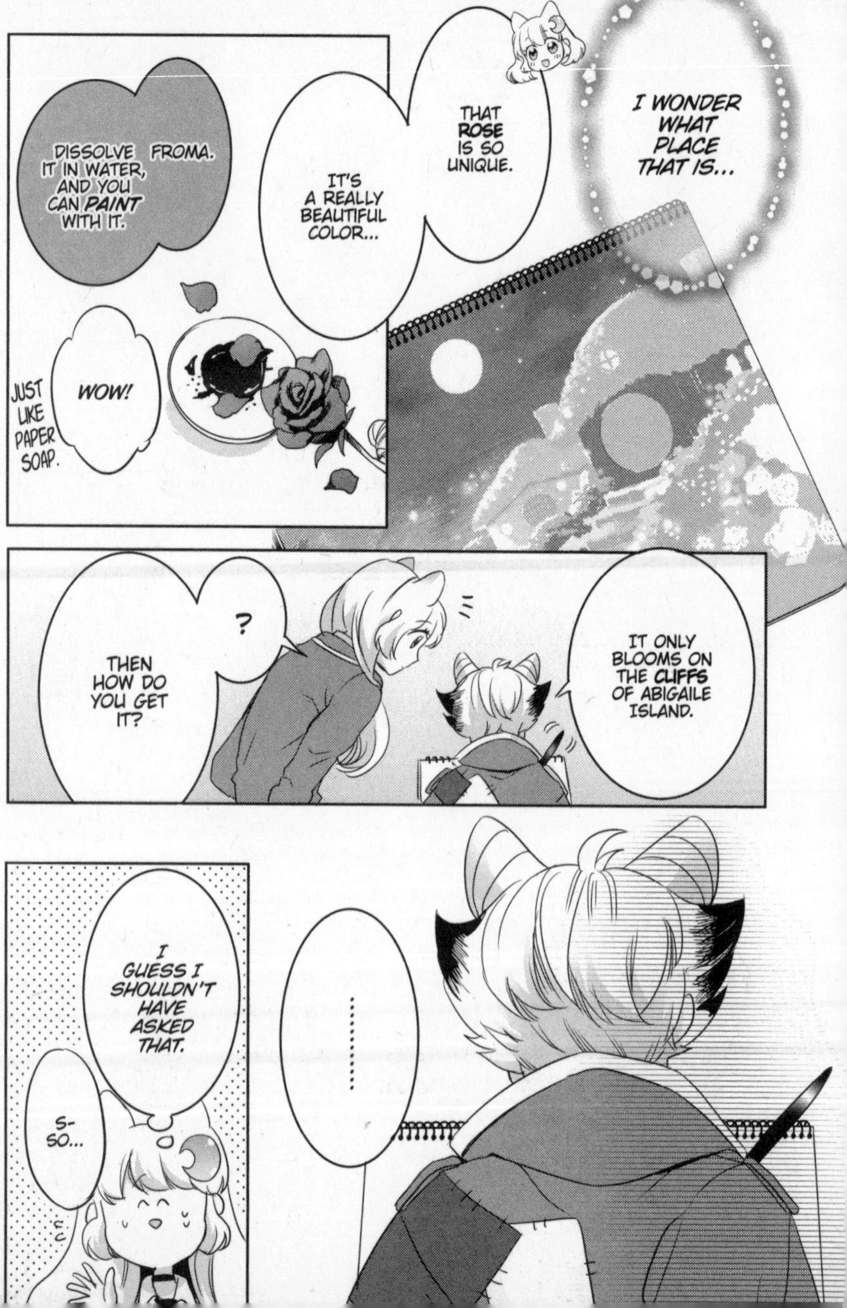
I WONDER WHAT PLACE THAT IS...
THAT ROSE IS SO UNIQUE.
IT'S A REALLY BEAUTIFUL COLOR...
FROMA.
DISSOLVE IT IN WATER, AND YOU CAN PAINT WITH IT.
WOW!
JUST LIKE PAPER SOAP.
IT ONLY BLOOMS ON THE CLIFFS OF ABIGAILE ISLAND.
?
THEN HOW DO YOU GET IT?
......
I GUESS I SHOULDN'T HAVE ASKED THAT.
S-SO...

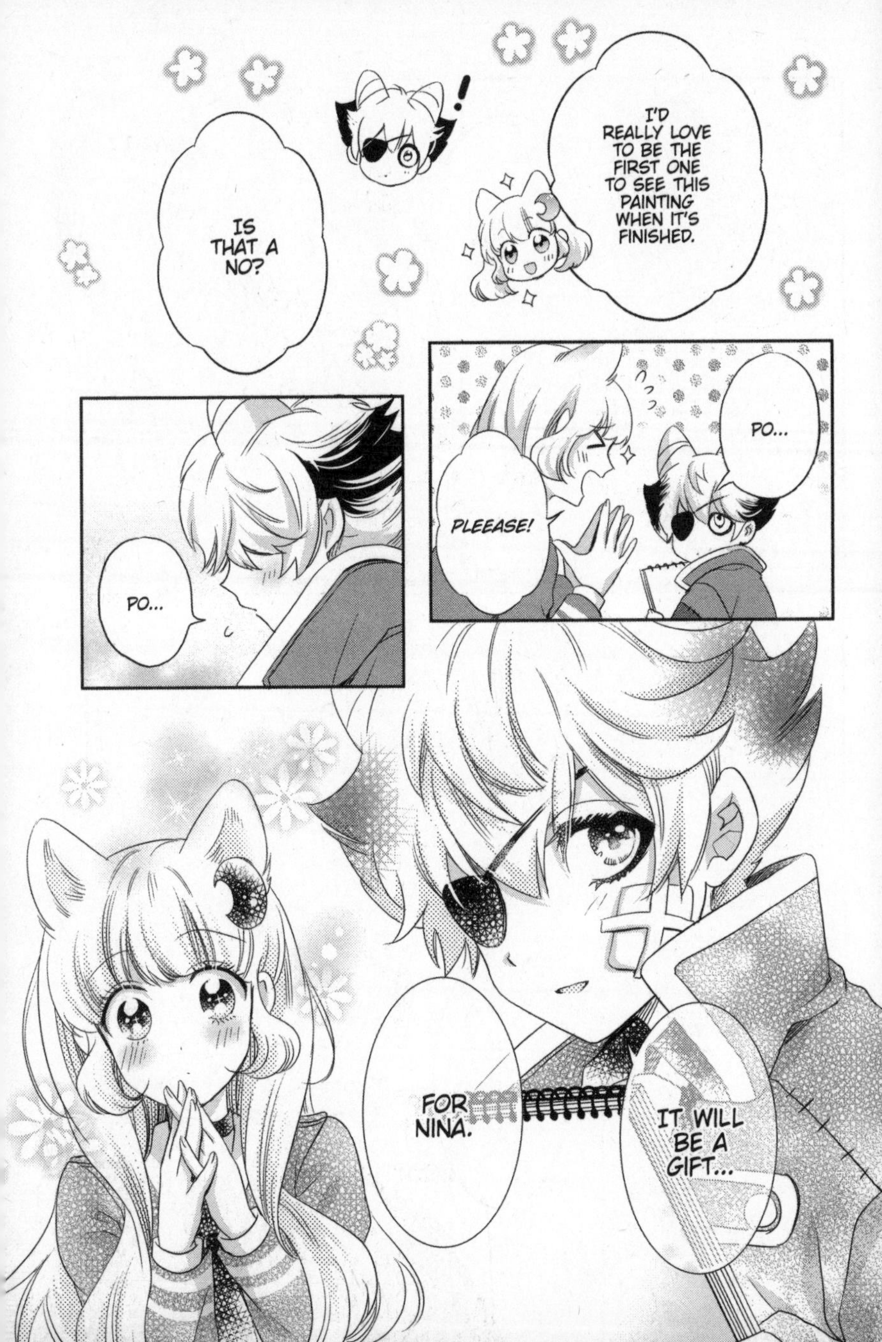
I'D REALLY LOVE TO BE THE FIRST ONE TO SEE THIS PAINTING WHEN IT'S FINISHED.
!
IS THAT A NO?
PO...
PLEEASE!
PO...
IT WILL BE A GIFT...
FOR NINA.

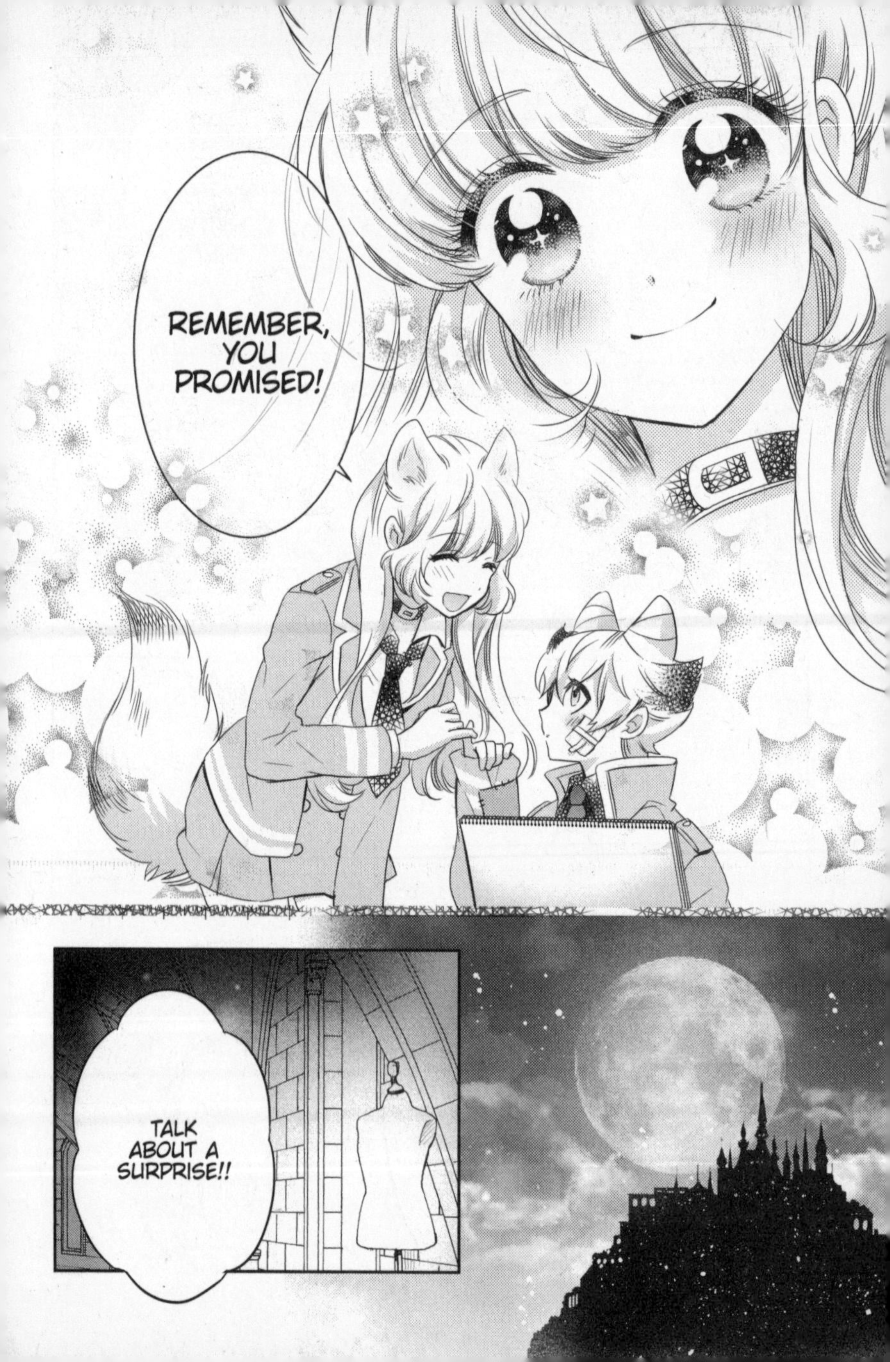
REMEMBER, YOU PROMISED!
TALK ABOUT A SURPRISE!!

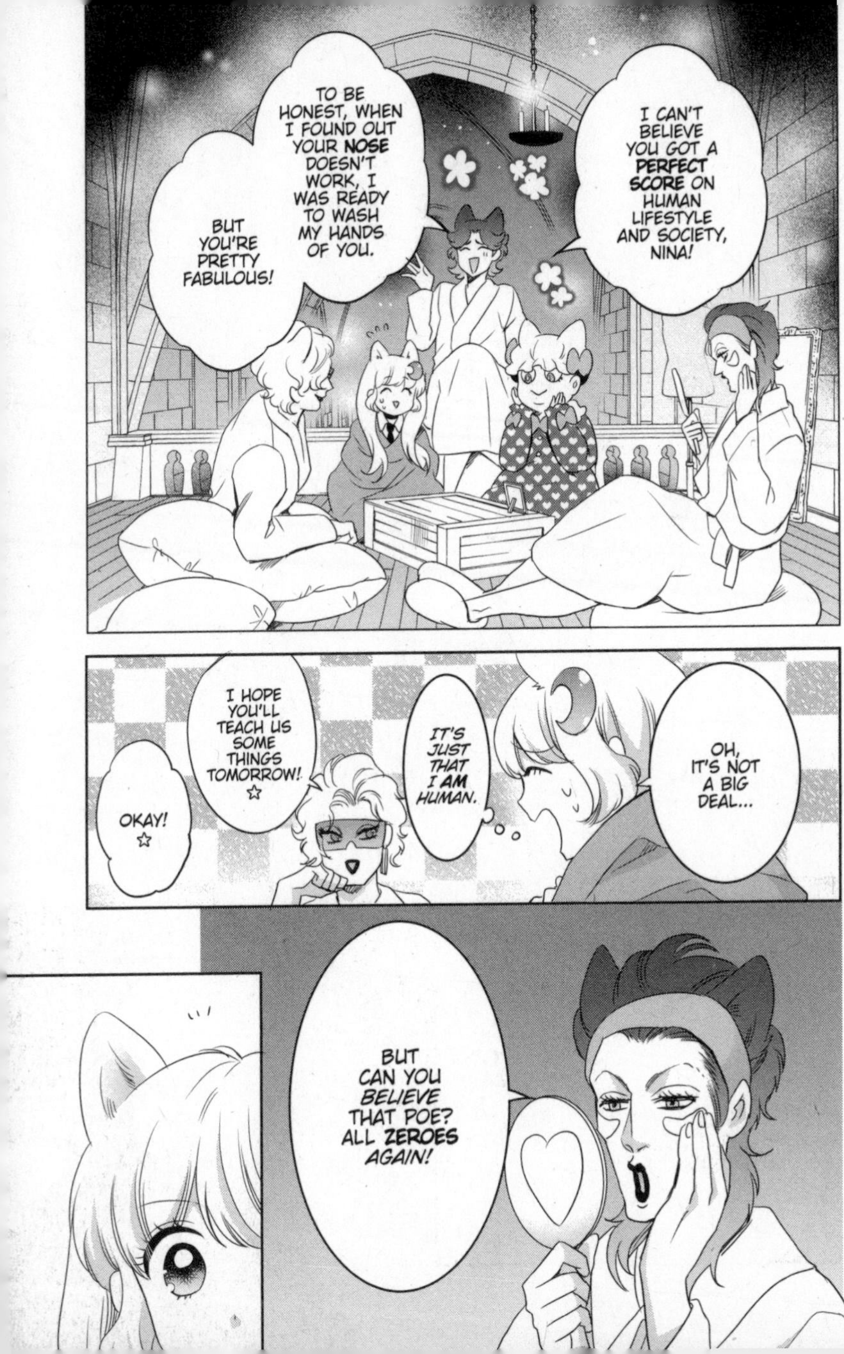
I CAN'T BELIEVE YOU GOT A **PERFECT SCORE** ON HUMAN LIFESTYLE AND SOCIETY, NINA!
TO BE HONEST, WHEN I FOUND OUT YOUR **NOSE** DOESN'T WORK, I WAS READY TO WASH MY HANDS OF YOU.
BUT YOU'RE PRETTY FABULOUS!
OH, IT'S NOT A BIG DEAL...
*IT'S JUST THAT I **AM** HUMAN.*
I HOPE YOU'LL TEACH US SOME THINGS TOMORROW! ☆
OKAY! ☆
BUT CAN YOU *BELIEVE* THAT POE? ALL **ZEROES** *AGAIN!*

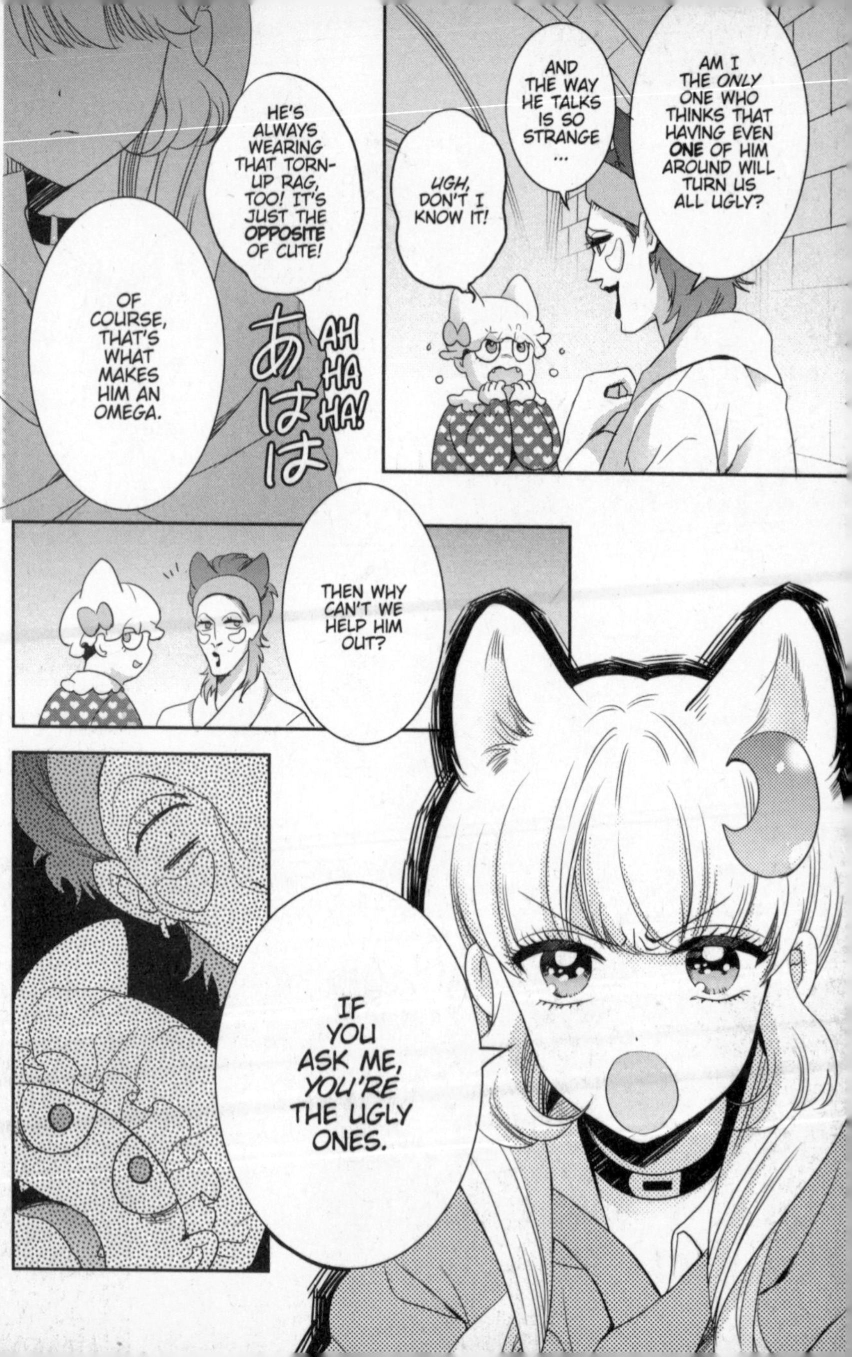
AM I THE ONLY ONE WHO THINKS THAT HAVING EVEN ONE OF HIM AROUND WILL TURN US ALL UGLY?
AND THE WAY HE TALKS IS SO STRANGE ...
UGH, DON'T I KNOW IT!
HE'S ALWAYS WEARING THAT TORN-UP RAG, TOO! IT'S JUST THE OPPOSITE OF CUTE!
OF COURSE, THAT'S WHAT MAKES HIM AN OMEGA.
あはは
AH HA HA!
THEN WHY CAN'T WE HELP HIM OUT?
IF YOU ASK ME, YOU'RE THE UGLY ONES.

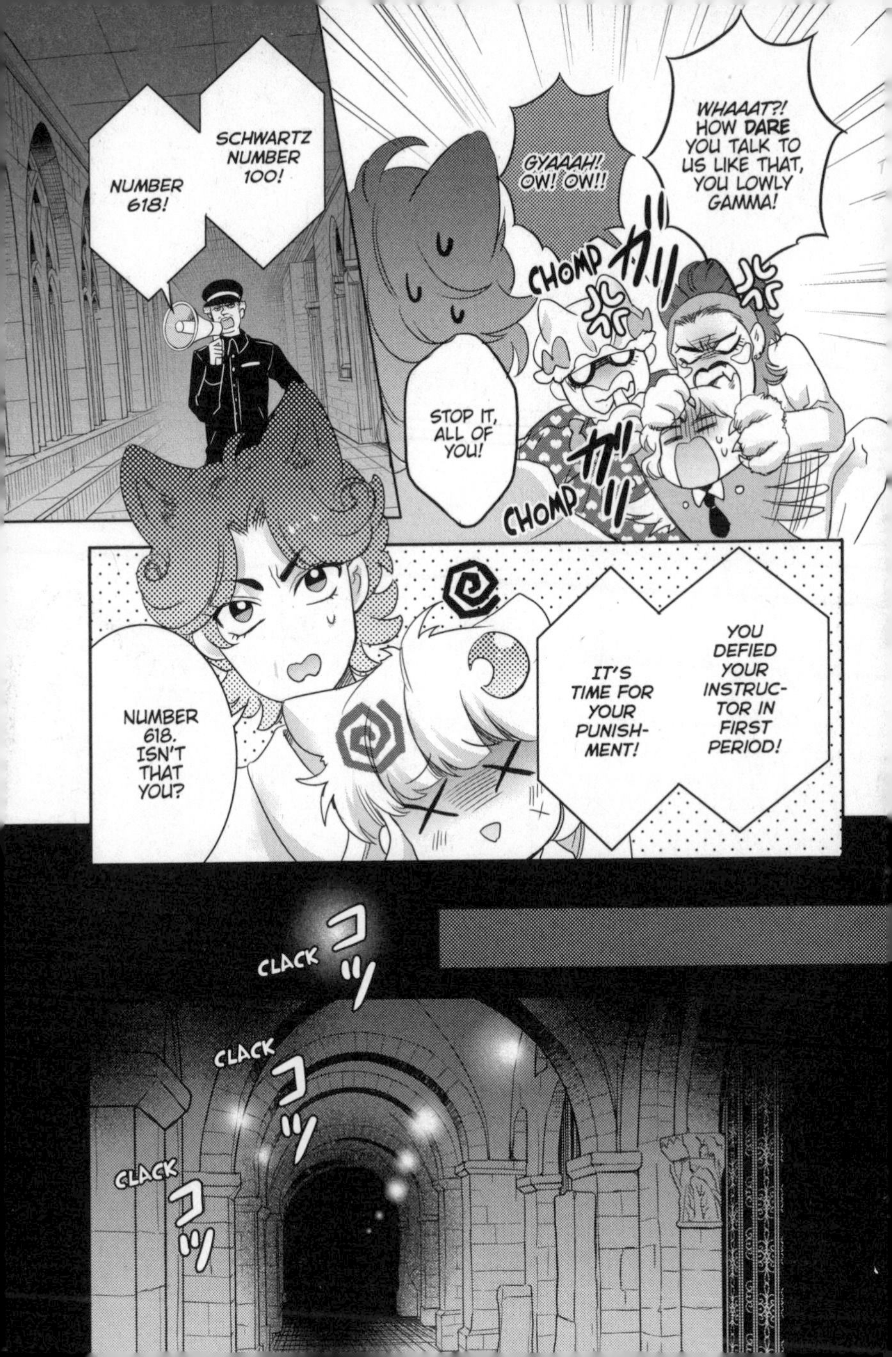
WHAAAT?! HOW DARE YOU TALK TO US LIKE THAT, YOU LOWLY GAMMA!
GYAAAH! OW! OW!!
CHOMP
STOP IT, ALL OF YOU!
CHOMP
SCHWARTZ NUMBER 100!
NUMBER 618!
YOU DEFIED YOUR INSTRUCTOR IN FIRST PERIOD!
IT'S TIME FOR YOUR PUNISHMENT!
NUMBER 618. ISN'T THAT YOU?
CLACK
CLACK
CLACK

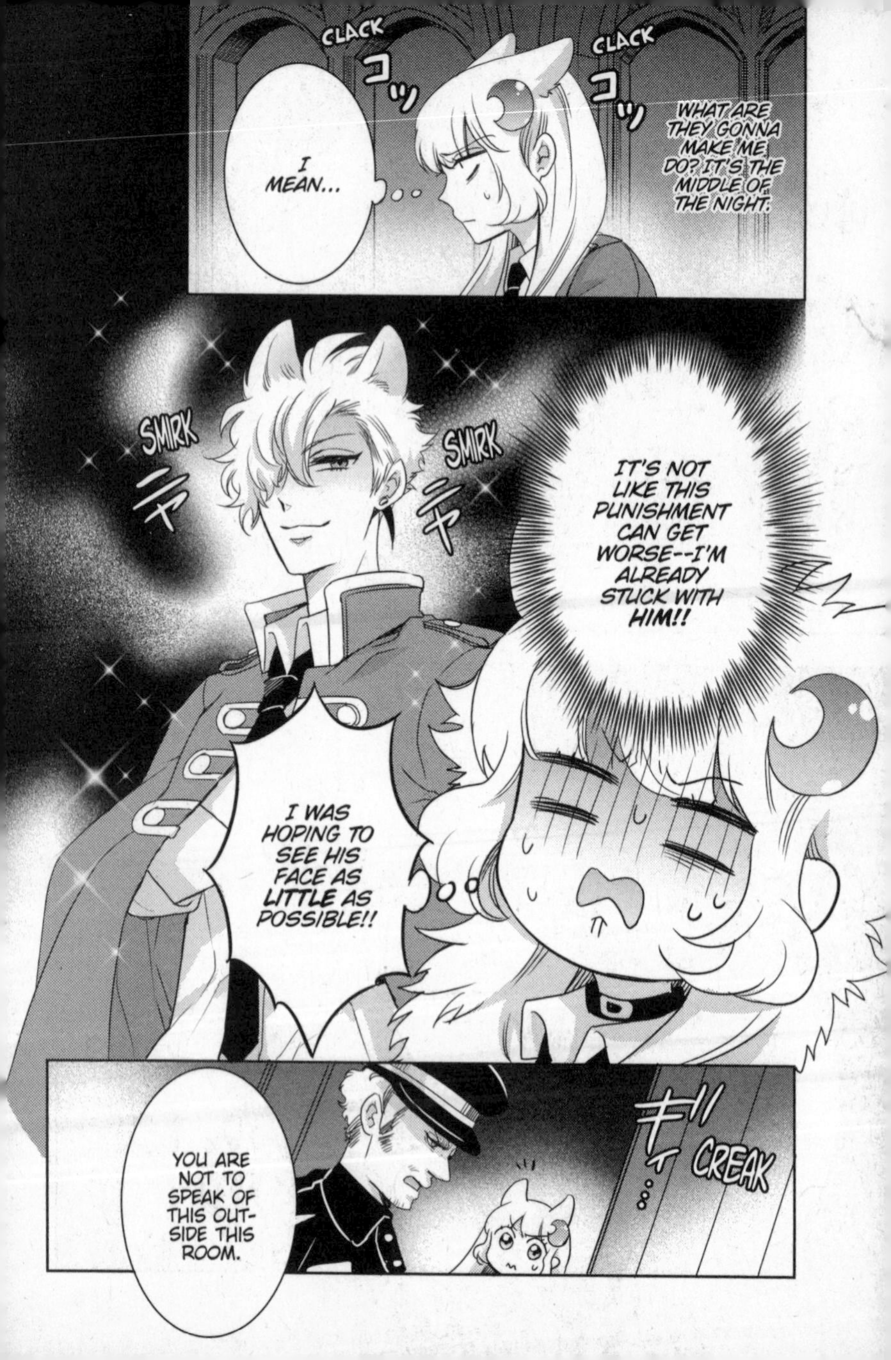
CLACK コッ
CLACK コッ
WHAT ARE THEY GONNA MAKE ME DO? IT'S THE MIDDLE OF THE NIGHT.
I MEAN...
SMIRK ニヤ
SMIRK ニヤ
IT'S NOT LIKE THIS PUNISHMENT CAN GET WORSE--I'M ALREADY STUCK WITH HIM!!
I WAS HOPING TO SEE HIS FACE AS LITTLE AS POSSIBLE!!
ギィ... CREAK
YOU ARE NOT TO SPEAK OF THIS OUT-SIDE THIS ROOM.

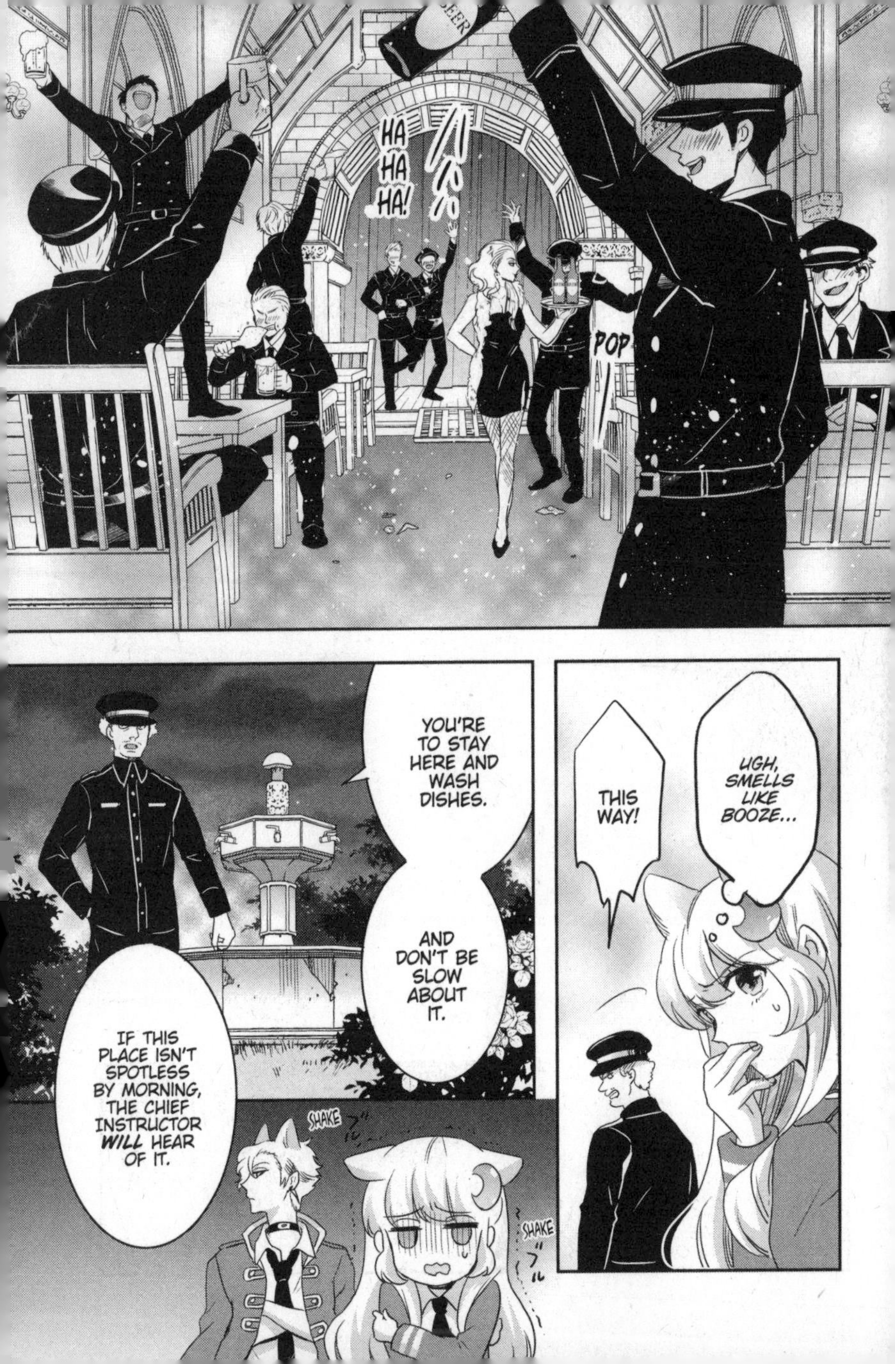
BEER
HA HA HA!
POP
UGH, SMELLS LIKE BOOZE...
THIS WAY!
YOU'RE TO STAY HERE AND WASH DISHES.
AND DON'T BE SLOW ABOUT IT.
IF THIS PLACE ISN'T SPOTLESS BY MORNING, THE CHIEF INSTRUCTOR ***WILL*** HEAR OF IT.
SHAKE
SHAKE

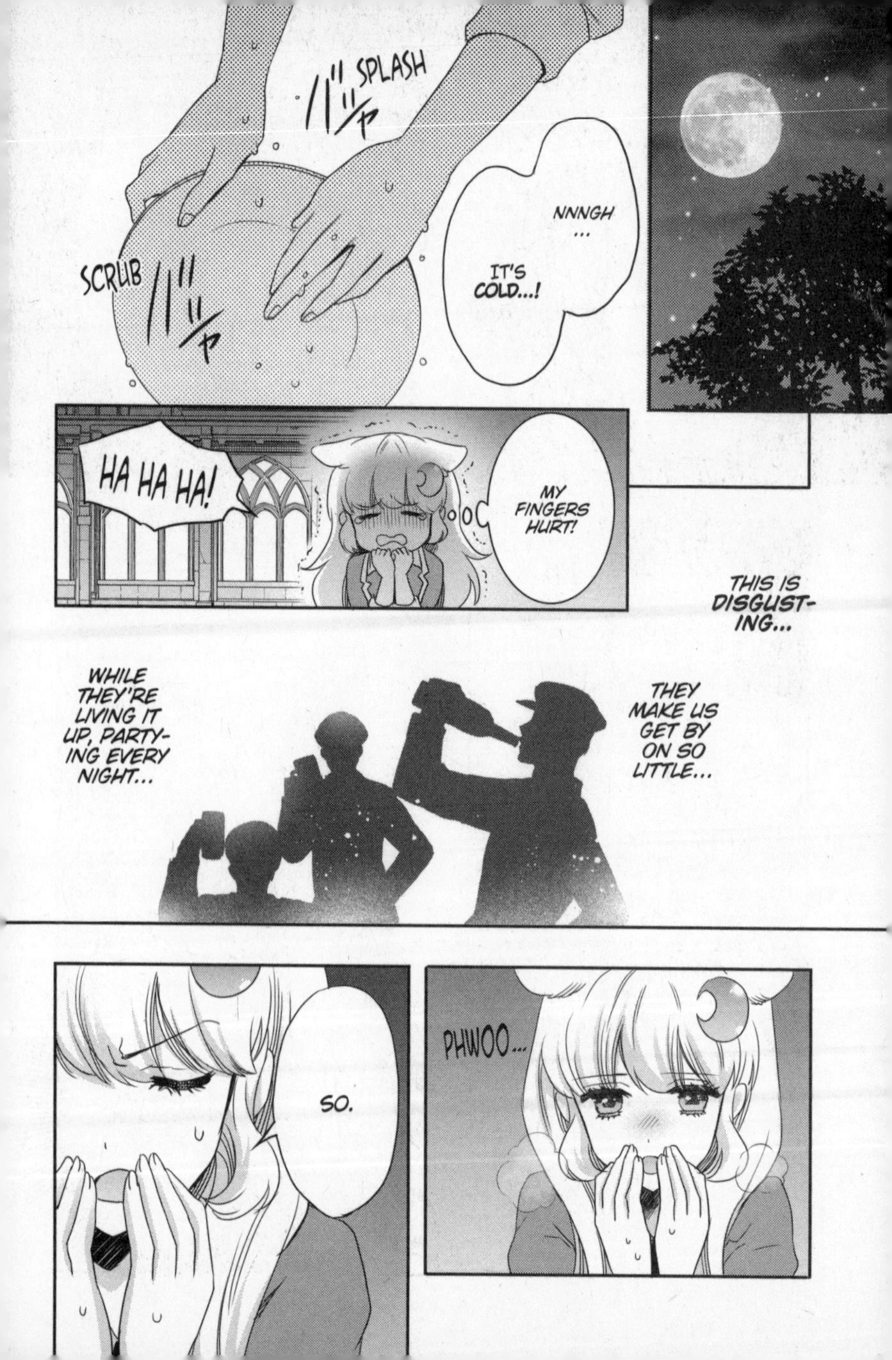
SPLASH
NNNGH... IT'S COLD...!
SCRUB
MY FINGERS HURT!
HA HA HA!
THIS IS DISGUST-ING...
THEY MAKE US GET BY ON SO LITTLE...
WHILE THEY'RE LIVING IT UP, PARTY-ING EVERY NIGHT...
PHWOO...
SO.

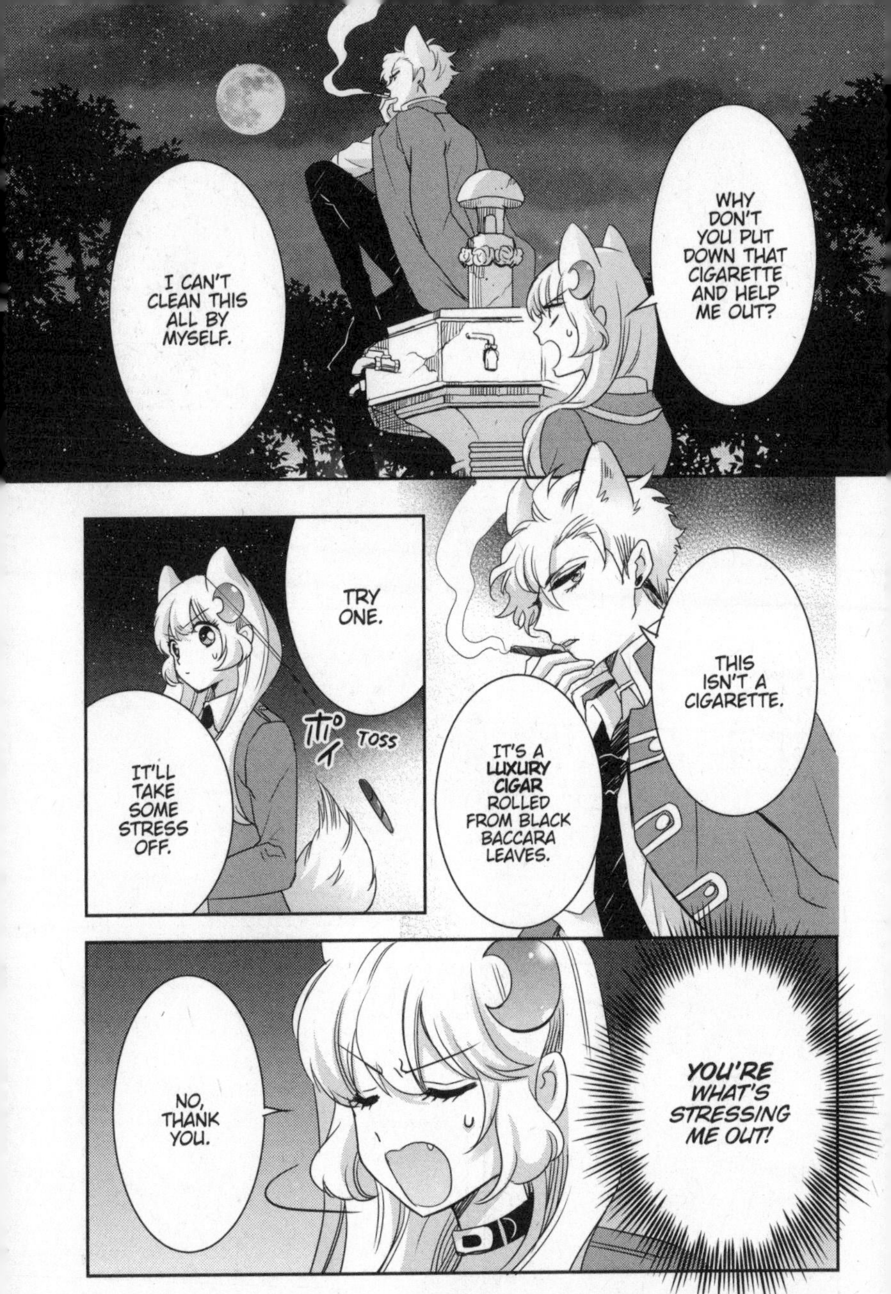
WHY DON'T YOU PUT DOWN THAT CIGARETTE AND HELP ME OUT?
I CAN'T CLEAN THIS ALL BY MYSELF.
THIS ISN'T A CIGARETTE.
IT'S A **LUXURY CIGAR** ROLLED FROM BLACK BACCARA LEAVES.
TRY ONE.
ポイ TOSS
IT'LL TAKE SOME STRESS OFF.
YOU'RE WHAT'S STRESSING ME OUT!
NO, THANK YOU.

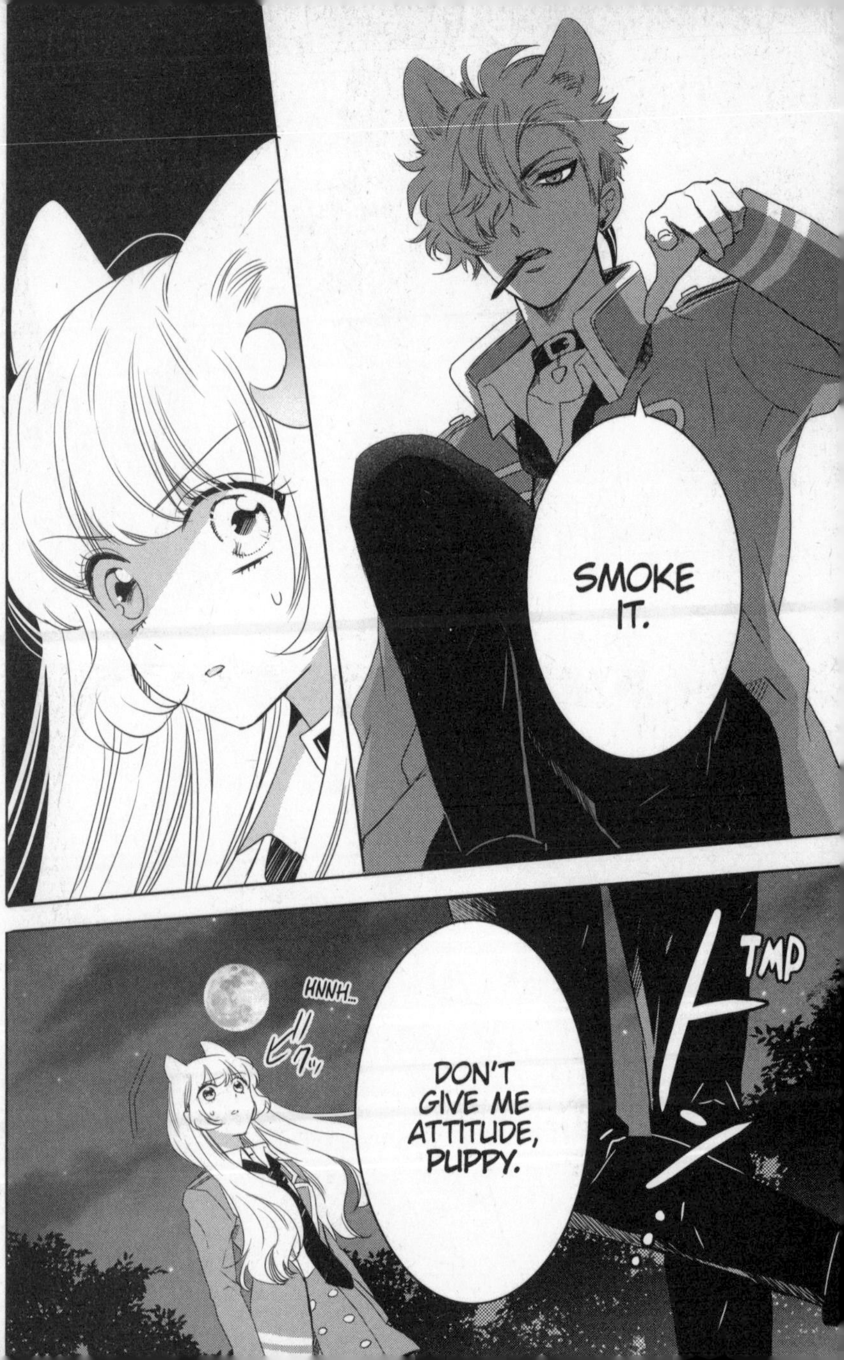
SMOKE IT.
TMP
DON'T GIVE ME ATTITUDE, PUPPY.
HNNH...

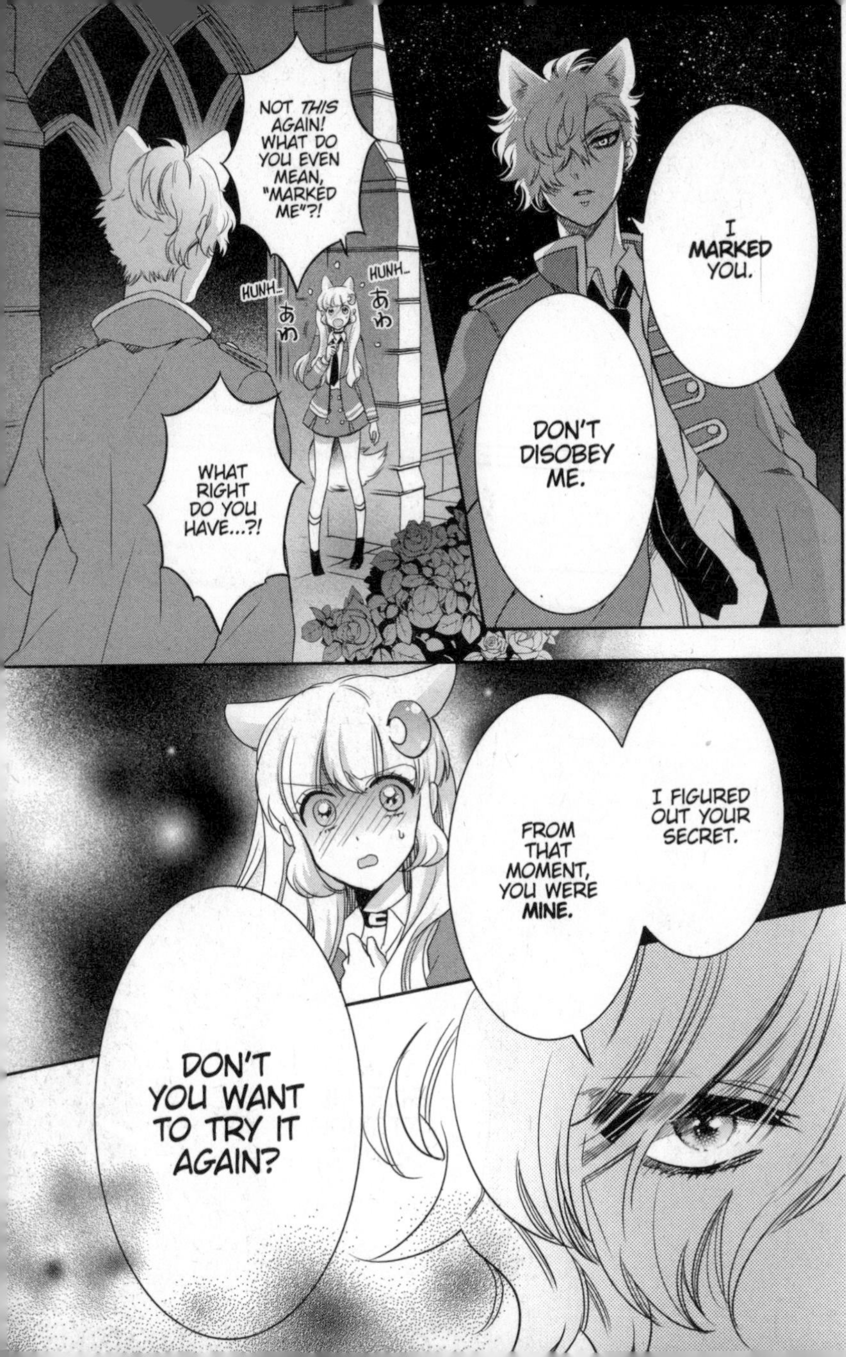
I MARKED YOU.
DON'T DISOBEY ME.
NOT *THIS* AGAIN! WHAT DO YOU EVEN MEAN, "MARKED ME"?!
HUNH.. あわ
HUNH.. あわ
WHAT RIGHT DO YOU HAVE...?!
I FIGURED OUT YOUR SECRET.
FROM THAT MOMENT, YOU WERE MINE.
DON'T YOU WANT TO TRY IT AGAIN?

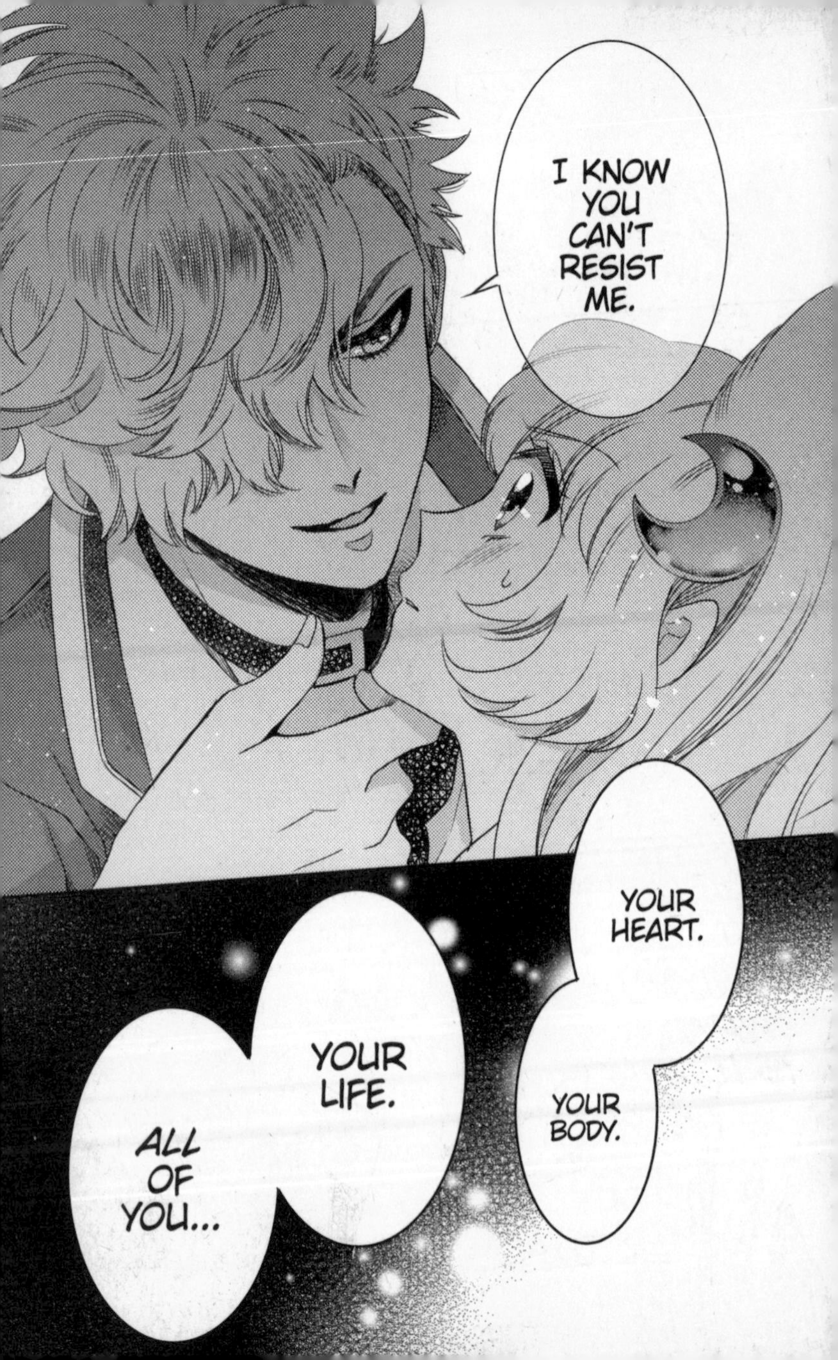
I KNOW YOU CAN'T RESIST ME.
YOUR HEART.
YOUR BODY.
YOUR LIFE.
ALL OF YOU...

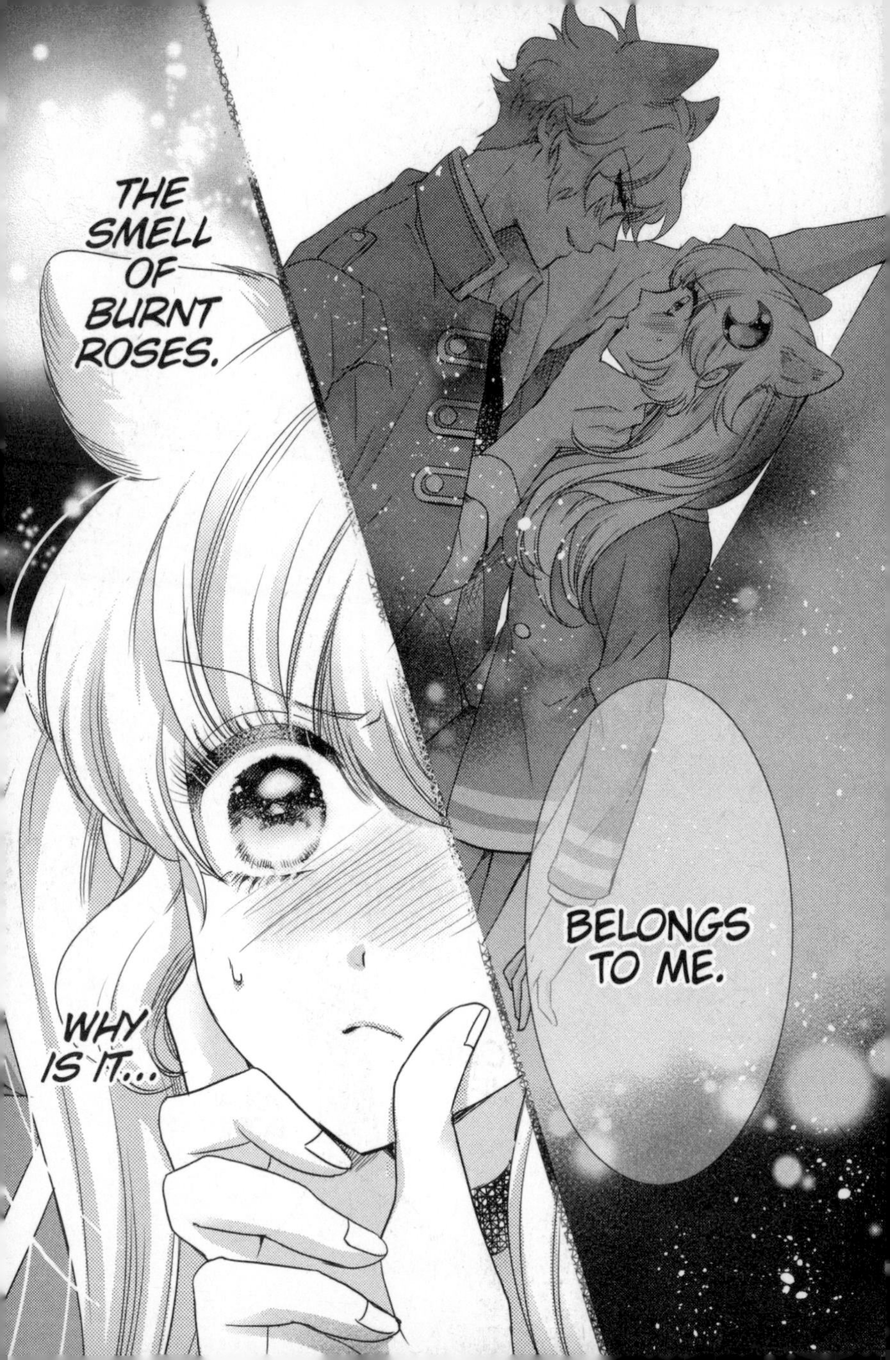
BELONGS TO ME.
THE SMELL OF BURNT ROSES.
WHY IS IT...

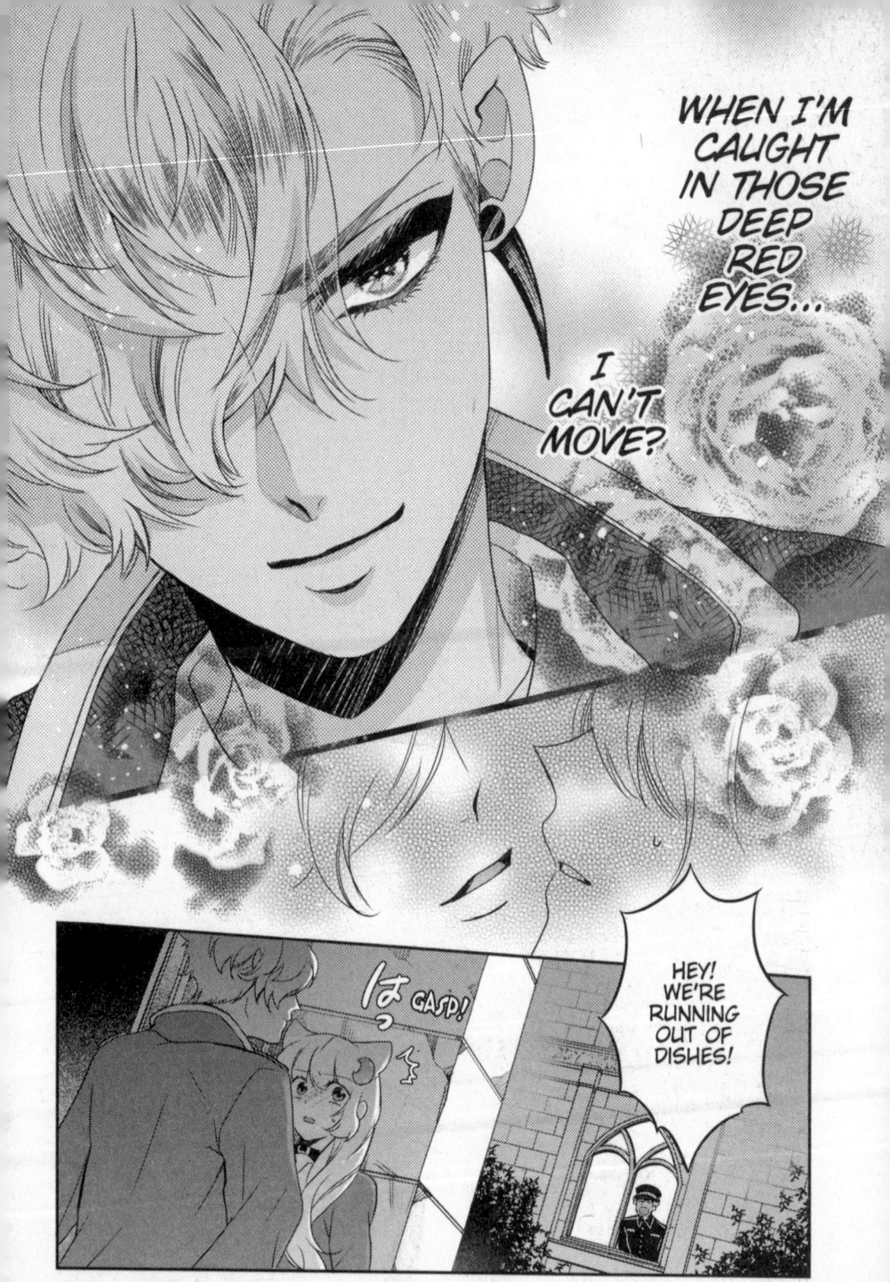
WHEN I'M CAUGHT IN THOSE DEEP RED EYES...
I CAN'T MOVE?
HEY! WE'RE RUNNING OUT OF DISHES!
GASP!

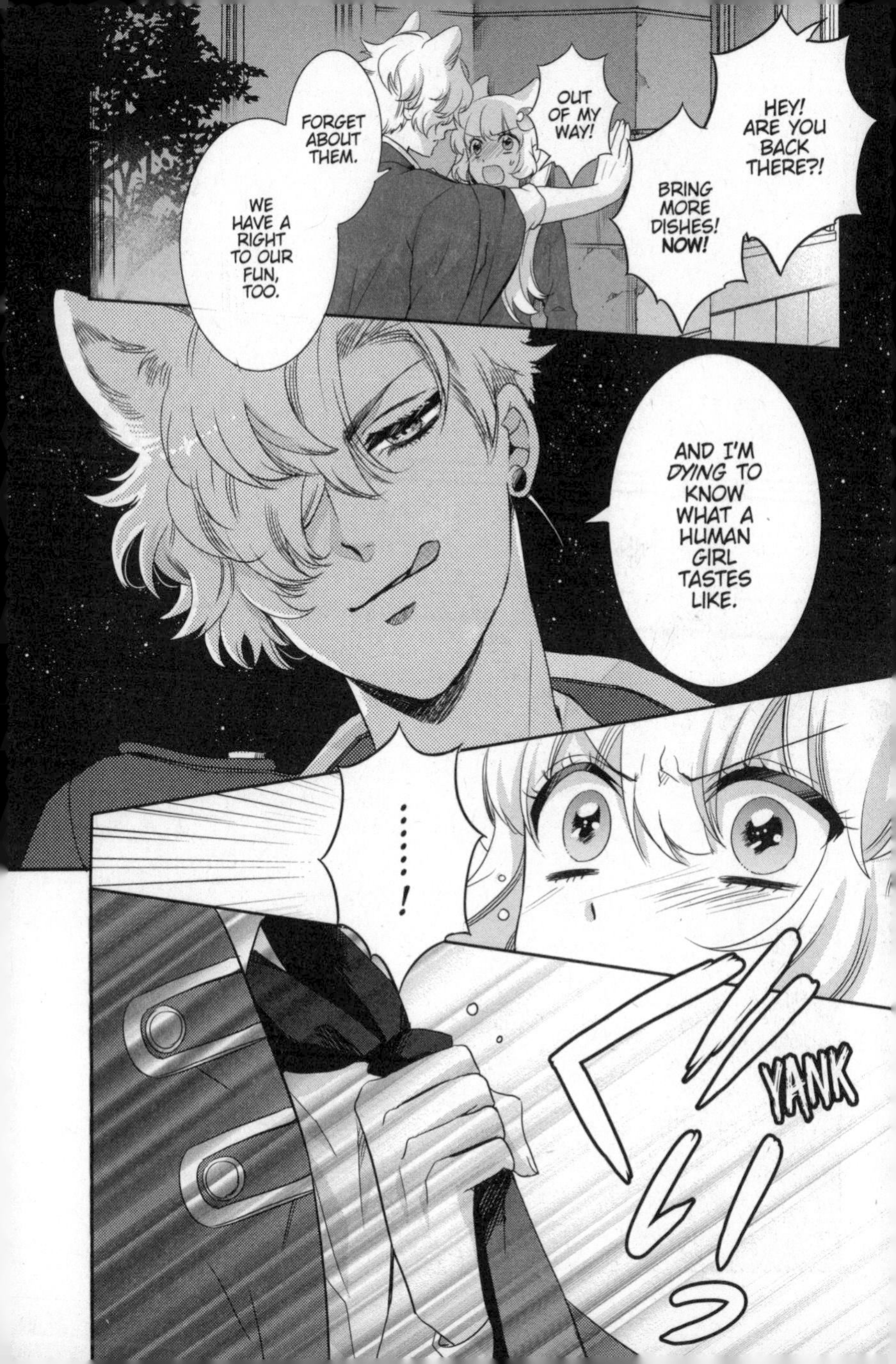
HEY! ARE YOU BACK THERE?!
BRING MORE DISHES! NOW!
OUT OF MY WAY!
FORGET ABOUT THEM.
WE HAVE A RIGHT TO OUR FUN, TOO.
AND I'M *DYING* TO KNOW WHAT A HUMAN GIRL TASTES LIKE.
......!
YANK

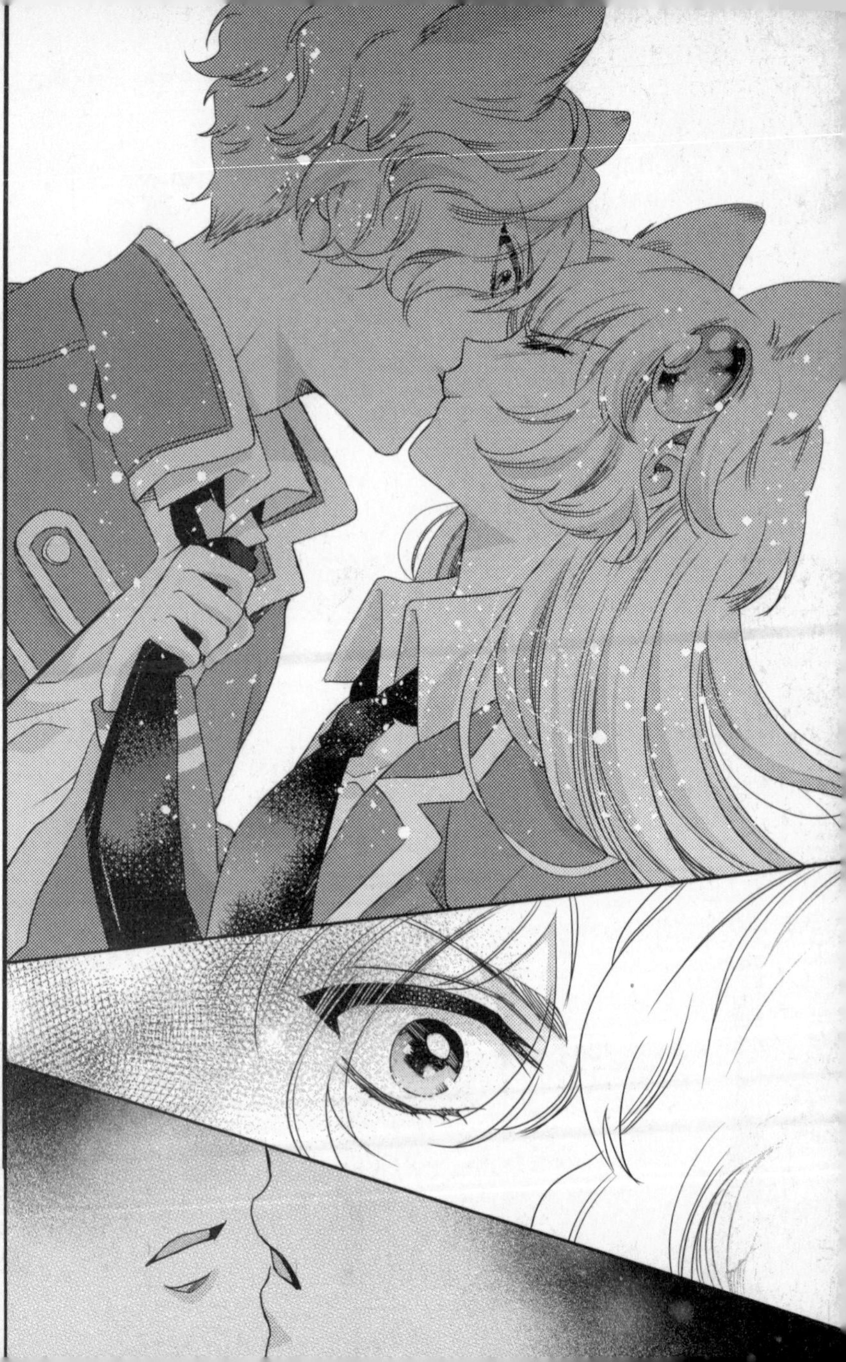

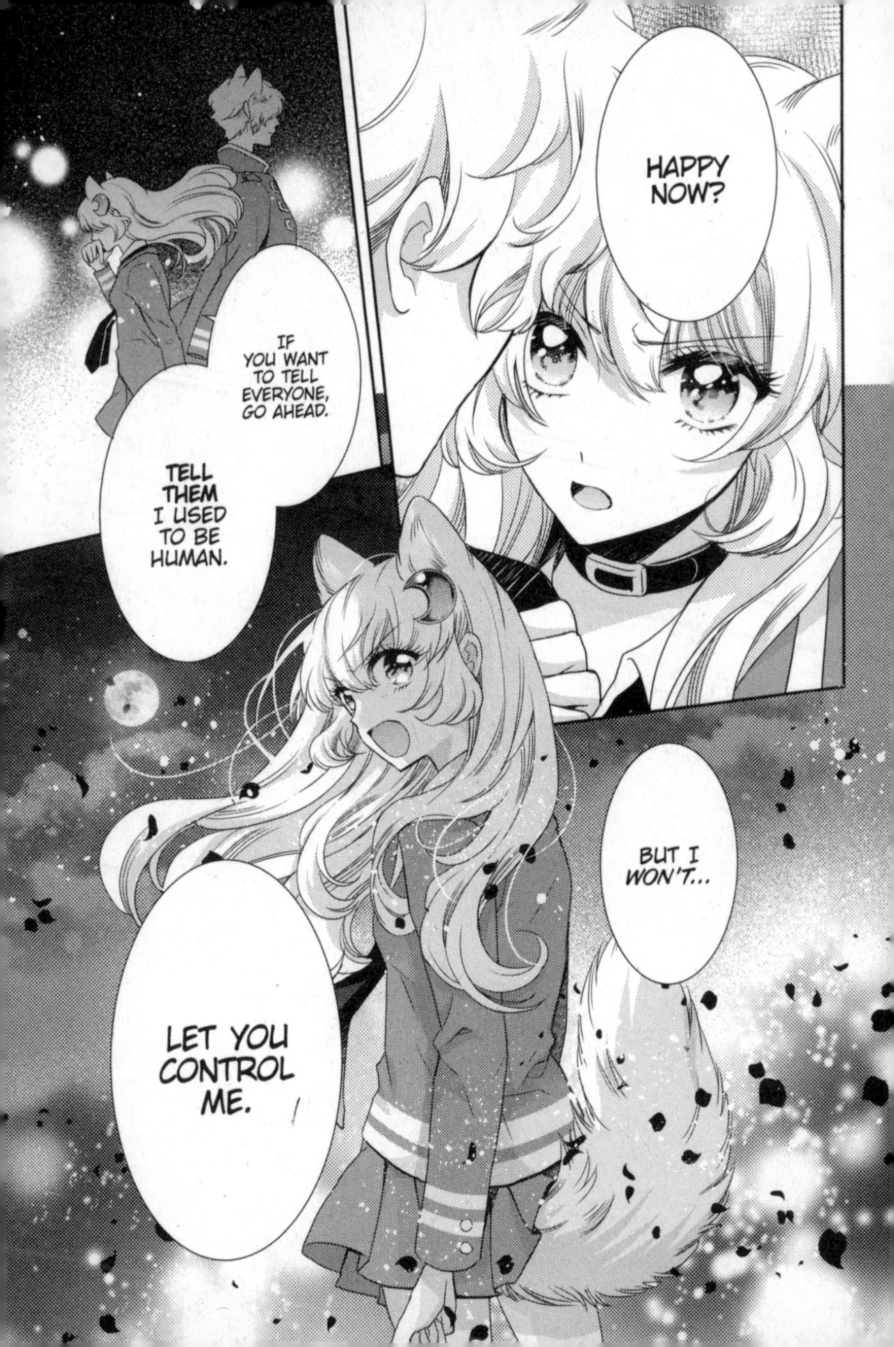
HAPPY NOW?
IF YOU WANT TO TELL EVERYONE, GO AHEAD.
TELL THEM I USED TO BE HUMAN.
BUT I WON'T...
LET YOU CONTROL ME.

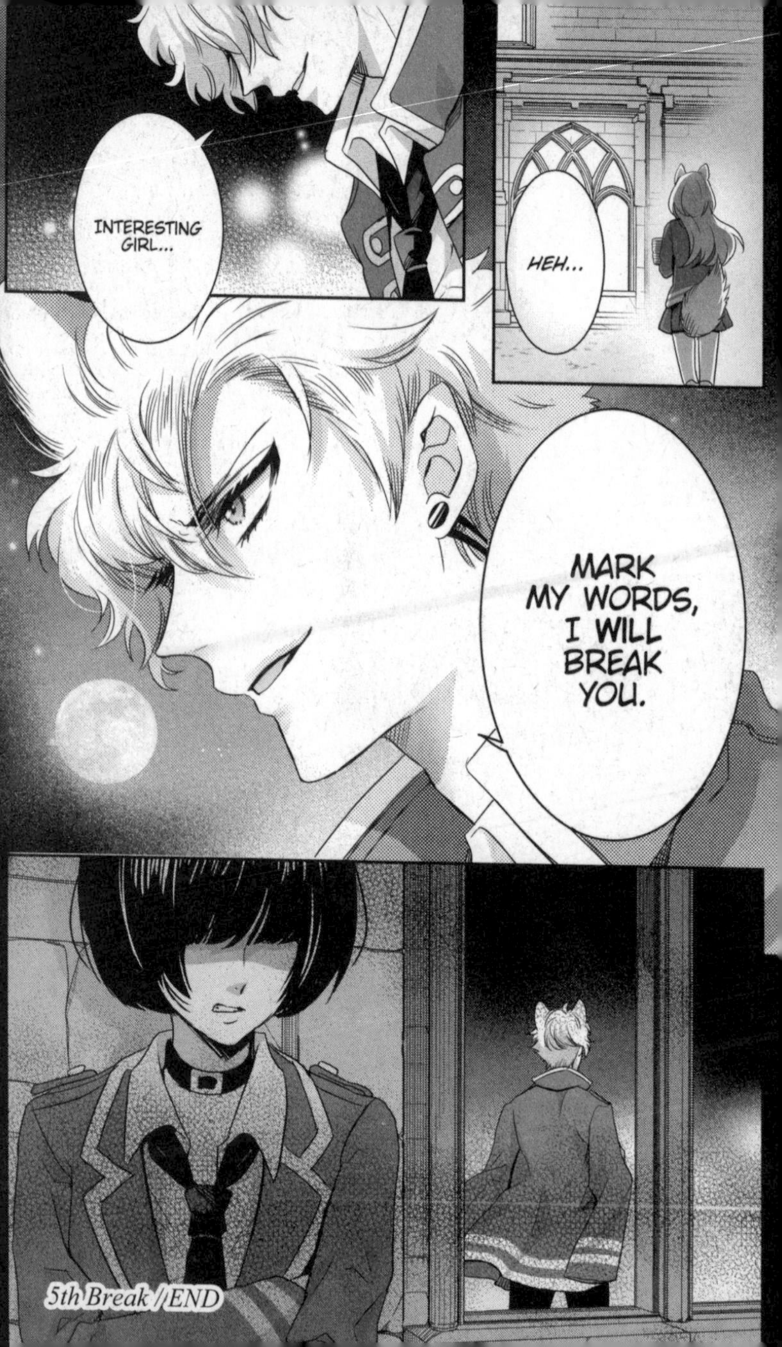
HEH...
INTERESTING GIRL...
MARK MY WORDS, I WILL BREAK YOU.
5th Break // END

No.618 Tsukishiro Nina

Birthday: 12/3

Height: 158cm (About 5'2")

Hobby: Watching sports

♥ Mint chocolate ice cream

Secret: Used to be human

Has a strong sense of justice and is kind at heart. She treats everyone equally, but sometimes lets her emotions drive her to dangerous behavior.

No.100 Roy Balfour

Birthday: 4/6

Height: 179cm (About 5'10")

Hobby: Expanding his territory

♥ Ear massage

Secret:

Wary and extremely aggressive. Very territorial. He is uncomfortable unless he has asserted his authority. But some of his homemates will vouch for his compassion.

Beasts of
Abigaile

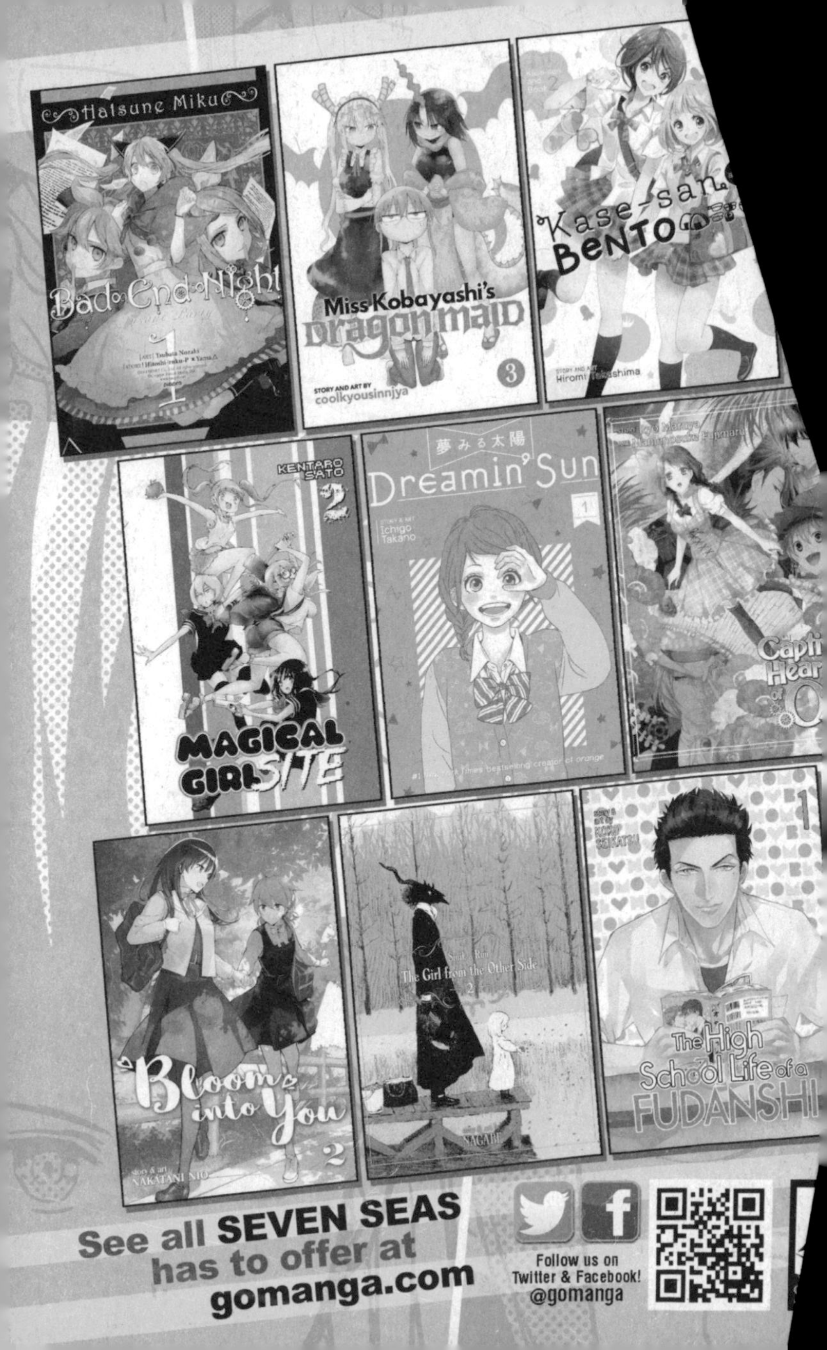

Hatsune Miku
Bad End Night
1
Miss Kobayashi's Dragon Maid
3
STORY AND ART BY coolkyousinnjya
Kase-san and Bento
KENTARO SATO
2
MAGICAL GIRL SITE
夢みる太陽
Dreamin' Sun
1
STORY & ART Ichigo Takano
Bloom into You
2
story & art NAKATANI NIO
The Girl from the Other Side
2
NAGABE
1
The High School Life of a FUDANSHI
See all SEVEN SEAS has to offer at gomanga.com
Follow us on Twitter & Facebook! @gomanga

AS ENTERTAINMENT PRESENTS

of Abigail

GA AOKI   VOLUME 1

SLATION
a Nibley

ADAPTATION
ykate Jasper

RING AND RETOUCH
Rina Mapa

COVER DESIGN
Nicky Lim

PROOFREADER
Janet Houck

ASSISTANT EDITOR
Jenn Grunigen

PRODUCTION ASSISTANT
CK Russell

PRODUCTION MANAGER
Lissa Pattillo

EDITOR-IN-CHIEF
Adam Arnold

PUBLISHER
Jason DeAngelis

ABIGAIL NO KEMONO TACHI VOL. 1
© SPICA AOKI 2016
Originally published in Japan in 2016 by Akita Publishing Co., Ltd..
English translation rights arranged with Akita Publishing Co., Ltd. through
TOHAN CORPORATION, Tokyo.

Seven Seas books may be purchased in bulk for educational, business, or pro-
motional use. For information on bulk purchases, please contact Macmillan Cor-
porate & Premium Sales Department at 1-800-221-7945 (ext 5442)
or write specialmarkets@macmillan.com.

Seven Seas and the Seven Seas logo are trademarks of
Seven Seas Entertainment, LLC. All rights reserved.

ISBN: 978-1-626925-35-9

Printed in Canada

First Printing: June 2017

10 9 8 7 6 5 4 3 2 1

FOLLOW US ONLINE: www.gomanga.com

READING DIRECTIONS

book reads from *right to left*, Japanese style.
s is your first time reading manga, you start
g from the top right panel on each page and
rom there. If you get lost, just follow the
d diagram here. It may seem backwards at
ou'll get the hang of it! Have fun!!

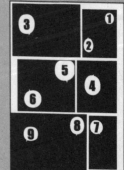